MPLS: Next Steps

The Morgan Kaufmann Series in Networking
Series Editor, David Clark, M.I.T.

MPLS: Next Steps

Bruce S. Davie and Adrian Farrel

AMSTERDAM • BOSTON • HEIDELBERG • LONDON
NEW YORK • OXFORD • PARIS • SAN DIEGO
SAN FRANCISCO • SINGAPORE • SYDNEY • TOKYO

Morgan Kaufmann is an imprint of Elsevier

Publishing Director: Chris Williams
Publisher: Denise E. M. Penrose
Acquisitions Editor: Rick Adams
Publishing Services Manager: George Morrison
Production Editor: Lianne Hong
Assistant Editor: Gregory Chalson
Design Direction: Alisa Andreola
Cover Design: Gary Ragaglia
Cover Image: iStockphoto
Composition: Charon Tec
Copyeditor: Jeanne Hansen
Proofreader: Charon Tec
Indexer: Broccoli Information Management
Interior printer: RR Donnelley, Harrisonburg
Cover printer: Phoenix Color Corporation

Morgan Kaufmann Publishers is an imprint of Elsevier.
30 Corporate Drive, Suite 400, Burlington, MA 01803, USA

Library of Congress Cataloging-in-Publication Data
Davie, Bruce S.
  MPLS : next steps / by Bruce S. Davie and Adrian Farrel.
    p. cm. — (Morgan Kaufmann series in networking)
  Includes index.
  ISBN-13: 978-0-12-374400-5 (hardcover : alk. paper) 1. MPLS standard. I. Farrel, Adrian. II. Title.
  TK5105.573.D39 2008
  621.382'16—dc22   2008004669

ISBN: 978-0-12-374400-5

For information on all Morgan Kaufmann publications, visit our
Web site at www.mkp.com or www.books.elsevier.com

Printed and bound by CPI Group (UK) Ltd, Croydon, CR0 4YY
Transferred to Digital Print 2012

Contents

About the Editors

Bruce Davie joined Cisco Systems in 1995, where he is a Cisco Fellow. For many years he led the team of architects responsible for Multiprotocol Label Switching and IP Quality of Service. He recently joined the Video and Content Networking Business Unit in the Service Provider group. He has 20 years of networking and communications industry experience and has written numerous books, RFCs, journal articles, and conference papers on IP networking. He is also an active participant in both the Internet Engineering Task Force and the Internet Research Task Force. Prior to joining Cisco he was director of internetworking research and chief scientist at Bell Communications Research. Bruce holds a Ph.D. in Computer Science from Edinburgh University and is a visiting lecturer at M.I.T. His research interests include routing, measurement, quality of service, transport protocols, and overlay networks.

Adrian Farrel has over two decades of experience designing and developing communications protocol software. At Old Dog Consulting he is an industry-leading freelance consultant on MPLS, GMPLS, and Internet routing. Formerly he worked as MPLS Architect for Data Connection Ltd., and as Director of Protocol Development for Movaz Networks, Inc. He is active within the Internet Engineering Task Force, where he is co-chair of the CCAMP working group responsible for GMPLS, the Path Computation Element (PCE) working group, and the Layer One VPN (L1VPN) working group. Adrian has co-authored and contributed to numerous Internet Drafts and RFCs on MPLS, GMPLS, and related technologies. This is his third book for Morgan Kaufmann.

About the Authors

Gerald R. Ash (Chapter 6) is from Glen Rock, New Jersey. He graduated from grammar school, high school, Rutgers, and Caltech, but got sent to Vietnam instead of being able to attend his Caltech graduation. He spent the first 20 years of his AT&T career as "the consummate BellHead" (as one colleague put it) but for the next 15 years sought to be a blossoming NetHead (although he never attempted the standard ponytail, beard, tee-shirt, shorts, and sandals). He does not claim to be a NetHead, but over the last 15 years has advanced to become perhaps 50% NetHead. He is happily married for over 40 years, has three children and four grandchildren. He is also the author of *Traffic Engineering and QoS Optimization of Integrated Voice & Data Networks*, published by Elsevier, 2006.

Igor Bryskin (Chapters 4, 5, 8, 9, and 14) is Chief Protocol Architect at ADVA Optical, Inc., where he is responsible for high–level and detailed architecture of the GMPLS control plane software running on Movaz's optical cross-connects. He has been involved in data communications since the 1980s and has worked since the 1990s primarily in the areas of IP/MPLS and ATM. Igor has served as principal author or co-author of several Internet drafts and RFCs in the area of MPLS and GMPLS. He is also a co-author of *GMPLS: Architecture and Applications*, published by Elsevier, 2005.

Bruce Davie (Chapters 2, 11, and 12) joined Cisco Systems in 1995, where he is a Cisco Fellow. For many years he led the team of architects responsible for Multiprotocol Label Switching and IP Quality of Service. He recently joined the Video and Content Networking Business Unit in the Service Provider group. He has 20 years of networking and communications industry experience and has written numerous books, RFCs, journal articles, and conference papers on IP networking. He is also an active participant in both the Internet Engineering Task Force and the Internet Research Task Force. Prior to joining Cisco he was director of internetworking research and chief scientist at Bell Communications Research. Bruce holds a Ph.D. in Computer Science from Edinburgh University and is a visiting lecturer at M.I.T. His research interests include routing, measurement, quality of service, transport protocols, and overlay networks. He is also a co-author of *MPLS: Technology and Applications*, published by Elsevier, 2000.

Piet Demeester (Chapter 7) received his doctoral degree from Ghent University at the Department of Information Technology (INTEC) in 1988. In 1993, he became a professor at Ghent University, where he is responsible for research on communication networks. He was involved in several European COST, ESPRIT, RACE, ACTS, and IST projects. He is a member of the editorial board of several international journals and has been a member of several technical program committees. His current interests are related to broadband communication networks (i.e., IP, G-MPLS, optical packet and burst switching, access and residential, active, mobile, CDN, grid) and include network planning, network and service management, telecom software, internetworking, and network protocols for QoS support. He has published over 250 journal or conference papers in this field. He also has been very active in the field of resilience in communication networks, both as founder of the DRCN conference and as editor of special issues on this subject in *IEEE Communication Magazine*. He is also a co-author of *Network Recovery: Protection and Restoration of Optical, SONET-SDH, IP, and MPLS*, published by Elsevier, 2004.

John Evans (Chapter 6), is a Distinguished Consulting Engineer with Cisco Systems, where he has been instrumental in the engineering and deployment of quality of service and policy control. His current areas of focus include policy/resource control, admission control, QOS, and traffic management with associated work in the DSL Forum, the Multiservice Forum, and ETSI/TISPAN. Prior to joining Cisco in 1998, John worked for BT where he was responsible for the design and development of large-scale networks for the financial community. Prior to BT, he worked on the design and deployment of battlefield communications networks for the military. He received a BEng (Hons) degree in Electronic Engineering from the University of Manchester Institute of Science and Technology (UMIST, now part of the University of Manchester), UK in 1991 and an MSc degree in Communications Engineering from UMIST in 1996. He is a Chartered Engineer (CEng) and Cisco Certified Internetwork Expert (CCIE). He is also a co-author of *Deploying IP and MPLS QoS for Multiservice Networks*, published by Elsevier, 2007.

Adrian Farrel (Chapters 1, 2, 3, 4, 5, 8, 9, 10, 12, 13, 14, and 15) has over two decades of experience designing and developing communications protocol software. As Old Dog Consulting he is an industry-leading freelance consultant on MPLS, GMPLS, and Internet routing. Formerly he worked as MPLS Architect for Data Connection Ltd., and as Director of Protocol Development for Movaz Networks, Inc. He is active within the Internet Engineering Task Force, where he is co-chair of the CCAMP working group responsible for GMPLS, the Path Computation Element (PCE) working group, and the Layer One VPN (L1VPN) working group. Adrian has co-authored and contributed to numerous Internet Drafts and RFCs on MPLS, GMPLS, and related technologies. He is also the author of *The Internet and Its Protocols: A Comparative Approach*, published by Elsevier, 2004, and a co-author of *GMPLS: Architecture and Applications*, published by Elsevier, 2005.

Clarence Filsfils (Chapter 6) is a Cisco Distinguished System Engineer and a recognized expert in Routing and Quality of Service. He has been playing a key role in engineering, marketing, and deploying the quality of service and fast routing convergence technology at Cisco Systems. Clarence is a regular speaker at conferences. He has published several journal articles and holds over 30 patents on QoS and routing mechanisms. He is also a co-author of *Deploying IP and MPLS QOS for Multiservice Networks*, published by Elsevier, 2007.

Monique Morrow (Chapter 12) is currently CTO Consulting Engineer at Cisco Systems. She has 20 years' experience in IP Internetworking, including design, implementation of complex customer projects, and service development. Morrow has been involved in developing managed network services such as remote access and LAN switching in a service provider environment. She has worked for both enterprise and service provider companies in the United States and in Europe, and led the Engineering Project team for one of the first European MPLS-VPN deployments in 1999 for a European service provider. Morrow has an M.S. in telecommunications management and an M.B.A. in marketing and is a Cisco Certified Internetworking Expert (#1711). She is also a co-author of *Developing IP-Based Services: Solutions for Service Providers and Vendors*, published by Elsevier, 2002.

Tom Nadeau (Chapter 9) Tom works at BT Group where is a Senior Network Architect responsible for the end-to-end network architecture of BT's 21C Network. Prior to BT, Tom worked at Cisco Systems where he was a Technical Leader responsible for the leadership and architecture of operations and management for MPLS-related components of Cisco IOS® and IOS-XR®. This included the areas of pseudo-wires, common optical control plane (GMPLS), Bi-directional Forwarding Detection, NetFlow, Service Assurance Agent, layer-2 and layer-3 VPN, Traffic Engineering, COPS, Diff-Serv, and SNMP in general.

Tom is an active participant in the IETF, ITU, and IEEE. He is co-author of all but one of the MPLS, PWE3, L2/L3 VPN and GMPLS-related IETF MIBs, as well as other IETF MIBs, numerous protocol and architecture documents in the MPLS, BFD, L2/L3 VPN, pseudo-wire, and traffic engineering areas. Tom has filed over 30 patents in the area of networking, and was granted US Patent #7,099,947. Tom is a member of the advisory board at of several network start-ups. Tom received his BSCS from The University of New Hampshire, and a M.Sc. from The University of Massachusetts in Lowell, where he has been an Adjunct Professor of Computer Science since 2000 and teaches courses on the topic of data communications. He is also on the technical committee of several prominent networking conferences where he provides technical guidance on their content, as well as frequently presents. He has been a guest editor for three issues of IEEE Communications magazine (October 2004, June 2005, and March 2008). He is the technical editor of *Enabling VPN Aware Networks with MPLS* (Prentice-Hall Publishers, 2001), and author of *MPLS Network Management: MIBs, Tools, and Technique*s (Morgan-Kaufman, 2002).

Mario Pickavet (Chapter 7) received a Master of Science degree and a Doctor of Electrical Engineering degree, specialized in telecommunications, from Ghent University in 1996 and 1999, respectively. Since 2000, he has been a full-time professor at the same university. His research interests are related to broadband communication networks (i.e., IP, MPLS, WDM, SDH, ATM) and include resilience mechanisms, design, and long-term planning of core and access networks. In this context, he was and currently is involved in European IST projects (i.e., LION, DAVID, STOLAS, ePhoton/One, LASAGNE) on IP over WDM next generation networks. He has published a number of international publications on these subjects, both in leading journals (e.g., *IEEE Journal on Selected Areas in*

Communications and *IEEE Communication Magazine*) and proceedings of conferences. He is also a co-author of *Network Recovery: Protection and Restoration of Optical, SONET-SDH, IP, and MPLS*, published by Elsevier, 2004.

Yakov Rekhter (Chapters 2 and 12) works at Juniper Networks, Inc. He is one of the leading designers of Tag Switching, BGP/MPLS VPNs, and MPLS Traffic Engineering. He is also one of the leading designers of Border Gateway Protocol (BGP). He is the author/co-author of many RFCs, as well as *MPLS: Technology and Applications*, published by Elsevier, 2000.

Jean-Philippe Vasseur (Chapter 7) has a French engineering degree in Network Computing and a Master of Science degree from the Stevens Institute of Technology, New Jersey. He worked as a network architect for several large national and international service providers in large multiprotocol environments (e.g., IP, ATM, X25) prior to joining Cisco Systems. After two years within the EMEA technical consulting group focusing on IP/MPLS routing, VPN, and traffic engineering designs for service providers, he joined the CISCO Engineering team as a Technical Leader with a particular focus on IP, MPLS traffic engineering, and recovery mechanisms. He is a regular speaker at various international conferences and is involved in several research projects in the area of IP and MPLS. In addition, he is an active member of the Internet Engineering Task Force (IETF) and has co-authored several IETF specifications. He is also a co-author of *Network Recovery: Protection and Restoration of Optical, SONET-SDH, IP, and MPLS*, published by Elsevier, 2004.

Kateel Vijayananda (Chapter 12) is currently a design consultant at Cisco Systems. He has 9 years' experience in data networking, including the design, implementation, and management of IP networks, and the development of software to implement the OSI protocol stack. He has also been involved in developing managed network services such as LAN switching and LAN interconnect in a service provider environment. Vijayananda has worked as a network engineer/architect for a European service provider where he was part of teams that designed and implemented an MPLS network and that developed and managed IP-based services on top of an MPLS network. Vijayananda has an M.S. and a Ph.D. in computer science and is a Cisco Certified Internetworking Expert (#4850). He is also a co-author of *Developing IP-Based Services: Solutions for Service Providers and Vendors*, published by Elsevier, 2002.

Introduction

Multiprotocol Label Switching (MPLS) is over 10 years old. Born at a time when the Internet had just become a household word, MPLS had a hugely enthusiastic childhood and rapidly became one of the hottest buzzwords in the networking industry. Deployment, however, followed much more cautiously, and it was some years before MPLS saw wide rollout to carry live traffic in real operators' networks. MPLS can certainly now be said to be a mature technology with extensive deployments around the world, and with new applications and enhancements being invented all the time.

Unlike some of its precursors (such as ATM and Frame Relay), MPLS deployments have seen extensive use of the control plane right from the very start. In part, that can be attributed to the fact that MPLS leveraged many already-mature control plane protocols from the TCP/IP suite of protocols, notably the routing protocols BGP, OSPF, and IS-IS. At times, it seemed that MPLS might suffer from a surplus of control plane protocols when the Constraint-based Routed Label Distribution Protocol (CR-LDP) and Traffic Engineering extensions to the Resource Reservation Protocol (RSVP-TE) were both fighting for the same role as members of the MPLS control plane to support constraint-based routing.

Plenty of books have been written to describe how MPLS works and to explain the signaling and routing protocols used in MPLS systems. It is not the objective of this book to revisit that ground, so Chapters 2 and 3 provide only a summary and overview of the basics of the MPLS data plane and control plane. Readers who want to know more about the background and fundamentals of MPLS could do worse than refer to *MPLS Technology and Applications* by Davie and Rekhter, while *The Internet and Its Protocols* by Farrel provides a detailed description of all the relevant protocols.

The main objective of this book is to introduce some of the newer developments in MPLS. These extensions to the protocols enable new applications and services—the next steps in MPLS. As a technology, MPLS is maturing beyond its roots as a useful forwarding mechanism to an advanced and highly functional technology that enables service providers to activate new sources of revenue and new network features for their customers. It is this ability to support new features and services that has ensured MPLS's success in the field, much more than any initial aspirations to provide higher speed or lower cost packet forwarding.

MPLS started out as a packet technology, but its core aspects—forwarding traffic based on some label associated with the traffic—have turned out to be applicable to other network technologies. Starting with lambda switching in WDM networks and rapidly extending to cover TDM and layer 2 technologies, the concept of label switching was generalized to produce Generalized MPLS (GMPLS). GMPLS placed new demands on the control protocols and resulted in a set of extensions to the MPLS protocols, but the very nature of GMPLS is that the solutions are generic, and so the GMPLS features have been fed back into the packet networks, and in many cases it is precisely these new protocol extensions that enable the advanced MPLS applications.

1.1 SOURCE MATERIAL

Of course, many of the topics covered in this book have already been described at length in other books. In fact, the Morgan Kaufmann Series in Networking includes a comprehensive range of titles that deal with many aspects of MPLS networking. However, each book in the series has as its main focus a particular function or technology, and only some of the chapters or sections are specifically relevant to MPLS.

Therefore, what we have done in this book is to bring together material from a number of sources to give you a thorough grounding in the new developments in MPLS. Where necessary, we have edited the source material or written new text to describe the latest technologies. Where the sections of the previous work provide adequate description, we have simply reproduced it here. This results in a single reference that introduces MPLS, explains the basics, describes the control protocols, and discusses advanced topics applicable to MPLS. Readers wanting to know more about a particular topic are encouraged to go to the sources and read more widely.

In producing this book, we have drawn on material from the following Morgan Kaufmann books.

MPLS Technology and Applications by Davie and Rekhter
Written by two experts who personally authored key parts of the MPLS standards, this book has been regarded for many years as the foundation text for all network operators and designers who are interested in MPLS. It has provided a definitive reference for engineers who are implementing MPLS-based products.

The Internet and It Protocols: A Comparative Approach by Farrel
This book covers all the common protocols and shows how they combine to create the Internet in its totality. Each protocol, including the various MPLS and GMPLS protocols, is described completely, with an examination of the requirements that the protocol addresses and the exact means by which it does its job.

GMPLS: Architecture and Applications **by Farrel and Bryskin**
The relatively new area of GMPLS is not covered in detail by many books, and this one, written by two leading engineers who have been involved in the design of the GMPLS protocols from the very start, presents a deep and broad view of GMPLS from the protocol essentials, through the early deployment functions, to advanced and future topics.

Deploying IP and MPLS QoS for Multiservice Networks: Theory & Practice **by Evans and Filsfils**
In this book, the authors have provided a comprehensive treatise on the subject of Quality of Service (QoS) in IP and MPLS networks. They have included topics such as traffic engineering, capacity planning, and admission control. This book provides real-world case studies of QoS in multiservice networks to help remove the mystery behind QoS by illustrating the how, what, and why of implementing QoS within networks.

Traffic Engineering and QoS Optimization of Integrated Voice & Data Networks **by Ash**
In over 35 years of industry research and leadership, Gerald Ash was involved in many projects that advanced the cause of network routing, planning, and optimization. In this book he provides an analysis of the latest thinking about methods for providing traffic engineering and quality of service optimization for integrated voice/data dynamic routing networks.

Network Recovery: Protection and Restoration of Optical, SONET-SDH, IP, and MPLS **by Vasseur, Pickavet, and Demeester**
Network Recovery is the first book to provide detailed information on protecting and restoring communications networks. It describes techniques that work at each layer of the networking hierarchy, including optical, SONET/SDH, IP, and MPLS, and it shows how multilayer networks can be constructed to leverage mechanisms that exist in the different layers.

MPLS Network Management by **Nadeau**
Practical information on managing MPLS networks remains scarce, but this book, written by the coauthor of most of the MPLS management standards, provides a comprehensive view of the relevant techniques and tools.

Developing IP-Based Services **by Morrow and Vijayanada**
This book meets the challenge of uniting business and technical perspectives to provide a cohesive view of the MPLS development and deployment process to enable networking organizations to leverage MPLS to drive traffic and boost revenue.

1.2 **CONTENTS OF THIS BOOK**

This book has 14 chapters following on from this introduction, and these are divided into four sections.

- Section A provides a refresher of MPLS Basics.
- Section B describes Advanced Techniques for providing high function services over an MPLS network.
- Section C examines the key features of Operations, Management, and Security that are necessary for a protocol to move from an experimental concept to a real technology that can be deployed and widely used.
- Section D looks at some of the techniques used to provide services to customers based on MPLS networks.

Chapter 2 provides a refresher and overview of the MPLS data plane. It describes how MPLS applies labels to packets and how labeled packets are forwarded through the network.

Chapter 3 gives a summary and reminder about the core MPLS control protocols with special reference to the Label Distribution Protocol (LDP) and RSVP-TE.

The fourth chapter introduces GMPLS and explains how the evolution from MPLS to GMPLS took place. It describes some of the new features brought in by the extensions to the MPLS protocols.

Chapter 5 discusses Traffic Engineering, one of the key aspects of MPLS that enables the provision of quality of service and allows an operator to manage the network for optimum performance and capacity.

Chapter 6 goes into the subject of quality of service in much more detail. When everything else has been described, the customer is usually not particularly interested in the networking technology that the operator uses to deliver services. What the customer really cares about is the quality of the service that is delivered, and this chapter looks at the techniques and mechanisms that are used in MPLS networks to ensure that the network meets the needs and expectations of the end customer.

Chapter 7 and Chapter 8 investigate the requirement for restoration and recovery techniques in MPLS networks. They look at how rapidly repairing end-to-end connectivity is an essential component in meeting the users' quality expectations, and they explore the techniques enabled by MPLS and GMPLS to achieve recovery through protection or restoration of the forwarding plane.

The ninth chapter begins the section on Operations, Management, and Security by describing the Management Information Base (MIB) definitions and tables that enable a consistent and standardized approach to managing MPLS networks, their protocols, and the equipment from which they are constructed.

Chapter 10 develops the management theme through an introduction to the monitoring and maintenance protocols that have been developed to check connectivity in MPLS networks, diagnose and isolate faults, and monitor data transfer through the networks.

Chapter 11 provides an overview of the importance of Security within MPLS. It describes how this function is relevant to clients of MPLS networks as well as within the networks themselves, and it provides an overview of the techniques applied to keep the networks and the data that traverse them safe.

The final section of the book begins with Chapter 12 on Virtual Private Networks (VPNs). VPNs have become one of the largest sources of revenue for Internet Service Providers and played a central role in the successful adoption of MPLS. VPNs offer a highly valuable service to customers that allows them to connect disparate sites (offices) and individual computers (such as home workers) to form one seamless network as though it was cabled using private network resources. MPLS offers a simple way for network operators to provide VPNs over a public network that shares resources and capacity with other VPNs and other applications, with relatively straightforward configuration and management.

Chapter 13 discusses MPLS pseudowires, another rapidly growing application of MPLS. An MPLS pseudowire is a way to provide emulated connectivity of some non-MPLS technology (such as TDM or Ethernet) across an MPLS network. As a service, pseudowires are critical for linking together isolated islands of some legacy or future technology to produce an integrated network, making them fundamental to many migration and installation plans.

Chapter 14 examines how MPLS techniques are applied to multidomain networks. Until recently, MPLS was applied only within a single network domain (for example, a routing area or an Autonomous System), with connectivity between MPLS domains being provided at a higher layer, such as by IP routing. But the increasing popularity of MPLS means that it makes sense to consider how the technology can be applied in multidomain networks to provide end-to-end MPLS services.

The final chapter, Chapter 15, is devoted to an introduction to multicast and point-to-multipoint MPLS. Multipoint services are gaining significant attention in the Internet with advances in technologies such as IPTV. It is becoming increasingly important to satisfy these services in a network-efficient way using MPLS, and this chapter looks at recent developments in the MPLS protocols to enable point-to-multipoint forwarding in the MPLS data plane.

We hope that this selection of material from some of the leading books on the associated topics will combine with the new chapters that we have written to give an up-to-date picture of MPLS and its applications in a rapidly evolving arena.

SECTION

MPLS Basics

A

This initial section introduces Multiprotocol Label Switching (MPLS). The basics of the MPLS data plane and control plane are covered in Chapters 2 and 3 respectively. Chapter 4 introduces the control plane and functional extensions to MPLS that create Generalized MPLS (GMPLS), and describes how those extensions are applicable to MPLS packet switching networks as well as the layer 1 optical networks more generally associated with GMPLS.

The material in these chapters, taken from *MPLS Technology and Applications* by Davie and Rekhter and *The Internet and Its Protocols* by Farrel, is intended as an overview and refresher. It does not give a detailed and thorough review of MPLS, and the reader should refer to the source texts for more details and deeper coverage.

Overview of the MPLS Data Plane

2

In this chapter, using information from *MPLS Technology and Applications* by Davie and Rekhter and from *The Internet and Its Protocols* by Farrel, we describe the fundamental concepts of label switching. Although there are differences among various approaches to label switching, certain concepts are common to all of these approaches—such concepts form the fundamental building blocks of label switching. A solid grasp of these concepts will help you understand and compare the individual approaches to label switching, and lays the groundwork for understanding the design decisions behind the MPLS standards.

We begin this chapter with a description of the functional decomposition of network layer routing into control and forwarding components. We then proceed to describe label switching forwarding and control components.

2.1 NETWORK LAYER ROUTING FUNCTIONAL COMPONENTS: CONTROL AND FORWARDING

Network layer routing can be partitioned into two basic components: control and forwarding. The forwarding component is responsible for the actual forwarding of packets from input to output across a switch or router. To forward a packet the forwarding component uses two sources of information: a forwarding table maintained by a router and the information carried in the packet itself. The control component is responsible for construction and maintenance of the forwarding table.

Each router in a network implements both control and forwarding components. The actual network layer routing is realized as a composition of control and forwarding components implemented in a distributed fashion by a set of routers that forms the network.

The control component consists of one or more routing protocols that provide exchange of routing information among routers, as well as the procedures (algorithms) that a router uses to convert this information into a forwarding table.

The forwarding component consists of a set of procedures (algorithms) that a router uses to make a forwarding decision on a packet. The algorithms define the

9

information from the packet that a router uses to find a particular entry in its forwarding table, as well as the exact procedures that the router uses for finding the entry. As an illustration, we consider three cases: (1) forwarding of unicast packets, (2) forwarding of unicast packets with Types of Service, and (3) forwarding of multicast packets.

For unicast forwarding, the information from a packet that a router uses to find a particular entry in the forwarding table is the network layer destination address, and the procedure that the router uses for finding the entry is the longest match algorithm.

For unicast forwarding with Types of Service, the information from a packet that a router uses to find a particular entry in the forwarding table is the network layer destination address and the Type of Service value, and the procedure that the router uses for finding the entry is the longest match algorithm on the destination address and the exact match algorithm on the Type of Service value.

For multicast forwarding, the information from a packet that a router uses to find a particular entry in the forwarding table is a combination of the network layer source and destination addresses and the incoming interface (the interface that a packet arrives on), and the procedure that the router uses for finding the entry uses both the longest match and the exact match algorithms.

2.1.1 Forwarding Equivalence Classes

We may think about procedures used by the forwarding component as a way of partitioning the set of all possible packets that a router can forward into a finite number of disjoint subsets. From a forwarding point of view, packets within each subset are treated by the router in the same way (e.g., they are all sent to the same next hop), even if the packets within the subset differ from each other with respect to the information in the network layer header of these packets. We refer to such subsets as Forwarding Equivalence Classes (FECs). The reason a router forwards all packets within a given FEC the same way is that the mapping between the information carried in the network layer header of the packets and the entries in the forwarding table is many-to-one (with one-to-one as a special case). That is, packets with different content of their network layer headers could be mapped into the same entry in the forwarding table, where the entry describes a particular FEC.

One example of an FEC is a set of unicast packets whose network layer destination address matches a particular IP address prefix. A set of multicast packets with the same source and destination network layer addresses is another example of an FEC. A set of unicast packets whose destination addresses match a particular IP address prefix and whose Type of Service bits are the same is yet another example of an FEC.

An essential part of a forwarding entry maintained by a router is the address of the next hop router. A packet that falls into an FEC associated with a particular forwarding entry is forwarded to the next hop router specified by the entry.

Therefore, the construction of a forwarding table by the control component could be modeled as constructing a set of FECs and the next hop for each of these FECs.

One important characteristic of an FEC is its forwarding granularity. For example, at one end of the spectrum, an FEC could include all the packets whose network layer destination address matches a particular address prefix. This type of FEC provides coarse forwarding granularity. At the other end of the spectrum, an FEC could include only the packets that belong to a particular application running between a pair of computers, thus including only the packets with the same source and destination network layer addresses (these addresses identify the computers), as well as the transport layer port numbers (these ports identify a particular application within a computer). This type of FEC provides fine forwarding granularity.

You could observe that coarse forwarding granularity is essential for making the overall system scalable. On the other hand, supporting only coarse granularity would make the overall system fairly inflexible, as it wouldn't allow differentiation among different types of traffic. For example, it would not allow different forwarding or resource reservations for traffic that belongs to different applications. These observations suggest that to build a routing system that is both scalable and functionally rich would require the system to support a wide spectrum of forwarding granularities, as well as the ability to flexibly intermix and combine different forwarding granularities.

2.1.2 Providing Consistent Routing

A correctly functioning routing system requires consistent forwarding across multiple routers. This consistency is accomplished via a combination of several mechanisms.

The control component is responsible for consistent distribution of routing information used by the routers for constructing their forwarding tables. The control component is also responsible for the consistency of the procedures that the routers use to construct their forwarding tables (and thus FECs and associated next hops) out of the routing information. Combining these two factors—consistent information distribution and consistent local procedures—results in consistency among forwarding tables, and therefore FECs and associated next hops, across routers that form a network.

The forwarding component is responsible for consistent procedures for extracting the information from packets, as well as for a consistent way of using this information to find an appropriate entry in a forwarding table, resulting in a consistent mapping of packets into FECs across multiple routers. Consistent mapping of packets into FECs, combined with the consistent forwarding tables across multiple routers, provides a correctly functioning routing system.

As an illustration, consider an example of unicast forwarding with OSPF as a routing protocol. The OSPF procedures guarantee (by means of reliable flooding) that the link-state information is consistent among a set of routers. The OSPF procedures also guarantee that all these routers will use the same procedure (the shortest path first algorithm) for computing their forwarding tables based on the link-state information. Combining these two factors results in consistent forwarding tables (consistent set of FECs and their next hops) among the routers. The forwarding component guarantees that the only information carried in the packets that will be used for making the forwarding decision will be the destination network layer address and that all the routers will use the longest match algorithm to find an appropriate entry in their forwarding tables.

2.2 LABEL SWITCHING: THE FORWARDING COMPONENT

Decomposition of network layer routing into control and forwarding components could be applied not only to the "conventional" routing architecture but to the label switching approach as well. In this section we describe some of the fundamental concepts associated with the label switching forwarding component.

The algorithm used by the label switching forwarding component to make a forwarding decision on a packet uses two sources of information: the first one is a forwarding table maintained by a Label Switching Router (LSR), and the second is a label carried in the packet.

2.2.1 What Is a Label?

A label is a short, fixed-length entity, with no internal structure. A label does not directly encode any of the information from the network layer header. For example, a label does not directly encode network layer addresses (neither source nor destination addresses). The semantics of a label are discussed in Section 2.2.4.

2.2.2 Label Switching Forwarding Tables

Conceptually, a forwarding table maintained by an LSR consists of a sequence of entries, where each entry consists of an incoming label, and one or more subentries, where each subentry consists of an outgoing label, an outgoing interface, and the next hop address (see Figure 2.1). Different subentries within an

Incoming label	First subentry	Second subentry
Incoming label	Outgoing label Outgoing interfaces Next hop address	Outgoing label Outgoing interfaces Next hop address

FIGURE 2.1

Forwarding table entry.

individual entry may have either the same or different outgoing labels. There may be more than one subentry in order to handle multicast forwarding, where a packet that arrives on one interface would need to be sent out on multiple outgoing interfaces.

The forwarding table is indexed by the value contained in the incoming label. That is, the value contained in the incoming label component of the Nth entry in the table is N.

In addition to the information that controls where a packet is forwarded (next hop), an entry in the forwarding table may include the information related to what resources the packet may use, such as a particular outgoing queue that the packet should be placed on.

An LSR could maintain either a single forwarding table or a forwarding table per each of its interfaces. With the latter option, handling of a packet is determined not just by the label carried in the packet but also by the interface that the packet arrives on. With the former option, handling of a packet is determined solely by the label carried in the packet. An LSR may use either the first or the second option, or a combination of both.

2.2.3 Carrying a Label in a Packet

Essential to the label switching forwarding component is the ability to carry a label in a packet. This can be accomplished in several ways.

Certain link layer technologies, most notably ATM and Frame Relay, can carry a label as part of their link layer header. Specifically, with ATM the label could be carried in the VCI and VPI fields of the ATM header. Likewise, with Frame Relay the label could be carried in the DLCI field of the Frame Relay header.

Using the option of carrying the label as part of the link layer header allows support of label switching with some but not all link layer technologies. Constraining label switching to only the link layer technologies that could carry the label as part of their link layer header would severely limit the usefulness of label switching (as it would immediately exclude the use of label switching over such media as Ethernet or point-to-point links).

A way to support label switching over link layer technologies where the link layer header can't be used to carry a label is to carry the label in a small "shim" label header. This MPLS shim label header is inserted between the link layer and the network layer headers (see Figure 2.2) and thus could be used with any link layer technology. Use of the shim label header allows support of label switching

Link layer header	"Shim" label header	Network layer header	Network layer data

FIGURE 2.2

Carrying label in the shim label header.

Label (20 bits)	Exp (3 bits)	Stack (1 bit)	TTL (8 bits)

FIGURE 2.3

The Shim Header carries a 20-bit label.

over such link layer technologies as Ethernet, FDDI, Token Ring, point-to-point links, and so on.

The MPLS shim header carries a 20-bit label. The other fields are listed here and shown in Figure 2.3.

- Three Experimental bits are used for grading services much as the IP Diff-Serv packet classification operates.
- One bit indicates that this label is the last in a stack of labels (see Section 2.2.8).
- Eight bits carry the time-to-live (TTL). The TTL is treated in the same way as an IP TTL (that is, decremented on a hop-by-hop basis) as the labeled packet is forwarded across the network.

2.2.4 Label Switching Forwarding Algorithm

The forwarding algorithm used by the forwarding component of label switching is based on label swapping. The algorithm works as follows. When an LSR receives a packet, the router extracts the label from the packet and uses it as an index in its forwarding table. Once the entry indexed by the label is found (this entry has its incoming label component equal to the label extracted from the packet), for each subentry of the found entry the router replaces the label in the packet with the outgoing label from the subentry and sends the packet over the outgoing interface specified by this subentry to the next hop specified by this subentry. If the entry specifies a particular outgoing queue, the router places the packet on the specified queue.

In the previous paragraph, our description assumes that an LSR maintains a single forwarding table. However, an LSR may also maintain a distinct forwarding table for each of its interfaces. In this case, the only modification to the algorithm is that after the LSR receives a packet, the LSR uses the interface on which the packet was received to select a particular forwarding table that will be used for handling the packet.

Readers familiar with ATM will notice that when an LSR maintains its forwarding tables on a per-interface basis, the forwarding algorithm just described corresponds to the algorithm used to forward cells in ATM switches.

The path that a data packet follows through the network is defined by the transition in label values. Since the mapping at each node is constant, the path is uniquely determined by the label value at the first node. Such a path is called a *Label Switched Path* (LSP). As described in Section 2.2.2, each node in an MPLS

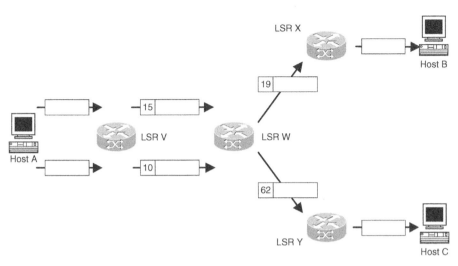

FIGURE 2.4

Label switched paths.

network maintains a look-up table that allows it to determine the next hop in the LSP. The table is known as the *Label Forwarding Information Base* (LFIB) and maps {incoming interface, incoming label} to {outgoing interface, outgoing label}. This is all the information necessary to forward labeled packets.

Note that once the LFIB has been populated there is no freedom of choice of label values. The process of populating the LFIB is controlled through configuration or through the label distribution protocols described in the next chapter. In general, the choice of label values to put in the LFIB is governed only by consideration of which labels are already in use, and the capabilities of the hardware/software that will be switching packets based on label values.

Figure 2.4 illustrates two LSPs carrying data from IP Host A to Hosts B and C. The MPLS network is made up of four *Label Switching Routers* (LSRs) that forward the packets. Host A sends normal IP packets to LSR V using its default route. LSR V is an ingress LSR and classifies the packets based on the final destination, assigns them to an LSP, and labels them. Those packets targeted at Host B are assigned to the upper LSP and are labeled 15; those for Host C are assigned to the lower LSP and are labeled 10. Once labeled, the packets are forwarded out of the appropriate interface toward LSR W.

At LSR W each labeled packet is examined to determine the incoming interface and incoming label. These are looked up in the LFIB (see Table 2.1) to determine the outgoing label and outgoing interface. The label values are swapped (incoming replaced with outgoing) and the packets are forwarded out of the designated interfaces. In the figure, packets labeled 15 are forwarded out of the interface to LSR X carrying the new label 19; packets labeled 10 are forwarded out of the interface to LSR Y carrying the new label 62.

Table 2.1 The LFIB at LSR W.

Incoming Interface	Incoming Label	Outgoing Interface	Outgoing Label
From LSR V	15	To LSR X	19
From LSR V	10	To LSR Y	62

LSR X and LSR Y are egress LSRs. They also perform a look-up into their LFIBs, but the entries indicate that they should remove the shim header and forward the packet as normal. This forwarding may be through the normal IP routing table, but can be optimized by the LFIB indicating the outgoing interface so that no routing look-up is required. So, in the example, if LSR V associates all packets for Host B with the upper LSP and labels them with the value 15, they will be successfully forwarded through the network and delivered to Host B.

A label always carries forwarding semantics and may also carry resource reservation semantics. A label always carries forwarding semantics because a label carried in a packet uniquely determines a particular entry in the forwarding table maintained by an LSR and because that particular entry contains information about where to forward a packet. A label may optionally carry resource reservation semantics because the entry determined by the label may optionally include the information related to what resources the packet may use, such as a particular outgoing queue that the packet should be placed on. When a label is carried in the ATM or Frame Relay header, the label has to carry both forwarding and resource reservation semantics. When a label is carried in the shim label header, then the information related to what resources the packet may use may be encoded as part of that header, rather than being carried by a label (so that the label will carry just forwarding semantics). Yet another option is to use both the label and the (nonlabel) part of the shim header to encode this information. And, of course, even with the shim header, the label may carry both forwarding and resource reservation semantics.

Simplicity of the forwarding algorithm used by the label switching forwarding component facilitates inexpensive implementations of this algorithm in hardware, which, in turn, enables faster forwarding performance without requiring expensive hardware.

One important property of the forwarding algorithm used by label switching is that an LSR can obtain all the information needed to forward a packet as well as to decide what resources the packet may use in just one memory access. This is because (a) an entry in the forwarding table contains all the information needed to forward a packet as well as to decide what resources the packet may use, and (b) the label carried in the packet provides an index to the entry in the forwarding table that should be used for forwarding the packet. The ability to obtain both forwarding and resource reservation information in just one memory access makes label switching suitable as a technology for high forwarding performance.

Routing function	Unicast routing	Unicast routing with Types of Service	Multicast routing
Forwarding algorithm	Longest match on destination address	Longest match on destination + exact match on Type of Service	Longest match on source address + exact match on source address, destination address, and incoming interface

FIGURE 2.5

Conventional routing architecture.

It is important to understand that the use of label swapping forwarding combined with the ability to carry labels on a wide range of link layer technologies means that many different devices can be used to implement LSRs. For example, carrying the label inside the VCI field of ATM cells enables unmodified ATM switch hardware to function as an LSR, given the addition of suitable control software. Similarly, the shim header described above appears in packets in a place where most conventional routers can process it in software. Thus, with the addition of suitable software, a conventional router can also become an LSR.

2.2.5 Single Forwarding Algorithm

In the "conventional" routing architecture, different functionality provided by the control component (e.g., unicast routing, multicast routing, unicast routing with Types of Service) requires multiple forwarding algorithms in the forwarding component (see Figure 2.5). For example, forwarding of unicast packets requires longest match based on the network layer destination address; forwarding of multicast packets requires longest match on the source network layer address plus the exact match on both source and destination network layer addresses, whereas unicast forwarding with Types of Service requires the longest match on the destination network layer address plus the exact match on the Type of Service bits carried in the network layer header.

One important property of label switching is the lack of multiple forwarding algorithms within its forwarding component; the label switching forwarding component consists of just one algorithm—the algorithm based on label swapping (see Figure 2.6). This forms one important distinction between label switching and the conventional routing architecture.

You may think that constraining the forwarding component to a single forwarding algorithm would significantly limit the functionality that could be

Routing function	Unicast routing	Unicast routing with Types of Service	Multicast routing
Forwarding algorithm	Common forwarding (label swapping)		

FIGURE 2.6

Label switching architecture.

supported with label switching. However, this is not the case. The ability to support a wide range of routing functionality with just one forwarding algorithm is one of the key assumptions behind label switching, and so far this assumption has proven to be correct. In fact, as we'll see later, the functionality that could be supported with label switching (using a single forwarding algorithm) could be richer than the functionality that could be accomplished with the conventional routing architecture (which uses multiple forwarding algorithms).

2.2.6 Forwarding Granularity

The label switching forwarding component, by itself, doesn't place any constraints on the forwarding granularity that could be associated with a particular FEC, and therefore with a label. The spectrum of forwarding granularities that could be associated with FECs, and therefore with labels, as well as the ability to intermix different forwarding granularities, is determined solely by the label switching control component. It is completely up to the control component to decide whether and how to exploit this.

2.2.7 Multiprotocol: Both Above and Below

From the previous description of the label switching forwarding component we can make two important observations. First of all, the forwarding component is not specific to a particular network layer. For example, the same forwarding component could be used when doing label switching with IP as well as when doing label switching with IPX. This makes label switching suitable as a multiprotocol solution with respect to the network layer protocols (see Figure 2.7).

Moreover, multiprotocol capabilities of label switching go beyond the ability to support multiple network layer protocols; label switching is also capable of operating over virtually any link layer protocol. This makes label switching a multiprotocol solution with respect to the link layer protocols.

These properties of label switching explain the name given to the IETF working group that is currently working to standardize this technology: Multiprotocol Label Switching (MPLS).

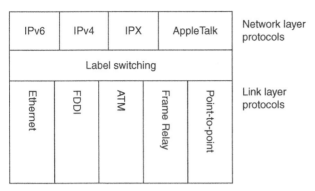

FIGURE 2.7

Multiprotocol: above and below.

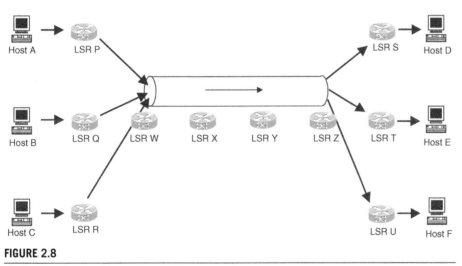

FIGURE 2.8

An LSP Tunnel carrying multiple LSPs.

2.2.8 **Hierarchies and Tunnels**

MPLS allows for LSPs to be nested or tunneled. This mechanism is useful for allowing many LSPs to be treated in the same way in the core of the network while preserving their individuality at the edges. Doing this enhances the scalability of LSRs in the core of the network and significantly improves the manageability of connections across the network.

Tunnels like the one between LSR W and LSR Z in Figure 2.8 may conveniently be presented to the routing protocol as virtual routing adjacencies or *forwarding adjacencies* (FAs). This allows other LSPs to be tunneled through these trunk

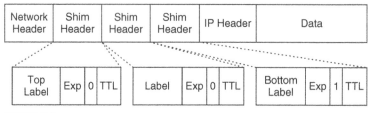

FIGURE 2.9

The label stack.

LSPs as though they were simply stepping from one LSR to the next (that is, from LSR W to LSR Z). There are many ways to achieve this, but a convenient one is to install the tunnel LSP as an interface at LSR W and to treat it as a virtual link between LSR W and LSR Z. Appropriate care must be taken to set the cost of this link correctly—it should be assigned a cost that is cheaper than taking the hop-by-hop route W-X-Y-Z, but not so cheap that a shorter route is excluded.

When MPLS packets are received at LSR Z in Figure 2.8, some identification is required so that LSR Z can easily determine the correct next label value and outgoing interface. It would be possible to match each packet against an FEC and so determine the correct LSP to use, but this would actually be a concatenation of LSPs—we require a way of stripping off the outer tunnel at Z, to be left with the inner LSP. This is achieved using a *label stack* on each packet. When each packet enters the tunnel at LSR W the label is replaced as usual, but an additional label is *imposed* on the packet. That is, a further label is pushed onto the label stack. This top-most label is used to forward the packet from LSR W to LSR Z. At LSR Z, the top label is popped from the stack, revealing the label of the tunneled LSP.

A label stack is achieved simply by adding additional shim headers to the data packet as shown in Figure 2.9. The first shim header encountered represents the top-most label (the one that is being actively used to forward the packet). The last shim header has the Stack bit set to indicate that it is the bottom of the stack.

Figure 2.10 illustrates how label stacks are used in the network shown in Figure 2.8. LSR P takes traffic from Host A targeted at Host D and imposes a label (5). Similarly, traffic from Host C to Host E is handled at LSR R where a label (8) is imposed. At LSR W, both LSPs undergo label swapping (5 to 3 and 8 to 7) and are tunneled into a new LSP where an additional label (9) is pushed onto the stack. Forwarding along the path W-X-Y-Z is as described before—the top label on the stack is swapped and the packet is forwarded. Note that the labels lower down the stack are not examined or processed. At LSR Z, the label that defines the tunnel is popped from the stack, and traffic is forwarded using the next label on the stack.

The actions needed for tunneling can be encoded in the LFIB by using an additional column. This is illustrated in Table 2.2.

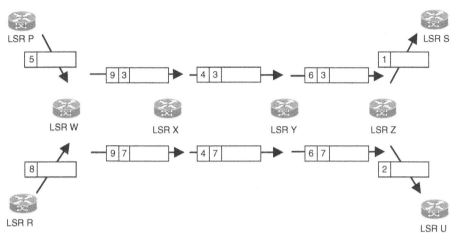

FIGURE 2.10

Label stacks in use.

Table 2.2 LFIBs at LSR W, LSR X and LSR Z for LSP Tunnels.				
Incoming Interface	**Incoming Label**	**Action**	**Outgoing Interface**	**Outgoing Labels**
LSR W				
From LSR P	5	Swap and Push	To LSR X	9, 3
From LSR R	8	Swap and Push	To LSR X	9, 7
LSR X				
From LSR W	9	Swap	To LSR Y	4
LSR Z				
From LSR Y	6	Pop	N/A	N/A
From Tunnel	3	Swap	To LSR S	1
From Tunnel	7	Swap	To LSR U	2

The LFIB in Table 2.2 shows how the processing at the tunnel egress (LSR Z) is a bit clumsy. First, a look-up in the LFIB is made for the received label (6), and then a second look-up must be made to process the labels of the tunneled LSPs (3 and 7) to determine how to forward the packets. The second look-up may be hard to perform in hardware implementations and is not actually required if the previous node performs *penultimate hop popping* (PHP). PHP is a process

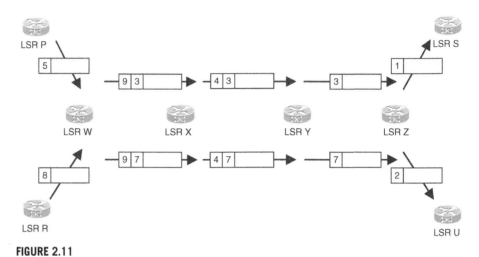

FIGURE 2.11

Label stacks with PHP.

Table 2.3 LFIBs at LSR Y and LSR Z for Previous Hop Popping.

Incoming Interface	Incoming Label	Action	Outgoing Interface	Outgoing Label
LSR Y				
From LSR X	4	Pop	To LSR Z	N/A
LSR Z				
From LSR Y	3	Swap	To LSR S	1
From LSR Y	7	Swap	To LSR U	2

in which the top label is popped from the stack one hop before the end of the tunnel. The packet is forwarded and the next LSR (the real end of the tunnel) processes the tunneled LSP. Figure 2.11 shows how PHP might be used in the previous example. LSR Y performs penultimate hop popping by stripping the top label (4) from the received packets, and forwarding the packets. Table 2.3 shows the LFIBs at LSR Y and LSR Z when PHP is used.

2.2.9 Label Switching Forwarding Component: Summary

As we discussed at the beginning of this section, the forwarding component of network layer routing defines (a) the information from a packet that a router uses for finding a particular entry in its forwarding table, as well as (b) the exact pro-cedures that a router uses for finding the entry. The label switching forwarding component defines a label carried in a packet as the information that an LSR uses to find a particular entry in its forwarding table. The label switching forwarding component defines the exact match on the label as the procedure for finding an entry in a forwarding table.

The following summarizes the rest of the key properties of the label switching forwarding component:

- The label switching forwarding component uses a single forwarding algo-rithm based on label swapping.
- The label carried in a packet is a short, fixed-length unstructured entity that has both forwarding and resource reservation semantics.
- The label switching forwarding component by itself doesn't place any con-straints on the forwarding granularity that could be associated with a label.
- The label switching forwarding component can support multiple network layer protocols as well as multiple link layer protocols.

2.3 LABEL SWITCHING: THE CONTROL COMPONENT

As we mentioned before, decomposition of network layer routing into control and forwarding components could be applied not only to the conventional routing architecture but to label switching as well. In this section we describe some of the fundamental concepts associated with the label switching control component.

The control component of label switching is responsible for (a) distributing routing information among LSRs and (b) the procedures (algorithms) that these routers use to convert this information into a forwarding table that is used by the label switching forwarding component. Just like a control component of any rout-ing system, the label switching control component must provide for consistent distribution of routing information among LSRs as well as consistent procedures for constructing forwarding tables out of this information.

There is a great deal of similarity between the control component of the con-ventional routing architecture and the label switching control component. In fact, the label switching control component includes all the routing protocols used by the control component of the conventional routing architecture. In this sense the control component of the conventional routing architecture forms a part (subset) of the label switching control component.

However, the control component of the conventional routing architecture is not sufficient to support label switching. This is because the information provided by the control component of the conventional routing architecture isn't sufficient to construct forwarding tables used by the label switching for-warding component, as these tables have to contain mappings between labels and next hops.

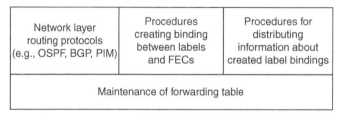

FIGURE 2.12

The label switching control component.

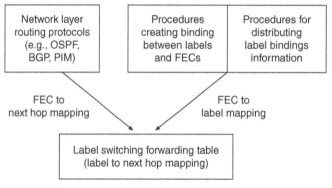

FIGURE 2.13

Construction of a label switching forwarding table.

To fill the void we need procedures by which an LSR can

1. Create bindings between labels and FECs
2. Inform other LSRs of the bindings it creates
3. Utilize both (a) and (b) to construct and maintain the forwarding table used by the label switching component

The overall structure of the label switching control component is shown in Figure 2.12.

The network layer routing protocols provide LSRs with the mapping between FECs and next hop addresses. Procedures for creating label binding between labels and FECs, and for distributing this binding information among label switches, provide LSRs with the mapping between FECs and labels. The two mappings combined provide the information needed to construct the forwarding tables used by the label switching forwarding component (see Figure 2.13).

2.3.1 Local versus Remote Binding

Recall that each entry in a forwarding table maintained by an LSR contains one incoming label and one or more outgoing labels. Corresponding to these two types of labels in the forwarding table, the label switching control component provides two types of label bindings. The first type of label binding occurs when the router creates the binding with a label that is chosen and assigned locally. We refer to such binding as local. The second type of label binding is when the router receives from some other LSR label binding information that corresponds to the label binding created by that other router. We refer to such binding as remote.

An important difference between a local and a remote binding is that with the local binding the label associated with the binding is chosen locally, by the LSR itself, whereas with the remote binding the label associated with the binding is chosen by some other LSR M.

2.3.2 Upstream versus Downstream Binding

The label switching control component uses both local and remote bindings to populate its forwarding table with incoming and outgoing labels. This could be done in two ways. The first method is when labels from the local binding are used as incoming labels and labels from the remote binding are used as outgoing labels. The second is exactly the opposite—labels from the local binding are used as outgoing labels, and labels from the remote binding are used as incoming labels. We examine each option in turn.

The first option is called *downstream* label binding because binding between a label carried by a packet and a particular FEC that the packet belongs to is created by an LSR that is downstream (with respect to the flow of the packet) from the LSR that places the label in the packet. Observe that with downstream label binding, packets that carry a particular label flow in the direction opposite to the flow of the binding information about that label.

The second option is called *upstream* label binding because binding between a label carried by a packet and a particular FEC that the packet belongs to is created by the same LSR that places the label in the packet; that is, the creator of the binding is upstream with respect to the flow of packets. Observe that with upstream label binding, packets that carry a particular label flow in the same direction as the label binding information about this label.

The names *upstream* and *downstream* seem to have caused considerable confusion, but no attempt to come up with less confusing names has yet succeeded. We have found that it helps to consider the flow of data packets—they flow toward the downstream end of the link—and then ask the question "At which end of the link were the bindings created: upstream or downstream?" Figure 2.14 illustrates flow of both data packets and label binding information for the downstream and upstream label binding modes. In each case data packets flow "down" to the right. In downstream allocation, binding is generated at the downstream end of the link; with upstream allocation, binding is generated at the upstream end.

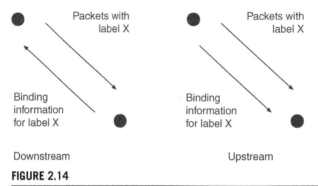

FIGURE 2.14

Downstream versus upstream label binding.

2.3.3 "Free" Labels

An LSR maintains a pool of "free" labels (labels with no bindings). When the LSR is first initialized, the pool contains all possible labels that the LSR can use for local binding. The size of this pool ultimately determines how many concurrent label bindings the LSR will be able to support. When the router creates a new local binding, the router takes a label from the pool; when the router destroys a previously created binding, the router returns the label associated with that binding to the pool.

Recall that an LSR could maintain either a single forwarding table or multiple forwarding tables—one per interface. When the router maintains a single label switching forwarding table, the router maintains a single pool of labels. When the LSR maintains a label switching table on a per-interface basis, the LSR maintains pools of labels on a per-interface basis as well.

2.3.4 Distributing Label Binding Information: What Are the Options?

Once an LSR creates or destroys a binding between a locally chosen label and an FEC, the LSR needs to inform other LSRs of that binding; this will provide other LSRs with the remote label binding information. Distributing label binding information can be accomplished in several ways.

Piggyback on Top of Routing Protocols

One way to distribute label binding information is to piggyback this information on top of the routing protocols. This approach is only possible in control-driven schemes, because it ties label distribution to the distribution of control (routing) information, and has some attractive properties. First of all, it makes the distribution of label binding information consistent with the distribution of routing information. It also allows race conditions to be avoided, where either the label binding information (binding between labels and FECs) would be available, but the associated routing information (and, more specifically, the binding between FECs and next hops) would not, or vice versa. Finally, it simplifies the overall system operation, as it eliminates the need for a separate protocol to distribute label binding information.

However, this approach has drawbacks as well. First of all, the routing information that is distributed by a particular protocol may not be suitable for distributing label binding information—only the protocols where distributed routing information explicitly contains mapping between FECs and next hops would be suitable for piggybacking label binding information. For this reason Link-State Routing Protocols (e.g., OSPF) make a rather poor match for what is required to distribute label binding information. On the other hand, for precisely the same reason, protocols such as BGP and PIM seem to be quite suitable for distributing label binding information as well.

Even if the routing information distributed by a protocol makes the protocol suitable for the distribution of label binding information, extending the protocol to carry this information may not always be feasible. This is because extending the protocol may involve changes to the format of the messages used by the protocol, which, in turn, may result in backward incompatibility. So, even if you view the option of piggybacking the label binding information on top of the routing protocol as desirable, it may not always be feasible.

You also have to be concerned about the possibility that a label, piggybacked in a protocol message, might be received by a device that does not understand labels. Either this must be prevented or the piggybacking must be done in a way that non-label switching devices are easily able to ignore label bindings received in this way.

Label Distribution Protocol

Constraining label switching to only the cases where the routing protocols can piggyback label binding information is undesirable. A way to circumvent this limitation is by distributing label binding information via a separate protocol.

The ability to support label switching with routing protocols that can't be used for piggybacking label binding information is perhaps the major advantage of using a separate label distribution protocol. But it is likely to be the only advantage of this approach.

On the negative side, this approach makes it more difficult to avoid race conditions—you may end up in a situation where an LSR would have label binding information (label to FEC binding), but not the routing information (FEC to next hop binding) needed to use the label binding information, or vice versa.

Another drawback of this approach is that it introduces yet another protocol into the system, which increases the overall complexity of the system.

If the label switching control component uses only one label distribution protocol, then this approach also makes it hard to make the distribution of label binding information consistent with the distribution of routing information. To see why this is true, observe that while some of the routing protocols exchange routing information based on the technique of incremental updates and explicit acknowledgments (e.g., BGP), other routing protocols use periodic refreshes of complete routing information (e.g., PIM).

A way to avoid this mismatch is to have more than one label distribution protocol. With this method you could make one label distribution protocol that will be used in conjunction with OSPF and will rely on incremental updates and explicit acknowledgments, while making another label distribution protocol that will be used in conjunction with PIM and will rely on periodic refreshes of complete binding information. But though this approach would solve the problem of consistent distribution of label binding information, it would introduce even more protocols into the system, which in turn would result in an even more complex system.

Based on the above discussion, the option of piggybacking label binding information on top of routing protocols should be viewed as preferred whenever possible or feasible; a separate label distribution protocol should be used only when piggybacking is not possible or feasible. By limiting the scope where a label distribution protocol is needed, you could hope to either reduce or avoid mismatch between the distribution of label binding information and the distribution of routing information while at the same time being able to stay with a single label distribution protocol.

2.4 EDGE DEVICES

So far we have described how LSRs forward packets that carry labels. But how do these packets get their labels in the first place? Turning "unlabeled" packets into "labeled" ones and vice versa is performed by the edge LSRs.

You can think of an edge LSR as a device that implements the control and forwarding components of both label switching and conventional routing. When an edge LSR receives a packet without a label, the LSR uses the conventional forwarding component to determine the FEC that this packet belongs to and the next hop that the packet should be sent to. If the next hop is an LSR, then the LSR uses the label switching forwarding component to determine the label that should be added to the packet. Likewise, when an edge LSR receives a packet with a label, the LSR uses the label switching forwarding component to determine the FEC that this packet belongs to and the next hop that the packet should be sent to. If the next hop is not an LSR, then the LSR just strips the label from the packet and hands the packet to its conventional forwarding component, which, in turn, sends the packet to the next hop.

The fact that both LSRs and conventional routers use the same set of routing protocols makes interworking between the conventional and the label switching control components trivial. The only thing that is required of the label switching control component is the ability to determine whether a particular (next hop) router is an LSR or not.

In some cases, a host may function as the edge device. Because hosts do not generally run routing protocols, there are some additional challenges to making a host capable of applying labels to packets.

2.5 RELATIONSHIP BETWEEN LABEL SWITCHING AND NETWORK LAYER ADDRESSING AND ROUTING

Label switching replaces forwarding algorithms used by various routing functions with a single forwarding component. At the same time, label switching doesn't replace procedures for establishing and maintaining routing information-label switching assumes the use of the existing procedures, such as OSPF, BGP, and so forth. Likewise, label switching doesn't replace the need for network layer (e.g., IP) addressing, as the network layer addressing information forms an essential part of routing information, and this information is used by the label switching control component.

How does label switching fit into the ISO 7-layer reference model? To answer this question observe that label switching doesn't fit into layer 2 (link layer), as label switching is independent of a particular link layer technology (we can use label switching over ATM, over Ethernet, over point-to-point links, etc.). Label switching doesn't form a layer 3 (network layer) on its own either, for the reasons outlined in the previous paragraph (as it doesn't have its own routing and addressing). Moreover, the ISO reference model assumes that a given link or a network layer uses a single format for the transport of the data from the layer above. Label switching clearly violates this assumption, as over ATM it uses the ATM header to carry the label information, while over Ethernet or point-to-point links it uses the "shim." So perhaps the answer to the question we asked at the beginning of this paragraph is that label switching just doesn't fit into the ISO reference model. The fact that at the time of this writing label switching has been already deployed suggests that there is a clear distinction between the reference model and the referenced reality, and moreover that this distinction has no impact on reality.

Overview of MPLS Protocols

3

The Multiprotocol Label Switching (MPLS) data plane described in Chapter 2 could be operated and controlled purely through management plane techniques. Network Management Systems (NMSs) and Element Management Systems (EMSs) could be used to program the forwarding behavior at each Label Switching Router (LSR) in the network. This would install Label Switching Paths (LSPs) across the network so that data packets are forwarded from end to end as described in Chapter 2.

However, controlling a highly dynamic network through the management plane is a significant overhead for the operator and makes it hard to provide advanced features and functions. In order to make MPLS networks more flexible and usable, a set of MPLS control plane protocols have been developed by the Internet Engineering Task Force (IETF). This chapter, taken from *The Internet and Its Protocols* by Farrel, provides an overview of those protocols and sets the scene for the remainder of the book.

3.1 FOUNDATIONS OF MPLS PROTOCOLS

Some process is needed to populate the look-up tables at each MPLS node. As well as the obvious possibility for manual configuration, several protocols have been developed to distribute labels and construct the look-up tables. Some of these protocols have been adapted from their previous uses, and a couple of new protocols have been invented. These protocols have been standardized by the IETF to give a full suite of routing and signaling protocols for MPLS. In all cases the control protocols utilize IP, but this has no bearing on whether the data switched through an MPLS network is IP traffic or not. For the sake of clarity, the remainder of this chapter will assume that the payload is IP data.

Note that the reason that MPLS is of interest to the IETF is not that IP traffic can be switched through an MPLS network. This is undoubtedly interesting to the participants in the IETF, but means of carrying IP traffic across networks are of only marginal concern to the IETF itself. The key reason for the IETF's involvement in MPLS is the fact that the control protocols are based on IP technology.

This chapter gives an overview of the Label Distribution Protocol (LDP) and the Traffic Engineering extensions to RSVP for LSP Tunnels (RSVP-TE), the two MPLS signaling protocols.

3.2 LABEL DISTRIBUTION PROTOCOL (LDP)

The Label Distribution Protocol (LDP) is one of the fundamental approaches to distributing labels between LSRs. It was worked on by the IETF's MPLS Working Group through the late 1990s, drawing ideas from TDP and ARIS, and was published as an RFC in January 2001.

LDP can be used to distribute labels that can be used for traffic that matches an FEC according to specific requests for such a label or in an unsolicited manner as new routes become available. These two distinct approaches provide significantly different network characteristics and each has its own benefits and disadvantages.

As a protocol, the activities of LDP can be separated into four categories.

1. Discovery of LDP-capable LSRs that are "adjacent"—that is, recognition by the nodes that are connected by a logical or physical link that they both support LDP
2. Establishment of a control conversation between adjacent LSRs, and negotiation of capabilities and options
3. Advertisement of labels
4. Withdrawal of labels

LDP exchanges messages between LDP-capable LSRs packaged into Protocol Data Units (PDUs). Each LDP PDU begins with a header that indicates the length of the whole PDU and is followed by one or more messages from one LSR to the same partner LSR. Each message is itself made up of a header that indicates the length of the message followed by the contents of the message. The message contents are built from TLV (type-length-variable) component objects so that as the message is read byte by byte there is first an identifier of the object type, then an indication of the length of the object, and then the contents of the object. TLVs may be nested so that the variable of one TLV is a series of sub-TLVs. In LDP, all lengths exclude any fields up to and including the length field itself so that, for example, the TLV length indicates the length of the variable and does not include the type field or the length field itself.

Building LDP messages from TLVs and packaging them in a PDU has made LDP highly extensible, allowing new features and functions to be supported easily and in a backwards compatible way, and making it possible to devise new protocol uses such as pseudowires (see Chapter 13).

The LDP message header includes a Message Type, a Message Length, and a Message Identifier that is used to correlate protocol responses and subsequent messages related to this message.

The message header is followed by a series of zero or more TLVs. Some of these are mandatory on a given message and others are optional. LDP specifies that mandatory TLVs must be present first, before any optional TLVs. Even the TLV has a common format in LDP. The first 2 bits of the TLV describe how the TLV should be handled by the receiver if it does not recognize or cannot process the TLV. If the first bit (the U bit) is set to zero the receiver must reject the whole message and send an error if the TLV is unknown or cannot be handled. If the U bit is set to 1 and the second bit (the F bit) is also set to 1, the receiver must forward the unknown TLV if it forwards the message. The TLV length gives the length of the TLV (including any sub-TLVs) but excluding the U-bit, F bit, TLV Type, and TLV Length fields.

TLVs may include fields that are designated as *reserved*. Reserved fields should be set to zero when an LSR sends a message and should be ignored when an LSR receives a message. This allows the protocol to be extended through the use of currently unused bits and bytes within TLVs without causing any backwards compatibility issues.

3.2.1 **Peers, Entities, and Sessions**

Two LSRs that use LDP to advertise labels to each other are referred to as *LDP peers*. An LSR introduces itself to its peers by multicasting an LDP Hello message using UDP. It periodically sends to the group address "all routers on this subnet" and targets a well-known UDP port reserved for LDP discovery (port 646 has been assigned by the Internet Assigned Numbers Authority, IANA).

When an LSR receives a Hello message it knows that a new peer has come on line or that an existing peer has sent another Hello message. The receiver keeps track of its peers by running a *Hold Timer* for each one, as identified by the LSR identifier in the PDU header. If the Hello is from an existing peer, the receiver restarts the hold timer using the value supplied in the Hello message. If the Hello is from a new peer, the receiver creates a *Hello Adjacency* with its peer and starts a hold timer using the value supplied in the Hello message.

If an LSR does not receive a new Hello message from a peer for which it is maintaining a Hello Adjacency before the hold timer expires, it declares the adjacency down and assumes that connectivity to with the peer has been lost. For that reason, the sender of a Hello message is recommended to resend the Hello at least every third of the value of the Hold Time that it advertises in the Hello Message.

If the receiving peer is not willing to accept the message, it simply ignores it. Reasons for ignoring a message might include LDP not being configured on the interface or the receiver having reached a maximum threshold for the number of peers that it can support. Optional TLVs can be included at the discretion of the sender and supply additional information for use in managing the connection between the peers.

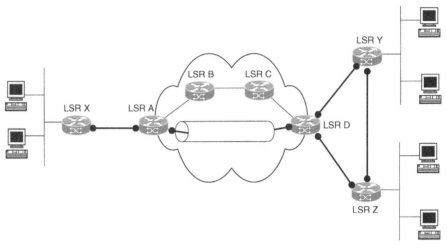

FIGURE 3.1

LDP Hello Adjacencies.

Although Hello messages are usually multicast, the UDP packets that carry the Hello messages can also be targeted at specific recipients. This is indicated by setting the T bit in the Hello message, and an LSR can request that it receives targeted Hellos in response by setting the R bit. An LSR receiving a targeted Hello will accept it if that LSR has been configured to accept all targeted Hellos or if it has been configured to send a targeted Hello to the originator of the message. Targeted Hellos have the advantage of reducing the LDP connectivity in a highly connected network at the expense of increased configuration. Alternatively, targeted Hellos can be used to set up Hello adjacencies between LSRs that are not on the same subnetwork, but that are connected, for example, by an MPLS tunnel. Figure 3.1 shows how this might work: LSR X and LSR A can exchange normal, untargeted Hellos. Similarly, LSRs D, Y and Z can use multicast Hellos to discover each other and set up adjacencies. However, in the core cloud there may be an MPLS tunnel from LSR A to LSR D. This tunnel (perhaps established for traffic engineering) will be used to forward packets across the cloud and it forms a virtual adjacency between LSR A and LSR D. These two LSRs can use targeted Hellos to set up a remote Hello adjacency.

Note that Hello messages are not responded to per se. However, an LSR that is configured to receive multicast Hellos will also be sending, them so both nodes will have a view of the Hello adjacency. Similarly, two nodes that are configured to send targeted Hellos to each other will each maintain a Hello adjacency. A node that is configured to accept all targeted Hellos must act as though it had been configured to send a targeted Hello to the originator, effectively responding with a Hello and making this mode of operation asymmetric.

Hello messages from one peer may identify different label spaces in the PDU header. Each time a Hello message is received for a new label space, the receiving

LSR establishes an *LDP session* with the peer over which to manage and exchange labels from the label space. Although LDP sessions are run between peers, some implementations and the LDP MIB refer to the logical end points of LDP sessions as entities. This allows the concept of multiple instances of the LDP code running in an LSR and makes more concrete the separate states that exist for each session.

An LDP session is a protocol conversation between LDP peers that is used to manage and exchange information about a single pair of label spaces, one at each peer. LDP assumes reliable transfer of its protocol message within a session, so sessions are run over TCP. TCP connections are set up between the peer LSRs using the well-known LDP port number 646, as for UDP carrying the Hello message. The IP address used for the TCP connection defaults to the LSR ID carried in the PDU header, but may be overridden by an optional Transport Address TLV in the Hello message itself. One single TCP connection may carry no more than one LDP session between a pair of LDP peers.

Protocol exchange on an LDP session can be categorized in five phases.

1. Session initialization (including TCP connection establishment)
2. Session maintenance
3. Address advertisement
4. Label advertisement and management
5. Error and event notification

Session initialization begins when a new Hello message is received, as described in the preceding paragraphs. As a first step, a new TCP session must be set up if one does not already exist between the addresses represented by the LSR identifiers in the exchanged Hello messages. Note that the LSR identifier is characterized as a Router ID, which is not necessarily an address—this fact appears to be glossed over in RFC 5036 and as a result, everyone assigns an address as the Router ID of their LDP router (or at least assigns an address for the LSR ID). Since only one TCP connection is required, it is set up by the *active* peer—the one with the greater LSR ID, where greater is defined by treating the LSR IDs as unsigned integers. Obviously, if the LSR IDs match there is an error and no attempt should be made to set up a connection.

Once the TCP connection is up, the active peer can initialize new sessions. The *passive* peer listens for new sessions and responds. Session initialization is achieved by exchanging Session Initialization messages. Although the Session Initialization message is described as negotiating session characteristics for use on the session, there is virtually no negotiation. The message describes the way the message sender intends to perform and may either be accepted or rejected.

The active peer sends a Session Initialization message advertising the behavior it intends to apply to the session. It contains information such as the version of LDP to be used, the timeout that will be applied to send periodic messages to keep the session open, and the largest size of LDP PDU that it is prepared to receive. The A and D bits describe the label distribution mode and the use of loop detection . If loop detection is in use, the sending node also indicates the

Path Vector Limit that it will use to detect loops—this is included for consistency checking within the network but is not otherwise used by the receiving node.

The Receiver LDP Identifier is used by the sender to indicate which label space the session is intended to control. This value is taken from the Hello message and allows the passive peer to correlate the requested session with the right internal state.

Optional parameters on session initialization are used to provide a detailed description of the label space if ATM or Frame Relay is used.

When the passive node receives a Session Initialization message it checks to see that it can handle the parameters. If it can't, it rejects the session by sending an Error Notification message (described in Section 3.2.7). An error code indicates that the session parameters were unacceptable, and the specific problem is indicated by including the received message up to the point of the bad parameter. Once a node has rejected a session it closes the TCP connection. Note that the next Hello exchange will cause the TCP connection to be reestablished and the session to be reattempted. To reduce the amount of network thrash when a pair of LDP LSRs disagree about session parameters, implementations should use an exponential back-off and not automatically attempt to set up a session on receipt of a Hello for a session that had previously failed. Since this might result in long delays in setting up adjacencies when the disagreement has been resolved by a change in configuration, the Hello message can carry an optional Configuration Sequence Number TLV—a change in the value of this TLV received from a peer indicates that some change has been made to the configuration and it is worth immediately trying to establish an adjacency.

If the passive node is happy with the received session parameters it must send a message to accept them and it must also send its own session parameters. Two separate messages are used: the passive node sends a Session Initialization message of its own containing its choices for protocol behavior on the session, and it acknowledges the received parameters by sending a KeepAlive message. The KeepAlive message is periodically retransmitted by both peers on a session when there is no other traffic to maintain the session, or more precisely, to make it possible to detect that the session has failed. This is necessary since TCP connection failure timeouts are typically quite large. Each node advertises in the Session Initialization message the time that it is prepared to wait without receiving any message on the session before it declares the session to have failed—both peers are required to use the same value on a session and this is taken to be the smaller of the two values exchanged on the Session Initialization message. Each node should send some message on the session so that its peer receives it within the KeepAlive period. If there is no other protocol message to be sent, a node can send a KeepAlive message. Since there is some possibility of delay in transmission and receipt of a message over TCP, the sender should make sure that it sends some message roughly every one third of the KeepAlive interval. Many implementations simply run a timer and send a KeepAlive message every one third of the KeepAlive interval regardless of whether it has sent another message or not. In the special case of session establishment, the first KeepAlive message is used to acknowledge the received Session Initialization message.

When the active peer receives a Session Initialization message it, too, checks that the received parameters are OK and acknowledges with a KeepAlive message. When both peers have received Session Initialization and KeepAlive messages, the session is active.

Note that the state machine for session initialization depicted in RFC 5036 is not complete. In particular, and contrary to the text of the RFC, it suggests that it would be invalid for the active peer to receive a KeepAlive message before it receives a Session Initialization message. Since implementations may have strictly followed the state machine, it would be best if all passive peers sent their Session Initialization message before sending the KeepAlive message that acknowledges the received session parameters.

Once the session has been established, but before it can be used, the peers must exchange information about the addresses that they support and use. This is done using Address messages, as described in Section 3.2.2.

3.2.2 Address Advertisement and Use

Immediately after the LDP session has been established, and before any protocol messages for label distribution are sent, the peers exchange addressing information using Address messages. This allows an LSR to map between IP routes distributed by routing protocols and LSPs. More precisely, it enables an LSR to know all of the next hop IP addresses that correspond to a particular adjacent LDP peer.

Consider the network in Figure 3.2. LSR E will advertise the FEC for Host Y together with a label for each interface—just one advertisement to LSR D. LSR D will advertise the FEC and a label to both LSR C and LSR G. In this way, LSR B will become aware of two LSPs that it could use to send traffic to Host Y, one to LSR C, and one to LSR F. It chooses between these routes using the routing protocol to advise it of the shortest/cheapest/best route and it installs an entry in its LFIB to map the label that it advertises to LSR A for this FEC to the label advertised to it by LSR C.

This process, however, is not absolutely simple. LSRs C and F have advertised labels using their LSR Identifier to identify themselves. The routing protocol will

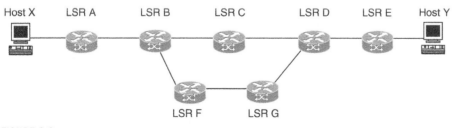

FIGURE 3.2

Using address information in LDP.

indicate the preferred path using interface addresses. LSR B needs a way to map from the address of the interface between LSRs B and C to the LSR ID of LSR C. Only then can it work out the correct label to use. If LSRs C and F advertise all of their addresses as soon as the LDP sessions with LSR B are established, LSR B can resolve the preferred path to an LSP.

Similar issues arise when a link fails. For example, if the link between LSRs C and D failed and the failure was reported by the routing protocol, LSR B would need to discover that the link to LSR F was currently the preferred path and work out which label to use.

The Address message can distribute one or more addresses belonging to a single address family (for example, IPv4 or IP6) but cannot mix addresses from multiple families. The body of the Address List TLV contains a family identifier followed by a list of addresses. Since the format of an address within a family is well known, the addresses in the list are simply concatenated and the TLV length is used to determine the end of the list.

New addresses may be added at any time during the life of the session simply by sending a new Address message. Addresses also may need to be withdrawn, for example, when an interface is taken out of service. This is done by sending an Address Withdraw message, which has the identical form to the Address message, but carries the message identifier 0x0301. When an LDP peer receives an Address Withdraw message it must remove all entries from its LFIB that utilized the address as a next hop, and should attempt to find an alternative label on another interface to carry the traffic. This is discussed further in the following sections.

3.2.3 Distributing Labels

LDP has two modes of label distribution: Downstream On Demand and Downstream Unsolicited. In both cases the downstream node is responsible for distributing the labels, but in the first case it does so only in response to a specific request from upstream, whereas in the second case the downstream node distributes labels whenever it can.

The mode of label distribution on any session is negotiated using the A bit in the Session Initialization message. If the A bit is set, Downstream On Demand is requested. If the bit is clear, Downstream Unsolicited is requested. If the peers request different modes of label distribution they should resolve their differences according to RFC 5036, which says that if the session is for an ATM or Frame Relay link Downstream On Demand should be used; otherwise Downstream Unsolicited must be used. An LSR can reject a label distribution mode that it doesn't want to support by rejecting the Session Initialization as described in the preceding paragraphs.

Both modes of label distribution can operate simultaneously in a single network with islands of LSRs or individual links given over to one mode or the other.

Label distribution uses the same mechanism in both distribution modes. The downstream LSR sends a Label Mapping message to the upstream node to let it know that if it wants to send a packet to any address represented by a particular FEC it may do so by sending a labeled packet on a particular interface to the downstream LSR. The interface to use is indicated by the LDP session on which the Label Mapping message arrives; the FEC and the label are carried in the message.

This appears to be a looser specification than for any of the LDP messages previously discussed because there are two variables being handled at once. First, recall that an FEC is the set of packets that are all forwarded in the same way. It may, therefore, be difficult to represent the FEC through a single identifier such as an IP address prefix, and a list of such identifiers may be needed. Although it is perfectly acceptable to send multiple Label mapping messages for the component elements of an FEC, it was recognized that it was far better to place all of the elements of the FEC on a single message so the Label Mapping can carry a series of FEC elements, each encoded as a single byte to identify the element type, followed by a well-known, context-specific number of bytes to carry the element. The number of elements is scoped by the length of the FEC TLV itself.

The Prefix FEC element represents an address prefix. The address family is indicated using the standard numbers from RFC 1700 (1 for IPv4, or 2 for IPv6) and the prefix length is in bits. The prefix itself is contained in the smallest number of bytes necessary and is right-padded with zeros. A default route can be conveyed in this way by specifying a prefix length of zero and supplying no bytes to carry the prefix itself.

The Host Address FEC element represents a fully qualified host address. The address family is indicated as before and the host address is presented, but in this case, the Length field indicates the length of the address in bytes. One might wonder at the presence of the address length here since the address family defines the address length, but including the length allows nodes that do not recognize a particular address family to easily parse the message, and indeed keeps all message parsing on the same footing of type-length-variable. Similarly, there is a question as to why the Host Address FEC element is needed at all, given that the Prefix element could be supplied with a prefix length indicating the whole address—a distinction is drawn in LDP so that an LSP associated with an FEC that contains a Host Address FEC element may carry only packets destined to that host address, whereas an LSP that uses a Prefix FEC element to represent the same fully qualified address may also include other Prefix FEC elements and so carry packets for multiple destinations. The second variable in the Label Mapping message is the label itself.

Label Mapping messages can be correlated to the Label Request that caused them (in Downstream On Demand label distribution) by the inclusion of the Message Identifier from the Label Request message as an optional TLV (the Label Request Message ID TLV-type 0x0600) in the Label Mapping message. In Downstream Unsolicited mode, the downstream LSR advertises a label to each upstream LSR every time a new route is added to its routing table. This may require it to update an existing label advertisement, but more likely it will advertise a new label.

When an upstream LSR receives an unsolicited Label Mapping message it must not simply make a new entry in its LFIB because it might receive a label advertisement for the same FEC from multiple downstream LSRs. Instead, it checks to see if there is already an entry in its FTN mapping table: if there isn't, it can create an entry, allocate local labels, advertise those labels, and populate the LFIB. On the other hand, if an entry already exists in the FTN mapping table for the received FEC, the LSR must consult the routing table to determine the preferred route and replace the outgoing interface and label in the LFIB. The addresses advertised using Address messages are important to correlate the next hop address in the routing table with the LSR advertising the new FEC/label.

In Downstream On Demand mode an upstream LSR makes a specific request for a label of one or more downstream LSRs for a specific FEC. The downstream LSRs do not advertise labels until they are requested to. The upstream LSR may be triggered to request a label by one of many factors, depending on the implementation and the use to which LDP is being put. In most cases, the decision is made based on the installation of a new route in the local routing table—this tells the LSR which way to route packets for a specific FEC and it can then ask the LSR that advertised the address that matches the routing next hop address for a label. In some cases (where it is desirable to keep the size of the LFIB small) the request is not made unless the rate of traffic flow for the FEC exceeds a threshold. Another mode of operation requests labels only for FECs that have been configured by the operator.

Triggers for label request can usually be left to the edges of the network or at least to the edges of regions within the network. When a node within the network receives a request for a label for an FEC for which it doesn't have a forward label, it can itself make a request downstream for a label.

Label requests are made in LDP using the Label Request message. The FEC is represented in the same way as on the Label Mapping message. The optional parameters can include a Hop Count TLV and a Path Vector TLV for use in loop detection, as discussed in the following paragraphs.

Label Mapping messages can be correlated to the Label Request that caused them by the inclusion of the Message Identifier from the label request message as an optional TLV (the Label Request Message ID TLV-type 0x0600) in the Label Mapping message.

3.2.4 Choosing a Label Distribution Mode

A key deployment decision for LDP networks is which label distribution mode to use. There is no simple answer, and the picture can be further confused by defining operation modes in which labels advertised from downstream are always propagated upstream (*ordered control*) and in which they are only propagated on request or when the local LSR sees a good reason for it (*independent control*).

In general, both distribution modes can be used in networks where label advertisement is driven by the availability of routes. Many systems use Downstream

Unsolicited distribution to advertise labels as routes become available—in this way, label advertisement models route advertisement and labels are available more or less as soon as routes are available. Other networks use Downstream On Demand distribution to request labels only when the new route reaches the edge of the network.

Note that Downstream Unsolicited label distribution with independent control may work badly in multi-area systems if the area border routers (ABRs) are configured to aggregate route information when they advertise it over the area border. This is because the first router to receive the advertisement may choose to advertise an FEC for the advertised aggregated route, and supply just a single label for the FEC. This means that when MPLS traffic reaches the ABR it will need to be decapsulated and examined before it can be assigned the right label to progress across the next area.

Where LSPs are required to meet specific services (such as traffic-driven LSPs, VPNs, or traffic engineering), label distribution is usually Downstream On Demand since this helps minimize the number of LSPs in the system, albeit at the expense of a small delay while the LSP is established in response to the demand. However, even this is not a golden rule, and many VPN models operate successfully using Downstream Unsolicited distribution.

Recall, however, that the label distribution mode is chosen on a per-link basis. This means that distribution modes may be mixed within a network, with islands of nodes using one mode of distribution and other islands using the other mode. A potential deployment of mixed modes would see the core of the network using Downstream Unsolicited distribution so that all core nodes had entries in their FTN mapping tables and LFIBs for all FECs, but the edge nodes exchanged labels only as demanded by traffic flows. The use of independent control at the edges of the core would ensure that labels were advertised from the core only on demand.

3.2.5 Choosing a Label retention Mode

When an upstream LSR replaces the labels in its LFIB because it has received an advertisement from a better downstream LSR, it can choose to retain the previous label (Liberal Label Retention) or to discard it (Conservative Label Retention). Conservative Label Retention obviously requires far less in the way of system resources; however, look again at the simple network in Figure 3.3. In this network LSR B will have an LFIB entry mapping a label from the interface with LSR A to a label on the interface with LSR C for use with the FEC of Host Y. It will also have received a label advertisement from LSR F for the same FEC but will not use it because the routing table shows that the route through LSR C is preferable. If the link between LSRs C and D fails, LSR B will notice the fact through the routing protocol and realize that the preferred route is now through LSR F. If it has discarded the label advertised by LSR F (Conservative Label Retention) it has no label to use to forward traffic to Host Y, but if it has used Liberal Label Retention it can install the label advertised by LSR F in its LFIB and continue to operate.

This distinction between label retention modes is equally applicable in Downstream Unsolicited and Downstream On Demand label distribution, but the effect of not retaining all labels is more significant in Downstream Unsolicited mode because if LSR B uses Downstream On Demand it can always issue a new Label Request message to rediscover the label advertised by LSR F.

This issue with Conservative Label Retention can be addressed in two ways. The downstream nodes can periodically re-advertise all labels—this ensures that the upstream node has the opportunity to reevaluate the best next hop for its LFIB, but is costly in terms of network usage, still leaves a window where the upstream node may be unable to forward labeled packets after a network failure, and requires that the downstream nodes be aware of the upstream node's label retention behavior. Alternatively, the upstream node may use a Label Request message to solicit a label from any of its preferred routes—this may appear to be strange in a system that is supposedly using Downstream Unsolicited label distribution, but is explicitly allowed by RFC 5036 to handle this problem. Thus, even in Downstream Unsolicited mode, Label Request messages can be sent and must be correctly handled and responded to. Note that an upstream node can tell whether a Label Mapping message is unsolicited or is a response to its Label Request message by looking for the Label Request Message ID TLV in the Label Mapping message.

3.2.6 Stopping Use of Labels

An LSR that has distributed a label for an FEC may decide that the label is no longer valid. There are many possible reasons for this, including local policy decisions to rearrange the use of labels or to reassign resources to more frequently used traffic flows. Obviously, when a link is decommissioned the labels previously advertised for the associated session with a peer are no longer valid.

The most common reason for a label to become incorrect is when the LSR is informed that it is no longer on any path for the FEC. It may discover this through the routing protocol or through LDP from the downstream LSRs.

Whenever an LSR decides that a label that it has previously advertised is no longer valid, it withdraws the advertisement by sending a Label Withdraw message. The receipt of a Label Withdraw message by one LSR may cause it to send a similar message to its upstream peers or, if liberal label retention is being used, may simply cause it to switch traffic to a different next hop.

There is good scope for network thrash when labels are withdrawn in networks in which conservative label retention is used. A trade-off is required between not immediately telling upstream nodes that traffic can no longer be forwarded (which will cause packets to be black-holed) and telling them too quickly when an alternative route is just one Label Request message exchange away.

The Label Withdraw message maps closely to a Label Mapping message, but note that the FEC can be a subset of that carried on a Label Mapping message to leave the label in place for a reduced FEC, the union of FECs from multiple Label Mapping messages to remove multiple labels at once, or a wildcard FEC to remove all advertised labels. The wildcard FEC is a single byte type identifier followed by no other data (none is required). If the wildcard FEC is used, no other FEC elements are valid on the message.

In this way, label withdrawal is really FEC withdrawal. The downstream node is saying which FECs can no longer be reached through it and asking that all associated labels that have no other use be released.

The Label Withdraw message may optionally include a Label TLV. This means that the specified label only is to be withdrawn from all uses where it matches the FECs carried in the message; other labels for those FECs are to remain in place. The most common usage of the Label TLV is with the wildcard FEC to show that the entire label is to be withdrawn from any FEC to which it is bound.

When an upstream node receives a Label Withdraw message, it must stop using the label in the way indicated by the message and must respond so that the downstream node knows that cleanup has completed. It does this using a Label Release message. This message is a direct copy of the received Label Withdraw message but carries the message type 0x0403.

Figure 3.3 shows the message exchanges in a simple network running Downstream Unsolicited label advertisement and demonstrates the use of Label Mapping, Label Withdraw, Label Release, and Label Request messages. Initially, LSR

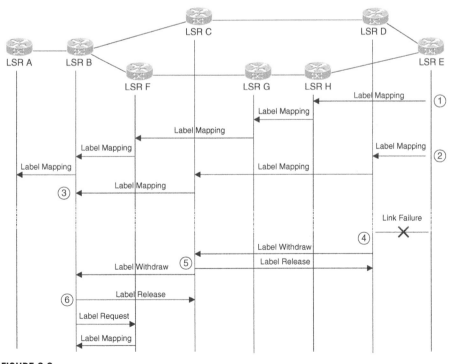

FIGURE 3.3

LDP message flows for Downstream Unsolicited label advertisement.

E advertises a label for an FEC by sending a Label Mapping message to LSR H (step 1). In turn, this FEC is advertised with a label by LSR H to LSR G, and so on hop by hop through LSR F and LSR B until it reaches LSR A. LSR E also advertises a label for the FEC by sending a Label Mapping message to LSR D (step 2). In turn, the FEC is advertised with a label by LSR D to LSR C and LSR C to LSR B.

When the advertisement reaches LSR B from LSR C (step 3), LSR B recognizes that the route through LSR C is preferable because it is shorter. Since it is using Conservative label retention, LSR B discards (but does not release) the label advertised by LSR F and uses the one advertised by LSR C. It does not need to tell LSR A about this operation—the only change is in the tables on LSR B.

After some time, the link between LSR D and LSR E fails (step 4). LSR D decides to withdraw the label it had previously advertised by sending a Label Withdraw message to LSR C. LSR C responds at once (step 5) with a Label Release message and, recognizing that it has no-one else to ask for a label, propagates the withdrawal by sending a Label Withdraw message to LSR B. In turn, LSR B responds at once with a Label Release message (step 6). Since LSR B has connectivity to more than one downstream node it is worth it trying to get another label from downstream before it withdraws its label from upstream. (Recall that LSR B is using Conservative label retention, so it no longer has the label originally advertised by LSR F). LSR B sends a Label Request to LSR F, which is able to respond at once with a Label Mapping message. LSR B updates its tables and does not need to tell LSR A about any changes.

A Label Release message can also be used by an upstream LSR to show that it no longer wishes to use a label that was previously advertised to it. As with the Label Withdraw message, the unit of currency on the Label Release message is the FEC so that the upstream node is saying that it is no longer interested in reaching the specified FEC(s) and that the downstream LSR may consider the associated labels released if they are not used for any other FECs. Again, if the optional Label TLV is present it indicates that only this label as applicable to the listed FECs should be released. This message is used in Downstream On Demand mode to release a label that was previously requested and advertised.

When an LSR receives a Label Abort Request message it may or may not have already sent a Label mapping message in response to the original Label Request. If it has not sent a Label Mapping message, it responds with a Notification message and may choose to forward the Abort request downstream. If it has already responded to the Label Request, it simply ignores the Label Abort Request. This means that an LSR that sends a Label Abort Request may still receive a Label Mapping message in response to the original Label Request message—it handles this by using the label as advertised, storing it in its FTN mapping table and LFIB, or by releasing it by sending a Label Release message.

3.2.7 Error Cases and Event Notification

In LDP, one LSR may need to inform another of errors or events that have occurred. For example, an LSR may want to reject parameters passed on a Session Initialization message and so prevent the establishment of an LDP session. Similarly, an LSR that receives a Label Abort Request message needs to inform the sender that the message has arrived.

Such notifications are carried in LDP using Notification messages. The Notification message includes a Status TLV which identifies the error or event that is being reported by including a Status Code. The first two bits in the Status Code indicate how the notification should be handled by the recipient. If the E bit is set, the notification is of a fatal error and both the sender and the recipient of the message should immediately close the LDP session—the setting of the E bit is defined for each of the Status Code values defined in RFC 5036. The F bit is set at the discretion of the LSR that sends the Notification message; when the F bit is set, the recipient of the Notification message is required to forward the message upstream or downstream along any LSP(s) or sessions associated with the original message, but when the F bit is clear, the recipient must not forward the message.

3.2.8 LDP Extensions

The message and TLV format of LDP means that new functions and features can be added easily, and additions have been happening almost since LDP was first published. Extensions cover network survivability, the ability to trace LSPs through a network, and MTU discovery. Many other extensions exist as proposals that have not yet been adopted by the MPLS Working Group.

When examining any extension to LDP, attention must be paid to the behavior of the extension when some nodes in the network do not support it. Most extensions are designed with backwards compatibility in mind so that use of the extension can be negotiated during session initialization. Others rely on the forwarding, untouched by an LSR, of TLVs that a node does not understand. In most cases, mixing LSRs that do and do not implement an extension to LDP will result in partial or poor support of the extension.

3.3 TRAFFIC ENGINEERING IN MPLS

Traffic Engineering is discussed in general later in this book. This section describes how MPLS can be used to achieve traffic engineering and examines the requirements on MPLS signaling protocols.

MPLS offers the ability to implement traffic engineering at a low cost in equipment and operational expenditure. Capital expenditure can be reduced because MPLS is able to supply much of the function of the traffic engineered overlay model in an integrated manner. Operational costs may be reduced by the use of automated provisioning of tunnels, proactive distribution of traffic between tunnels, and dynamic computation of optimal routes through the network. In many cases, this pushes the intelligence for operation of a traffic engineered network into the network itself and away from central management stations.

MPLS has many components that make it attractive for use in a traffic engineered network. These aspects are examined in the sections that follow. They include the following.

- MPLS has the ability to establish an LSP that follows a path other than the one offered as preferred by the routing protocol and forwarding algorithm.

- Resources within the network can be dynamically reserved as LSPs are established and can be dynamically updated as the needs of the LSPs change so that traffic flows can be guaranteed a level and quality of service. Routing of the LSPs can be made dependent on the resource requirements.

- Traffic can be groomed on to "parallel" LSPs. That is, multiple LSPs can be established between a pair of source and destination end points, and traffic can be distributed between the LSPs according to any number of algorithms. The parallel LSPs can take significantly different paths through the network.

- Network resources can be automatically managed with new LSPs set up to meet the immediate demands of the network, and with resources freed up again as old LSPs that are no longer required are released.

- The network can be managed centrally through a common set of management options and with a common underlying granularity of managed object—the LSP.

- Recovery procedures can be defined describing how traffic can be transferred to alternate LSPs in the event of a failure and indicating how and when backup and standby LSPs should be set up and routed.

Ultimately, MPLS scores over previous traffic engineering implementations because the load-sharing, traffic grooming decisions need only be made once (at the entry point into the LSPs) rather than at each node within the network. This makes traffic propagation considerably more efficient.

3.3.1 Extensions to RSVP for LSP tunnels (RSVP-TE)

A second protocol suitable for label distribution in a traffic engineered MPLS networks is based on the Resource Reservation Protocol (RSVP). RSVP is suitable for extension to the MPLS world because it deals with end-to-end reservation of resources for traffic flows, a concept similar to traffic engineered MPLS. On the other hand, it does not address all of the requirements needed for MPLS (most notably label distribution and control of paths through explicit routes).

RSVP was first extended for this kind of application by Cisco when it was developing Tag Switching. Since then the IETF has published *RSVP-TE: Extensions to RSVP for LSP Tunnels* as RFC 3209.

3.3.2 **Reuse of RSVP Function**

RSVP-TE manages to reuse RSVP fairly comprehensively. All seven of the RSVP messages find a use in RSVP-TE, although the ResvConf is less significant than it is when used for RSVP. RSVP is essentially a request/response protocol with Path messages being used to navigate a path and request resources for traffic flows, and Resv messages returning along the path to indicate what resources should be reserved. This flow of messages matches the requirements for Downstream On Demand label distribution and can be extended easily by adding information to the messages. Since RSVP messages are built from *objects*, which are basically LTV structures, this is easily achieved (recall that in RSVP, objects are presented as Length-Type-Variable triplets in which the Length field defines the length of the triplet, including the Length and Type fields.)

Although RSVP contains good mechanics for describing traffic and for specifying reservation requirements, it does not have facilities for other aspects necessary in a traffic engineered MPLS protocol. Extensions are necessary to cover the following features, which are described in more detail in the following sections.

- Label management
- Requesting and controlling routes
- Preempting resources
- Maintaining connectivity between RSVP-TE LSRs.

Additionally, a big concern inherited from RSVP is the processing overhead associated with the soft state nature of the protocol. In traffic engineered MPLS LSPs do not always need to fluctuate according to changes in the routing database; In fact, if an LSP has been set up using a strict explicit route, it doesn't need to change at all. Furthermore, there are satisfactory methods in RSVP-TE for controlled rerouting of an LSP. For these reasons, the techniques of refresh reduction described in *RSVP Refresh Overhead Reduction Extensions* (RFC 2961) are very relevant to MPLS.

One of the objectives of the designers of RSVP-TE was to allow RSVP and RSVP-TE to operate in the same networks at the same time. This has not led to any startling design choices, but has resulted in a few small quirks, which are highlighted in the following sections.

3.3.3 **Distributing Labels**

LSP setup is requested in RSVP-TE using Downstream On Demand label distribution by the inclusion of a Label Request Object on a Path message. It is the presence of this object that distinguishes this and all other messages on this session as RSVP-TE rather than RSVP transactions.

The requester indicates the type of label that it is interested in (general, ATM, or Frame Relay) by the C-type of the object, and if the label is for ATM or Frame Relay the requester also indicates the range of acceptable labels as governed by the hardware capabilities of local policy. All three formats of the Label Request Object also carry a Layer Three Protocol ID to indicate to the egress of the LSP what kind of traffic it should expect to discover when it removes the shim header from the MPLS packets.

The Resv message that successfully responds to the Path message that carried a Label Request Object advertises a label using the Label Object. The label is conveyed within a 32-bit field and is right-justified and left-padded with zero bits.

3.3.4 Identifying LSPs

RSVP sessions are identified using a Session Object present on all RSVP messages, and this practice is continued in RSVP-TE. Two new C-types are introduced to distinguish the IPv4 LSP Tunnel Session and the IPv6 LSP Tunnel Session.

The destination address field is common between the RSVP and RSVP-TE Session Objects, but from there on the fields are different (although you will find some implementers and implementations so entrenched in RSVP that they refer to the new tunnel ID field as the port ID). To ensure that there is no accidental overlap or interpretation of the Protocol ID and Flags fields from the RSVP Session Object, the Reserved field of the RSVP-TE Session Object must be set to zero. The Tunnel ID field is used to give a unique identifier to the tunnel, and the Extended Tunnel ID gives context to the name space from which the Tunnel ID was chosen—it is usually set to the source address of the tunnel.

If LSP merging is desirable, all ingresses must use the same session identifier. This means that the Tunnel ID must be known to all sources (possibly as a feature of the application that requests the tunnel, or possibly through a management protocol) and that each source must use the same Extended Tunnel ID. This last point means that for LSP merging, the Extended Tunnel ID cannot be the source address of the tunnel and a well-known value (usually zero) must be used.

The Sender Template is used to identify traffic flows in RSVP within the context of a session. In RSVP-TE there may often be little difference between a traffic flow and a tunnel, and the RSVP-TE form of the Sender Template Object includes a Source Address as in RSVP and an LSP ID to replace the Source Port. The LSP ID is unique within the context of the Source Address and in many implementations represents an *instance* of the tunnel identified by the Tunnel ID of the Session Object.

This concept of tunnel instances is useful in configurations in which a series of alternative routes are configured for the same tunnel for use either as alternatives when one route fails, or in parallel to offer distribution of traffic along different paths.

3.3.5 Managing Routes

Explicit routes can be signaled in RSVP-TE by the inclusion of an Explicit Route Object. This object is a single header followed by a series of subobjects. Perversely, the subobjects are encoded as TLVs not LTVs, but the value of the Length field still includes the Type and Length fields. Each subobject begins with a single-bit flag to indicate whether the hop is strict or loose.

RSVP-TE also includes a mechanism known as route recording. The Record Route Object may be present on Path or Resv messages and it records the hops through which the message has been routed. When received at the egress or ingress, the Record Route Object gives a full picture of the path of the tunnel. At transit nodes, the Record Route Object from the Path and Resv messages must be combined to see the full route.

The rules for including the Record Route Object are simple: If the object is present on a received message, it should also be present on the message when it is forwarded. The ingress node is free to choose whether to include the Record Route Object on a Path message. The egress LSR must include the Record Route Object in the Resv it sends if it was present in the received Path message.

Each node processing the Record Route Object adds itself to the head of a list of nodes. RFC 3209 is careful to say that the address added may be "any network-reachable interface address," but conventionally the address used is the address through which the Path message was received or the address out of which the Path message was sent. When a Record Route Object is received on a Resv at the ingress node, it therefore carries the precise sequence of addresses necessary to form a strict explicit route that follows the course of the LSP, and in this way route pinning can be achieved even if the LSP was originally set up using loose routes.

In fact, the Record Route Object is structured so that it may be converted to an Explicit Route Object with the minimum of effort. The fields are precisely aligned—note that there is no strict/loose bit in the Record Route Subobjects, and that this is consistent with the fact that any explicit route generated from a Record Route Object would have the strict/loose bits set to zero to indicate strict hops. Note that all of the hops in the Record Route Object are explicit nodes; that is, there are no prefixes and no abstract nodes-again, this is a feature of the recorded route representing every node in the path.

A Flags field (which corresponds to a reserved field in the Explicit Route sub-objects) has two settings, both of which are permissible only if support for local protection was indicated in the Session Attributes Object in the original Path message. The value 1 indicates that the link downstream of the node represented by this subobject can be protected through a local repair mechanism. The value 2 indicates that a local repair mechanism is currently in use to maintain this LSP.

A flag in the Session Attributes Object is used to request that the Record Route Object will also collect information about the labels allocated at each hop. This is particularly useful for analyzing the behavior of the network and tracing data. Note that the Label Subobject breaks the formatting conventions of the other subobjects by putting the Flags field before the rest of main value of the sub-object—this is permissible because there is no Label Subobject in the Explicit Route Object. The Flags field in the Label Subobject has value 1 to indicate that the label comes from the Global Label Space and zero to show that this is a per-interface label. The Label C-Type is copied from the C-type of the corresponding

Label Object (which is limited to the value 1 for RSVP-TE, but has extended use in Generalized MPLS).

It is possible that the construction of a Record Route Object will cause the Path or Resv message to grow to larger than the maximum MTU size. In this case the Record Route is abandoned (that is, dropped from the message) and an error (PathErr or ResvErr) is sent to inform the ingress/egress of the problem.

3.3.6 **Resource Requests and Reservation**

FlowSpec objects are inherited from RSVP without any change. Recall that IntServ encodings are a little unusual in that the length counting the number of words in the IntServ descriptor does not include the header.

RSVP defines three reservation styles that allow for different modes of resource sharing. Two of these, Fixed Filter (FF) and Shared Explicit (SE), are supported in RSVP-TE, but the Wildcard Filter (WF) is not considered appropriate for traffic engineering since its real application is for multipoint to point flows in which only one sender sends at any time.

In RSVP-TE the choice of style is made by the egress node, but should be heavily influenced by the setting of the SE Style Desired bit in the Session Attributes Object (see the following section). If FF is used, a unique label and unique resource reservations are assigned to each sender (as specified in the Sender Template)—this means that there is no resource sharing and no merging of LSPs. SE style, on the other hand, allows sharing and merging, which is particularly useful in rerouting techniques such as make-before-break. Note that once SE style has been selected it is often necessary to take explicit action to prevent sharing of resources between LSPs targeted at the same egress, because the Tunnel ID may accidentally be the same for two distinct LSPs from two separate sources. This prevention is achieved by setting the Extended Tunnel ID to the IP address of the source node.

The choice between FF and SE styles is therefore governed by the function within the network. If resource sharing and LSP merging are not supported, FF must be used. Many existing MPLS implementations do not support SE style and will clear the SE Style Desired bit in the Session Attributes object as they forward the path message. This act in itself does not guarantee that the egress will not select the SE style, but may help to prevent it.

The Adspec object plays an important part in RSVP in recording what resources are available along a path to help the egress determine appropriate reservations to make. In RSVP-TE, however, Adspec is rarely used.

Note that, as in RSVP, the resources in RSVP-TE are technically not reserved until the Resv message reaches a node. However, in practice, it is simple in RSVP-TE for a transit node to make a reliable guess as to the reservation requirements of an LSP, and so most implementations make a provisional resource reservation as they process the Path message. The final reservation requirements are still carried on the Resv message with the label, and may require a modification (which might fail) to what has already been reserved, but this is generally more efficient than handling resource contention when processing Resv messages.

3.3.7 Priorities, Preemption, and Other Attributes

The Session Attribute Object is an optional object that contains additional qualifying details for the session and hence the tunnel. The setup and holding priorities necessary for preemption control are carried as values in the range zero to 7 (zero is the highest priority) and no default values have been defined to cover the case in which the Session Attribute Object is absent. Using a value of 4 is not unreasonable, but one might consider that the absence of any specified value should mean that the tunnel be treated as the lowest priority, that is, 7.

RSVP also contains a more complex priority scheme in the Preemption Priority Policy element. In practice, MPLS systems will likely use only the Session Attribute Object, but RFC 3209 explains in detail how to handle the case when both are present or when only the Preemption Priority Policy element in RSVP-TE.

Three bits are defined within the Flags field and are interpreted as follows.

- **0x01, Local protection desired:** This flag indicates that local repair mechanisms may be used to reroute the LSP around network faults after the LSP has been established and in violation of the explicit route.
- **0x02, Label recording desired:** This flag requests that the recorded route includes label information.
- **0x04, SE style desired:** This flag is used by the ingress node to state that it may wish to reroute the tunnel without first tearing it down. This is a request for the egress node to use the SE Style in the corresponding Resv.

The last element of the Session Attribute Object is a name. The name length gives the length in bytes, but note that the name field itself must be increased to a multiple of 4 bytes and right-padded with zeros. The name is intended to be a user-friendly printable string for diagnostics and management, but many implementations have found this a convenient place to hide additional control information, so don't be surprised to find strange, unprintable characters at the end of the name.

3.3.8 Coloring the LSP

RSVP-TE supports routing tunnels through the network using resource affinities. This can be used to help control free routing when there is no explicit route present or when loose or nonexplicit hops are encountered. The individual links in the network are "colored" and the Path message is flagged with the colors that must not be used (exclude any), the colors at least one of which must be used (include any), and the colors that must be used (include all). These three values are carried within a variant of the Session Attribute Object indicated by a different C-Type value. Only one Session Attribute Object may be present on a Path message.

The Exclude Any Affinities might more reasonably be know as the Exclude All Affinities since the inclusion of any of the listed affinities on a link renders the link unacceptable, but the logic says that it is the link that is excluded if any affinity matches, so the name is not wrong.

3.3.9 Detecting Errors and Maintaining Connectivity

In classic RSVP, if a network link fails, the routing protocol at both ends of the link will become aware of the problem through the failure of its Hello exchanges and will start to route packets down an alternative route (not withstanding the fact that resources have not been reserved on that alternative route). This approach does not work for RSVP-TE because the packets are labeled and routing is not involved in their forwarding.

What is needed is for the control plane (that is, RSVP-TE signaling) to become aware of the network failure and to rapidly reroute the affected tunnels or report the failure to the ingress node. The existing methods of state refresh provide a mechanism to detect failures, but since state refresh is designed to tidy up after failure rather than to trigger recovery, the process is typically too slow. Any attempt to increase the refresh time on a per-LSP basis to be fast enough to handle errors would swamp the network with refresh messages.

This issue is combated in RSVP-TE by the introduction of a new message exchange. Each pair of adjacent LSRs exchanges Hello messages to keep the control connection between them open. It should be noted that this exchange is NOT a discovery mechanism as in LDP, but is more akin to the KeepAlive processing of those protocols.

The new Hello message has a single mandatory object, the Hello Object. The Hello Object has two C-types: the value 1 indicates a Hello Request, and the value 2 indicates a Hello Ack. Both variants of the object carry a source and destination instance number. When an LSR becomes aware of the existence of an RSVP-TE-capable neighbor through the receipt of a path or Resv message it may start the Hello exchange.

The initiator of the Hello exchange uses a Hello Request object and sets the source instance to some reference number (perhaps random, perhaps time dependent) and the destination instance to zero. The receiver of such a Hello message responds with a Hello Ack Object carrying its own source instance and returning the received instance as the destination instance. The messages can now bounce back and forth, certifying that the link is active. RFC 3209 recommends that the default retransmission time for Hello messages is 5 milliseconds, and that a link should be declared down if no response is received in three-and-a-half times this interval. In practice, somewhat larger timer values are used, with the norm often being around one second.

If a node restarts after a failure of its software or of the link, it is required to select a new value for its source instance, allowing the following procedure to apply. If a Hello message is received with a destination identifier set to zero it indicates that the previous Hello message was not received. After this has happened a configurable number of times in a row the link should be declared to have failed. If the received Hello message does not reflect the correct destination identifier (that is, local source identifier) it also indicates some failure in the link. Finally, if a node detects a change in the remote instance identifier (that is, the received source identifier) it knows that the remote node has detected a link failure and has restarted. The Hello exchange is usually (although not necessarily) stopped when the last piece of state between a pair of LSRs is removed.

3.4 PRIORITIZING TRAFFIC IN MPLS

IP traffic flows may be prioritized within the Internet through the use of Differentiated Services. This allows higher-priority packets to overtake those of lower priorities, making preferential use of queuing mechanisms, resource availability, and fast links.

The use of resource affinities within RSVP-TE allows LSPs to be set up using specific link types, and explicit routing allows LSPs to be directed down chosen paths. This provides some of the function for Differentiated Services over MPLS, but it does not cover the full range. Specifically, it does not define how an LSR should prioritize the traffic on one LSP compared to that on another, and it does not indicate how individual labeled packets on an LSP should be handled.

RFC 3270 defines procedures and protocol extensions for the full support of Differentiated Services over MPLS by describing how LSPs may be set up with specific priorities, and how packets within an individual LSP may be assigned priorities.

3.4.1 Inferring Priority from Labels

If each LSP that is set up is associated with a DiffServ Ordered Aggregate (OA), then all of the traffic on the LSP can be assigned the same Per Hop Behavior Scheduling Class (PSC) and drop precedence at an LSR. This allows traffic from different LSPs to be differentiated at transit LSRs. If the ingress LSR places traffic onto LSPs according to its DiffServ Behavior Aggregates (BAs), then the features of DiffServ can be achieved within an MPLS network. LSPs that are established to carry traffic associated with specific OAs by associating the DiffServ class with a label are called L-LSPs.

For this process to operate, it is necessary that the relationship between the L-LSP and the PSC and drop precedence be understood at each transit LSR. This information can be statically configured across the network or can be signaled through the MPLS label distribution protocol. Note, however, that as with DiffServ there is no obligation on an LSR to prioritize the LSPs in the same way or even to differentiate between the traffic flows at all.

New objects are added to RSVP-TE and to LDP to signal the PSC mapping for an L-LSP. These objects are added to the Path and Label request messages, respectively, as optional objects. In RSVP-TE the new DiffServ Object should be placed between the Session Attributes object and the Policy Object. In LDP the new DiffServ TLV should be placed with the optional TLVs. Note that L-LSPs can be supported in LDP by placing the DiffServ TLV in the Label Mapping message. The PSC is encoded as a 16-bit number.

In the LDP DiffServ TLV the setting of the U and F bits are up to the source LSR and could be both set to zero if the ingress wishes full DiffServ support across all LSRs in the network, or both set to 1 if the ingress is content to have the DiffServ function applied within the network wherever it can be.

3.4.2 Inferring Priority from Experimental Bits

Recall that an MPLS label includes 3 bits called the experimental bits (EXP bits). If not used for any other purpose, these bits allow an MPLS packet to be assigned to one of eight categories. If each bit setting is assigned to a DiffServ BA, basic differentiation of traffic may be achieved on the LSP within the network. More precisely, each EXP bit setting can be interpreted as specifying a specific PSC and drop precedence. This provides considerably more granularity than simply inferring priority from labels, and can help to reduce the number of LSPs required to provide extensive differentiation of traffic but does require that the label switching engine is able to examine the EXP bits. LSPs that use the EXP bits to differentiate traffic are called E-LSPs.

Two pieces of information must be signaled by the MPLS traffic engineering protocol for this process to work. First, all LSRs on the LSP must be made aware that they can interpret the EXP bits as indicating a PSC, and second, the LSRs must have a common understanding of the meanings of the EXP bits and the ranking of the PSCs that they encode. Note, however, that as with DiffServ there is no obligation on an LSR to prioritize the packets in the same way or even to handle the EXP bits at all.

The mapping from the EXP field to the PSC and drop precedence can be different for each LSP and can be preconfigured at each LSR or signaled during LSP setup. Preconfigured mappings can be defined as defaults for the LSR or can be derived from other information such as the source and destination points of the LSP. Signaling the EXP bit to PSC mapping requires the addition of extra information to the signaling messages.

A counter in the new objects indicates how many EXP bit to PSC mappings are defined—this is not strictly needed since it can be deduced from the length of the object. Each EXP to PSC mapping contains the setting of the EXP bits and a PHBID encoded as a 16-bit number.

In the LDP DiffServ TLV the T bit is used to indicate that the TLV defines an E-LSP and is set to zero. The settings of the U and F bits are as described in the preceding section.

It is acceptable for fewer than eight mappings to be signaled, in which case it is a local configuration matter how each LSR will handle traffic with other EXP bit settings.

From MPLS to GMPLS

Multiprotocol Label Switching (MPLS), as described in Chapters 2 and 3, is concerned with data forwarding in packet, frame, and cell networks. Generalized MPLS (GMPLS) is concerned with extending the MPLS concepts so that a uniform control plane can be applied to any transport technology including the MPLS packet-based data plane described in Chapter 2.

Traditionally, network elements of transport networks were provisioned via manual planning and configuration. It could take days (if not weeks) to add a new service and have it operate properly because careful network planning was required, and because network downtime might be needed to reposition other services. Removing services was also slow and painful because any mistakes could affect other services. It is obvious that the larger and more sophisticated transport networks become, the more demand there will be for dynamic provisioning using some sort of control plane and, as a consequence, for traffic engineering.

This chapter taken from *GMPLS: Architecture and Applications* by Farrel and Bryskin, examines how GMPLS came about and how the concepts of MPLS can be applied to transport networks that use packet and non-packet technologies. GMPLS is important in the context of MPLS because it opens up new control plane mechanisms that enhance the capabilities of MPLS-based networks and deepens the set of functions and features that an MPLS network can offer to the application or user.

4.1 THE ORIGINS OF GMPLS

As interest grew in offering a control plane solution to provisioning in transport networks, one option was to develop a new set of protocols from scratch for all types of transport network: one for WDM networks, one for TDM networks, and so forth. The obvious advantage of such an approach would be that each control plane could be designed to be very efficient for the target network. For example, a control plane designed for photonic networks could have built-in mechanisms to take care of optical impairments and wavelength continuity constraints, whereas

55

one designed for TDM networks could take advantage of the SDH overhead bits for signaling.

The obvious disadvantage to individual, specifically tailored control planes is the enormous amount of effort needed to develop the many new sets of signaling, routing, and traffic engineering protocols and applications. Another disadvantage is the fact that services have a tendency to span networks of different types: Some segments are built from IP routers and layer 2 switches, others from SONET/SDH switches, while the core network could interconnect optical add-drop multiplexers and cross-connects. End-to-end provisioning on such heterogeneous networks, each with its own separate control plane, would be a formidable task.

4.1.1 Lambda Switching

With the rapid rise in popularity of WDM networks at the end of the 1990s, vendors and Service Providers started to search for an intelligent control plane that could simplify provisioning, reduce operational expenditure, and offer the ability to provide new services. It was noticed that the basic switching operation in a WDM network was logically very similar to that in an MPLS device. That is, a switch was required to convert an input wavelength on an incoming interface to an output wavelength on an outgoing interface in an operation so similar to the MPLS mapping of {input label, incoming interface} to {output label, outgoing interface} that it made obvious sense to attempt to reuse MPLS signaling techniques. From this initial observation, Multiprotocol Lambda Switching (MPLambdaS or MPλS) was born.

The initial MPλS protocol specifications borrowed heavily from the MPLS signaling and routing protocols. They worked on the basic assumption that, although the LFIB was logically embedded in a physical switching device (such as a set of mirrors in a MEMS), the cross-connect operations in the switch were identical to those in an LFIB. The MPλS protocols needed to install mappings of {incoming lambda, incoming interface} to {outgoing lambda, outgoing interface}.

4.1.2 Generalizing the Technology

It wasn't long before other optical switching technologies were put forward as candidates for a similar control plane. What about fiber or port switches? Could they use techniques like MPLambdaS? How about TDM networks? Isn't a device that switches timeslots doing exactly the same type of functional operation?

Fortunately, the techniques and procedures of MPLS represented a proven technology with similar switching notions that work on heterogeneous network and solve the traffic engineering issues that need to be addressed for all types of transport network. So the MPLambdaS work was broadened to cover not just lambda switching, but also fiber switching, TDM, layer 2 switching, and the existing packet/frame/cell switching technologies. The concepts were truly generalized, and the work was named Generalized MPLS.

But are all of the concepts of MPLS applicable? Not completely. Some MPLS techniques were focused on establishing LSPs that matched the IP routing tables;

these functions (such as that provided by the LDP signaling protocol) are not applicable to non-packet transport networks. Transport networks are more concerned with the provisioning of end-to-end connections or circuits. The MPLS protocols on which GMPLS is built were designed and implemented to apply traffic engineering to MPLS networks. Traffic engineering is the process of placing traffic on selected, pre-computed paths within the network in order to maximize revenues from the available resources. In practical terms, this means routing traffic away from congested "hot spots," picking links that provide the desired quality of service or satisfying other application constraints, or directing data so that it utilizes underused links. But these are all packet-based, statistical concepts. Can they also apply to transport networks or should GMPLS be limited to simple control operations? Is the requirement for a rapid provisioning system that offloads some of the burden of operator function or can we take advantage of the capabilities of the MPLS traffic engineering protocols and place intelligence within the network?

It turns out that traffic engineering has its place in a transport network. This certainly isn't every Service Provider's cup of tea. Many take the view that, although signaling and network discovery are valuable control plane tools, there is no way that they want to allow the network to make decisions about the placement of services, no matter how clever the software. Still others prefer to limit their view of GMPLS to an operator aid—a process that allows the network manager to provision services rapidly, monitor their status, and tear them down in a coordinated way. These uses of GMPLS are sufficient to make OPEX savings and get better leverage of existing equipment, but other Service Providers are enthusiastic to embrace the possibilities of a fully functional GMPLS control plane that will discover resources, advertise their availability and usage, compute paths for complex services such as path protection, and install trails to support the services.

In general, many or most of the techniques in MPLS traffic engineering are applicable to the generalized problem of the control of an arbitrary transport network. So why not just adopt the MPLS control plane and make it work on transport networks? After all, if it can handle ATM switches, why wouldn't it work, say, for digital cross-connects?

4.2 BASIC GMPLS REQUIREMENTS

In order to understand the way that GMPLS protocols and concepts were developed out of MPLS, it is necessary to examine some of the basic requirements of a transport network. How do the connections in a transport network differ from those in an MPLS TE packet network?

4.2.1 What is a Label?

In MPLS a label is an arbitrary tag for a data packet that is used as an index into the LFIB. MPLS labels and resources are not tightly coupled. As often as not, resource management in MPLS is purely statistical, such that the available bandwidth on an interface is only logically divided up between the LSPs that use the interface. In this case the label will indicate the amount of resources statistically reserved, but does not identify any specific physical resources. Reservations represent a percentage of the available resources (for example, bandwidth), but no resources (such as buffers) are actually dedicated to supporting the flow, and the total resource reservation may actually be allowed to exceed the available bandwidth to allow for the fact that it is unlikely that all flows will be at their maximum capacity at the same time.

Where real resource reservations are used, the label on a data packet may still not identify specific physical resources. For example, network resources in MPLS may be a set of buffers used to receive data for a particular LSP from the wire and to forward it through the switch. But the resource reservation may be made from a pool of buffers that is shared between multiple LSPs—that is, no buffer is specifically allocated to one LSP, but the total number of buffers allocated for LSPs defines the size of the pool. On the other hand, an LSP may have specific resources (buffers or queues) dedicated to it, and in this case the label is more closely tied to the resources, because it identifies exactly which resources may be used for the LSP. Should an LSR decide to share resources between two LSPs, it may allocate two separate labels and map them to the same set of resources.

In transport networks the physical resources are exactly the switchable quantities. That is, in a WDM network the lambdas are switched, in a TDM network the timeslots are switched, and so forth. Thus a label that identifies a switchable data stream in GMPLS also precisely identifies a physical resource. So in a lambda switching network a label identifies a specific wavelength, in a TDM network a label identifies a specific timeslot, and in a fiber switching network a label identifies a specific port or fiber. This fact brings challenges that are not found in packet switching environments. One implication, for example, is that labels come from a disjoint set (for example, identifying the frequencies of the lambdas) rather than being arbitrary integers. Similarly, the set of valid labels is likely to be much smaller in a transport switch. Further, the interpretation of a label must be carefully understood—no longer is this an arbitrary tag, but it identifies a specific resource, and both ends of a link must have the same understanding of which resource is in use.

In GMPLS the meaning of a label is private between two adjacent LSRs, but they must have the same understanding of that meaning. TDM labels are given a special encoding so that the referenced timeslot may be deduced, but for lambda and fiber switching the meaning of the label is left as a matter for configuration or negotiation through the Link Management Protocol.

4.2.2 Switching Types

The switching type of a network node defines the data units that the device can manage and switch—that is, the level to which it can demultiplex the data signal from an incoming interface, switch it, and send it out of another interface. For

---

Table 4.1 The GMPLS Switching Types

Packet (switching based on MPLS shim header)
Layer 2 (switching based on layer 2 header such as ATM VPI/VCI)
Timeslot (TDM)
Lambda
Waveband (contiguous collection of lambdas)
Fiber (or port)

---

example, MPLS routers are *packet switch capable (PSC)*—they can receive data
on an interface (which may be an Ethernet port, a SONET port, and so forth), identify the packets in the data stream, and switch each packet separately. A photonic
cross-connect is *lambda switch capable (LSC)* and can demultiplex individual
lambdas from a single fiber before switching each lambda in a different direction.
A *time division multiplex capable (TDM)* switch is able to recognize individual
timeslots within a lambda.

Note that the grade of data signal that a switch can identify is not the same as
the granularity of bandwidth that the switch can process. A lambda switch may
deal in lambdas that carry 2.5, 5, or 10 Gbps signals, and if it is a photonic cross-
connect it is very probably unaware of the different bandwidths. A TDM switch that
can process VC-192 signals may be handling greater units of bandwidth than some
lambda switches, even though it is switching a finer grade of data signal. In fact, we
should really describe the switching capabilities of interfaces rather than switches,
because a single network device may support a variety of interfaces with different
switching capabilities, and because some devices may be capable of discriminating
the signal at different levels (for example, lambda and TDM) on the same interface.

GMPLS recognizes a list of switching types that is consistent with the quantities that may be labeled (see Table 4.1). There is an obvious logic to this because it
is precisely those things which can be switched that must be labeled.

4.2.3 What is a Label Switched Path?

Now that we have defined the switchable and labeled quantities in GMPLS,
we need to decide what we mean by a Label Switched Path (LSP). In any transport
network, regardless of the switching type, we are concerned with the establishment
of connections that carry data between two specific end points. This connection
is sometimes called a circuit or a trail, and the end points are not necessarily the
points of delivery of the service, but may be intermediate switches that need to
be connected in order to help facilitate the provision of the service.

At each switch along the connection or trail, resources are *cross-connected*.
That is, the switch is programmed to take traffic from an incoming resource and
send it to an outgoing resource (recall that a resource may be a timeslot, lambda,
and so forth, on a specific interface). Because these resources are associated directly

with labels, we are able to define an LSP as a contiguous series of cross-connected resources capable of delivering traffic.

In the data plane this gives us a trail of {interface, label, cross-connect} triplets (where a label is synonymous with a resource). Note that the LSP is not a service but supports a service by providing full or partial connectivity.

The term *label switched path* is also meaningfully applied in the control or management plane to describe the state (that is control blocks, memory, and so forth) that is used to manage the LSP within the data plane. Thus, if the data plane is programmed manually, there is a record of the LSP within the management plane, whereas if the LSP is established through the exchange of control plane signaling messages, there is LSP state in the control plane.

4.2.4 What is Bandwidth?

In MPLS, bandwidth—specifically bandwidth requested for an LSP—can be measured down to the finest granularity in bytes per second. The available bandwidth on a link may be divided up in any way between the LSPs that use the link. In GMPLS transport networks, because an LSP is directly related to a physical and switchable resource, the bandwidth can only be divided up according to the capabilities of the switching device—this typically forces the bandwidth division to be in large units of bytes per second. For instance, if a service over a wavelength switching network requires bandwidth of, say, 10 Kbps, then 2.5, 10, or 40 Gbps (depending on the capacity of one lambda channel) will be allocated on every link of the service path. This means that only a fraction of the allocated bandwidth will actually be used, which is clearly very wasteful.

On the other hand, in a GMPLS transport network there is no danger that a traffic flow will violate the user-network agreement and consume more than the allotted bandwidth that was allocated during service setup. This problem can easily occur in a packet network, especially if only statistical admission control is applied, but the limits of the physical resources in a transport network mean that it is absolutely impossible to over-consume bandwidth.

Various advanced techniques (such as the use of hierarchical LSPs and Forwarding Adjacencies) have been developed to help GMPLS make optimal use of bandwidth where the service needs to use only a small proportion of the available resources. This is easier in some technologies than in others because, for example, TDM readily supports the aggregation of multiple small data flows into one larger flow.

4.2.5 Bidirectionality of Transport Connections

MPLS LSPs are unidirectional—that is, they provide connectivity for unidirectional transfer of data within the network. Services offered by transport network Service Providers are almost always bidirectional, offering equal connectivity and data transfer capabilities in both directions. Further, there is often a requirement for the connectivity in each direction to share common links (such as fiber pairs) to provide *fate sharing*. It is possible, of course, to construct bidirectional connectivity from a pair of unidirectional LSPs that have the same end points and run in opposite directions. However, there are numerous advantages to having a single signaling exchange establish a bidirectional LSP and a single control plane state managing both directions instead of having two unidirectional LSPs. For example, from the fate sharing and recovery point of view it is advantageous that if one direction becomes inoperable, resources associated with the other direction are immediately released. Resource contention, which may happen when two bidirectional tunnels are established simultaneously from both directions under conditions of limited link label spaces—the usual case on transport networks—can be resolved in a simple way if resources for both directions are allocated simultaneously. Besides, a single bidirectional LSP requires only one control plane state on each node, and hence consumes half as much memory as two unidirectional LSPs. It can also be set up more smoothly, quickly, and with less processing because it needs only one set of control plane messages to be exchanged.

4.2.6 Separation of Control and Data Planes

In a packet switching environment, control plane messages can be delivered through the same links as the data packets. Thus, control and data channels can be considered coincident. This is not the case for transport networks. One of the reasons why transport network nodes can forward large volumes of data with such great speed is that the nodes switch entire timeslots, wavelengths, bands of wavelengths, or entire fibers without recognizing individual packets. This feature means that control plane messages cannot be delivered through the same channels as the data traffic.

In some cases one "data" channel on every link is dedicated for control traffic delivery—for example, a lambda on a WDM link, or a timeslot on a TDM link (the in-fiber-out-of-band model). In other cases, control traffic uses separate links or even separate networks (out-of-fiber-out-of-band model). It is not unusual for a control message to pass through several controllers before it reaches its destination—the controller that controls the next data switch on the LSP. There are also configurations when a separate single broadcast network interconnects all controllers so that each of them is only one hop away from any other.

The separation of control and data plane channels brings a lot of complications and challenges for the GMPLS protocols. For example, identification of data links is no longer implicit in the signaling message, but must be made explicit. Similarly, additional control plane techniques are needed to verify the connectivity and aliveness of data plane links, because the successful delivery of signaling messages can no longer be used. Further, mechanisms need to be added to the signaling protocols to allow the management of data plane failures. For example, if some controller is notified by a data plane hardware component about a failure, it should be able to send an appropriate notification to a node that is responsible for service recovery. It also should be possible to set up and shut down services in an alarm-free manner, so that no false alarms are raised.

The corollary of control and data plane separation is that failures on one or more controllers or control plane connections do not necessarily mean that there is any problem delivering data traffic. In fact, data services, albeit only partially controlled, can continue to function properly indefinitely. New features are needed in the signaling mechanisms so that the control plane can recover from failures and re-assume control of existing data services.

4.2.7 Tunneling and Hierarchies

LSP tunneling using hierarchical LSPs is an MPLS concept supported by label stacking. But label stacks are only efficacious where shim headers are used to encode the labels. That is, they can only be used in packet, cell, or frame networks. In non-packet environments, where the label is implicit and directly associated with a physical resource, it is not possible to produce a label stack. Consider, for example, a lambda network: Although it is conceptually possible to encapsulate the signal from one lambda LSP into another lambda LSP, this encapsulation can only be done on a one-for-one basis, and it is impossible to determine the correct lambda to use for the encapsulated LSP when it emerges from the far end of the tunnel. There is no mechanism to encode this information with the data.

However, the concept of hierarchical LSPs does have a different meaning in GMPLS. Because we are now dealing with a variety of switching types (packet, TDM, lambda, and so forth), we can observe that there is a natural hierarchy of switching based on the granularity. LSPs may be nested according to this hierarchy just as the physical resources are nested. So, as shown in Figure 4.1, lambdas may be nested within a fiber, timeslots within a lambda, and packets within a timeslot.

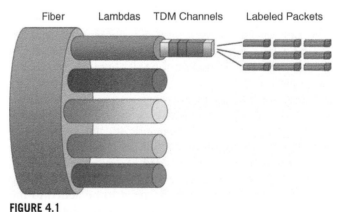

Fiber   Lambdas   TDM Channels   Labeled Packets

FIGURE 4.1

The hierarchy of switching types.

This form of LSP hierarchy allows for aggregation of tunnels offering more scalable traffic engineering, and more efficient use of bandwidth in core transport networks, as well as facilitating the integration of different switching types to provide end-to-end connectivity.

Various techniques are needed in GMPLS signaling and routing to make hierarchical LSPs properly useful. These include the Hierarchical LSP (H-LSP), where an LSP tunnel is presented as offering point-to-point connectivity across the network so that LSPs may be routed through the tunnel; non-adjacent signaling that allows control messages to be exchanged between the ends of a tunnel; and LSP stitching, which brings the concepts of the H-LSP into the single switching-type network.

Advanced Techniques

As MPLS deployments have become more extensive and more customer services are provided over MPLS networks, it is increasingly important that those networks include sophisticated functions to add value and quality to the features offered to the customers. This section looks at some of the most critical advanced techniques that are applied within MPLS networks to provide these benefits.

Chapter 5 discusses Traffic Engineering, one of the key aspects of MPLS that enables the provision of quality of service and allows an operator to manage the network for optimum performance and capacity. Chapter 6 describes the subject of quality of service and looks at the techniques and mechanisms that are used in MPLS networks to ensure that the networks meet the needs and expectations of the end customer. Chapters 7 and 8 investigate the requirement for restoration and recovery techniques in MPLS networks and look at how MPLS and GMPLS can achieve recovery through protection or restoration of the forwarding plane.

Traffic Engineering

This chapter draws on material from *The Internet and Its Protocols* by Farrel, and from *GMPLS: Architecture and Applications* by Farrel and Bryskin to introduce the concept of traffic engineering (TE) as applied to MPLS traffic in the Internet. Traffic engineering has long been a familiar concept to town planners and road safety engineers—they are concerned with how to get the best flows of vehicles through congested streets with the minimum number of accidents. A road planner is concerned about the effects of road junctions, merging traffic flows, and sudden turns. When they build a new road will a single lane street be sufficient or do they need an eight-lane highway? What are the optimum speed limits they should set, and how should they coordinate traffic light phasing? Can they prioritize certain traffic (buses, high-occupancy vehicles, or emergency services) without causing additional disruption to the lower-priority traffic.

Most of these concepts apply within packet switched networks. A data packet is equivalent to an individual car, the links (cables, fibers, etc.) can be compared with roads, and the junctions are the switches and routers within the network. Just as vehicular traffic congestion causes delays and accidents, so data traffic congestion results in slow delivery times and lost packets.

This chapter examines some of the concepts used to manage the traffic within an IP network to make better use of the available resources, and looks at the extensions to the IGP routing protocols that are being developed within the IETF to make available information about the capabilities of and stresses on the network.

5.1 WHAT IS IP TRAFFIC ENGINEERING?

The Internet is a collection of nodes and links with the purpose of delivering IP datagrams from a source host to a destination host. The source does not, in general, care how the data is delivered so long as it arrives in a timely and reliable way. The conventional routing protocols are based on "shortest path first" (SPF) routing, in which each datagram is routed on the shortest path between the source and the destination.

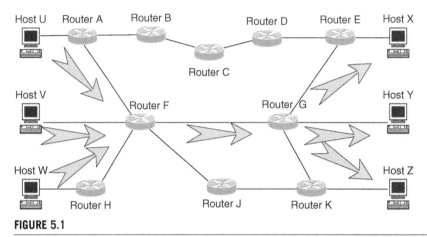

FIGURE 5.1

Shortest path first routing may result in unnecessarily congested links and nodes.

In an otherwise unused network, SPF routing is ideal: datagrams are delivered expeditiously with the least use of network resources. However, as network traffic increases it may be the case that a link or router is saturated and cannot handle all of the traffic that it receives. When this happens, data will be lost either in a random way through data collisions or through an organized scheme within routers.

The techniques to increase the reliability of traffic delivery within an SPF routing system are useful, but they do not increase the amount of traffic the network can handle. Consider the network shown in Figure 5.1. In this network traffic from Hosts U, V, and W is routed across the network to Host X, Y, and Z. Using SPF routing, traffic tends to converge on the link between Routers F and G. This is fine until the link or the Routers become overloaded, at which time data is dropped. But what about the other links in the network? Surely they could be used to reduce the burden on the congested resources. For example, if traffic between Hosts U and X was sent through Routers B, C, and D the datagrams would take a slightly longer path but would avoid the congested link.

Traffic Engineering is all about discovering what other paths and links are available in the network, what the current traffic usage is within the network, and directing traffic to routes other than the shortest so that optimal use is made of the resource in the network. This is achieved by a combination of extensions to the existing IGP routing protocols, traffic monitoring tools, and traffic routing techniques, respectively. The remaining sections in this chapter examine these mechanisms.

5.2 ROUTING IP FLOWS

Equal cost paths may be selected by a router for different flows to help balance the load within the network. But suppose that some observer of the network (an operator or an application program) determines that there is a longer, more expensive, underused path that is suitable for the traffic: Can the data be sent down that path without having to modify path costs as described in the previous section? If this could be achieved, network congestion could be avoided (the drivers could download new routes from their GPS navigation systems and find a way around the traffic jams).

In source routing, each datagram contains a list of IP addresses of the links or nodes it must pass through, in order, on the way to its destination. SPF routing is performed at each stage on the next address in the list so that the datagram may be sent along a path under the control of the source application. This is ideal because it gives complete control to the sender, allowing it to choose whether to use the shortest (lowest cost) path (which may be congested) or some other more expensive path that would otherwise not be chosen by the network.

But, notwithstanding the limitations of IP source routing, source routing is also not ideal because it forces the hosts to make routing decisions. This is both too much function to place in a host and too much responsibility. Proper choice of routes requires detailed analysis of traffic flows and available resources, and this requires a sophisticated application. At the same time, if each individual traffic source makes uncoordinated routing decisions based on the same network data, the result may be the sudden and simultaneous transferal of all traffic from one overused link to another (formerly underused link) in a way that may cause even more serious congestion. (Compare this with the rush hour traffic that responds to a radio traffic report by diverting en masse from the slightly congested freeway to the single-lane country road.)

A better model, therefore, might have paths selected in coordination with a centralized traffic control station. This sort of model is applied very successfully in vehicular traffic engineering when a city or motorway network is controlled through an operational headquarters that can control speed limits, traffic lights, diversions, and lane assignments. An individual host may, however, find that the overhead of soliciting a path for its traffic is unacceptably high given the small amount of data it wants to send.

On the other hand, significant traffic management can usefully be performed within the core of the network where the traffic volumes are greater. Here individual flows from host to host can be bundled together and treated in the same way for forwarding down routes that are not necessarily the shortest. The easiest way to handle this is through a process known as *tunneling*. A tunnel is a well-defined path from one point in the network to another, and flows may be injected into the tunnel at one end to emerge at the other end, as shown in Figure 5.2.

Tunnels may run from one edge of the network to another, or may be used to bypass an area of congestion. The simplest way to achieve a tunnel is to impose a source route on each datagram that enters the tunnel. In this way the router at the head end of the tunnel determines the path of the datagram until it reaches the end of the tunnel. Other, more sophisticated, IP tunneling techniques may be used. Note that tunnels may themselves be routed through other tunnels, providing a hierarchy or nesting of tunnels.

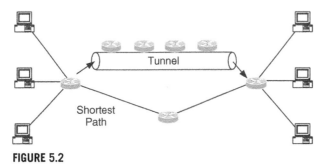

FIGURE 5.2

A tunnel carries a collection of flows from one point in the network to another by a path that may not be the shortest.

Tunneling may also be achieved at a level below IP in the network. A good example of this is MPLS. When sub-IP tunnels are established, they may be defined to the network as *virtual links*, which are logical point-to-point connections between routers that are not actually physically connected. These virtual links may be assigned costs and can be advertised through the routing protocols in just as physical links are, resulting in traffic being routed down the tunnels rather than across the physical links.

5.3 CHOOSING OFFLINE OR DYNAMIC TRAFFIC ENGINEERING

Various comments in the previous sections have indicated the problems with making traffic engineering routing decisions dynamically within the network. Among these concerns are problems caused by routers that do not share the same routing paradigms as the rest of the network—they may place traffic using different rules and this unpredictability may cause links to be overloaded. Conversely, the simultaneous application by multiple routers of the same routing and traffic balancing rules may result in decisions to move lots of traffic from several slightly overused links to a single underused link, making the one link congested. These difficulties arise to a lesser extent if the traffic engineering routing decisions are made only by the data sources or by TE tunnel head-end routers within the network, but even then the reactivity of a single network node to changes within the network is limited by the node's view of the network.

A more controlled approach favored by many network operators is *offline traffic engineering*. In this mode of operation, all decisions about how to route traffic are made by one (or a few) centralized servers. Such servers can keep a coordinated view of the network and react to changes in traffic loads. They can supply source routes to hosts, tunneling information to selected routers, or constraint-based routing instructions to all routers in the network. These instructions from the traffic engineering server can be applied to new flows or to existing flows, making it possible for the traffic to be dynamically redistributed within the network.

One key advantage of offline traffic engineering is that more time can be taken to perform complex calculations and modeling before the new flow paradigms are applied within the live network. This reduces the chance of a major mistake — it is better to have traffic continue to flow with some congestion than it is to bring complete gridlock to the network.

Offline traffic engineering is best suited to a tunneling model. This may use IP tunnels as described in the previous sections or lower-layer tunneling using MPLS of layer two tunnels.

5.4 CHOOSING TO USE TRAFFIC ENGINEERING

Traffic engineering maximizes the performance of existing network connections, allowing more traffic to be carried. This increases revenues from deployed equipment and an increase in revenue without an increase in expenditure should imply increased profits. Further, maximizing the performance of the existing infrastructure delays the point at which more money has to be spent to add links and nodes to the network.

Of course, if the network is massively over-provisioned there is nothing the operator needs to do other than possibly monitoring the most congested links to check that traffic is well within the safe parameters. A network provider who considers himself lucky in this situation should appreciate that although he is able to satisfy his customers' Service Level Agreements (SLAs) he is not generating as much revenue from his network as he could. More traffic means higher revenues.

Traffic engineering is a tool for operators of well-used networks who need to move the traffic around to take the pressure off congested links without compromising the SLAs they are contracted to meet. Path computation engines can run offline or can be dynamic, as already described. Path computation can be a single shot for each flow (that is, the route is computed when the flow is first established) or can be adaptive, adjusting the routes of the flows in the network according to the pressures of traffic.

Additionally, the rules for computing paths can be based on a variety of constraints above and beyond the volume of the flows and the available bandwidth on the links. Constraints can cover priority, quality of service, reliability, and security. Other constraints can be used to ensure that flows include or exclude specific resources (such as links that are known to be vulnerable, or paths that are used to provide diverse backup routes), nodes, or groups of resources known as *shared risk link groups* (SRLGs) that share the same risk of failure.

The greater the complexity of the applied traffic engineering scheme, the more sophisticated are the features that can be sold to customers and the more flexible are the management options for the network provider. At the same time, increased complexity demands more detailed and reliable collection of network statistics as well as increased processing resource. The trade-off between cost and benefit will be met at a different level for each network, and it should be born in mind that with increased complexity may come a greater risk of a mistake that could cause severe perturbations within the network.

5.4.1 Limitations of IP Traffic Engineering

There are some distinct limitations to the way traffic engineering can be performed using IP. If forwarding rules are modified, then the routers in the network need to be kept synchronized and must all operate with the same level of function, or loops and increased congestion may result. On the other hand, IP source routing is limited both by the size of the route that may be specified (just nine hops) and the fact that not all routers support IP source routing in a consistent way (or at all).

Other IP tunneling techniques may help to direct traffic around hot spots and do have some efficacy, especially as they allow data flows to be grouped together and handled in the same way. But even these tunneling techniques really need some form of source routing to route them through the network. Clearly, some other form of tunneling is really needed.

5.4.2 Future Developments in Traffic Engineering

Traffic engineering is increasingly utilizing Multiprotocol Label Switching (MPLS) to meet its tunneling needs. MPLS provides data tunnels through the network that can be placed according to explicit routes calculated offline or online and modified in real time. These tunnels rely on IP routing information gathered through the TE extensions to the IGPs for computation of their paths and distribution of tunnel forwarding information, but do not use the IP addresses of the datagrams to actually forward the data within the tunnels. This gives the best of both worlds because all the information from the IP world can be used to determine paths to forward IP data, but the issues with IP forwarding can be overcome by using non-IP forwarding techniques.

Note that preexisting layer two forwarding protocols such as Frame Relay and ATM have offered the same sort of tunneling as MPLS for some time. MPLS just brings them together under one generic protocol umbrella for ease of management and the construction of heterogeneous networks.

5.5 TRAFFIC ENGINEERING IN MPLS

This section describes how MPLS can be used to achieve traffic engineering and examines the requirements on MPLS signaling protocols.

MPLS offers the ability to implement traffic engineering at a low cost in equipment and operational expenditure. Capital expenditure can be reduced because

MPLS is able to supply much of the function of the traffic engineered overlay model in an integrated manner. Operational costs may be reduced by the use of automated provisioning of tunnels, proactive distribution of traffic between tunnels, and dynamic computation of optimal routes through the network. In many cases, this pushes the intelligence for operation of a traffic engineered network into the network itself and away from central management stations.

MPLS has many components that make it attractive for use in a traffic engineered network. These aspects are examined in the sections that follow. They include the following.

- MPLS has the ability to establish an LSP that follows a path other than the one offered as preferred by the routing protocol and forwarding algorithm.
- Resources within the network can be dynamically reserved as LSPs are established and can be dynamically updated as the needs of the LSPs change so that traffic flows can be guaranteed a level and quality of service. Routing of the LSPs can be made dependent on the resource requirements.
- Traffic can be groomed on to "parallel" LSPs. That is, multiple LSPs can be established between a pair of source and destination end points, and traffic can be distributed between the LSPs according to any number of algorithms. The parallel LSPs can take significantly different paths through the network.
- Network resources can be automatically managed with new LSPs set up to meet the immediate demands of the network, and with resources freed up again as old LSPs that are no longer required are released.
- The network can be managed centrally through a common set of management options and with a common underlying granularity of managed object—the LSP.
- Recovery procedures can be defined describing how traffic can be transferred to alternate LSPs in the event of a failure and indicating how and when backup and standby LSPs should be set up and routed.

Ultimately, MPLS scores over previous traffic engineering implementations because the load-sharing, traffic grooming decisions need only be made once (at the entry point into the LSPs) rather than at each node within the network. This makes traffic propagation considerably more efficient.

Consider the gratuitously complex but miraculously symmetrical network in Figure 5.3. There are five data sources, all sending traffic to a single data sink. Left to itself, a shortest path first algorithm will serve to converge all of the traffic onto the link between node H and the sink. This might unnecessarily overload that link even though the network contains sufficient independent routes, as illustrated by the heavy lines in the figure.

Some diversity can be achieved by modifying the costs of key links. For example, if the link from Source 5 to node J is made expensive, the SPF algorithm will choose to send traffic via node M. But this approach cannot address the whole of the problem for our network since all of the traffic from Sources 2, 3, and 4 converges on node G, and so we might need to implement some form of Constraint-based routing

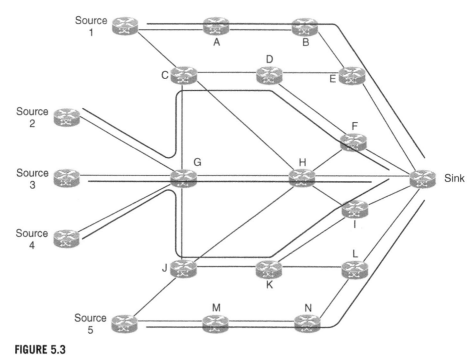

FIGURE 5.3

Explicit path control in an MPLS network.

at node G to send some traffic through node C and some through node J. Even then the problems are not over because the traffic tends to converge again at node H, so we would need to increase the costs of links CH and JH or do more constraint-based routing at node H to split the traffic through nodes F and I. This all becomes very complicated and might be entirely broken if a new traffic flow were added through a new source or sink.

However, if MPLS LSPs are used, the computation of diverse paths can be performed offline and no changes to the behavior of the routing or forwarding code are needed. LSPs are simply established (manually or through the signaling of explicit paths) to follow the computed routes shown in bold and data flows without congestion.

5.5.1 Explicit Routes

MPLS LSPs can be set up using signaling protocols utilizing the existing routing protocols. This is how LDP Downstream On Demand label distribution works and is also used by MPLS traffic engineering protocols in the absence of any explicit route control.

The request to set up an LSP includes the address of the end point or egress LSR. The first LSR in the network performs a routing look-up based on the egress address and sends a signaling message to the next hop. This process is repeated LSR by LSR through the network until the egress is reached.

One of the main issues in a network is that preferred routes tend to converge. This serves to place much traffic onto a few links while other links remain relatively free of traffic. A key aim of traffic engineering is to distribute traffic across the links to ensure that the load is shared. If LSPs can be forced to follow other routes, the traffic can be made to traverse underutilized links and so take the pressure off busy links.

The fundamental facility that MPLS brings to traffic engineered networks is the ability to set up a virtual circuit switched overlay to the Internet routing model. In a manually provisioned MPLS network this is simple—the LSRs can have their FTN mapping tables and LFIBs explicitly set to send traffic down specific paths. This process can be automated through the use of a management protocol (such as SNMP) or the use of any form of remote access (such as Telnet) to configure the LSRs.

Ideally, however, MPLS signaling protocols like those discussed in Chapter 3 will allow the path, the explicit route, of the LSP to be specified to the head end of the LSP and will traverse the chosen path establishing the LSP. Explicit routes are specified as a well-ordered series of hops expressed as IP addresses, IP prefixes, or identifiers of autonomous systems. The LSP must traverse the hops in order.

Because each hop can be an expression of multiple nodes (as a prefix or as an autonomous system), the elements of an explicit route are referred to as *abstract nodes*. The LSP must traverse the abstract nodes in the order that they are specified in the explicit route, and where the abstract node defines more than one node the LSP must traverse at least one LSR that is a member of the abstract node.

The fully specified addresses used in explicit routes give rise to some confusion. If loopback addresses are used, it is clear that the path must include the node with the specified address, but if an interface address is used, consideration must be given as to whether this refers to an incoming address or an outgoing address. Some systems prefer the interface address to indicate the outgoing interface because this does not require any routing look-up as the route is processed at a node, but others consider that a precise interpretation of the explicit route processing rules (see the following section) require that addresses always indicate the next hop. It is important when building an MPLS network that you understand the processing rules applied to explicit routes by the various equipment vendors who supply you—many switches now support both modes of operation at the same time, but others require configuration to select the mode, and a few utilize one mode only. Failure to harmonize this aspect of explicit route processing will possibly prevent LSP setup in your network.

The abstract node hops in the explicit route may each be defined as *strict* or *loose*. If a hop is strict, no LSR may be inserted in the actual path of the LSP between LSRs that are members of the previous abstract node and those that are members of the current hop. If the hop is loose, the local routing decisions may fill in additional nodes necessary to reach an LSR that is a member of the abstract node that is the current explicit route hop. Loose and explicit hops can be explained further with reference to Figure 5.4. Suppose we want to set up an LSP from the ingress LSR to the egress LSR. The simplest explicit route we can give is a single loose hop specifying the loopback address of the egress LSR that leaves the network free to choose a route in between.

Now, suppose further that we want to include the link between LSR E and the egress because we know that it is currently underutilized. There are several options that force the route through LSR E (for example, including a hop that specifies the loopback address of LSR E), but these rely on the CSPF algorithm at LSRE not choosing to pick a route back through LSRs B and D. The best option is to include an address that forces the link to be used—192.168.253.10 as a loose hop would achieve the desired result in some networks and 192.168.253.9 would be satisfactory in others. This explicit route looks like {loose(192.168.253.9), loose (egress LSR)}.

So far we have left the choice of route in the upper part of the network open and that still allows routes to be picked through LSR A and LSR D. In particular, it is possible that a path {Ingress, LSR A, LSR D, Egress, LSR E} would be chosen to reach the first hop in the explicit route given in the preceding paragraph. We need to apply more control. Suppose we would rather not use any path through LSR A, but we don't have any preference between LSRs B and C. If we include a strict abstract node hop with prefix 63.217.244.248/29 we will ensure that the path goes in the right direction, but there is still a possibility of a path through LSR B and LSR D that misses our objectives, so it is necessary to include a strict hop to LSR E.

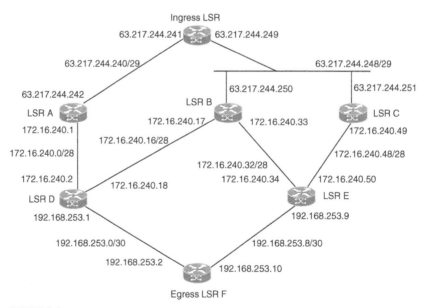

FIGURE 5.4

Strict and loose hops in explicit path control in an MPLS network.

This gives us the explicit route of {strict(63.217.244.248/29), strict LSR E, …}. Now we will definitely reach LSR E and we may simplify the remaining route to the egress as a strict hop to its loopback address, or (depending on the system) a strict hop to 192.168.253.9 or 192.168.253.10. The final explicit route is {strict (63.217.244.248/29), strict LSR E, strict (LSR F)}.

Explicit Route Processing Rules

The processing rules for MPLS explicit routes are laid out in the definition of the IETF's signaling protocol for traffic engineered MPLS (RSVP-TE in RFC 3209). When an LSP setup request message carrying an explicit route object is received by an LSR it must follow the simple steps in the following list. These steps all follow the assumption that as the message propagates through the network, the explicit route on the message is trimmed so that only parts of the route relevant to the nodes that have not yet been reached remain in the message.

1. On receipt, the LSR must check that it is a member of the first abstract node in the explicit route. If it isn't, processing must fail.
2. If there is only one abstract node in the explicit route it must be removed. Processing continues at step 8.
3. If the LSR is also a member of the second abstract node, the first node is removed and processing continues at step 2.
4. If the LSR determines that it is topologically adjacent to (that is, only one hop away from) some node that is a member of the second abstract node, it selects the next hop, removes the first abstract node and continues at step 9.
5. The LSR attempts to find a next hop that is a member of the first abstract node and is on the route toward the second abstract node. Note that if the first abstract node is explicit (that is, not a prefix or an autonomous system) this attempt will fail, but it is at this point that the difference in processing for interface addresses as incoming or outgoing addresses can be applied. If such a next hop is found, processing continues at step 9.
6. If the second abstract node is a loose hop, the LSR chooses any next hop toward the second abstract node, removes the first, and continues at step 9.
7. If no route has been found (which includes no route available, and second abstract node is a strict hop) the LSP setup fails.
8. There being no more explicit route present, the LSR may insert a fresh series of abstract nodes as a new explicit route toward the destination. If it does, processing continues with step 10, otherwise, the LSP setup continues but is routed on a hop-by-hop basis across the rest of the network.
9. If the selected next hop is a member of the (new) first abstract node in the explicit route, and that abstract node is not an explicit address, the LSR may insert additional abstract nodes at the head of the explicit route as a result of local path computation. The one proviso is that all inserted abstract nodes must be subsets of the first abstract node.

10. If the selected next hop is not a member of the (new) first abstract node in the explicit route (possible if the first abstract node is a loose hop) the LSR must insert a new abstract node that the next hop is a member of at the start of the explicit route. This ensures that the explicit route is accepted at the next node.

5.5.2 **Reserving Resources and Constraint-Based Routing**

It can be desirable to specify the characteristics of traffic flows so that resources can be reserved to help to satisfy quality of service requirements and to implement service level agreements (SLAs). Overlay of a virtual circuit-switched overlay is established using MPLS and if specific reservation requirements are associated with each LSP it becomes possible to reserve precisely enough resources for each flow and to guarantee SLAs based on a much more precise allocation of network capabilities. This can lead to considerable savings or, more precisely, it can allow network operators to make full use of their networks without needing to over-provision resources to play it safe with their SLAs.

The following features are necessary for MPLS to fully provide this service.

- The routing protocol must advertise the capabilities and available resources on each link.
- The requester of a flow of LSP must indicate the characteristics of the flow (average bandwidth, peaks, quality requirements).
- The engine that computes the paths must take into account the requirements of the LSP and the availability of network resources by performing constraint-based routing.
- The MPLS signaling protocol must support setting up explicitly routed LSPs.
- The MPLS signaling protocol must be able to signal the LSP resource requirements so that the appropriate reservations can be made at each LSR along the path.
- The routing protocol must re-advertise the modified resource availabilities for each link on the LSP so that subsequent path computations at other nodes can know the current state of the network.

Even when all of the available resources have been used, it is still possible to set up a new LSP by commandeering the resources used by one or more existing LSPs. This process of LSP *preemption* needs some form of policing, otherwise the network will simply thrash with LSPs alternately replacing each other. In MPLS preemption is achieved by using two priority values associated with each LSP. The *holding priority* indicates how hard an existing LSP will hold on to resources once it has them and the *setup priority* says how important the setup of the new LSP is. An LSP with a greater setup priority may preempt an LSP with a lower holding priority. Obviously, network thrash will be avoided only if LSPs have holding priorities greater than or equal to their own setup priorities (and if operators show a modicum of self-discipline about their choice of priorities).

5.5.3 **Grooming Traffic**

In some cases there will be multiple traffic flows between a source and a sink. Perhaps there are multiple applications, some serving high-bandwidth, low-priority file transfers, and others serving low-bandwidth, rapid-response user interfaces. In these cases it is desirable to keep the flows separate as they pass through the network, allowing the high-priority traffic to overtake the larger quantity of low-priority traffic. This is the sort of behavior that DiffServ can provide in an IP forwarding network.

In an MPLS network, the same effect can be achieved by establishing two LSPs between the same source and destination. The LSPs can follow the same route and be given different characteristics to prioritize the traffic. Alternatively, the LSPs can follow diverse paths. All that is necessary once the LSPs are established is for the source node to decide which LSP to assign each packet to based on the source application or the DiffServ packet color.

5.5.4 **Managing the Network**

Managing the network as a mesh of LSPs allows regulated predictability to be applied to the traffic flows. This makes it much easier to handle planned network outages in a seamless way since the LSPs can be rerouted around the resource that is going to be taken out of service to preserve traffic. At the same time, management techniques can be applied to predict future flows and control current demands so that congestion is avoided and quality of service is provided to users.

Such network management can be centralized or operated from multiple sites, all using the topology and resource information supplied by the routing protocols and establishing new LSPs as required. Such management can even be distributed to the LSRs, building an intelligent network that is capable of routing and rerouting LSPs according to the current traffic load conditions.

5.5.5 **Recovery Procedures**

In the event of unplanned network outages, traffic engineering with MPLS can define how data flows can be protected. Backup or protection LSP can be presignaled using disjoint paths through the network so that when there is a failure on the primary or working LSP the data can immediately be switched to the backup path. In the same way, single LSPs called bypass tunnels can provide protection for a group of working LSPs, a physical link, or even a bundle of physical links.

Presignaled backup LSPs utilize network resources without carrying traffic until there is a failure. There are a host of schemes to mitigate this issue, ranging from LSPs that reserve resources only when they start to see traffic, through LSPs that support low-priority preemptable traffic until the failure occurs, to backup LSPs that are signaled only after the failure. The choice between these different protection models is complicated by the configuration of the network and the capabilities of the LSRs.

5.5.6 **Choosing to Use a Constraint-Based Signaling Protocol**

Traffic engineered LSPs can be configured manually. That is, the operator can pre-compute the path of the LSP, perhaps using a path computation engine fed by topology and availability information from the routing protocol and by traffic statistics gathered from the edges and core of the network. Having selected a path for the LSP, the operator can visit each LSR in the network to configure the LFIB and install the LSP. Finally, the operator can configure the ingress LSR through the FTN mapping table and through the routing table so that the correct traffic is placed on the LSP. How the operator achieves this will depend on the devices, but might include using command line interfaces through Telnet, configuration through Management Information Bases (MIBs) using SNMP, or proprietary configuration protocols.

The manual configuration process is time consuming and error-prone. One of the requirements of traffic engineering is that it must be able to respond quickly to changes within the network, and operator intervention is unlikely to achieve this.

A signaling protocol reduces the number of configuration steps and allows a spectrum of control from full operator selection of paths, through offline traffic engineering, to on-demand traffic engineering with intelligence within the network. The use of a software application determines the need to establish new LSPs or to reposition existing ones and issues a request to the ingress of the LSP. From there, the request is signaled along the path of the LSP conventionally using Downstream On Demand label distribution.

5.6 GMPLS AND TRAFFIC ENGINEERING

Service Providers have come to realize the importance of traffic engineering techniques because they allow them to optimize utilization of network resources and bring more revenues. In fact, one of the biggest reasons for the success of MPLS as a technology is its ability to implement traffic engineering at a low cost, especially in terms of operational expenditure. Dynamic computation of optimal paths through the network, dynamic provisioning of tunnels, and proactive distribution of traffic between the tunnels are examples of how MPLS pushes the intelligence for operation of a traffic engineered network into the network itself and away from proprietary central management stations, thus allowing for the building of efficient and cost-effective multi-vendor networks. In this chapter we will discuss what traffic engineering is, how it applies to GMPLS-controlled transport networks, and how it is different from traffic engineering in packet switching networks. We will define the notions of a transport service, network controller, data switch, and control channel, as well as control interface, data interface, data link, and link attributes in the context of traffic engineering. We will go on to discuss ways that GMPLS nodes learn about other nodes and links, so that path computation elements can determine optimal paths for services with specified attributes.

Finally, we will analyze the peculiarities of traffic engineering on networks that span multiple regions and administrative domains.

5.6.1 Evolution of Traffic Engineering

RFC 2702, *Requirements for Traffic Engineering Over MPLS*, states that traffic engineering is a technology that is concerned with performance optimization of operational networks. In general, this is a set of applications, mechanisms, tools, and scientific principles that allow for measuring, modeling, characterization, and control of packet-based user data traffic in order to achieve specific performance objectives. What are these objectives? There are two classes.

The first class is traffic-oriented and hence directly visible to end users. The performance objectives of this class include Quality of Service (QoS) enhancement of traffic streams, minimization of data loss, minimization of delay, and the provision of a certain level of throughput for high-priority traffic flows in conditions when some network links are congested.

The second class of performance objectives is resource-oriented. These objectives are important only to Service Providers and irrelevant to users of services they sell. The objectives concern optimization of resource utilization. To put it more simply, traffic engineering in this respect is a technology that can answer questions like these: Given the network resources that I have, how can I keep all my users happy? Can I sell more services without adversely affecting my current users? How can I avoid the situation where some network resources are severely overused while others are underused or not used at all? What network assets can I add, and where do I need to add them, in order to improve my network performance? How can I protect the services that I sell from network outages? To be competitive, Service Providers must find good answers to all these questions and in a timely manner.

Note that traffic engineering is most important only for well-used networks. Under-provisioned networks that provide simple services to a few clients do not experience congestion and, therefore, do not need traffic engineering. For networks that provide constantly growing amounts of service of different types and levels of complexity, on the other hand, traffic engineering is very important because it can yield substantial savings in capital and operational expenses. Note that this draws a distinction between traffic engineering as a function and the act of computing paths through the network. The latter is also required to provide protection and recovery services. Because both traffic engineering and other path-specific services use the same features of path computation, we consider them together in this chapter.

Traffic engineering is an important function of the network control plane. Originally, it was introduced to fight congestion on overloaded links that were caused by its routing protocols (more specifically, their shortest-path-first nature).

There are two reasons why congestion can happen.

- The network is under-provisioned; that is, the amount of traffic is such that one or more network links cannot accommodate it, and there are no alternative paths that can deliver the traffic to its destination.
- Traffic is mapped onto paths that use overloaded links despite one or more alternative paths available in the network that could deliver the traffic, which, albeit more expensive, would use under-subscribed links. Congestions of this type happen because routing protocols that are used to determine the paths are oblivious of the bandwidth usage on network links. They determine paths that are shortest; ones that have the minimal sum of metrics associated with path links.

Congestion of the first type is of no concern to traffic engineering because no action in the control plane can possibly make up for the lack of physical resources in the network, but congestion of the second type can be mitigated through traffic engineering. As is pointed out in RFC 2702, traffic engineering is useful when a service path is dynamically computed, and there is more than one path available that can deliver the service traffic. Traffic engineering is all about learning what resources are available on the network, determining feasible paths, and choosing the optimal ones.

Traffic engineering has gone through an interesting evolution. The major problems it was created to address are as follows.

1. How to control paths taken by services without changing Internet routing protocols in a fundamental way.
2. How to make sure that a service path can always deliver QoS no worse than that pledged for the service in the Service Level Agreement.
3. How to guarantee that service resilience to network failures is at least no worse than committed.
4. If a better path becomes available after a service has been established, how to make the service switch to this path with minimal user traffic disruption. How to guarantee that this kind of optimization will not violate network stability.
5. How to bill services so that users will be interested in paying more for better services.

Traffic Engineering Through Modifying Network Link Metrics

One might suggest controlling traffic flows by modifying the metrics associated with network links. After all, that is what link metrics are for—to make links (and the paths composed of the links) more or less attractive depending on some operator-controlled policies. What about the traffic engineering goals for the policies?

Consider the network shown in Figure 5.5. Note that each link metric has a value of 1. Suppose that there are two services provisioned on the network: service 1 taking path AFGE and service 2 going over path HFGI. Note that both services are directed to use link FG by the Shortest Path First algorithm. Suppose also that there is some entity (human or application) that is monitoring the level of congestion on the links. When it is detected that the congestion on link FG exceeds some threshold, some logic could increase the link metric by some value (say, 2 to a value of 3). This would force service 1 to switch onto the preferable (lower cost) path ABCDE and would make link FG less congested because it will be relieved from carrying traffic for service 1. When some time later the level of congestion goes below some other threshold, the same logic could decrease the metric for link FG—say, by 1. The new metric assignment would keep service 1 on path ABCDE, but might attract other services to use link FG.

Unfortunately the tweaking of link metrics is not so straightforward. Neither is it harmless. In fact, it may cause much more severe problems than the ones it is trying to solve. The tricky part is to decide which metrics to modify, when, and by how much. If one performs the modification too early, traffic can be switched from slightly congested to uncongested low capacity links, immediately causing more severe congestion. If one does it too late, the traffic may experience a hit because it will take at least a few seconds before the routing tables converge and services take the intended new paths. And what if the traffic bursts that triggered the congestion come and go in quick successions? This might cause continual modification of the network metrics, which results in significant load on the routing protocols and disruption to traffic. It is quite obvious that modifications of link metrics require very careful network planning: Mistakes can be very costly, and there is no guarantee that such modifications will not affect services that are perfectly healthy and even going over paths disjoint from the links whose metrics are going to be modified.

Traffic Engineering Through ECMP

Suppose the metric of link FG in Figure 5.5 has a value of 2 instead of 1. We then have two paths from node A to node E, ABCDE and AFGE, that have equal costs (4).

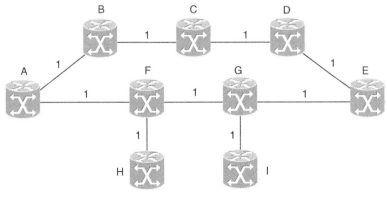

FIGURE 5.5

Traffic engineering through modifying link metrics and ECMP.

In such cases a routing protocol running on node A would normally pick one of the paths (say, AFGE) and create a forwarding table entry instructing node A to forward packets going to node E through link AF. However, with relatively small modifications, the routing protocol could provide next hop forwarding information for all paths that have equal costs (in our example, it would be links AF and AB) and let the data plane forwarder decide which of the paths to take for any given packet.

The most obvious and straightforward way to take advantage of several paths is simply to alternate between them in a round-robin way so that the traffic load is evenly distributed. This, however, would almost certainly break the order of data flows and might trigger higher layer IP protocols such as TCP to perform numerous unnecessary retransmissions. The smarter way to use parallel paths is to segregate flows according to packet source IP address, destination IP address, transport level ports, payload protocol type, DiffServ color, or any combination of the above and forward different flows over different paths. This is called *Equal Cost Multi-Path (ECMP)* forwarding.

Many existing routing protocol implementations support ECMP. It is useful because it provides an easy and safe way for load balancing; however, it is not much help. The same reasons that have made links of one path congested may cause congestion on two or three equal cost paths, and we might start losing data despite the fact that some other slightly more expensive but completely unused paths are available. Besides, if we do have congestion, how do we make sure that packets of a lower priority service are dropped before packets of a higher priority service?

Traffic Engineering Through Service Type Based Routing

The next attempt to achieve the traffic engineering goals was through separate routing of data flows that are associated with different service types. A limited number of application types that have different network services requirements can be identified. For instance, a Voice Over IP (VoIP) service imposes tight constraints on end-to-end packet delivery, delay, and delay variation, but can tolerate occasional packet drops; a file transfer service does not care much about the delay but expects minimal packet drops. The main concerns for a WEB browsing application is speed (especially in the download direction) and low cost. Once application/service types are identified, it is possible to:

- associate with each link on the network graph, not one but a set of link metrics (one per service type), and have a routing protocol build separate forwarding tables for each service type;
- have the packet forwarder on every node determine the service type associated with a packet (perhaps by looking into the DiffServ color or other bytes within the packet header or payload), and choose the appropriate forwarding table for forwarding the packet.

This method achieves two goals. First, some kind of load balancing is provided: Data flows associated with different service types are routed over different paths even if they originated on the same source and are directed to the same destination. Secondly, the data plane can be provisioned in such a way that QoS requirements for different service types are appropriately accommodated, so that data packets get respective forwarding treatment. As a result, the network is in a position to meet committed SLAs and bill its clients accordingly.

However, there are some issues with this approach. It is assumed that each router on the network applies the same forwarding policy on any given packet as the rest of the routers. But what if packet forwarding rules (which can be very complex, and cannot be dynamically provisioned or updated) on one router are different from the others? In this case the router might make forwarding decisions that are not expected by other routers, and loops can easily occur. Besides, this approach does not help if the network is used predominantly for one service type.

Traffic Engineering Using Overlays

Introducing overlay networks was a big step forward in traffic engineering. In this model (see Figure 5.6) a Service Provider core network is built of layer 2 switches (ATM or Frame Relay) that are good at providing QoS support; whereas the overlay network is composed of Service Provider edge IP routers interconnected via layer 2 virtual channels provisioned by the core network. Each pair of edge routers is usually connected by more than one channel. Extra channels are needed for load balancing, delivering different QoS, and for recovery purposes.

The great thing about this model is that each data flow can be routed individually, even if all of them are associated with the same service type. When a packet enters the Service Provider network, it can be classified depending on the ingress data port and/or the contents of the packet header and/or the payload. Once the packet is classified (and, thus, the associated data flow is identified), it can

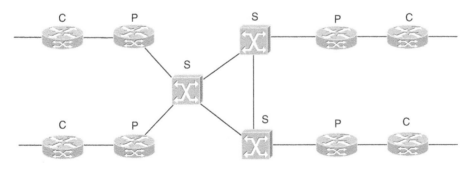

C—customer site IP router
P—provider IP router
S—ATM or Frame Relay switch

FIGURE 5.6

IP overlay network.

be placed on a virtual channel that connects the ingress and egress edge routers along the data flow path and supports the expected QoS. The user network
can shape the traffic so that it will not violate the SLA contract, and the provider
network can police traffic that "behaves badly," so that it will not adversely affect
data flows of other users. The forwarding decision for every packet is made only
once (by the ingress router and not by any core network element), hence loops
could not be produced. The load balancing can be easily achieved by provisioning parallel (not necessarily equal cost) virtual channels. In the case of network
failures, traffic can be switched onto pre-provisioned virtual channels that are disjoint from the channels affected by the failures.

One of the problems with the overlay model is its poor scalability: Each layer 2
virtual tunnel requires a direct routing adjacency (peering) between its ends. This
results in the well-recognized n-squared problem in the control plane. The major
inconvenience with overlays is the complexity required to support two control
and management planes—IP and ATM/Frame Relay—and, consequently, high operational costs. It would be simpler, cheaper, and better overall to provision virtual
QoS channels on heterogeneous networks using a single unified control plane.

Traffic Engineering Based on MPLS

The innovation of MPLS technology offered simple, efficient, and elegant answers
to many of the questions raised by traffic engineering.

MPLS Traffic engineering protocols allow nodes to advertise not just their
presence and topological connectivity, but attributes of their links as well. This
makes it possible for provider network edge nodes or off-line path computation elements to compute paths with the necessary constraints; therefore, services taking the paths have a good likelihood to be successfully established and
operational.

MPLS signaling protocols make it possible to set up services along dynamically computed or manually provisioned paths that could be different from those
that are identified by routing protocols. If a better path becomes available for
some active service, the latter can be re-routed onto the new path with little or
no affect on the user traffic. In case some high priority service cannot be placed
on the network because the required resources are not available; it is possible to
automatically preempt the resources from some lower priority service.

The Label Switched Paths (LSPs) produced by the MPLS signaling protocols
have similar qualities to the virtual paths of the overlay model. A service mapped
onto an MPLS LSP can deliver the required QoS because the necessary resource
reservations were made during the LSP setup; data packets are switched based on
MPLS labels without looking into packet headers or payloads.

The big advantage of the MPLS model versus the overlay model is the ability of MPLS LSPs to be dynamically provisioned in heterogeneous networks (for
example, composed of IP routers, ATM switches), using a single unified control
plane. It is possible to set up multiple LSPs between any pair of edge routers for
the purpose of load balancing. MPLS LSPs also naturally eliminate the n-squared

problem intrinsic to the overlay model of virtual tunnels because there is no need for a routing peering between the ends of an LSP.

From the service resilience point of view, MPLS networks perform much better than overlay networks. The MPLS signaling protocols have an in-built mechanism to notify an LSP ingress node, or any other node responsible for service recovery, about LSP failures. Thus, the ingress node can take service recovery actions without waiting for routing tables to converge. For example, the node can establish an LSP diverted from the failed links and switch traffic onto it away from the LSP affected by the failures. To get an even better recovery time, a service can be mapped on multiple LSPs—one working and one or more protection LSPs separately protecting one link, one node, or one segment of the working LSP—so that recovery actions can be performed on a node close to the point of failure. Once network failures are repaired, the affected services can be automatically switched back (restored) onto the original LSPs.

The MPLS node graceful restart procedures allow for a failed node to quickly synchronize its control state with its neighbors; thus LSPs going through the failed node can be managed via the control plane, and all other nodes can have the correct representation of the node resources available for other LSPs.

Probably the best part of MPLS traffic engineering for Service Providers is that the bulk of its components and mechanisms are built into MPLS protocols and standard applications. Therefore, the network can be built of devices of different types and from different vendors. As a result, multiple services can be offered on a single infrastructure.

5.6.2 Traffic Engineering in Transport Networks

Automatic traffic engineering is not needed on networks that are manually provisioned. It is the responsibility of the network operators and planners to direct services through parts of the network that have sufficient resources to support the services. Congestion is usually discovered at the planning stage and is handled by manually redirecting other services during a period of network maintenance, or by installing new equipment (such as additional fibers or lasers) within the network. If congestion occurs in a live network, it is the direct result of a provisioning or planning error.

When transport networks were provisioned manually, traffic engineering did not need to be a dynamic process. Network operators examined the current state of the network and placed each new circuit according to the available resources. If there was a shortage of resources, or some form of congestion, the operator might reposition existing service, or commission the installation of new equipment. This contributed to the slow speed of service provisioning.

Further, most transport networks were built on ring-based technologies that made the networks topologically quite simple, which meant that traffic engineering could only add limited value.

As transport networks became more complex, with the interconnection of rings and the topology beginning to look more like a mesh, GMPLS was introduced to handle the dynamic provisioning of services. Traffic engineering in these networks began to look more interesting.

Because GMPLS is based on MPLS technology, it makes sense to consider employing the MPLS traffic engineering techniques in transport networks, but there are several ways in which a transport network differs from an MPLS packet-based network.

Transport Connections are Bidirectional

MPLS LSPs are unidirectional, while services offered by transport network Service Providers are almost always bidirectional. So, while MPLS services may also be bidirectional (constructed from an LSP that runs in each direction), transport services must attempt to use the same physical resources (fibers) in both directions to give a level of *fate sharing* for the forward and reverse data flows. This means that the traffic engineering algorithms used must manage the availability of resources in both directions.

Labels Identify Resources

In MPLS labels and associated resources are decoupled; there is no correlation between a label and the resources that are allocated to support the LSP that uses that label. In transport networks, however, the label is synonymous with the resource. A label indicates exactly which resource is reserved—for example, in a lambda switching network—and the label precisely identifies the WDM wavelength of the transport circuit LSP that has been established.

This means that some simple tunneling techniques that "pick up" an LSP and redirect it down a tunnel and are used for MPLS traffic engineering cannot be applied in transport networks. Also, resource sharing, which is necessary for make-before-break operations that are fundamental to the operation of the repositioning of LSPs during traffic engineering, needs a new mechanism in transport networks.

Bandwidth is Less Granular

Traffic engineering in MPLS networks can theoretically be managed as bandwidth measured down to individual bytes per second. In practice (partly because of the floating point notation used to encode the bandwidths and partly for sanity) bandwidth is usually measured and reserved in larger units reflecting the type of service required. This may be 10 or 100 Kb/sec for a typical end-user service, but larger amounts are reserved for aggregated flows. A key aspect of MPLS traffic engineering is that multiple flows can be aggregated onto a single link to share the total available bandwidth.

In a transport network, as already described, the resources reserved for an LSP are associated with physical resources. Simple traffic engineering aggregation is not possible. Thus, if a WDM laser provides a 2.5 Gbps, a 10-Kbps LSP that uses that laser (wavelength) will demand the full 2.5 Gbps and waste most of the bandwidth. The case is even worse if the laser provides a 10- or 40-Gbps service.

Traffic engineering in a transport network, therefore, requires careful consideration of bandwidth wastage, and needs new aggregation techniques to carry multiple traffic flows using the same resources. Note that traffic policing is not necessary in a transport network because a single flow is physically incapable of exceeding the bandwidth reserved for it.

Path Computation Needs More Constraints

The traffic engineering problem for transport networks is generally more complex than for packet networks simply because there is a tendency toward a greater number of constraints on the paths that can be selected. These constraints may be fixed, such as switching capabilities of the hardware, or the data encoding mechanism. Alternatively, the constraints may be dynamic, such as the optical impairments of the signals in the network.

To impose such constraints the computing node or workstation needs to obtain information about pertinent link attributes. Hence more traffic engineering information needs to be advertised. The increased volume of advertising causes scalability concerns; therefore, mechanisms to make the TE advertising more scalable are very much desirable.

Control Plane and Data Plane Channels are Separated

The separation of control and data planes in transport networks means that there has to be a clean separation of the TE information advertised so that the topology built into the TED reflects the data plane connectivity and not the control plane connectivity.

Further, the routing and TE advertising protocols cannot be relied on to detect link failures, because the failures they will discover are failures in the control plane. The Link Management Protocol (LMP) is used to detect and correlate data plane TE links and to isolate failures, whereas failures in the control plane are usually allowed to happen without disruption to the data plane.

All these aspects cause fundamental conceptual differences in the TE mechanisms in transport networks compared to MPLS networks, where the control and data links are congruous.

Usage of Hierarchical LSPs

Hierarchical LSPs (referred in this book as H-LSPs) provide a significant scaling advantage in TE networks where they allow multiple end-to-end LSPs to be clustered and tunneled down a single H-LSP. This results in considerable simplification and reduction of the control and data plane state at transit nodes. In packet switched networks, this is the limit of their benefit, but in transport networks H-LSPs play a much more important role.

Note that a transport network service can span links with different switching capabilities. For instance it can start on a segment with TDM links, go through

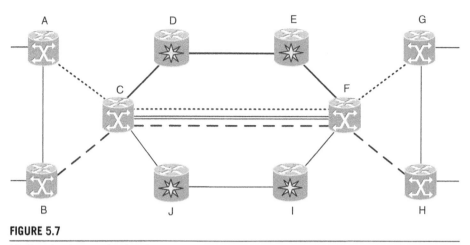

FIGURE 5.7

Multi-region transport network.

several wavelength switches, and terminate within some other TDM segment (as shown in Figure 5.7).

In this example, the node that is located on the boundary between the first TDM network and the optical network (node C) cannot allocate individual times-lots on the link facing the optical network (link CD). The only reasonable option for the node C in this case is to create an H-LSP going through the optical seg-ment (CDEF) and nest all TDM level LSPs within the H-LSP. The alternative would be to allocate a separate lambda channel for each TDM LSP and utilize only a frac-tion of the allocated resources, and as already discussed, this would result in a lot of wasted bandwidth.

H-LSPs define data links that traverse the network between nodes that are not necessarily physically adjacent, but rather, adjacent in a particular network layer. These data links are available to carry LSPs and form part of the network topology—that is, provide extra network flexibility—and are used during traf-fic engineering. In transport networks, H-LSPs form an important part of the TE mechanism and must be carefully planned (as is the case for the static topology) and advertised with their TE properties.

Traffic Engineering in Photonic Networks

Optical networks built of photonic cross-connects present additional challenges for traffic engineering. One of the problems with photonic cross-connects is that they cannot perform wavelength conversion; that is, they cannot convert a signal received with one wavelength to be sent out using a different wavelength. This limitation results in the wavelength continuity constraint for paths in such net-works. That is, for a path to be considered a feasible candidate for some service, each data link of the path must have at least one lambda channel of the same fre-quency available for reservation. To honor such a constraint, a much larger volume of TE advertising is required (information about every individual channel on every link must be available for path computing nodes) and more complex path computation algorithms must be applied (paths have to be computed not in terms of TE links but in terms of lambda channels). On the other hand, signaling of such paths is simpler than signaling of conventional GMPLS LSPs: there is no need for label negotiation during the optical trail setup—the path computing node selects lambda channels and hence assigns all labels.

The other class of challenges in photonic networks comes from the fact that because of signal attenuation and optical impairments, and because the photonic network cannot regenerate the signal, the quality of the optical signal deteriorates while the signal travels over data links and cross-connects in the network. By the time the signal arrives at the service destination, it might not be possible to transform the optical signal back into an electrical signal with an acceptable quality. Path computation needs to account for all contributions to the signal degradation by all devices—fibers, amplifiers, cross-connects, DWDMs, DCMs, and so forth—that constitute the path. It needs to do this while deciding whether the path is feasible or not. It is a formidable task, because these contributions to the signal degradation are not always linear or accumulative. Sometimes the degradations are also wavelength dependent, and sometimes they are also a function of other signals going through the same devices or fibers.

From the traffic engineering point of view the challenges described here result in more advertisements (more TE link attributes), and a completely new class of path computation algorithms to be introduced.

5.7 GMPLS TRAFFIC ENGINEERING DEFINITIONS

Analyzing objectives, requirements, and peculiarities of traffic engineering in transport networks leads to an obvious conclusion: For a transport network, MPLS traffic engineering is good but not perfect. Numerous extensions, and brand new principles and paradigms are necessary for every aspect of the MPLS control plane to make traffic engineering attractive for transport Service Providers.

Fortunately, GMPLS technology is flexible enough to accommodate the necessary extensions in such a way that they work and are very useful in packet switching networks as well. To develop such extensions is exactly the goal of the GMPLS technology in general and GMPLS traffic engineering in particular.

This section describes the key terms and concepts necessary to enable traffic engineering in a GMPLS network.

It is convenient to decompose a transport network into the following abstract components: network, control channels, control interfaces, data switchers, data links, and data interfaces (see Figure 5.8).

The *Controller* is where all control plane intelligence (routing, TE and signaling protocols, and path computation elements) is located. Controllers communicate with each other over *control channels*. Locally, controllers are connected to

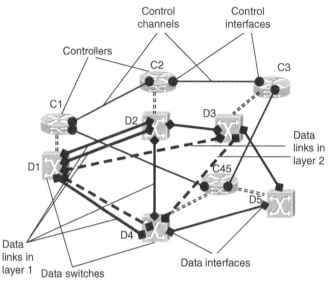

FIGURE 5.8

Transport network elements.

control channels through *control interfaces*. For example, controllers C1 and C2 in Figure 5.8 use their control interfaces in order to establish an OSPF adjacency over control channel C1C2.

A *data switch* (also referred as a *transport node*) is a component capable of terminating a data traffic flow and/or forwarding it on the route to its destination. A *data link* (or simply a *link*) is a construct used in network topology that characterizes a set of network resources that are used to deliver traffic between two data switches that are adjacent in a particular network layer. For example, the data link D2D3 in Figure 5.8 delivers all traffic going from D2 to D3 in network layer 1, while the data link D4D3 carries data between D4 and D3 in network layer 2.

The *network layer* (or *layer*) is an abstraction representing a collection of network resources of the same type.

Data links on transport networks are usually bidirectional; hence data link D5D4 (which will sometimes be known as D4D5) also delivers traffic going from D4 to D5. A pair of data switches can be interconnected within the same layer by more than one data link. For instance, switches D1 and D2 are interconnected by two parallel data links in layer 1. And, of course, a pair of data switches could be interconnected by multiple data links in different network layers (like switches D1 and D4).

Locally, data switches are connected to data links through *data interfaces* (also referred as *link interfaces* or simply *interfaces*). As we will see later, the most important characteristics of a data interface are its switching, termination, and adaptation capabilities. A data switch can be connected to the same data link via several data interfaces with one of them modeling the switching function, while the rest encompass different termination/adaptation functions.

A GMPLS-based control plane distinguishes data links of two types: *dynamic* data links and *static* data links. The former are completely under the control of the GMPLS control plane. Such data links could be added to or removed from the network topology of a particular layer by setting up or tearing down LSPs in different layers. What is important about dynamic data links from the GMPLS point of view is that they could be added/removed "on the fly" to achieve certain traffic engineering objectives like adding additional network flexibility to provide a path for a particular service. For example, data link D4D3 in layer 2 could be realized by establishing an LSP in layer 1 going through nodes D4, D5, and D3. As mentioned earlier, LSPs that are created to be used as data links in different layers are called *Hierarchical LSPs*. Static data links are those that are either manually provisioned (for example, ATM PVCs) or created by a non-GMPLS control plane (for example, ATM SVCs).

Controllers discover network resources that they manage (that is, local network resources) in the form of data links. Local data link ends are learned via configuration, whereas the information about the remote data link ends is provided by the Link Management Protocol (LMP) or configuration. However, network resources are advertised into the TE routing domain in the form of *TE links*. In contrast to a data link, which is a "real" network topology construct, a TE link is a *logical* grouping of network resources for the purposes of routing. It is important to keep in mind that paths for a particular service are computed in terms of TE links, whereas the LSPs onto which a service is mapped are provisioned over data links. One of the functions of a controller that takes part in setting up a particular LSP is to translate a local TE link found in the explicit path of the LSP Setup message into a local data link where resources must be allocated. Usually one TE link reflects exactly one data link. However, it is possible to advertise resources of two or more parallel data links (that is, data links connecting the same pair of data switches within the same network layer) as one TE link (this is called TE bundling). It is also possible to advertise any fraction of a data link as a separate TE link, while reserving the rest of the data link resources for other purposes, such as recovery.

The controllers managing the ends of a data link (and, hence, the associated TE link) need to have control plane connectivity with each other to make use of the link during dynamic LSP provisioning. Such connectivity could be achieved via a parallel plane channel connection (for example, link D2D3 in layer 1 has a parallel control plane connection C2C3) or a sequence of control plane connections (for link D1D3 in layer 2 control plane connectivity could be achieved via the connections C1C2 and C2C3). The control plane connectivity is termed a *control channel*, and care should always be taken to ensure that such control plane connectivity exists.

However, there are some links for which control plane connectivity is guaranteed. Let us consider the link D1D3 in layer 2. This link could be constructed using an H-LSP established in layer 1 going over the links D1D2 and D2D3, and the link could be advertised as a TE link. An LSP advertised as a TE link is called *TE-LSP* and could be advertised into the same or a different instance of the control plane from that used for advertising the constituent links from which the TE-LSP was constructed. The former case is interesting because the TE-LSP has *guaranteed* control plane connectivity between its ends. The fact that the TE-LSP was successfully created means that each of its constituent links has control plane connectivity within the instance of the control plane that was used to provision the TE-LSP. Because the TE-LSP is advertised into the same instance of control plane, the control plane connectivity between the TE-LSP ends is guaranteed to be at worst a concatenation of control plane connections connecting the end points of each of its links. In GMPLS such dynamic links that have intrinsic control plane connectivity between their ends are called *Forwarding Adjacencies (FAs)*.

One controller can manage one or several data switches. For example, controller C45 manages two switches, D4 and D5. In most of the cases, controllers and the data switches they manage are arranged in a one-to-one relationship and are physically collocated within the same devices. It is fair to note, however, that, at least theoretically, the controller and the switches could be separate devices, even coming from separate vendors. It is possible to imagine, for example, a model where an intelligent protocol-rich control box controls one or several simple optical cross-connects, and this is often proposed as the migration path for including legacy (or dumb) switching equipment in GMPLS networks. In the case when a controller manages a single data switch it is useful to denote the combination of the controller and the switch as a *node*.

One of the most remarkable differences between transport and packet switching networks is the relationship between control channels and data links. On packet switching networks control packets are usually delivered over the same links as the data. This is possible because data switchers forward data on a packet-by-packet basis. To do so they need to understand packet boundaries, headers, and so forth. They can easily detect control packets destined to local devices and pass such packets to local controllers. Data switchers on transport networks, on the other hand, forward entire signals based on wavelengths or timeslots. They cannot distinguish the boundaries of individual packets. Hence, for control plane packets to be terminated at each switch, the control plane traffic must use separate channels specifically dedicated for this purpose. A control channel and associated data link represent totally different sets of network resources. It is important to understand why path computation for transport services must consider only network TE information and disregard IP related advertising: Data paths have nothing to do with control plane paths. *For a transport service, IP routing reachability between the service source and destination is of no importance.* The fact that two controllers can exchange control messages does not mean that the associated data switches are interconnected through a sequence of links with available resources (fibers, wavelength channels, timeslots) to deliver the traffic. Likewise, a sudden loss of control plane connectivity does not necessarily mean a user traffic hit. Also, there are no guarantees that a fiber cut disconnecting a service can be detected via the control plane.

Transport Service, Path, and LSP

Let us define a point-to-point transport service as a way to deliver user traffic of specified parameters with specified QoS between specified user-network inter-faces. A transport service should be distinguished from a transport service path, which we define as a sequence of Service Provider network TE links that have appropriate resources to deliver the service. A transport LSP is the path that is adequately provisioned over data links (that is, all resources are allocated, bound, and committed) for the service delivery. A transport service is a routable object; that is, it can be placed on one or more LSPs. It can be also re-routed over different LSPs when the original ones become inoperable

5.7.1 TE Link Attributes

TE link attributes as well as attributes of the data interfaces that connect associated data link(s) to a data switch are configured on and advertised by the associated controller. Let us assume that each data link in Figure 5.8 is advertised as a separate TE link. Thus, controller C2 in Figure 5.8 advertises attributes of TE link D2D3 and also attributes of the data interface that connects data switch D2 to the link D2D3. Likewise, controller C3 advertises attributes of TE link D3D2 and attributes of the data interface that connects data switch D3 to the link D3D2. From the perspective of any given controller in the network, a TE link is denoted as *synchronized* if the controller has received valid and consistent advertisements related to both sides of the link. Only synchronized TE links are installed as edges into the local TE network graph and, thus, made available for local path computation elements.

The following link attributes are introduced for the purpose of link synchronization.

1. Link type
2. Link ID
3. Local interface IP address (for numbered TE links)
4. Remote interface IP address (for numbered TE links)
5. Local link identifier (for unnumbered links)
6. Remote link identifier (for unnumbered links).

The *Link type* attribute identifies the TE link type. Two link types are currently defined (1: point-to-point; 2: multi-access). Only links of type 1 are relevant for transport networks, since multi-access optical or TDM networks have not yet been deployed.

The *Link ID* attribute has a very confusing name. For point-to-point links it identifies a Router Address of a controller associated with the *other* side of the link. By a controller Router Address we define some routable IP address configured on the controller, which is always available and associated with the data switch that originates/terminates the link. It could be also defined as an IP routable data switch identifier. Note that a controller needs to have several Router Addresses if it manages several data switches (one per data switch).

The end points of the TE link are identified by a local and a remote link identifier. A TE link can be either numbered or unnumbered. A TE link is numbered if its link identifiers on both sides are four-byte network-wide unique numbers (usually, but not necessarily, IPv4 addresses). A TE link is unnumbered if its link identifiers are four-byte numbers unique within the scopes of the two local controllers. Thus, in order to uniquely identify an unnumbered TE link within the whole network, one needs to augment its local identifier with the Router Address of the advertising controller.

The *Local interface IP address* and *Remote interface IP address* attributes identify, respectively, local and remote link identifiers for numbered TE links. These attribute names are also confusing. They are inherited from MPLS, where control channels and data links are inseparable, and the control interface IP address is used as an identifier of the associated TE link. In GMPLS, numbered TE link identifiers do not have to relate to associated control interfaces—there might not even be any associated control interfaces. The numbered TE link identifiers also do not need to be routable.

The *Local link identifier* and *Remote link identifier* attributes denote, respectively, local and remote link identifiers for unnumbered TE links. There are multiple ways that advertising controllers may learn about remote link identifiers. For example, they can learn about them the same way they learn about local link identifiers—through configuration. Remote link identifiers can be also learned via the LMP link auto-discovery mechanism.

TE link advertising is consistent if all the following conditions hold.

1. TE link attributes are advertised by controllers associated with both ends of the link.
2. The Link type attribute is the same in both advertisements and equal to one (point-to-point).
3. The Link ID attribute in one advertisement matches the controller Router Address of the other and vice versa.
4. The non-zero Local interface IP address attribute in one advertisement matches the Remote interface IP address attribute of the other and vice versa (only for numbered TE links).
5. The non-zero Local link identifier attribute in one advertisement matches the Remote link identifier attribute of the other and vice versa (only for unnumbered TE links).

As was mentioned earlier, from the perspective of a controller on the domain, a TE link can be considered synchronized if both advertisements are consistent and valid. The advertisement validity means the following.

■ TE link attributes that the processing controller can understand are advertised in a proper format defined by the TE protocol in use—OSPF-TE or ISIS-TE.

Note that unknown link attributes are usually simply disregarded, as they do not prevent the link from becoming synchronized.

- There is always a way for the advertising controllers to withdraw their advertisements. That is, the processing controller is connected to each of the advertising controllers via a sequence of active routing adjacencies. This is necessary because once the processing controller loses routing connectivity with any of the advertising controllers, it might use stale information in its local path computations for a considerable period of time (up to 60 minutes in the case of OSPF) until the advertisements are withdrawn from the local TED due to their timeout.

All other GMPLS TE link attributes are intended for use in constraint-based path computation.

The *Traffic engineering metric* attribute is used as a cost of the arc that represents the TE link on the TE network graph in the direction *from* the data switch with which the advertising controller is associated. For example, controller C2 (Figure 5.8) may advertise the Traffic engineering metric attribute 10 for the TE link D2D3. This piece of information instructs every network controller to assign cost 10 to arc D2D3 in the direction from D2 to D3 on the locally built TE network graph. Note that controller C3 may advertise a different traffic engineering metric for TE link D3D2 (say, 15). For every path computing controller this will make the link more attractive in the direction D2D3 than in the direction D3D2.

The *Administrative group* attribute is a 32-bit number that may be advertised for a TE link. Each bit of the administrative group represents some network-wide known quality of the link (link color), so that a path computation process can be constrained to avoid or force the use of TE links with particular colors, depending on the service for which the path is computed.

The *Link protection type* attribute represents the TE link protection capabilities. The link protection capabilities are 'Extra Traffic', 'unprotected', 'shared', 'dedicated 1:1', 'dedicated 1+1', 'enhanced'.

The link protection attribute is used to constrain the path computation algorithm to consider only links that can guarantee some acceptable level of protection on every link. The definition of acceptable will depend on the particular service; for example, if there is a need to compute a path for a service that expects shared protection, all links with the link protection attribute 2 or lower are supposed to be excluded from the path computation.

The *Shared Risk Link Group* attribute identifies all SRLGs to which the link belongs. As mentioned earlier, several links can constitute an SRLG if they share a network resource whose failure may affect all links in the group. For instance, if two fibers belonging to two separate data links are located within the same conduit, and there is a cut in the conduit, both links may fail. Hence, the two links belong to an SRLG associated with the conduit. Every SRLG on the network is identified by a 32-bit network-wide unique number. Any given TE link may belong to multiple SRLGs, thus, the SRLG link attribute may include more than one SRLG ID.

The SRLG attribute is very useful for the computation of recovery paths. It is always desirable for a service recovery LSP to be as disjoint as possible from the service working LSP, so that a failure of a single network resource would not affect both LSPs. It is reasonable to instruct the path computation to make sure that the union of SRLGs of all links belonging to the resulting working path and the union of SRLGs of all links that belong to the resulting recovery path have zero SRLGs in common.

Unlike all other TE link attributes, the *Interface Switching Capability (ISC) descriptor* attribute describes the characteristics not of a TE link, but of a data interface. As we discussed earlier, a data switch is locally connected to the near side of an associated data link via a data interface. For example, data switch D3 in Figure 5.8 is connected to the link D3D5 via a data interface (marked as a black diamond). As part of advertising the TE link D3D5, controller C3 advertises parameters of the data interface connecting the associated data switch D3 to the link D3D5. Likewise, controller C5 advertises the characteristics of the data interface that connects switch D5 to the link D5D3.

The following information is provided by the ISC descriptor attribute.

- Interface switching capability type
- Data encoding type
- Maximum LSP bandwidth available for reservation for each (0–7) priority level

For Packet Switch capable interfaces the ISC descriptor additionally includes the following.

- Minimum LSP bandwidth
- Interface Maximum Transmit Unit (MTU)

For TDM capable interfaces the descriptor additionally includes the following.

- Minimum LSP bandwidth
- Indicator of whether the Standard or Arbitrary SONET/SDH is supported

The most important data interface parameter is its switching capability type. This describes how and with what granularity data can be switched from/onto the link connected through the interface. Some interfaces can distinguish individual data packets within the data flow received over connected link, look into packet headers, and make forwarding decisions depending on the headers contents. Other interfaces may not be capable of distinguishing packet boundaries, but can switch individual channels within an SDH payload. There are also interfaces that can only switch individual wavelength channels, or entire traffic received over individual fibers. The importance of switching capabilities within GMPLS networks is described later in this chapter. It should be noted here that when a path is computed across a network it must use TE links that provide the right level of switching capabilities.

Data encoding type is another data interface attribute. It is always associated with a switching capability type within the *ISC* descriptor attribute and provides information about encoding supported by the interface.

The data encoding type describes the format of data presentation to the transport medium. Fundamentally this is a characteristic of a traffic flow and not of an attribute of a link of link interface. For example, the ANSI PDH type defines how DS1 or DS3 traffic is presented on the wire. One may find it particularly confusing to see this parameter among TE link and link interface attributes. For instance, if it is said that a link interface has *Lambda* for switching capability type and *Lambda* for the encoding type, what does it really mean? It means that the link interface can multiplex/de-multiplex entire wavelength channels, and it does not know how the data is structured within the channels. A link interface that has the *Packet* switching capability type and *Ethernet* data encoding type is capable of switching individual packets based on 801.3 headers. Thus, in the context of traffic engineering the data encoding type has a different meaning. This is the extent to which a data interface understands how data is encoded within the traffic flows they switch. Again, this is important information during path computation because consistent TE links must be selected.

Link interface switching capability type and encoding type parameters are always associated with the third component of the *ISC descriptor* attribute: *Maximal LSP Bandwidth available* at each of the eight priority levels. Some descriptors also include switching capability specific information. For example, the TDM descriptor additionally includes Minimal LSP bandwidth and indicates whether Standard or Arbitrary SONET/SDH concatenation is supported. This information along with the Data encoding type is particularly important for identification of network layers and layer boundaries within a single network region. For instance, a TDM region (identified by TE links with the TDM switching type) may be (and usually is) comprised of multiple layers. Each such layer is identified by a layer *switching capability*—a combination of switching capability type, data encoding type, the arbitrary concatenation indicator, and the minimal LSP bandwidth—describing the data format and switching granularity of the links comprising the layer.

There are several reasons why a data switch can be locally connected to a data link by more than one link interface. Suppose a data link carries 40 wavelength channels. It is possible that, say, 30 of these channels could be switched only as lambdas. In GMPLS this is modeled by connecting the link to the switch via a link interface providing the *switching* function. For the remaining ten channels, however, there could be termination and adaptation function in place, so that lambda channels can be terminated and individual TDM channels can be extracted from the SDH payload of the terminated lambda channels and switched onto separate TDM interfaces. This is modeled by connecting the link to the switch by an additional link interface providing the termination function for the lambda channels as well as adaptation of the TDM channels onto them.

It is not required for a data switch to be locally connected to all data links with link interfaces of the same switching capability or even the same switching capability type. An optical cross-connect, which is also an STS cross-connect, will be connected to some links via LSC interfaces and to others with TDM interfaces.

The ISC descriptor link attribute serves two purposes.

- To identify TE region and layer boundaries on the network.
- To constrain the path computation to consider only TE links with appropriate switching capability.

5.8 GMPLS TRAFFIC ENGINEERING PROTOCOLS

Controllers need to exchange control messages in order to operate signaling protocols to establish LSPs in the data plane. To do so, they encapsulate the messages within IP packets and use the IP infrastructure for message delivery. IP transport requires IP forwarding tables on all controllers, so that each of them knows how to forward IP packets. The forwarding tables must be built and updated in a dynamic way without management interference, since at any point of time new controllers might be added to or removed from the network, and control channels might go in and out of service. The dynamic management of forwarding tables is solved by running a link state IP routing protocol (OSPF or ISIS) on every controller. Specifically, each controller advertises information about itself and the control channels to which it is connected. The advertisements are distributed to all other protocol speakers in a reliable and efficient way. Thus, any given controller also receives similar advertisements from all other controllers, and builds the Link State Database (LSD) that contains a complete view of the network topology. Periodically, each controller runs the Shortest Path First (SPF) algorithm on the LSD and determines the shortest IP paths to all other controllers. Finally, it uses the SPF outcome to build and update the local IP forwarding table.

A controller component that applies TE policies also requires accurate network representation, only in this case it needs to view the topology not in terms of controllers and control channels, but in terms of data switches and TE links. This information is needed for building the TED. Once the TED is built, a local path computation element can run constraint-based path computation algorithm(s) to determine optimal path(s) for any given data service.

It is tempting, and seems natural and straightforward, to use a link state IP routing protocol for the distribution of TE advertisements in the same way as it is used for IP forwarding—related advertisements. That is exactly how the Traffic Engineering protocols (OSPF-TE and ISIS-TE) were introduced in MPLS: the transport of respective protocols was exposed to the TE layer, so that it could distribute the TE related information in a way that was opaque for the routing protocols.

One can find numerous statements in MPLS-related books or specifications saying that OSPF-TE is OSPF extended to support the traffic engineering. Conceptually this statement is not correct. It is true that OSPF-TE distributes its advertisements using OSPF mechanisms (for example, OSPF data base synchronization,

LSA flooding) and may share those mechanisms with a running instance of OSPF; however, this is the full extent of the commonality between the two protocols. They advertise completely unrelated information, which is used for entirely different purposes.

5.8.1 OSPF-TE

OSPF-TE makes use of the OSPF opaque LSA option introduced in RFC2370— *The OSPF Opaque LSA Option*. TE-related advertisements are encapsulated into OSPF opaque LSAs and presented for distribution to OSPF, which acts as a transport mechanism. The TE LSAs are of type 10 (area scope); thus, they are flooded only within the LSA originator's OSPF area, and their payload is delivered to the TE layer of every OSPF-TE speaker within the area. The TE layer is responsible for building and managing the local TED. It also produces the network TE graph with data switches represented as graph vertices and synchronized TE links as edges or arcs. It is this network graph that is used to compute paths through the network for data services (LSPs).

The TE LSA payload is structured as a set of Type-Length-Value blocks (TLVs). Top-level TLVs may nest other TLVs (sub-TLVs) within themselves. Two types of TE top-level TLVs are currently defined:

- Router Address
- TE Link

Only one top-level TLV is permitted per opaque LSA to facilitate small updates when one of the TLVs changes.

The Router Address TLV is used so that the advertising controller can specify one of its IP addresses that is always routable (for example, a loopback address). This address may be used to uniquely identify the advertising controller so that if both OSFP-TE and ISIS-TE are used to advertise TE links, a connection can be made between the two advertisements and they can be collected into a single TED. At the same time, the address provides a routable target for control plane messages (that is, signaling messages) that concern the resources associated with the TE links terminated on a locally managed data switch. As was mentioned earlier, it also provides a good candidate for the data switch identifier.

The TE Link TLV is used to advertise attributes of one TE link. Each TE link attribute is encoded as a separate sub-TLV.

Currently, there are several restrictions on the use of TE TLVs. No router may advertise more than one Router Address TLV, and there is no way to segregate the TE links advertised by a router to apply to distinct data switches. Thus, if a router controller wishes to manage more than one data switch (as shown by C45 in Figure 5.8), it has two somewhat contrived options.

1. It can impersonate multiple routing controllers by having distinct Router IDs and Router Addresses for each controller. In this way, each controller

can continue to control a single data switch. The disadvantage of this approach is that it does not fit well with the necessary topology in the control plane, but with some care and some virtual control plane connections between the distinct routers, this approach can be made to work.

2. The set of data switches that are managed by a single controller can be presented to the outside world as a single switch. That is, a composite logical switch can be constructed from the real component switches. Only the external TE links are advertised. Clearly a good degree of care must be taken to manage the effect on the externally visible TE links of switching data through component switches. The effect of depleting the resources on an "internal" link may be to remove the ability to establish an LSP across the composite logical switch, thereby introducing a horizontal switching constraint that is hard to explain to external path computation algorithms.

A more comprehensive solution is being worked out between the IETF's CCAMP Working Group and ITU-T Study Group 15. The ideal solution will allow for clear differentiation of data switches in the TE advertisements of a single routing controller, so that each router controller may advertise the capabilities and TE links belonging to more than one data switch.

GMPLS extensions to OSPF-TE introduce additional TE Link sub-TLVs for the purpose of advertising the following new GMPLS TE link attributes.

5.8.2 ISIS-TE

ISIS-TE serves the exactly the same purpose as OSPF-TE. The choice between ISIS-TE and OSPF-TE depends simply upon which routing protocol, IS-IS or OSPF, is used in the control plane. In theory one could use one protocol to distribute IP reachability and the other to distribute TE information, but this would be unusual because there is no necessity to run both protocols.

To advertise their information to the network, IS-IS speakers use Link State Protocol Data Units that are composed of multiple TLVs. ISIS-TE defines two new types of TLVs: the Traffic Engineering Router ID TLV and the Extended IS Reachability TLV. Both new TLVs contain the same information and are used for the same purpose as the OSPF-TE Router Address and Link TLVs, respectively.

GMPLS ISIS-TE introduces some new sub-TLVs for the Extended IS Reachability TLV to make it possible to advertise such TE link attributes as link local and remote identifiers for unnumbered TE links, link protection types, ISC descriptors, and SRLGs.

5.9 TRAFFIC ENGINEERING LINK BUNDLING

GMPLS constraint-based path computation requires more TE information to be advertised than in MPLS, and this causes legitimate scalability concerns. TE link bundling is one way to decrease the volume of TE advertisement as well as to control the TED size.

Consider the network represented in Figure 5.8. Suppose controller C3 determines a path in layer 1 going from switch D3 to switch D1 as D3-D2-D1. There are two parallel data links between D2 and D1, which could be advertised as separate TE links; however, provided that both TE links have equal TE metrics and satisfy all computation constraints, controller C3 would not normally care which of the data links the service takes. In fact, all it needs to know is that at least one of the two links satisfies the service requirements. It can be left for controllers C2 and C1 to agree upon which data link to use during the LSP setup. Thus, both data links can be advertised as a single TE link by both controllers without adversely affecting the accuracy of the path computation on controller C3 or any other network controller.

TE link bundling introduced in an IETF Internet-Draft *Link Bundling in MPLS Traffic Engineering* specifies a way of summarizing attributes of parallel data links and advertising the whole bundle as a single TE link (that is, within a single OSPF-TE link TLV or ISIS-TE Extended IS Reachability TLV).

A data link within a bundle is called a *component link*. Component link IDs are relevant only for controllers that handle switches on either side of the bundle and are of no importance to the rest of the controllers in the network, although there may be some value to diagnostic service mapping, to see which component link an LSP has actually used. According to the IETF Internet-Draft, the controller handling the upstream side (with respect to the direction of LSP establishment) of a TE bundle is responsible for choosing which component link to use to support the LSP. It signals the chosen component link ID to the controller handling the other side of the bundle in the LSP Setup message.

Perhaps surprisingly, there are currently no mechanisms to consistently let the transit controllers report which component links they use, or to allow negotiation between adjacent controllers about which component link to use (in the manner of GMPLS label negotiation). Considering severe limitations and binding constraints on transport data switches, one would think such mechanisms would be very practical mechanisms to have. Consider a situation where there is a bundle with ten component links, and the service requirements are such that the downstream controller (perhaps because of some switching limitations) can accept only one particular component link. Rather than signal to the upstream controller which of the component links is acceptable, it has the option only of rejecting successive setup requests and letting the upstream controller try again and again until it finally guesses the right component link.

The following conditions must hold for two or more component links to become a part of the same bundle.

- They must begin and end on the same pair of data switches.
- They must belong to the same network layer; that is, must have the same ISC descriptor.

- They must have the same traffic engineering metric attribute.
- They must have the same administrative group attribute.

Note that apart from the traffic engineering metric and administrative group, all other attributes of bundle components could be different. For instance, the component links may provide different protection capabilities, SRLGs, and so forth. A TE bundle advertisement includes the highest protection capability provided by any of the components, and the union of all SRLGs associated with each component.

Just like simple TE links, TE bundles could be numbered or unnumbered. Parallel TE-LSPs (see the following section) could also be bound into bundles provided that they satisfy the restrictions on what links can be components of the same bundle.

5.10 TRAFFIC ENGINEERING REGIONS AND SWITCHING LAYERS

Initial GMPLS implementation and deployment efforts targeted single, homogeneous transport networks. Those were networks built of elements with a single switching type. Examples of such networks are G.707 SONET/SDH and G.709 optical transport networks. The level of complexity of a GMPLS control plane that manages a homogeneous transport network is roughly equal to the level of complexity of an MPLS control plane working on a classical IP packet switching network. For example, TE link switching capability need not be a constraint during path computations on such networks; a single round-trip exchange of signaling messages is sufficient to establish a GMPLS LSP, and so forth. In general, the size of a homogenous transport network is considerably smaller than an MPLS network.

Because the GMPLS control plane works equally well for many different types of network (packet and transport), it is realistic to consider how it may be applied to heterogeneous networks built from component networks that have different switching capabilities. In the transport data world this is known as network layering, and a network of one switching capability provides connectivity for a pair of nodes in a network of a different switching capability. There is generally considered to be a hierarchy of network layers, which follows exactly the hierarchy of GMPLS switching capabilities.

Consider the network represented in Figure 5.7, where two TDM network segments (built of digital cross-connects A, B, C and F, G, H) are interconnected with a wavelength switching network (built of optical switches D, E, J, and I). Although it is possible to use separate control planes for the TDM and wavelength networks, it would be cumbersome in such a small network, and would require significant error-prone configuration efforts for maintaining and integrating the two control planes—recall the IP/ATM overlays! Therefore, the idea of using a single unified control plane that can manage both networks at once is appealing.

A heterogeneous network managed by a single instance of the GMPLS control plane can be decomposed into TE regions and switching layers. A *TE region* (also referred as an *LSP region* or simply a *region*) is a set of data links that are connected to data switches via interfaces of a particular switching type. In other words, a TE region is a set of data links associated with a particular data plane technology. Examples of TE regions are IP, ATM, TDM, photonic, and fiber switching. A *switching layer* (also referred as a *network layer* or simply a *layer*) is defined as a set of data links with interfaces that have the same switching and data encoding types and switching bandwidth granularity. It is obvious from this definition that a single TE region can contain and manage one or more switching layers. Examples of switching layers are SDH VC12, SDH VC4, ATM VP, ATM VP/VC, Ethernet, and IP.

It is important to note that a network should not be viewed as a single stack of layers. Generally it is comprised of multiple independent stacks of layers where the server-client relationships can be established between layers within a stack, but not between layers that belong to different stacks. For instance, a single TDM device may support multiple SDH branches, with each of them representing a separate stack of layers, and with termination and adaptation functions existing only within the branches, but not across the branches.

Network decomposition into TE regions is significant only from the control plane point of view. Regions and region boundaries are important for the signaling sub-system of the control plane because connections (LSPs) are signaled somewhat differently (that is, they use different signaling object formats and semantics) in different regions. Furthermore, TE advertising, routing, and path computation could be performed differently in different regions. For example, computation of paths across photonic regions requires a wider set of constraint (for example, optical impairments, and wavelength continuity) and needs to be performed in different terms (for example, in terms of individual resources such as lambda channels, rather than in terms of TE links) from path computation in other regions like IP or TDM.

Regions and region boundaries, however, are of little (if any) importance from the data plane point of view. What is significant for the data plane is switching layers and the server-client relationships by which LSPs in one (server) layer may provide network flexibility (that is, data links) for other (client) layers. Whether the server and client layers belong to the same or different regions is insignificant. It is important to understand that an LSP is always provisioned within a particular switching layer despite the fact that it can trigger re-provisioning in multiple layers and even regions.

It should be noted that the level of the GMPLS control plane complexity increases when more than one switching layer is supported. This is because, from the control plane point of view, such networks require *vertical integration*. This can be defined as a set of collaborative mechanisms within a single instance of the control plane driving multiple (at least two) switching layers and the *adaptation* between the layers. The notion of vertical integration should not be confused with the notion of *horizontal integration*, which is defined as a way of handling the situation when a single instance of a control plane manages networks that belong to separate routing areas or autonomous systems, and hence having separate TE advertising domains. We will discuss the horizontal integration later in this chapter. For now it is important to understand that the horizontal integration happens within a *single* switching layer, whereas the vertical integration involves *multiple* switching layers.

So, what exactly is vertical integration, where does it occur in the network, and which of the control plane sub-systems does it affect? In the examples described in this chapter it is assumed (unless explicitly stated otherwise) that each region has exactly one switching layer. This is done for reasons of simplicity, and the reader must keep in mind that all inter-layer relationships described in the examples are also true for layers that belong to the same multi-layer region.

Refer once again to the example network in Figure 5.7. Suppose no LSPs have been set up anywhere yet, and we need to place a service carrying SDH traffic from node A to node G. The path computation on node A needs to constrain the path selection to TDM switching capable links. Such links are AC, BC, FG, and FH. Thus, we have problem number one: No sequence of TDM switching capable links can be found that interconnects the source and destination nodes, and hence the path computation fails. Apart from this, even if we could somehow force the path computation to define a path (say, ACDEFG), the subsequent LSP setup could fail because either link CD or link EF might not have an adaptation function that could place or extract an SDH payload onto or from the wavelength channels on links CD and EF (problem two). Finally, suppose we are lucky, and the necessary adaptation function is available on both links, and the LSP is successfully established and carries traffic—in this case, the capacity of the wavelength channels allocated for the service will only be fractionally used, while the rest of the allocated channel's bandwidth will not be available for any other services and thus will be wasted. This is problem three.

All three problems can be solved through vertical integration. H-LSPs, introduced in MPLS as pure abstractions for the purpose of scalability improvements through the reduction of required control plane states, turn out to be a crucial tool for vertical integration.

Let us define a layer boundary node as a data switch that is connected to TE links with interfaces of multiple (at least two) switching capabilities and with an adaptation function to place/extract a layer corresponding to the lower switching capability into/from a layer associated with the higher switching capability. In our example the layer boundary nodes are C and F, assuming, of course, that they have the adaptation function.

Node A can solve the first problem during path computation simply by relaxing the switching capability constraint. Instead of limiting candidates to TDM links, it considers links that have the switching capability type numerically equal to or larger than the TDM switching capability type. Note that PSC links are still not considered. That is, it can compute an end-to-end path that crosses all three layers and changes switching capabilities at the boundary nodes (C and F). In a more complex network, the computation might be arranged to:

- make as much use of the original switching capability as possible;
- minimize the number of changes in switching capability;
- not attempt to use switching capabilities lower down the hierarchy than the source capability.

This third point is most important because, for example, a lambda service cannot be carried on a TDM link.

Such a path is highly dependent on the existence of suitable adaptation components at the layer boundaries. In our example, node C must be capable of adapting a TDM signal onto a lambda channel (not technically hard, but it does require special equipment), and node F must be capable of extracting the TDM signal from the lambda channel and sending it onward. As the second problem indicates, this method of end-to-end or *contiguous* LSP establishment in a particular layer that requires involvement of other layers is vulnerable to nodes that lie on layer boundaries that do not have the requisite adaptation capabilities. The obvious solution is for the node that performs the path computation to generate the LSP's route by excluding those boundary nodes that do not have the necessary capabilities. Unfortunately, there is currently no means for the boundary nodes to advertise their adaptation capabilities—the default assumption is that a node that has links of two different switching capabilities has the means to switch between those links, but that need not be a valid assumption. It is likely that further extensions will be made to the TE information advertised by the routing protocols so that the adaptation capabilities can be known.

Even if a contiguous LSP is set up and can carry the end-to-end data, the third problem shows how this is sub-optimal and can waste a high percentage of the bandwidth in the server layer (that is, a layer providing necessary network flexibility for the successful LSP setup). Consider the relatively reasonable example of an OC-48 service from A to G. As this crosses the LSC layer from C to F it will require a full lambda channel. Now, a single lambda channel can often carry 10 Gbps, but OC-48 only actually uses 2.488 Gbps, thus 7.5 Gbps (or 75%) of the lambda channel's bandwidth is wasted. Because the lambda channel cannot be subdivided (the transit switches are only LSC and so cannot switch subdivisions), what is clearly required is some way to multiplex additional TDM signals onto the lambda channel to make use of the spare bandwidth.

Real vertical integration happens on the layer boundary nodes and offers a solution to this third problem. When the LSP Setup message arrives at node C, it recognizes that the LSP is about to enter a layer of a coarser level switching capability. It suspends the setup of the end-to-end LSP and triggers the setup of a H-LSP (in this case an LSC LSP) across the LSC layer, between itself and the remote layer boundary node located on the path (node F). Once the H-LSP is established, it could be used as a data link of the TDM switching layer—the layer where our original LSP is provisioned node C can resume the setup of the original LSP.

To do this it sends the LSP Setup message direct to the far end of the new link (node F), requesting a TDM label and resource reservation on the link. Finally, the two nodes provision their local adaptation functions so that the service traffic could be carried over the LSC layer within the dynamically created link. As we see, on layer boundary nodes, vertical integration involves both control and data planes.

Note that an explicit path supplied in the LSP Setup message must not reference nodes or links entirely within the server layer. This is because the H-LSC LSP is going to be used as a data link in its own right, and it will constitute a single hop in the end-to-end LSP.

Since the H-LSP is now used as a TDM data link, the nodes at its two ends can (but do not have to) advertise the LSP to the TE routing domain as a TE link with TDM switching capability. This makes the LSP (which becomes a TE-LSP) more generally available for use by other end-to-end LSPs. Let us consider what happens if, some time later, node B decides to establish a TDM LSP going to node H. First, there will be no problems for path computation on node B, since both TDM segments are now interconnected by a TDM TE link that has resources available for an additional LSP; that is, the TE-LSP advertised by nodes C and F. Secondly, when the second LSP Setup message arrives at node C, it will realize that it does not have to establish a new LSC LSP for this LSP, because there is already a suitable TDM link in place (provided by the TE-LSP). All that it has to do is to continue the LSP setup by sending the LSP Setup message direct to node F and requesting a label and resource reservation within the dynamic TDM link. Thus, the third problem is resolved as well.

The process that is responsible for placing finer grained tunnels within a coarser grained tunnel is called *traffic grooming*. It allows for efficient network utilization when the bandwidth on links can be allocated in chunks of a significant size. Layer boundary devices are particularly well suited to traffic grooming.

5.10.1 Virtual Network Topology

In our example an LSC LSP provided a necessary connectivity to deliver TDM traffic over the optical layer. Generally speaking, a set of such H-LSPs provides a *Virtual Network Topology* (VNT) for routing the traffic for higher layers requiring a finer switching granularity. For example, a set of LSC HLSPs can provide a TDM VNT. Likewise, TDM LSPs can be also used as H-LSPs and constitute a VNT for PSC or L2SC traffic, and so forth. Note here that in the hierarchy of switching types, fiber switch capable (FSC) is usually referred to as the highest switching type with packet switch capable (PSC) the lowest type. However, in layered networking, the layer that supports other layers (that is, the server layer) is the lowest layer; thus FSC networks form the lowest layer and PSC networks the highest layer.

There are four ways in which a TE link supported by an H-LSP can be added to the VNT, and the choice has some impact on the way the network operates. As described in the example above, an H-LSP can be created on demand by the boundary node that provides access to the lower layer. The associated TE link can then be advertised for use by other end-to-end LSPs. This technique is effective, but it requires the node that computes the path to make assumptions about the behavior of the two boundary nodes that it selects to provide ingress to and egress from the server layer. There is an implicit cooperation between the ingress and the boundary nodes so that the H-LSP is established. The mechanism also requires that the computing node has full visibility into the topology of the server layer so that it can be reasonably certain that it is actually possible to establish the desired LSP in the server layer.

An alternative approach is to pre-establish a set of H-LSPs that traverse the server layer and to ensure that these are advertised as TE links so that they can be sued for path computation. This brings us to the situation in the second half of the example where the H-LSP has already been established. Such a network of H-LSPs is clearly useful and simplifies the path computation problem, but it requires an element of network planning and configuration. Which boundary nodes will need to be connected? How much bandwidth will be required—that is, how many parallel H-LSPs are needed? Note that in an LSC network where there are multiple parallel lambda paths across a layer, the H-LSPs do not need to be advertised as individual TE links. Instead, they can be formed into a bundle that is advertised as a single TE link in its own right.

In practice, such network planning questions are likely to give rise to the construction of a full mesh of H-LSPs between all boundary nodes. Low bandwidth requirements will be assumed, and some trigger mechanism will be used to ensure that further H-LSPs are set up as the resources on the existing ones become depleted. This technique is all very well, but it actually wastes considerable bandwidth in the core of the server layer—resources are reserved for H-LSPs that carry no traffic, and they could be allocated for other services.

What we need is some way to trigger the H-LSPs on demand, but to make the associated TE links visible to the computing node *before* the LSPs are actually created. This is achieved through the third method of managing the VNT—the use of *virtual H-LSPs*. The H-LSPs are configured at the boundary nodes and are advertised as TE links as part of the VNT, but the H-LSPs themselves are not signaled until a LSP Setup message arrives for an end-to-end LSP that needs to use the H-LSP. Obviously, there is some risk that the H-LSP will fail to establish, but apart from that, this technique gives the flexibility of easy computation through a richly populated VNT without the consequent resource wastage in the server layer.

One interesting alternative to virtual H-LSPs on which the CCAMP community has begun to work is the concept of *soft H-LSPs* (method number four). These are dynamic links provided by H-LSPs that are only half-pre-provisioned. The necessary resources are allocated on all links, but are not bound into the LSP cross-connects. Such soft H-LSPs can share resources with other soft H-LSPs. Additionally, their resources could be used to support protection LSPs and can even carry extra traffic. When the LSP Setup message of the first, higher layer LSP to be nested inside a soft H-LSP arrives at the ingress node for the soft H-LSP, the soft H-LSP is activated—an LSP Modify message is sent hop-by-hop to every controller that is involved in the soft H-LSP requesting that the H-LSP resources are bound into the cross-connects. Thus, two goals are achieved: the resources allocated for a soft H-LSP are not wasted when the H-LSP is idle, and the resources are guaranteed to be available and in place when they are actually needed.

Note that a virtual H-LSP requires more configuration and management coordination than a real (also referred as hard) or a soft H-LSP because the latter is able to allocate and signal interface identifiers when it is set up, but the virtual H-LSP must have these identifiers configured in matching pairs (just as for a physical link that does not use LMP). The interface identifiers are needed, of course, so that the TE links can be advertised to form part of the TED.

Ultimately, a network operator may choose some mix of all four mechanisms. That is, the TED used in the higher layer will include TE links associated with static data links that belong to this layer as well as any H-LSPs (hard, soft, and/or virtual) contributed by the VNT. The balance between the four modes of operation will obviously depend on the predicted network usage.

Routing of user traffic over a transport network depends on the network topology in general and VNTs in particular, and can be impaired if the topology changes too frequently. For example, if TE links are frequently added and removed from the TED, there will be a continual need to flood new TE state information and repeated attempts may be made to re-optimize the active LSPs to make better use of the available resources. In our example there is one aspect that we have not considered yet: When should the TE link associated with LSC H-LSP be removed? One may guess that the H-LSP should be torn down and the associated TE link advertisement should be withdrawn from the domain immediately after the last nested end-to-end LSP is removed. Imagine the situation when for some reason a single TDM LSP ACFG (Figure 5.7) is set up and torn down in quick succession. This would cause the LSC H-LSP to be constantly set up and torn down as well, and the associated TE link will be also frequently advertised, removed, re-advertised again and so on, which is not good. It would be much better to apply some hysteresis to the H-LSP removal. Thus, routing robustness must be traded with adaptability with respect to the change of incoming traffic requests.

On the other hand, it may actually be optimal to tear down an H-LSP even when it is carrying end-to-end LSPs that have active traffic. Recall that an unused H-LSP wastes resources in the server layer and that those resources might be better used for a new H-LSP between some other pair of boundary nodes. In the same way, an H-LSP that carries an end-to-end LSP that uses only a small percentage of the H-LSP's resources is also wasting server layer resources. In the first instance it may be possible to *re-groom* the end-to-end LSP onto some other existing H-LSP between the two boundary nodes—this can be achieved by using make-before-break on the end-to-end LSP. If no such second H-LSP is available between the boundary nodes, it is possible that a different path is available through the higher layers and over the server layer using another H-LSP between a different pair of boundary nodes. Again, make-before-break can be used to re-position the end-to-end LSP. As a final resort, preemption may be used within the transit network so that a low priority H-LSP may be displaced by a higher priority service request. When this happens, the end-to-end LSPs carried on the displaced H-LSP are broken and must be repaired or discarded.

5.10.2 **Hierarchical LSP Protection**

When a layer boundary node decides to establish an H-LSP, it may choose for recovery purposes to set up two disjoint H-LSPs rather than one. The first will carry higher layer LSPs, while the other will stand by, so that if the first H-LSP fails, the nested tunnels can be rapidly re-routed onto the second H-LSP. Note that in this case, despite there being more than one H-LSP, only one TE link will be advertised. The Link Protection Capability attribute of the TE link will depend on the nature of the second H-LSP (whether it is 1 + 1, dedicated 1:1, shared, and so forth). It is also possible to have a configuration where two or more parallel H-LSPs are advertised as a single TE link (that is, a bundle) with the Link Protection attribute set to "Shared M:N." In this case, in the steady (fault-free) mode, the protecting H-LSPs may nest extra traffic LSPs. The latter are subject to preemption during protection switchover. It is important to keep in mind that TE links associated with H-LSPs are no different from "normal" (static) TE links, and hence parallel H-LSPs bundled into TE links can provide all types of link protection.

Alternatively, the layer boundary node could form two parallel links based on each of the H-LSPs and advertise two separate TE links (let us call this scheme 2). Although it is similar in spirit—the nested tunnels can be switched onto the parallel H-LSP if the working one fails—conceptually it is different from the model of a single link associated with two H-LSPs (scheme 1) for the following reasons.

- In scheme 1, the second H-LSP cannot be used for unprotected nested tunnels (with the exception of extra traffic tunnels in some link protection schemes); all its resources are entirely dedicated to protecting the nested tunnels carried by the first H-LSP. In scheme 2 both H-LSPs can be used to carry unrelated unprotected nested tunnels.
- In scheme 1 it is guaranteed that if there are available resources on the first H-LSP sufficient to nest a particular tunnel, there are also resources on the second H-LSP to carry the same nested tunnel during protection. This is not the case in scheme 2, because other tunnels may have been nested into the second H-LSP and so depleted the resources.
- In scheme 1, service recovery is realized on the link level, whereas in scheme 2 it is achieved on the level of nested tunnels (that is, path level).

5.10.3 **Adaptation Capabilities**

At this stage it should be absolutely clear that at least one TE link attribute of great importance is currently missing. This is the attribute advertising interface *adaptation* capabilities. We may call it the Interface Adaptation Capability (IAC)

Descriptor (similar to the ISC Descriptor). For example, the fact that a node has some TDM interfaces and some LSC interfaces does not necessarily mean that on a particular LSC interface the node can:

- originate/terminate a TDM-level H-LSP (for example, there is no suitable transceiver on the link);
- adopt/extract a particular TDM traffic flow onto/from the H-LSP (that is. the transceiver may not be able to cross-connect to the proper SIM card, or there may simply be no hardware capable of performing the necessary adaptation).

We need this attribute to constrain the hierarchical (that is, multi-layer) path computation to those links that can actually provide such adaptation that will decrease LSP setup blocking probability. At a minimum an IAC Descriptor entry should include the following fields.

- Switching layer (which is identified via switching and bandwidth encoding types, and by switching bandwidth granularity) of the signal to be adopted/ extracted (inner LSP traffic parameters).
- Switching layer of the H-LSP to be created.
- Bandwidth (on per-priority level) available for the termination/adaptation purposes.

This problem is an example of a vertical binding constraint. It is not to be confused with a horizontal binding constraint—a limited ability to bind together data links of the same switching level that might exist in some switching platforms, for example, where the hardware is implemented as "switchlets." Horizontal constraints might also need to be advertised, but on a TE node basis (rather than on a TE link basis as for the IAC Descriptor).

As multi-region/multi-layer traffic engineering work is extended within the IETF, it is likely that both the vertical and horizontal constraints will need to be added to the TE advertisements.

5.11 INTER-DOMAIN TRAFFIC ENGINEERING

A GMPLS LSP may span different routing areas or even administrative domains. As was mentioned earlier, such LSPs require horizontal integration on area/domain borders. From the traffic engineering perspective, provisioning inter-domain LSPs implies an environment of partitioned TE advertising domains. It has both path computation and signaling challenges.

5.11.1 Path Computation with Limited TE Visibility

Let us consider a very simple multi-area network presented in Figure 5.9. Suppose there is a request to establish a service going from node A to node M. As the service

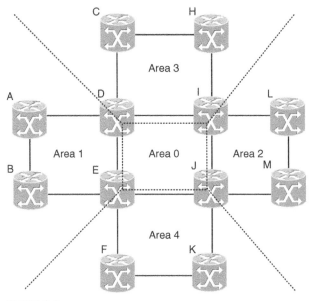

FIGURE 5.9

Multi-area network.

head-end node, node A attempts to compute a path for the service. Recall that TE advertisements are only of area scope, hence node A knows only about the four TE links AD, DE, EB, and BA. Thus, it cannot compute a full path. It does not even know where the path should exit from the first area.

There are two ways that path computation can be performed under these conditions of limited TE visibility.

- Using distributed path computation (method 1)
- Using remote path computation element(s) (method 2)

In method 1, the service ingress node (node A) first requests from its local routing sub-system a list of nodes that advertise IP reachability to the service destination. If the list is empty, the path computation request and the service setup are failed with the reason code "unknown service destination." Otherwise, node A assumes that the nodes in the list are area/domain border nodes with a wider TE network view and will be capable of determining the service path over the next area/domain (fortunately, this assumption is true in most of the cases). The ingress node computes the TE paths to those list members (border nodes) that have entries in the local TED (in our example nodes D and E), and selects the shortest path to signal the LSP Setup message. The message contains detailed path information only up to the selected border node (node D), although the destination is obviously also part of the message.

When the message arrives at the border node, it attempts a path computation to extend the path to the service destination. If this is still not possible, the border node performs the same operations as the ingress node. Specifically, it determines its own set of next area/domain border nodes (nodes I and J), computes paths to them, and sends the LSP Setup message toward the closest one (say, node I). The process repeats itself on all border nodes that lie on the path until one of them (node I) sees the destination in its local TED and is able to complete the path computation and the service setup.

A protected service requires one or more paths disjoint from the working path. When a service spans multiple TE domains, each domain is usually responsible for recovery of the service LSP segment that belongs to the domain. That is, recovery paths are computed and provisioned between the border nodes within domains. If in our example the service working LSP is ADILM, the recovery path in areas 1, 0, and 2 would be ABED, DEJI, and IJM, respectively. In this mode of protection, inter-domain services do not present additional challenges from the point of view of recovery path computation, because each recovery path is computed with full TE visibility. However, such a recovery scheme makes border nodes single points of failure, and can lead to over-provisioning of resources on links that run between border nodes (such as the link DE). One way to address this problem involves applying the segment recovery technique, it is possible to install additional recovery schemes to protect against border node failures. However, there are also reasons why some services require end-to-end node disjoint recovery paths rather than allowing protection to be performed per domain. One way to compute such paths is by using the distributed path computation mechanism just described, but with the following modifications.

- The ingress node computes disjoint paths to all border nodes returned by the routing sub-system.
- The ingress node selects the closest border node (one with the shortest path) and sends the LSP Setup message to it.
- The message includes the path to the selected border node as the working path as well as paths to all other border nodes as alternate paths.

In our example the LSP Setup message going out of node A would contain path AD as the working path and path ABE as the alternate path.

When the message arrives at the first border node, it expands the working and alternate paths. To do so it computes disjoint paths from each of the last nodes found in the working and alternate paths to all of the next domain border nodes returned by the local routing sub-system. In our example node D computes a pair of shortest disjoint paths, one from node D to one of node J or node I, and the other from node E to the other of node J and node I. One of the paths (DI) extends the working path, while the other (EJ) extends the alternate path. Similar path computations are repeated on each border node on the working path. When the LSP Setup message reaches the destination, the alternate path is copied into the LSP Accept message (RSVP Resv) and thus sent back to the ingress. When the ingress node receives the LSP Accept message for the working path, it will have complete path information to set up the end-to-end recovery path.

Note that this algorithm will miss alternate paths that go through domains other than those traversed by the working path. To compute such paths using distributed path computation is quite a challenging task and is likely to involve a degree of trial and error. Note also that the mechanism described is suitable for domains where there are no confidentiality issues (such as IGP areas), but may be seen as a concern in inter-AS traffic engineering, since the alternate path provides information about the topology of the neighboring AS.

In method 2, paths for inter-domain services are computed using remote path computation elements (PCEs). PCEs can be collocated with domain border nodes (border nodes have a wider TE view of the network than other nodes and hence are a good choice for hosting PCEs), or they can be placed on off-line servers. Path computing nodes learn about the location of PCEs either through configuration or dynamically. In the latter case nodes hosting PCEs may advertise their ability to accept remote path computation requests by making use of protocols similar to the TE information distribution protocols. For example, there are proposals within the IETF to introduce a way for OSPF speakers to advertise their PCE capability within OSPF areas or across an entire AS using the OSPF opaque LSA.

When path computation on some node fails because the path request destination cannot be found in the local TED, the node performing the path computation may select a remote PCE and request a remote path computation. This process obviously requires a protocol for communication between the LSR controller and the PCE, and the IETF is currently working to develop such a protocol.

Suppose, in our example, node A learns that it can use nodes D and E as remote PCEs. In order to compute one or several disjoint paths to node M it can send an appropriate path computation request to node D or node E, or to both. Once node A receives path computation responses from all PCEs, it picks the optimal set of paths and sets up working and, if necessary, recovery LSPs.

A PCE, while trying to satisfy a path computation request, might use other PCEs. The PCE on node D, for example, will not be capable of computing a path from node A to node M on its own, because node M is not in its local TED either. Thus, it might send a request to, say, the PCE on node I to compute path(s) from itself and/or from node E to node M. Once node D receives a response with the requested path(s), it is capable of building the proper response for node A's request.

The advantage of method 1 is simplicity: there is no need to support yet another communication protocol. It will also usually provide better service setup times because there is no need to wait for remote PCEs to respond. Method 2 also has a problem with PCEs as potential bottlenecks and single points of failure. However, method 2 produces paths of a better quality: They are potentially more efficient and the setup of the paths is less likely to be blocked; hence service setup time on some configurations can be even better than the setup time for services that take paths computed with method 1.

5.11.2 **Provisioning of Inter-Domain LSPs**

When a service LSP Setup message arrives at a domain border node, the latter is supposed to perform the integration of LSP segments that belong to the neighboring domains. This procedure is called the *horizontal LSP integration*. Its complexity depends on the similarity of signaling protocols running in each domain and on local policies.

When both domains run the same signaling protocols, the border node is likely to continue the service LSP setup as a contiguous LSP. It performs the usual functions of an intra-domain transit node. In this case no special integration is necessary. If the signaling protocols are slightly different (for example, each or one of them is using a set of domain proprietary signaling objects), the LSP is still likely to be set up as a contiguous LSP. However, in this case the border nodes might remove the objects specific to the previous domain, and add the objects specific to the next domain to the signaling messages.

It is also possible that neighboring domains run entirely different signaling protocols, or that one of them uses only static provisioning. In such cases a mechanism called *LSP stitching* is used for the horizontal integration. In this model some or all intra-domain LSP segments could be pre-provisioned, while the provisioning of others could be induced by receipt of inter-domain LSP Setup messages. In any case, when an inter-domain LSP Setup message arrives, the border node conducts the following operations.

- It performs data plane binding of the inter-domain LSP with a suitable intra-domain LSP segment that starts on the processing border node and terminates on the next domain border node.
- It tunnels the inter-domain LSP Setup message to the next domain border node, so that the latter could perform data plane binding on the remote end of the LSP segment and continue the setup of the inter-domain LSP.

Inter-domain LSP Accept messages (RSVP Resv) are tunneled between domain border nodes in the opposite direction.

It could be that the neighboring domains are built of devices with different switching capabilities. In this case the border node needs to perform both horizontal integration and vertical integration (that is, the integration between data layers). The vertical integration is accomplished via H-LSPs. The only peculiarity about H-LSPs established on border nodes is that they could be provisioned statically or by using a signaling protocol that is different from one used for the provisioning of nested (in our case inter-domain) LSPs. Note that the latter are likely to be contiguous in this case. But they can also be stitched if, for example, intra-domain stitching LSP segments are pre-provisioned within H-LSPs.

5.11.3 **Handling Inter-Domain LSP Setup Failures**

The goal of constraint-based path computation is to produce paths that have a good likelihood of successful service established. However, despite that, a service LSP setup can fail. There are numerous reasons for that. For example:

- The local TED on a path computing node might not adequately reflect the current state of the network resources.
- The path computation request might not take into account all necessary constraints, perhaps because not all link attributes were advertised.
- Unexpected hardware problems might be detected during programming of the data plane on some links.

Normally the LSP ingress node handles LSP setup failures by re-computing the path with a constraint exclude all previously failed links, and re-attempts the LSP establishment over the new path. This is quite straightforward to do in the single TE domain environment, where information about all network TE links is available.

It is not so simple when paths are computed in a distributed way under conditions of limited TE visibility. Suppose, the setup of an inter-domain service LSP was attempted over path ADILM (Figure 5.9), and the setup failed because of some problem with link DI. When node A computes a new path, it cannot exclude the failed link (or rather, excluding the link will make no difference), because the latter belongs to a different area. But node A can constrain the path computation to avoid using node D. Suppose it does this and attempts to set up the LSP over intra-domain segment ABE. Unfortunately, by the time the LSP Setup message arrives at node E, the information about the previously failed link is lost (that is, it is known by node A but not by node E), and nothing prevents node E from selecting a path that traverses the failed link DI for the LSP segment going though area 0. Thus, the setup will repeatedly fail despite the existence of paths that would lead to the successful LSP setup.

The solution to inter-domain setup failures was proposed in two IETF Internet-Drafts that define Crankback and Route Exclusion. The former introduces a way to carry summarized or detailed information about all link failures in the LSP Upstream Error message (RSVP PathErr). It also suggests recovering LSP setup failures on domain border nodes before attempting end-to-end recovery. In our example, the first attempt to re-establish the LSP would happen on node D. This seems to be the correct thing to do because node D is responsible for path computation of the LSP segment over area 0, and it can exclude the failed link from the computation of an alternate path. If node D fails to compute the new path or to setup the LSP over the new segment, it is supposed to send the LSP Upstream Error message upstream, adding itself to the crankback information as a point of blockage. According to the proposed solution, the next computation recovery attempt happens on the next closest upstream border node or, as in our example, on the ingress node (node A). Computation is constrained to avoid using the nodes and links in the crankback information (node D). Provided that an alternate path segment can be computed (segment ABE), a new LSP Setup message will be sent out over the new path.

The route exclusion proposals allow the LSP Setup message to contain a list of all links and nodes that must be excluded from subsequent path computations. Thus, when node E computes the LSP path segment over area 0, it will not consider the failed link DI.

5.12 SERVICE PATH RE-OPTIMIZATION

It is possible that after a service has been established, a more efficient path for the service becomes available, perhaps because one or more new TE links have been advertised or because some other services have been torn down causing resources in the network to be released. A path computation element could be designed so that it keeps track of all path requests and paths it has determined for all locally collocated and remote applications. When a better path can be found for one of the previously computed paths, the node or component that originally requested the path can be notified. In order to take advantage of the new path, the service ingress node must re-route the service onto the new path using the *make-before-break* technique.

Such optimization is simpler to do in the single TE domain environment, where service path computation is normally performed only once on the service ingress node. In the TE multi-domain environment it is the responsibility of every PCE that has participated in the distributed path computation to notify the ingress node about availability of better paths for its LSP segments. A further proposal in the IETF introduces signaling and procedural extensions to RSVP-TE to provide this information and allow the control of head end path re-optimization from remote nodes.

Service path re-optimization is not always desirable because it may also impose a traffic hit even using make-before-break techniques. Therefore, it is important to be able to provision a service as *pinned*. Once established, a pinned service cannot be re-routed away from the paths taken during the setup.

Frequent service path re-optimizations, especially involving multiple services, could also be dangerous for network stability. Hence there should always be a configurable limit on how often service path re-optimization can be triggered on a particular node.

Providing Quality of Service

6

As the applications using the Internet become more sophisticated, so it becomes increasingly more important to provide a variety of grades of service to distinguish different uses and service demands. These grades of service are termed Quality of Service (QoS) and provide a new set of challenges to network operators.

This chapter draws on material from *Deploying IP and MPLS QoS for Multi-service Networks: Theory & Practice* by Evans and Filsfils, and from *Traffic Engineering and QoS Optimization of Integrated Voice & Data Networks* by Ash. The text examines issues of how to provide QoS across packet switched networks, and investigates how MPLS can be used to enhance the service levels that can be provided to the network users. In the process, lessons are learnt from the experiences of transport networks to evolve a generic traffic engineering quality of service optimization technique.

6.1 WHAT IS QUALITY OF SERVICE?

In networking, the term quality of service (QOS) can mean many different things to different people, hence it is key that we start this chapter by defining what "QOS" means in the context of this book.

Firstly, how do we define a "service" in the context of IP networking? We consider that a service is a description of the overall treatment of a customer's traffic across a particular domain. A service is only practically useful if it meets the requirements of the end-user applications it is intended to support. Hence, the aim of the service is to maximize end-user satisfaction with the applications that the service is supporting. Maximizing user satisfaction requires that the end-user applications work effectively.

How then do we define "quality" in the context of a particular IP service? We can define service quality in terms of the underlying requirements for an application which can be defined in terms of the SLA metrics for IP service performance: delay, jitter, packet loss, throughput, service availability, and per flow sequence preservation.

QOS, however, implies more than just ensuring that a network service is able to support the SLA requirements of the applications it is aiming to support.   **119**

The problem of ensuring that a network can meet these requirements is fundamentally a problem of managing the available network capacity relative to the service load, i.e. a problem of managing congestion. If it is possible to ensure that there is always significantly more capacity available than there is traffic load then delay, jitter and loss will be minimized, throughput will be maximized, and the service requirements will be easy to meet. In practice, however, ensuring that the network is always overprovisioned relative to the actual traffic load is not always cost-effective. Hence, in engineering the QOS of a network service there is implicitly another important constraint, which is to minimize cost. If there is more traffic load than there is capacity to support it, i.e. if congestion occurs, then some traffic will either need to be delayed until there is capacity available or it will need to be dropped. Minimizing cost may demand that multiple services are supported or multiplexed on the same network, by classifying traffic into discrete classes, such that the problem of engineering traffic load relative to capacity can be performed on a per-class basis allowing per-class service differentiation.

In summary, at a high level we can describe QOS in terms of the goals that it is trying to achieve, which effectively define an optimization problem of trying to maximize end-user satisfaction (utility or efficacy) while minimizing cost. Maximizing user satisfaction requires that the end-user applications work effectively, for example, that a voice over IP call quality is acceptable, which requires that the application's SLA requirements are met. Minimizing cost requires that we do not overengineer the network in order to deliver that call quality, which may require the need to differentiate the service levels offered to different applications.

6.1.1 Quality of Service vs Class of Service or Type of Service?

The terms "class of service" (COS) and "type of service" (TOS) are sometimes used interchangeably with quality of service; for the purposes of this book, we explicitly define them here to avoid confusion:

Class of service. As well as being used interchangeably with quality of service, class of service is also sometimes used to refer to the layer 2 QOS capabilities provided by Ethernet or ATM. We prefer to use neither of those definitions but rather use "class of service" or COS purely in the context of traffic classification. We define the concept of a traffic class as a set of traffic streams that will have common actions applied to them. Hence, to avoid confusion, we use the term "classes of service" to refer to the classification of an aggregate traffic stream into a number of constituent classes, where different actions will be applied to each individual "class of service."

Type of service. We use the term "type of service" to refer specifically to the use of the Type of Service Octet in the IPv4 packet header.

6.1.2 Best-effort Service

Networks engineered to deliver a particular quality of service are often contrasted to "best-effort" networks. "Best-effort" describes a network service which attempts to deliver traffic to its destination, but which does not provide any guarantees of delivery, and hence is without any commitments for delay, jitter, loss, and throughput.

The term best-effort, however, is often misused. Where a network supports multiple service classes simultaneously, best-effort is often used to refer to the service which offers the lowest SLA commitments. By definition, best-effort infers no SLA commitments and hence a service which provides any SLA commitments cannot be defined as best-effort, however lowly those commitments might be. Even if a network supports only a single service class, i.e. where packet forwarding is egalitarian and all packets receive the same quality of service, if that service provides defined SLA commitments, we contend that it cannot be considered a best-effort network service.

Confusion is also sometimes caused because IP can be referred to as a "best-effort" network layer protocol, in that it does not implicitly provide any capabilities to detect or retransmit lost packets. Despite this, however, with appropriate network engineering, it is possible to support IP services which have defined SLA commitments and hence an IP service does not imply a best-effort service. Conversely, TCP is sometimes considered to be a guaranteed transport layer protocol in that it provides the capability to detect and retransmit lost packets. This capability, however, may be of no practical use if the underlying IP service cannot deliver the TCP segments with the SLAs required by applications; the effective SLA of the TCP service is implicitly constrained by the SLA commitments provided by the underlying IP service.

In order to avoid any potential for confusion, we intentionally try not to use the term "best-effort."

6.1.3 The Timeframes that Matter for QOS

We find it useful to consider three timeframes relevant to engineering the quality of service of a network; different QOS techniques are applied in each timeframe:

O(milliseconds). The first timeframe we consider is in the order of milliseconds. Within this timeframe bursts of individual traffic streams or the aggregation of bursts for different streams at network aggregation points can cause congestion, where the traffic load exceeds the available capacity. QOS mechanisms relevant to this timescale include applying per-hop queuing, scheduling and dropping techniques to provide differentiation and isolation between different types of traffic, to prioritize some types of traffic over others thereby managing delay, and to ensure fair bandwidth allocations.

O(100 milliseconds). The next timeframe we consider is in the order of 100s of milliseconds. This is the timeframe which defines network round trip times (RTT). This is the timeframe which is important to applications that used closed-loop feedback between sender and receiver to apply flow control mechanisms, such as TCP-based applications. QOS mechanisms relevant to this timeframe therefore include active queue management (AQM) congestion control techniques such as random early detection (RED).

O(10 seconds) or more. Timeframes of seconds and minutes are relevant to the management of the long-term average network traffic rates and capacity, which is achieved through capacity planning and traffic engineering.

6.1.4 Why IP QOS?

Layer 2 technologies such as ATM and Ethernet have their own defined QOS capabilities, hence it is a valid question to ask: "why use IP QOS rather than layer 2 QOS mechanisms?" The main reasons for using IP QOS stem from the fact that IP is the end-to-end network layer technology used by the vast majority of applications today. Added to this QOS is an end-to-end discipline where the service that a particular class of traffic receives is limited by the element on the end-to-end path which provides the worst service. Hence, in order to provide a low-delay, low-jitter and low-loss service (thus maximizing user satisfaction) the network must be engineered to remove all points of congestion on the end-to-end path for that service; in order to assure different SLAs for different classes of traffic (hence minimizing cost), we must apply differentiation at all points of congestion. Different underlying layer 2 technologies may be used for different legs of an end-to-end

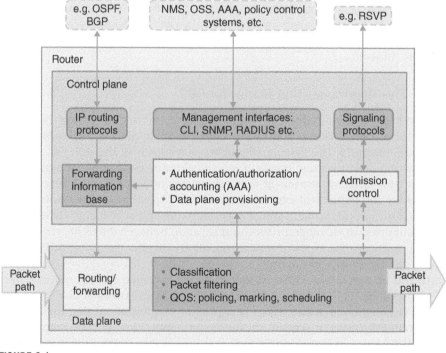

FIGURE 6.1

Control plane and data plane QoS functions.

layer 3 path. Therefore, as IP is the lowest common end-to-end layer, it makes fundamental sense to use IP QOS techniques where possible, and to map them to underlying QOS capabilities in lower layer technologies, where required, rather than to attempt to map layer 2 QOS capabilities for one leg to the layer 2 QOS capabilities of the next leg. The SLAs provided at the IP layer, however, are implicitly limited by the SLAs of the underlying Layer 2 technology.

6.1.5 **The QOS Toolset**

In practical terms, QOS involves using a range of functions and features (e.g. classification, scheduling, policing, shaping), within the context of overriding architecture (e.g. Integrated Service, Differentiated Services) in order to ensure that a network service delivers the SLA characteristics that the applications targeted by that service need to work effectively. The mechanisms used for engineering the QOS in a network can be broken down into data plane and control plane mechanisms applied on network devices such as routers, as shown in Figure 6.1 and which are introduced here and described in detail in the proceeding sections.

Data plane. Data plane QOS mechanisms are applied at network nodes and can directly impact the forwarding behavior of packets. They are processing intensive functions; in high-performance routers, they are typically implemented in hardware, along with other data plane functions such as packet forwarding lookups and packet filtering. Such data plane QOS mechanisms can be categorized in terms of the primitive behavioral characteristics that they impart to traffic streams to which they are applied:

- *Classification*. Classification is the process of categorizing an aggregate traffic stream into a number of constituent classes, such that any of the following actions can be applied to each individual "class of service."
- *Marking*. Traffic marking is the process of explicitly setting the value of the fields assigned for QOS classification in the IP or MPLS packet headers so that the traffic can subsequently be easily identified.
- *Maximum rate enforcement*. Policing and shaping can be used to enforce a maximum rate for a traffic class.
- *Prioritization*. Techniques such as priority scheduling are used to prioritize some types of traffic over others thereby managing delay and jitter.
- *Minimum rate assurance*. Scheduling techniques such as Weighted Fair Queuing (WFQ) and Deficit Round Robin (DRR) can be used to provide different traffic classes with different minimum bandwidth assurances.

Control plane. Control or signaling plane QOS mechanisms typically deal with admission control and resource reservation, and may in some cases be used to set up the data plane QOS functions. Control plane QOS functions are typically implemented as software processes, along with other control plane functions such as routing protocols. In practice, there is only one protocol widely used for control plane QOS signaling; that signaling protocol is RSVP. RSVP is used in several different contexts:

- *Integrated services architecture*. RSVP is used in the context of the Integrated Services architecture to perform per flow resource reservation and admission control.
- *MPLS traffic engineering*. RSVP is used in the context of MPLS traffic engineering, for admission control and to set up MPLS traffic engineering tunnels.

These QOS functions and mechanisms are, however, not generally used in isolation, but rather they are used together in concert, within the framework of an overriding QOS architecture, where mechanisms are combined for end-to-end effect. There are two defined IP QOS architectures: the Integrated Services architecture and the Differentiated Services architecture.

6.2 MPLS TRAFFIC ENGINEERING FOR QOS

6.2.1 Diffserv-aware MPLS Traffic Engineering

MPLS TE and Diffserv can be deployed concurrently in an IP backbone, with TE determining the path that traffic takes on aggregate based upon aggregate bandwidth constraints, and Diffserv mechanisms being used on each link for differential scheduling of packets on a per-class of service basis. TE and Diffserv are orthogonal technologies which can be used in concert for combined benefit: TE allows distribution of traffic on non-shortest paths for more efficient use of available bandwidth, while Diffserv allows SLA differentiation on a per-class basis. As it was initially defined and has been described in the previous section, however, MPLS TE computes tunnel paths for aggregates across all traffic classes and hence traffic from different classes may use the same TE tunnels. In this form MPLS TE is aware of only a single aggregate pool of available bandwidth per link and is unaware of what specific link bandwidth resources are allocated to which queues, and hence to which classes.

Diffserv-aware MPLS TE (DS-TE) extends the basic capabilities of TE to allow constraint-based path computation, explicit routing and admission control to be performed separately for different classes of service. DS-TE provides the capability to enforce different bandwidth constraints for different classes of traffic through the addition of more pools of available bandwidth on each link. These bandwidth pools are sub-pools of the aggregate TE bandwidth constraint, i.e. the sub-pools are a portion of the aggregate pool. This allows a bandwidth sub-pool to be used for a particular class of traffic, such that constraint-based routing and admission control can be performed for tunnels carrying traffic of that class, with the aggregate pool used to enforce an aggregate constraint across all classes of traffic. There are two different models that define how the sub-pool bandwidth constraints are applied:

- *Maximum allocation model.* RFC4127 defines the maximum allocation bandwidth constraints model (MAM) for Diffserv-aware MPLS TE. With the MAM, independent sub-pool constraints can be applied to each class, and an aggregate constraint can be applied across all classes.
- *Russian doll model.* RFC4125 defines the Russian dolls bandwidth constraints model (RDM) for Diffserv-aware MPLS TE. With the RDM, a hierarchy of constraints is defined, which consists of an aggregate constraint (global pool), and a number of sub-constraints (sub-pools) where constraint 1 is a sub-pool of constraint 0, constraint 2 is a sub-pool of constraint 1, and so on.

The choice of which bandwidth allocation model to use depends upon the way in which bandwidth allocation and pre-emption will be managed between tunnels of different classes. It is noted that if traffic engineering is required for only one of the deployed traffic classes, e.g. for EF traffic only, then DS-TE is not required and standard single bandwidth pool TE is sufficient.

In support of DS-TE, extensions have been added to IS-IS and OSPF RFC4124 to advertise the available sub-pool bandwidth per link. In addition, the TE constraint-based routing algorithms have been enhanced for DS-TE in order to take into account the constraint of available sub-pool bandwidth in computing the path of sub-pool tunnels. RSVP has also been extended RFC4124 to indicate the constraint model and the bandwidth pool, for which a tunnel is being signaled.

Setting an upper bound on the EF class (e.g. VoIP) utilization per link is necessary to bound the delay for that class and therefore to ensure that the SLA can be met. DS-TE can be used to assure that this upper bound is not exceeded. For example, consider the network in Figure 6.2, where each link is 2.5 Gbps and an IGP and TE metric value of one is applied to each link.

DS-TE could be used to ensure that traffic is routed over the network so that, on every link, there is never more than a defined percentage of the link capacity for EF class traffic, while there can be up to 100% of the link capacity for EF and AF class traffic in total. In this example, for illustration we assume that the defined maximum percentage for EF traffic per link is 50%. LSR1 is sending an aggregate of 1 Gbps of traffic to LSR8, and R2 is also sending an aggregate of 1 Gbps of traffic to LSR8. In this case, both the IGP (i.e. if TE were not deployed) and non-Diffserv aware TE would pick the same route. The IGP would pick the top route (R1/R2 → R3 → R4 → R5 → R8) because it is the shortest path (with a metric of 4). Assuming 1 Gbps tunnels were used from both LSR1 and LSR2 to LSR8, TE would also pick the top route, because it is the shortest path that has sufficient bandwidth available (metric of 4, 2.5 Gbps bandwidth available, 2 Gbps required). The decision to route both traffic aggregates via the top path may not seem appropriate if we examine the composition of the aggregate traffic flows.

If each of the aggregate flows were composed of 250 Mbps of VoIP traffic and 750 Mbps of standard data traffic, then in this case the total VoIP traffic load on the

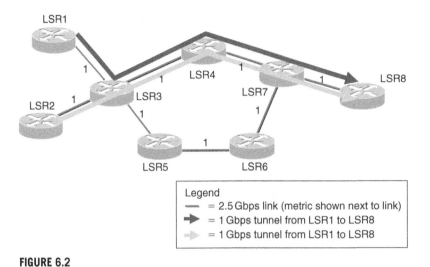

FIGURE 6.2

DS-TE deployment example 1.

top links would be 500 Mbps, which is within our EF class per link bound of 50%
5 1 Gbps. If, however, each traffic aggregate is comprised of 750 Mbps of VoIP and
250 Mbps of standard data traffic then such routing would aggregate 1.5 Gbps of
VoIP traffic on the R3 → R4 → R5 links, thereby exceeding our EF class bound of
50%. DS-TE can be used to overcome this problem if, for example, each link is configured with an available aggregate bandwidth pool of 2.5 Gbps, and an available
VoIP class sub-pool bandwidth of 1.25 Gbps (i.e. 50% of 2.5 Gbps). A VoIP class sub-
pool tunnel of 750 Mbps is then configured from R1 to R8, together with a standard
class aggregate pool tunnel of 250 Mbps. Similarly, from R2 to R8 a VoIP class sub-
pool tunnel of 750 Mbps and a standard class aggregate pool tunnel of 250 Mbps
are configured from R2 to R8. The DS-TE constraint-based routing algorithm would
then route the VoIP sub-pool tunnels to ensure that the 1.25 Gbps bound is not
exceeded on any link, and of the tunnels from R1 and R2 to R8, one VoIP sub-pool
tunnel would be routed via the top path (R1/R2 → R3 → R4 → R5 → R8) and the
other via the bottom path (R1/R2 → R6 → R7 → R5 → R8). In this particular case,
there would be enough available bandwidth for both aggregate pool tunnels to be
routed via the top path (R1/R2 → R3 → R4 → R5 → R8), which is the shortest path
with available aggregate bandwidth, possibly as shown in Figure 6.3, for example.

Hence, DS-TE allows separate route computation and admission control for different classes of traffic, which enables the distribution of EF and AF class load over
all available EF and AF class capacity making optimal use of available capacity. It
also provides a tool for constraining the class utilization per link to a specified
maximum thus ensuring that the class SLAs can be met. In order to provide these
benefits, however, the configured bandwidth for the sub-pools must align to the
queuing resources that are available for traffic-engineered traffic.

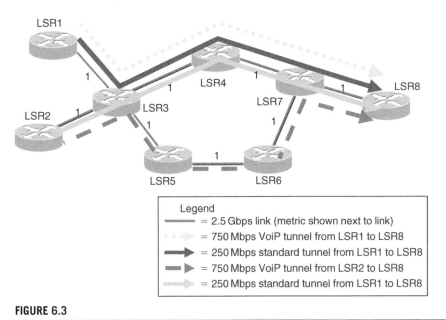

FIGURE 6.3

DS-TE deployment example 2.

6.2.2 **MPLS TE Deployment Models and Considerations**

MPLS TE can be deployed either in an ad hoc fashion, with selective tunnels configured tactically to move a subset of traffic away from congested links, or systematically, with all backbone traffic transported in TE tunnels.

Tactical TE Deployment

MPLS TE can be used tactically in order to offload traffic from congestion hotspots; this is an ad hoc approach, aimed at fixing current problems and as such is generally a short-term reactive operational/engineering process. When used in this way, rather than all traffic being subjected to traffic engineering, TE tunnels are deployed to reroute a subset of the network traffic from a congested part of the network, to a part where there is more capacity. This can be done by explicitly defining the path that a tunnel should take on a head-end router.

Consider Figure 6.4, for example; in this case there are two links of unequal capacity providing the connectivity between two POPs; one 622 Mbps, the other 2.5 Gbps. Using IGP metrics proportional to link capacity, e.g. a link cost of 1 for the 2.5 Gbps links and a link cost of 4 for 622 Mbps link, in normal working case conditions, the bottom path would be the lowest cost path and the top path would remain unused. Hence, even though there is over 3 Gbps of capacity between the POPs, this capacity could not all be used. If, however, two TE tunnels were configured between LSR 1 and LSR 2, one explicitly defined to use the

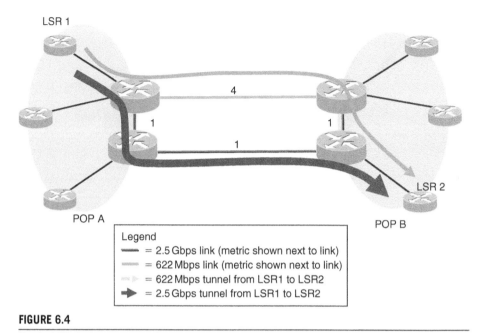

FIGURE 6.4

Tactical TE deployment—enables unequal cost load balancing.

top path and the other the bottom path, then as MPLS TE supports unequal cost load balancing (which normal IGP routing does not), the traffic demand between Router 1 and Router 2 could be balanced over the tunnels in proportion to the bandwidths of those paths, i.e. 1/5 of the total demand using the top path and 4/5 of the total demand on the bottom path.

Systematic TE Deployment

With a systematic TE deployment, all traffic is subjected to traffic engineering within the core; this is a long-term proactive engineering/planning process aimed at cost savings. Such a systematic approach requires that a mesh of TE tunnels be configured, hence one of the key considerations for a systematic MPLS TE deployment is tunnel scaling; a router incurs control plane processing overhead for each tunnel that it has some responsibility for, either as head-end, mid-point, or tail-end of that tunnel. The main metrics that are considered with respect to TE tunnel scalability are the number of tunnels per head-end and the number of tunnels traversing a tunnel mid-point. We consider the key scaling characteristics of a number of different systematic MPLS TE deployment models:

- *Outer core mesh.* In considering a full mesh from edge-to-edge across the core (i.e. from distribution router to distribution router), as MPLS TE tunnels are unidirectional, two tunnels are required between each pair of edge routers hence $n * (n - 1)$ tunnels are required in total where n is the number of edge routers or head-ends. The example in Figure 6.5 shows the tunnels that would

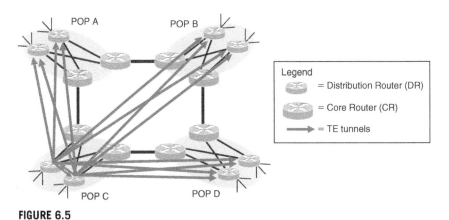

FIGURE 6.5

Outer core TE mesh.

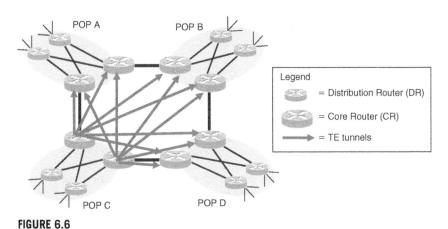

FIGURE 6.6

Inner core MPLS-TE mesh.

be required from the distribution routers within one POP to form a mesh to the distribution routers in other POPs. If TE is required for m classes of traffic each using Diffserv-aware TE then $m * n * (n - 1)$ tunnels would be required.

- *Inner core mesh.* Creating a core mesh of tunnels, i.e. from core routers to core routers, can make tunnel scaling independent of the number of distribution routers (there are normally more distribution routers than core routers), as shown in Figure 6.6, which illustrates the tunnels that would be required from the core routers within one POP to form a mesh to the core routers in other POPs.

- *Regional meshes.* Another way of reducing the number of tunnels required and therefore improving the tunnel scalability is to break the topology up

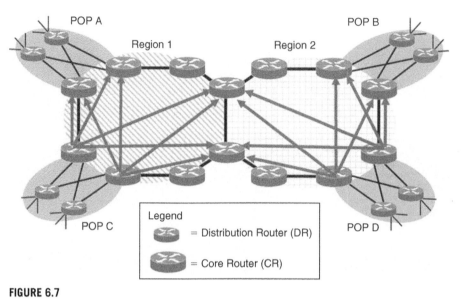

FIGURE 6.7

Regional MPLS-TE meshes.

into regions of meshed routers; adjacent tunnel meshes would be connected by routers which are part of both meshes, as shown in Figure 6.7, which shows meshes within each of two regions. Although this reduces the number of tunnels required, it may result in less optimal routing and less optimal use of available capacity.

To put these options into context, the largest TE deployments at the time of publication have a full mesh between ~120 head-ends, which results in ~120^2 = ~14400 tunnels in total with a maximum of ~120 tunnels per head-end and a maximum of ~1500 tunnels traversing a mid-point.

6.2.3 Setting Tunnel Bandwidth

Having decided on a particular MPLS TE deployment model, the next most significant decision is how to set the bandwidth requested for TE tunnels. The bandwidth of tunnels is a logical (i.e. control plane) constraint, rather than a physical constraint, hence if the actual tunnel load exceeds the reserved bandwidth, congestion can occur. Conversely, if a tunnel reservation is greater than the actual tunnel load, more bandwidth may be reserved than is required, which may lead to needless rejection of other tunnels and hence underutilization of the network.

The principles of over-provisioning could be applied to traffic engineering deployments. The bandwidth pools on each link should be set taking the required over-provisioning ratios into account for that particular link speed. For example, if Diffserv is not deployed in the core network and an OP of 1.42 is determined

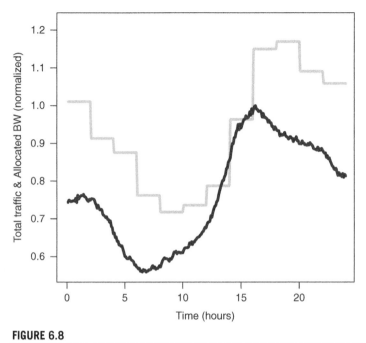

FIGURE 6.8

Automatic tunnel bandwidth sizing.

to be required to achieve a target P99.9 queuing delay of 2 ms on a 155 Mbps link, then the aggregate TE bandwidth pool should be set to 155/1.42 5 109 Mbps. Each tunnel (which represents a traffic demand across the network) should then be sized based upon the measured average tunnel load (or a percentile thereof). This will ensure that the measured average aggregate load on each link will be controlled such that the per-link over-provisioning factor is always met, and hence the target SLAs can be achieved, even when there are potentially multiple tunnels that may traverse the link.

Tunnel resizing can be performed online, by the head-end routers themselves, or by an offline system. When online tunnel resizing is used, algorithms run on the head-end routers to automatically and dynamically resize the tunnels which originate from them, based upon some measure of the traffic load on the tunnel over previous measurement periods. Simple algorithms can lead to inefficiencies, however. Consider, for example, an algorithm that sizes the tunnel based upon the peak of the 5-minute average tunnel loads in the previous interval; when traffic is ramping up during the day, the algorithm needs to take into account the traffic growth during the next interval, or else it will under-provision the tunnel. Consequently, in the interval following the peak interval of the day, significantly more tunnel bandwidth will be reserved than is necessary, as illustrated by the example in Figure 6.8.

Figure 6.8 plots the total traffic load across all TE tunnels (black line) in a network with a TE tunnel full mesh during a single day. The corresponding sum of the reserved TE tunnel bandwidth is plotted in grey. The tunnel resizing algorithm used in this case resized each tunnel every 2 hours to a multiple of the peak of the 5-minute average load for that tunnel experienced during the preceding 2 hour period. In order to cope with the rapid ramp up in traffic load before the daily peak, a high multiple needed to be used; in this case the multiple was 1.2 times. As a consequence, the reserved tunnel bandwidth is significantly greater than the actual tunnel load during the period after the daily peak load, due to the resizing lag. Hence, tunnel resizing algorithms are most efficient when they rely on a longer history of measurements for tunnel sizing, i.e. day, week, or month.

6.3 TRAFFIC ENGINEERING AND QOS OPTIMIZATION OF MPLS-BASED INTEGRATED VOICE/DATA DYNAMIC ROUTING NETWORKS

This section and the subsequent sections set out the TE and QoS Optimization (TQO) evolution discussion and focus on QoS resource management in an IP/MPLS-based, converged voice/data network architecture. It draws on material from *Engineering and QoS Optimization of Integrated Voice & Data Networks* by Ash. AT&T's internal RATS team performed evolution studies of an IP/MPLS-based architecture. In the course of this work, a wide range of alternative architectures were considered, and the modeling and analysis studies and conclusions reached are described in the sections that follow, with an emphasis on the analysis of QoS resource management approaches.

RATS had widely divergent opinions as to the right architectural approach. Some participants came from the TDM voice world and thought in terms of highly successful voice/ISDN network dynamic routing strategies such as RTNR and STT-EDR. Some participants came from the IP data world, where dynamic routing strategies such as OSPF and MPLS were fast becoming the de facto technologies of choice for networks worldwide. Some participants came from an ATM world, where PNNI was proving to be a revolutionary dynamic routing technology and some pushed hard on ATM SVP overlays using ATM data switching and cross-connect technology. Spirited (should I say heated?) arguments were the norm, with the TDM, IP, and ATM technology RATS all feeling confident on the basis of representing highly successful, well-entrenched technologies that were already the basis for lucrative service offerings.

In the end, the analysis and detailed case studies proved to be the vehicle for consensus on innovative architecture directions that incorporated the best ideas of both worlds. What emerged is a Generic TQO (GTQO) design.

This chapter captures the wide range and diversity of ideas, architectures, alternatives, and technologies that were considered by RATS. While the range considered is not exhaustive, it is certainly comprehensive.

The problem statement for TQO design in this chapter includes the following:

- Traffic/application layer design: Find an optimal class-of-service routing design for arbitrary traffic loads and network topology, which yields minimum cost capacity and maximum flow/revenue, subject to meeting performance constraints.
- MPLS LSP dynamic routing and bandwidth allocation layer 3 design: Find an optimal connection/bearer-path routing design and MPLS LSP dynamic routing and bandwidth allocation strategy for arbitrary traffic loads and network topology, which yields minimum cost capacity and maximum flow/revenue, subject to meeting performance constraints.

QoS resource management (sometimes called QoS routing) functions include class-of-service identification, routing table derivation, connection admission control, bandwidth allocation, bandwidth protection, bandwidth reservation, priority routing, priority queuing, and other related resource management functions. QoS resource management methods have been applied successfully in circuit-switched networks and are being extended to packet-switched, IP/(G)MPLS-based networks. In this chapter we define and analyze a wide variety of MPLS-based QoS resource management methods, in which bandwidth is allocated to each of several virtual networks (VNETs) and VNETs are assigned a priority corresponding to either high-priority key services, normal-priority services, or best-effort low-priority services. VNETs are formed by MPLS LSPs routed on layer 2 logical links between nodes. Traffic routers dynamically route connections in response to call/session requests that fall within classes of service assigned to VNETs. A VNET is allocated bandwidth on layer 2 logical links, and the bandwidth allocation is managed to meet performance requirements. For example, real-time voice traffic may form one VNET made up of MPLS (LSPs) between the network nodes. Premium private data traffic may form another VNET made up of separate and additional MPLS LSPs between the nodes. The TQO design analyzed in this chapter optimizes the routing and bandwidth allocation of the LSP mesh forming the VNETs, with traffic for various classes of service (also known as QoS classes) carried on the VNET bandwidth so as to satisfy various performance objectives. This mesh of MPLS LSPs forming the VNETs is carried in turn by GMPLS LSPs forming the layer 2 logical link network. Bandwidth allocated to VNETs can be shared with other VNETs when relatively idle, but is protected for exclusive use by traffic assigned to the particular VNET when necessary. This is accomplished through dynamic bandwidth reservation mechanisms explained in this chapter. Changes in VNET bandwidth capacity can be determined by edge nodes on a per-flow (per-connection) basis or based on an overall aggregated bandwidth demand for VNET capacity (not on a per-connection demand basis). In the latter case of per-VNET bandwidth allocation, based on the aggregated bandwidth demand, edge nodes make periodic discrete changes in bandwidth allocation, i.e., either increase or decrease bandwidth, such as on the constraint-based routing label switched paths

(CRLSPs) constituting the VNET bandwidth capacity. It is shown that aggregated per-VNET bandwidth allocation is preferred to per-flow bandwidth allocation lower routing table management overhead, thereby increasing scalability. STT-EDR path selection combined with per-VNET bandwidth allocation dramatically reduce flooding of network status changes and control overhead, such as used in SDR approaches (e.g., OSPF). Alternatives to VNET architectures are considered as well, for example, where (a) no VNETs exist but rather all traffic is combined on available bandwidth, (b) services are differentiated only by queuing mechanisms such as DiffServ, and (c) other architecture alternatives. It is shown in these studies that the VNET approach is superior to other alternatives and is the basis for a GTQO protocol.

Capacity design of VNET architectures considers all VNETs at once in an integrated network design, in which all the complex dynamic functions are considered together, including per-VNET dynamic routing, per-VNET dynamic bandwidth allocation, bandwidth sharing, bandwidth reservation, and per-VNET queuing. In short, the integrated VNET design takes into account the complex dynamics, and efficiencies, of statistical multiplexing in packet networks where bandwidth is maximally shared. This full sharing approach avoids the network inefficiencies that would result from designing separate VNETs, one at a time, in which bandwidth is not shared and statistical multiplexing is not realized. All of these dynamics are considered at once in the capacity design while meeting multidimensional performance objectives using the discrete event flow optimization (DEFO) method.

QoS resource management therefore can be applied on a per-flow (or per-call/session request or per-connection-request) basis or can be applied beneficially to traffic trunks (also known as "bandwidth pipes" or "virtual trunks") in the form of CRLSPs in IP/(G)MPLS-based networks.

QoS resource management provides integration of services on a shared network for many classes of service such as the following:

- Constant bit rate real-time services, including voice, 64-, 384-, and 1536-Kbps ISDN switched digital data, international transit, priority defense communication, virtual private network, 800/FreePhone, fiber preferred, and other services.
- Variable bit rate real-time services, including IP-telephony, compressed video, and other services.
- Variable bit rate nonreal-time services, including WWW file transfer, credit card check, and other services.
- Unassigned bit rate best-effort services, including voice mail, email, file transfer, and other services.

Examples of service priorities within these VNET categories include the following:

- High-priority key services such as constant/variable rate real-time emergency and defense voice communication

- Normal-priority services such as constant/variable rate real-time voice; variable rate non-delay-sensitive WWW file transfer
- Low-priority best-effort services such as variable rate non-delay-sensitive voice mail, email, and file transfer

A key requirement of the GTQO QoS resource management function is class-of-service identification/routing. Class-of-service identification/routing provides a means to define network services through table-driven concepts rather than software development and new network deployment. Whereas the historical model of new service development always led to a "stovepipe" approach with specialized software development to implement the service and hardware development to build a new network and network elements, class-of-service routing defines service and network capabilities in tables within the network nodes. That is, definitions of new services capabilities are table driven and require no software development or network element development.

Bandwidth allocation control in the GTQO method is based on estimated bandwidth needs, bandwidth use, and status of links in the VNET. The edge node, or originating node (ON), determines when VNET bandwidth needs to be increased or decreased on a CRLSP and uses an illustrative MPLS CRLSP bandwidth modification procedure to execute needed bandwidth allocation changes on VNET CRLSPs. In the bandwidth allocation procedure the resource reservation protocol (e.g., RSVP-TE, RFC3209) could be used, for example, to specify appropriate parameters in the resource reservation message (a) to request bandwidth allocation changes on each link in the CRLSP and (b) to determine if link bandwidth can be allocated on each link in the CRLSP. If a link bandwidth allocation is not allowed, a crankback notification message allows the ON to search out possible bandwidth allocation on another CRLSP. In particular we illustrate a depth-of-search (DEPTH) parameter in the resource reservation message to control the bandwidth allocation on individual links in a CRLSP. In addition, we illustrate a modify parameter in the resource reservation message to allow dynamic modification of the assigned traffic parameters (such as peak data rate, committed data rate, etc.) of an already existing CRLSP. Finally, we illustrate the crankback notification message to allow an edge node to search out additional alternate CRLSPs when a given CRLSP cannot accommodate a bandwidth request.

As shown in this chapter, dynamic bandwidth reservation, a network capability that enables preferential treatment for "preferred" traffic over "nonpreferred" traffic, is an essential GTQO capability for a converged MPLS-based network.

The conclusions reached in this chapter are that (a) class-of-service routing is an important capability of converged TQO networks to define table-driven service elements and component application/network capabilities to avoid software development, network element development, and new network implementation for new service deployment, (b) bandwidth reservation is critical to the stable and efficient performance of TQO methods in a network and to ensure the proper operation of multiservice bandwidth allocation, protection, and priority treatment, (c) per-VNET bandwidth allocation is essentially equivalent to per-flow bandwidth allocation in network performance and efficiency, with much lower routing table management overhead requirements compared to per-flow allocation, (d) QoS resource management is shown to be effective in achieving key-service, normal-service, and best-effort service differentiation, and (e) both MPLS QoS and bandwidth management and DiffServ priority queuing management are important for ensuring that multiservice network performance objectives are met under a range of network conditions.

We now illustrate the principles of QoS resource management, identify many alternative approaches to QoS resource management, and finally analyze the tradeoffs in the various approaches.

6.4 CLASS-OF-SERVICE ROUTING

QoS resource management functions include class-of-service routing, routing table derivation, connection admission, bandwidth allocation, bandwidth protection, bandwidth reservation, priority routing, and priority queuing. In this section we discuss class-of-service identification and routing table derivation.

Class-of-service routing provides a means to define network services through table-driven concepts rather than software development and new network deployment. In the class-of-service routing model, tables are installed in network elements, such as edge routers, and updated through provisioning of the tables through automated management systems. The historical model of new service development always led to the latter, i.e., specialized software had to be developed to implement the service and network features particular to the service usually required a new network to be built with new network elements and capabilities being required. This process was slow and expensive and led to a proliferation of networks—"stovepipes" as they are sometimes called.

Class-of-service routing is the antithesis of the historical stovepipe approach and is fully consistent with converged network evolution and deployment. Class-of-service routing defines elements of a service in terms of application and network capabilities, which can then be specified and provisioned in tables within the network nodes. That is, definition of new services capabilities are table driven and require no software development or network element development. An illustration of table-driven class-of-service routing capabilities is given in the following sections. Such capabilities have been in operation in AT&T's network for about 15 years, with great success. New services have been defined along the way, including 800 Gold Service, International Priority Routing, Emergency Services Priority Routing, and others. Class-of-service routing should be an important element of future converged TQO network capabilities.

6.4.1 Class-of-Service Identification

QoS routing and resource management entails first identifying the required class of service (or QoS class) and determining the class-of-service parameters, which may include, for example, service identity (SI), virtual network (VNET), link capability (LC), and QoS and traffic threshold parameters.

The SI describes the actual service associated with the connection. The VNET describes the bandwidth allocation and routing table parameters to be used by the connection. The LC describes the link hardware capabilities, such as fiber, radio, satellite, and digital circuit multiplexing equipment (DCME), that the connection should require, prefer, or avoid. The combination of SI, VNET, and LC constitutes the class of service, which together with the network node number is used to access routing table data.

In addition to controlling bandwidth allocation, the QoS resource management procedures can check end-to-end transfer delay, delay variation, and transmission quality considerations such as loss, echo, and noise.

Determination of class of service begins with translation at the originating node. The number or name is translated to determine the routing address of the destination node. If multiple ingress/egress routing is used, multiple destination node addresses are derived for the connection. Other data derived from connection information, such as link characteristics, Q.931 message information elements, and service control point routing information, are used to derive the class of service for the connection.

6.4.2 Routing Table Derivation

Class of service is identified at the network edge, and it is important that the identification be uniform at all edge points throughout the network in order to avoid inconsistent treatment within the network. Inconsistent treatment, for example, could lead to some services hogging bandwidth to the detriment of other services in the network. Class-of-service parameters are derived through application of policy-based routing. Policy-based routing involves the application of rules applied to input parameters to derive a routing table and its associated parameters. Input parameters for applying policy-based rules to derive SI, VNET, and LC could include numbering plan, type of origination/destination network, and type of service. Policy-based routing rules may then be applied to the derived SI, VNET, and LC to derive the routing table and associated parameters.

Hence policy-based routing rules are used in SI derivation, which, for example, uses the type of origin, type of destination, signaling service type, and dialed number/name service type to derive the SI. The type of origin can be derived normally from the type of incoming link to the connected network domain, connecting to a directly connected (also known as nodal) customer equipment location, an access node within a local exchange carrier domain, or an international carrier location. Similarly, based on the dialed numbering plan, the type of destination network is derived and can be a directly connected customer location if a private numbering plan is used (e.g., within a VPN), a domestic access node within a local exchange carrier domain location if a domestic E.164 number is used to the destination, or an international access node location if the international E.164 numbering plan is used. Signaling service type is derived based on bearer capability within signaling messages, information digits in dialed digit codes, numbering plan, or other signaling information and can indicate constant-bit-rate voice service (CVS), virtual private network (VPN) service, ISDN switched digital service (SDS), and other service types. Finally, dialed number service type is derived based on special dialed number codes such as 800 numbers or 900 numbers and can indicate 800 (FreePhone) service, 900 (mass announcement) service, and other service types. Type of origin, type of destination, signaling service type, and dialed number service type are then all used to derive the SI.

The following examples use policy-based routing rules to derive class-of-service parameters. A CVS SI, for example, is derived from the following information:

- The type of origination network is a domestic access node within a local exchange carrier domain because the connection originates from a domestic local exchange carrier node.
- The type of destination network is a domestic access node within a local exchange carrier domain, based on the domestic E.164 dialed number.
- The signaling service type is long-distance service, based on the numbering plan (domestic E.164).
- The dialed number service type is not used to distinguish the CVS SI.

An 800 (FreePhone) service SI, for example, is derived from similar information, except that the dialed number service type is based on the 800 dialed "FreePhone" number to distinguish the 800 service SI.

A VPN service SI, for example, is derived from similar information, except that the signaling service type is based on the originating customer having access to VPN-based services to derive the VPN service SI.

A service identity mapping table uses the four inputs listed above to derive the service identity. This policy-based routing table is changeable by administrative updates, in which new service information can be defined without software modifications to the node processing. From the SI and bearer service capability the SI/bearer-service-to-virtual network mapping table is used to derive the VNET.

Here the SIs are mapped to individual virtual networks. Routing parameters for priority or key services are discussed further later in this section.

Link capability selection allows connections to be routed on links that have the particular characteristics required by these connections. A connection can require, prefer, or avoid a set of link characteristics such as fiber transmission, radio transmission, satellite transmission, or compressed voice transmission. LC requirements for the connection can be determined by the SI of the connection or by other information derived from the signaling message or from the routing number. Routing logic allows the connection to skip those links that have undesired characteristics and to seek a best match for the requirements of the connection. For any SI, a set of LC selection preferences is specified for the connection request. LC selection preferences can override the normal order of selection of paths. If an LC characteristic is required, then any path with a link that does not have that characteristic is skipped. If a characteristic is preferred, paths having all links with that characteristic are used first. Paths having links without the preferred characteristic will be used next. An LC preference is set for the presence or absence of a characteristic. For example, if fiber-optic transmission is required, then only paths with links having *Fiberoptic* = *Yes* are used. If we prefer the presence of fiber-optic transmission, then paths having all links with *Fiberoptic* = *Yes* are used first, followed by paths having some links with *Fiberoptic* = *No*.

6.4.3 **Class-of-Service Routing Steps**

The class-of-service routing method consists of the following steps:

- At the ON, the destination node (DN), SI, VNET, and QoS resource management parameters are determined through the number/name translation database and other service information available at the ON.
- The DN and QoS resource management parameters are used to access the appropriate VNET and routing table between the ON and the DN.
- The connection request is set up over the first available path in the routing table with the required transmission resource selected based on QoS resource management data.

In the first step, the ON translates the dialed digits to determine the address of the DN. If multiple ingress/egress routing is used, multiple destination node addresses are derived for the connection request. Other data derived from connection request information include link characteristics, Q.931 message information elements, information interchange (II) digits, and service control point (SCP) routing information and are used to derive the QoS resource management parameters (SI, VNET, LC, and QoS/traffic thresholds). Each connection request is classified by its SI. A connection request for an individual service is allocated an equivalent bandwidth equal to EQBW and routed on a particular VNET. For CBR services the equivalent bandwidth EQBW is equal to the average or sustained bit rate. For VBR services the equivalent bandwidth EQBW is a function of the sustained bit rate, peak bit rate, and perhaps other parameters. For example, EQBW equals 86.8 Kbps of bandwidth for CBR voice service (CVS) connections, which includes the G.711 voice payload, RTP/UDP/IP headers, PPP header, and MPLS labels.

In the second step, the SI value is used to derive the VNET. In the multiservice, QoS resource management network, bandwidth is allocated to individual VNETs, which is protected as needed but otherwise shared. Under normal nontraffic-lost/delayed network conditions, all services fully share all available bandwidth. When traffic loss/delay occurs for VNET i, bandwidth reservation acts to prohibit alternate-routed traffic and traffic from other VNETs from seizing the allocated capacity for VNET i. Associated with each VNET are average bandwidth *(BWavg)* and maximum bandwidth *(BWmax)* parameters to govern bandwidth allocation and protection, which are discussed further in the next section. As discussed, LC selection allows connection requests to be routed on specific transmission links that have the particular characteristics required by a connection request.

In the third step, the VNET routing table determines which network capacity is allowed to be selected for each connection request. In using the VNET routing table to select network capacity, the ON selects a first choice path based on the routing table selection rules. Whether or not bandwidth can be allocated to the connection request on the first choice path is determined by the QoS resource management rules given later in this section. If a first-choice path cannot be accessed, the ON may then try alternate paths determined by FXR, TDR, SDR, or EDR path selection rules. Whether or not bandwidth can be allocated to the connection request on the alternate path again is determined by the QoS resource management rules now described.

6.5 DYNAMIC BANDWIDTH ALLOCATION, PROTECTION AND RESERVATION PRINCIPLES

As mentioned earlier, QoS resource management functions include class-of-service identification, routing table derivation, connection admission, bandwidth allocation, bandwidth protection, bandwidth reservation, priority routing, and priority queuing. In this section we discuss connection admission, bandwidth allocation, bandwidth protection, and bandwidth reservation. Note that other QoS routing constraints are taken into account in the QoS resource management and route selection methods, including end-to-end transfer delay, delay variation, and transmission quality considerations such as loss, echo, and noise.

This section specifies the resource allocation controls and priority mechanisms, and the information needed to support them. In the illustrative QoS resource management method, the connection/bandwidth-allocation admission control for each link in the path is performed based on the status of the link. The ON may select any path for which the first link is allowed according to QoS resource management criteria. If a subsequent link is not allowed, then a release with crankback (bandwidth not available) is used to return to the ON and select an alternate path. This use of EDR path selection, which entails the use of the release with crankback/bandwidth-not-available mechanism to search for an available path, is an alternative to SDR path selection, which may entail flooding of frequently changing link state parameters, such as available bandwidth. There are trade-offs between EDR with crankback and SDR with link-state flooding. In particular, when EDR path selection with crankback is used in lieu of SDR path selection with link-state flooding, the reduction in the frequency of such link-state parameter flooding allows for larger domain (area, peer group, etc.) sizes. This is because link-state flooding can consume substantial processor and link resources in terms of message processing by the processors and link bandwidth consumed by messages on the links.

Two cases of QoS resource management are considered in this chapter: per-virtual-network (per-VNET) management and per-flow management. In the per-VNET method, such as for IP-based MPLS networks, aggregated LSP bandwidth is managed to meet the overall bandwidth requirements of VNET service needs. Individual flows are allocated bandwidth within the CRLSPs accordingly, as CRLSP bandwidth is available. In the per-flow method, bandwidth is allocated to each individual flow, such as in SVC setup in an ATM-based network, from the overall pool of bandwidth, as the total pool bandwidth is available. A fundamental principle applied in these bandwidth allocation methods is the use of bandwidth reservation techniques. We first review bandwidth reservation principles and then discuss per-VNET and per-flow QoS resource allocations.

Bandwidth reservation (called "trunk reservation" in TDM network terminology) gives preference to the preferred traffic by allowing it to seize any idle bandwidth in a link, while allowing nonpreferred traffic to only seize bandwidth if there is a minimum level of idle bandwidth available, where the minimum bandwidth threshold is called the reservation level. P. J. Burke first analyzed bandwidth reservation behavior from the solution of the birth-death equations for the bandwidth reservation model. Burke's model showed the relative lost-traffic level for preferred traffic, which is not subject to bandwidth reservation restrictions, as compared to nonpreferred traffic, which is subject to the restrictions. Figure 6.9 illustrates the percentage lost traffic of preferred and nonpreferred traffic on a typical link with 10% traffic overload. It is seen that the preferred lost traffic is near zero, whereas the nonpreferred lost traffic is much higher; this situation is maintained across a wide variation in the percentage of the preferred traffic load. Hence, bandwidth reservation protection is robust to traffic variations and provides significant dynamic protection of particular streams of traffic.

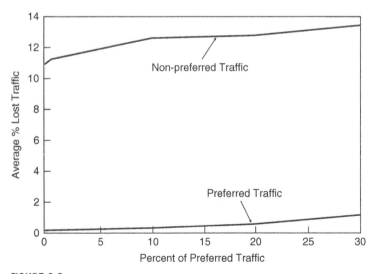

FIGURE 6.9

Dynamic bandwidth reservation performance under 10% overload.

Bandwidth reservation is a crucial technique used in nonhierarchical networks to prevent "instability," which can severely reduce throughput in periods of congestion, perhaps by as much as 50% of the traffic-carrying capacity of a network. The phenomenon of instability has an interesting mathematical solution to network flow equations, which has been presented in several studies. These studies have shown that nonhierarchical networks exhibit two stable states, or bistability, under congestion and that networks can transition between these stable states in a network congestion condition that has been demonstrated in simulation studies. A simple explanation of how this bistable phenomenon arises is that under congestion, a network is often not able to complete a connection request on the primary shortest path, which consists in this example of a single link. If alternate routing is allowed, such as on longer, multiple-link paths, which are assumed in this example to consist of two links, then the connection request might be completed on a two-link path selected from among a large number of two-link path choices, only one of which needs sufficient idle bandwidth on both links to be used to route the connection. Because this two-link connection now occupies resources that could perhaps otherwise be used to complete two one-link connections, this is a less efficient use of network resources under congestion. In the event that a large fraction of all connections cannot complete on the direct link but instead occupy two-link paths, the total network throughput capacity is reduced by one-half because most connections take twice the resources needed. This is one stable state; i.e., most or all connections use two links. The other stable state is that most or all connections use one link, which is the desired condition.

Bandwidth reservation is used to prevent this unstable behavior by having the preferred traffic on a link be the direct traffic on the primary, shortest path, and the nonpreferred traffic, subjected to bandwidth reservation restrictions as described above, be the alternate-routed traffic on longer paths. In this way the alternate-routed traffic is inhibited from selecting longer alternate paths when sufficient idle trunk capacity is not available on all links of an alternate-routed connection, which is the likely condition under network and link congestion. Mathematically, studies of bistable network behavior have shown that bandwidth reservation used in this manner to favor primary shortest connections eliminates the bistability problem in nonhierarchical networks and allows such networks to maintain efficient utilization under congestion by favoring connections completed on the shortest path. For this reason, dynamic bandwidth reservation is applied universally in nonhierarchical TDM-based networks, and often in hierarchical networks. As shown in this chapter, bandwidth reservation is an essential capability for a converged MPLS-based network.

There are differences in how and when bandwidth reservation is applied, however, such as whether the bandwidth reservation for connections routed on the primary path is in place at all times or whether it is dynamically triggered to be used only under network or link congestion. This is a complex network throughput trade-off issue because bandwidth reservation can lead to some loss in throughput under normal, low-congestion conditions. This loss in throughput arises when bandwidth is reserved for connections on the primary path, but these connection requests do not arrive and then the capacity is needlessly reserved when it might be used to complete other traffic, such as alternate-routed traffic that might otherwise be lost. However, under network congestion, the use of bandwidth reservation is critical to preventing network instability, as explained above.

It is beneficial for bandwidth reservation techniques to be included in IP-based and ATM-based routing methods in order to ensure the efficient use of network resources, especially under congestion conditions. Path selection methods such as optimized multipath for traffic engineering in IP-based MPLS networks or path selection in ATM-based PNNI networks give no guidance on the necessity for using bandwidth-reservation techniques. Such guidance is essential for acceptable network performance.

Alternative approaches are given for dynamically triggered bandwidth reservation techniques, where bandwidth reservation is triggered only under network congestion. Such methods are shown to be effective in striking a balance between protecting network resources under congestion and ensuring that resources are available for sharing when conditions permit. Simulation studies illustrate the phenomenon of network instability, and the effectiveness of bandwidth reservation in eliminating the instability is demonstrated. Bandwidth reservation is also shown to be an effective technique to share bandwidth capacity among services on a primary path, where the reservation in this case is invoked to prefer link capacity on the primary path for one particular class of service as opposed to another class of service when network and link congestion are encountered.

6.5.1 Per-VNET Bandwidth Allocation, Protection, and Reservation

Through the use of bandwidth allocation, reservation, and congestion control techniques, QoS resource management can provide good network performance under normal and abnormal operating conditions for all services sharing the integrated network. Such methods have been implemented and analyzed in practice for TDM-based networks and analyzed in detailed modeling studies for IP/MPLS-based networks in this chapter.

The per-VNET bandwidth allocation approach to QoS resource management is where bandwidth is allocated to the individual VNETs (high-priority key services VNETs, normal-priority services VNETs, and best-effort low-priority services VNETs). This allocated bandwidth is protected by bandwidth reservation methods, as needed, but otherwise shared. Each ON monitors VNET bandwidth use on each VNET CRLSP and determines when the VNET CRLSP bandwidth needs to be increased or decreased. Bandwidth changes in VNET bandwidth capacity are determined by ONs based on an overall aggregated bandwidth demand for VNET capacity (not on a per-connection demand basis). Based on the aggregated bandwidth demand, these ONs make periodic discrete changes in bandwidth allocation, i.e., either increase or decrease bandwidth on the CRLSPs constituting the VNET bandwidth capacity. For example, if connection requests are made for VNET CRLSP bandwidth that exceeds the current CRLSP bandwidth allocation, the ON initiates a bandwidth modification request on the appropriate CRLSP (s). For example, this bandwidth modification request may entail increasing the current CRLSP bandwidth allocation by a discrete increment of bandwidth denoted here as delta-bandwidth (DBW). DBW is a large enough bandwidth change so that modification requests are made relatively infrequently. Also, the ON periodically monitors CRLSP bandwidth use, such as once each minute, and if bandwidth use falls below the current CRLSP allocation, the ON initiates a bandwidth modification request to decrease the CRLSP bandwidth allocation by a unit of bandwidth such as DBW.

In making a VNET bandwidth allocation modification, the ON determines the QoS resource management parameters, including the VNET priority (key, normal, or best-effort), VNET bandwidth in use, VNET bandwidth allocation thresholds, and whether the CRLSP is a first-choice CRLSP or alternate CRLSP. These parameters are used to access a VNET depth-of-search table to determine a DEPTH load state threshold (Di), or the "depth" to which network capacity can be allocated for the VNET bandwidth modification request. In using the DEPTH threshold to allocate VNET bandwidth capacity, the ON selects a first-choice CRLSP based on the routing table selection rules.

Path selection in this IP network illustration may use open shortest path first (OSPF) for intranetwork routing. In OSPF-based layer 3 routing, as illustrated in Figure 6.10, ON A determines a list of shortest paths by using, for example, Dijkstra's algorithm.

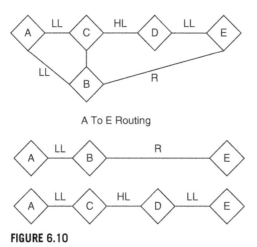

A To E Routing

FIGURE 6.10

Label switched path selection for bandwidth modification request.

This path list could be determined based on administrative weights of each link, which are communicated to all nodes within the autonomous system (AS) domain. These administrative weights may be set, for example, to [1 + ex distance], where s is a factor giving a relatively smaller weight to the distance in comparison to the hop count. The ON selects a path from the list based on, for example, FXR, TDR, SDR, or EDR path selection.

For example, in using the first CRLSP A-B-E in Figure 6.10, ON A sends an MPLS label request message to VN B, which in turn forwards the label request message to DN E. VN B and DN E are passed in the explicit routing (ER) parameter contained in the label request message. Each node in the CRLSP reads the ER information and passes the label request message to the next node listed in the ER parameter. If the first path is congested at any of the links in the path, an MPLS notification message with a crankback parameter is returned to ON A, which can then attempt the next path. If FXR is used, then this path is the next path in the shortest path list, for example, path A-C-D-E. If TDR is used, then the next path is the next path in the routing table for the current time period. If SDR is used, OSPF implements a distributed method of flooding link status information, which is triggered either periodically and/or by crossing load state threshold values. This method of distributing link status information can be resource intensive and may not be any more efficient than simpler path selection methods such as EDR. If EDR is used, then the next path is the last successful path, and if that path is unsuccessful another alternate path is searched out according to the EDR path selection method.

Hence in using the selected CRLSP, the ON sends the explicit route, the requested traffic parameters (peak data rate, committed data rate, etc.), a DEPTH parameter, and a modify parameter in the MPLS setup message IE to each VN and the DN in the selected CRLSP. Whether or not bandwidth can be allocated to the bandwidth modification request on the first choice CRLSP is determined by each VN applying the QoS resource management rules. These rules entail that the VN determine the CRLSP link states, based on bandwidth use and bandwidth available, and compare the link load state to the DEPTH threshold Di sent in the MPLS signaling parameters, as explained further later in this section. If the first-choice CRLSP cannot admit the bandwidth change, a VN or DN returns control to the ON through the use of the crankback parameter in the MPLS release message IE. At that point the ON may then try an alternate CRLSP. Whether or not bandwidth can be allocated to the bandwidth modification request on the alternate path again is determined by the use of the DEPTH threshold compared to the CRLSP link load state at each VN. Priority queuing is used during the time the CRLSP is established, and at each link the queuing discipline is maintained such that the packets are given priority according to the VNET traffic priority.

Hence determination of the CRLSP link load states is necessary for QoS resource management to select network capacity on either the first-choice CRLSP or alternate CRLSPs. Four link load states are distinguished: lightly loaded (LL), heavily loaded (HL), reserved (R), and busy (B). Management of CRLSP capacity uses the link state model and the DEPTH model to determine if a bandwidth modification request can be accepted on a given CRLSP. The allowed DEPTH load state threshold Di determines if a bandwidth modification request can be accepted on a given link to an available bandwidth "depth." In setting up the bandwidth modification request, the ON encodes the DEPTH load state threshold allowed on each link in the DEPTH parameter Di, which is carried in the MPLS setup message IE. If a CRLSP link is encountered at a VN in which the idle link bandwidth and link load state are below the allowed DEPTH load state threshold Di, then the VN sends an MPLS release message IE with the crankback parameter to the ON, which can then route the bandwidth modification request to an alternate CRLSP choice. For example, in Figure 6.10, CRLSP A-B-E may be the first path tried where link A-B is in the LL state and link B-E is in the R state. If the DEPTH load state allowed is $Di = HL$ or better, then the CRLSP bandwidth modification request in the MPLS setup message IE is routed on link A-B but will not be admitted on link B-E, wherein the CRLSP bandwidth modification request will be cranked back in the MPLS release message IE to the originating node A to try alternate CRLSP A-C-D-E. Here the CRLSP bandwidth modification request succeeds, as all links have a state of HL or better.

Per-VNET Bandwidth Allocation/Reservation: Meshed Network Case

For purposes of bandwidth allocation reservation, two approaches are illustrated: one applicable to meshed network topologies and the other to sparse topologies. In meshed networks, a greater number of logical links result in less traffic carried per link, and functions such as bandwidth reservation need to be controlled more carefully than in a sparse network. In a sparse network the traffic is concentrated on much larger, and many fewer, logical links, and here bandwidth reservation does not have to be managed as carefully. Hence in the meshed network case, functions such as automatically triggering of bandwidth reservation on and off, dependent on the link/network congestion level, are beneficial to use. In the sparse network case, however, the complexity of such automatic triggering is not essential and bandwidth reservation may be permanently enabled without performance degradation.

This section discusses a meshed network alternative approach for bandwidth allocation/reservation and the following section discusses the sparse network case.

The DEPTH load state threshold is a function of bandwidth-in-progress, VNET priority, and bandwidth allocation thresholds.

Note that BWIP, BWavg, and BWmax are specified per ON-DN pair and that the QoS resource management method provides for a key-priority VNET, a normal-priority VNET, and a best-effort VNET. Key services admitted by an ON on the key VNET are given higher priority routing treatment by allowing greater path selection DEPTH than normal services admitted on the normal VNET. Best-effort services admitted on the best-effort VNET are given lower priority routing treatment by allowing lesser path selection DEPTH than normal. The quantities $BWavg_i$ are computed periodically, such as every week, w, and can be averaged exponentially over a several-week period, as follows:

$$BWavg_i(w) = .5 \times BWavg_i(w - 1) + .5 \times [BWIPavg_i(w) + BWOVavg_i(w)]$$

$BWIPavg_i$ = average bandwidth in progress across a load set period on VNET i
$BWOVavg_i$ = average bandwidth allocation request rejected (or overflow) across
a load set period on VNET i

where all variables are specified per ON-DN pair and where $BWIP_i$ and $BWOV_i$ are averaged across various load set periods, such as morning, afternoon, and evening averages for weekday, Saturday, and Sunday, to obtain $BWIPavg_i$ and $BWOVavg_i$.

QoS resource management implements bandwidth reservation logic to favor connections routed on the first-choice CRLSP in situations of link congestion. If link congestion (or traffic lost/delayed) is detected, bandwidth reservation is immediately triggered and the reservation level N is set for the link according to the level of link congestion. In this manner bandwidth allocation requests attempting to alternate route over a congested link are subject to bandwidth reservation, and first-choice CRLSP requests are favored for that link. At the same time, the LL and HL link state thresholds are raised accordingly in order to accommodate the reserved bandwidth capacity N for the VNET. Figure 6.11 illustrates bandwidth allocation and the mechanisms by which bandwidth is protected through bandwidth reservation. Under normal bandwidth allocation demands, bandwidth is fully shared, but under overloaded bandwidth allocation demands, bandwidth is protected through the reservation mechanisms wherein each VNET can use its allocated bandwidth. Under failure, however, the reservation mechanisms operate

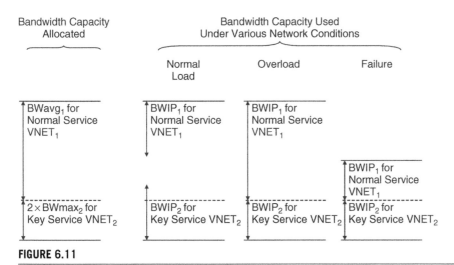

FIGURE 6.11

Bandwidth allocation, protection, and priority routing.

to give the key VNET its allocated bandwidth before the normal-priority VNET gets its bandwidth allocation. The best-effort, low-priority VNET is not allocated bandwidth nor is bandwidth reserved for the best-effort VNET.

The reservation level N (e.g., N may have one of four levels) is calculated for each link k based on the link traffic lost/delayed level of bandwidth allocation requests. The link traffic lost/delayed level is equal to the total requested but rejected (or overflow) link bandwidth allocation (measured in total bandwidth), divided by the total requested link bandwidth allocation, over the last periodic update interval, which is, for example, every 3 min. That is,

$BWOV_k$ = total requested bandwidth allocation rejected (or overflow) on link
$BWOF_k$ = total requested or offered bandwidth allocation on link k
$LLDL_k$ = link traffic lost/delayed level on link k = $BWOV_k/BWOF_k$

If $LLDL_k$ exceeds a threshold value, the reservation level N is calculated accordingly. The reserved bandwidth and link states are calculated based on the total link bandwidth required on link k, $TRBW_k$, which is computed on-line, for example, every 1-min interval m, and approximated as follows:

$$TRBW_k(m) = .5 \times TRBW_k(m - 1) + .5 \times [1.1 \times TBWIP_k(m) + TBWOV_k(m)]$$

$TBWIP_k$ = sum of the bandwidth in progress ($BWIP_i$) for all VNETs i for bandwidth requests on their first-choice CRLSP over link k
$TBWOV_k$ = sum of bandwidth overflow ($BWOV_i$) for all VNETs i for bandwidth requests on their first choice CRLSP over link k

Therefore the reservation level and load state boundary thresholds are proportional to the estimated required bandwidth load, which means that the bandwidth reserved and the bandwidth required to constitute a lightly loaded link rise and fall with the bandwidth load, as, intuitively, they should.

Per-VNET Bandwidth Allocation/Reservation: Sparse Network Case

Here we discuss a sparse network alternative approach for bandwidth allocation/reservation. For the sparse network case of bandwidth reservation, a simpler method is illustrated that takes advantage of the concentration of traffic onto fewer, higher capacity backbone links. A small, fixed level of bandwidth reservation is used and permanently enabled on each link.

The DEPTH load state threshold again is a function of bandwidth-in-progress, VNET priority, and bandwidth allocation thresholds; however, only the reserved (R) and nonreserved (NR) states are used.

The corresponding load state table for the sparse network case shows that the reservation level is fixed and not dependent on any link lost/delayed level (*LLDL*) calculation or total required bandwidth (*TRBW*) calculation. Therefore *LLDL* and *TRBW* monitoring are not required in this candidate bandwidth allocation/protection method.

6.5.2 **Per-Flow Bandwidth Allocation, Protection, and Reservation**

Per-flow QoS resource management methods have been applied successfully in TDM-based networks, where bandwidth allocation is determined by edge nodes based on bandwidth demand for each connection request. Based on the bandwidth demand, these edge nodes make changes in bandwidth allocation using, for example, a per-flow CRLSP QoS resource management approach illustrated in this section. Again, the determination of the link load states is used for QoS resource management in order to select network capacity on either the first-choice path or alternate paths. Also the allowed DEPTH load state threshold determines if an individual connection request can be admitted on a given link to an available bandwidth "depth." In setting up each connection request, the ON encodes the DEPTH load state threshold allowed on each link in the connection-setup IE. If a link is encountered at a VN in which the idle link bandwidth and link load state are below the allowed DEPTH load state threshold, then the VN sends a crank-back/bandwidth-not-available IE to the ON, which can then route the connection request to an alternate path choice. For example, in Figure 6.10, path A-B-E may be the first path tried where link A-B is in the LL state and link B-E is in the R state. If the DEPTH load state allowed is HL or better, then the connection request is routed on link A-B but will not be admitted on link B-E, wherein the connection request will be cranked back to the originating node A to try alternate path A-C-D-E. Here the connection request succeeds, as all links have a state of HL or better.

Per-Flow Bandwidth Allocation/Reservation: Meshed Network Case

Here again, two approaches are illustrated for bandwidth allocation reservation: one applicable to meshed network topologies and the other to sparse topologies. In meshed networks, a greater number of links result in less traffic carried per link, and functions such as bandwidth reservation need to be controlled more carefully than in a sparse network. In a sparse network the traffic is concentrated on much larger and many fewer links, and here bandwidth reservation does not have to be managed as carefully (such as automatically triggering bandwidth reservation on and off, dependent on the link/network congestion level).

This section discusses a meshed network alternative approach for bandwidth allocation/reservation, followed by the sparse network case.

The illustrative DEPTH load state threshold is a function of bandwidth-in-progress, service priority, and bandwidth allocation thresholds. Note that all parameters are specified per ON-DN pair and that the QoS resource management method provides for key service and best-effort service. Key services are given higher priority routing treatment by allowing greater path selection DEPTH than normal services. Best-effort services are given lower priority routing treatment by allowing lesser path selection DEPTH than normal. The quantities $BWavg_i$ are computed periodically, such as every week w, and can be averaged exponentially over a several-week period, as follows:

$$BWavg_i(w) = .5 \times BWavg_i(w - 1) + .5 \times [BWIPavg_i(w) + BWOVavg_i(w)]$$

$BWIPavg_i$ = average bandwidth-in-progress across a load set period on VNET i
$BWOVavg_i$ = average bandwidth overflow across a load set period

where $BWIP_i$ and $BWOV_i$ are averaged across various load set periods, such as morning, afternoon, and evening averages for weekday, Saturday, and Sunday, to obtain $BWIPavg_i$ and $BWOVavg_i$.

The illustrative QoS resource management method implements bandwidth reservation logic to favor connections routed on the first-choice path in situations of link congestion. If link traffic lost/delayed is detected, bandwidth reservation is immediately triggered and the reservation level N is set for the link according to the level of link congestion. In this manner traffic attempting to alternate route over a congested link is subject to bandwidth reservation, and the first-choice path traffic is favored for that link. At the same time, the LL and HL link state thresholds are raised accordingly in order to accommodate the reserved bandwidth capacity for the VNET. The reservation level N (e.g., N may have one of four levels) is calculated for each link k based on the link traffic lost/delayed level and the estimated link traffic. The link traffic lost/delayed level is equal to the equivalent bandwidth overflow count divided by the equivalent bandwidth peg count over the last periodic update interval, which is typically 3 min. That is,

$BWOV_k$ = equivalent bandwidth overflow count on link k
$BWPC_k$ = equivalent bandwidth peg count on link k
$LLDL_k$ = link traffic lost/delayed level on link k = $BWOV_k/BWPC_k$

If $LLDL_k$ exceeds a threshold value, the reservation level N is calculated accordingly. The reserved bandwidth and link states are calculated based on the total link bandwidth required on link k, TBW_k, which is computed on-line, for example, every 1-min interval m, and approximated as follows:

$$TBW_k(m) = .5 \times TBW_k(m - 1) + .5 \times [1.1 \times TBWIP_k(m) + TBWOV_k(m)]$$

$TBWIP_k$ = sum of the bandwidth in progress ($BWIP_i$) for all VNETs i for connections on their first-choice path over link k
$TBWOV_k$ = sum of bandwidth overflow ($BWOV_i$) for all VNETs i for connections on their first-choice path over link k

Therefore the reservation level and load state boundary thresholds are proportional to the estimated required bandwidth traffic load, which means that the bandwidth reserved and the bandwidth required to constitute a lightly loaded link rise and fall with the traffic load, as, intuitively, they should.

Per-Flow Bandwidth Allocation/Reservation: Sparse Network Case

Here we discuss a sparse network alternative approach for bandwidth allocation/reservation. For the sparse network case of bandwidth reservation, a simpler method is illustrated that takes advantage of the concentration of traffic onto fewer, higher capacity backbone links. A small, fixed level of bandwidth reservation is used on each link.

The DEPTH load state threshold again is a function of bandwidth-in-progress, VNET priority, and bandwidth allocation thresholds; however only the R and NR states are used.

Note that reservation level is fixed and not dependent on any *LLDL* calculation or *TRBW* calculation. Therefore *LLDL* and *TRBW* monitoring is not required in this alternative approach to QoS resource management.

6.6 QUEUING MECHANISMS

QoS resource management functions include class-of-service identification, routing table derivation, connection admission, bandwidth allocation, bandwidth protection, bandwidth reservation, priority routing, and priority queuing. This section discusses priority queuing as an illustrative traffic scheduling method and further assumes that a traffic shaper function is employed, such as a leaky-bucket model, to determine out-of-contract traffic behavior and appropriately mark packets for possible dropping under congestion. These scheduling and shaping mechanisms complement the connection admission mechanisms described in the previous sections to appropriately allocate bandwidth on links in the network.

Note that priority queuing is used as an illustrative scheduling mechanism, whereas other methods may be used. DiffServ does not require that a particular queuing mechanism be used to achieve EF, AF, etc. QoS. Therefore the queuing implementation used for DiffServ could be weighted fair queuing (WFQ), priority queuing (PQ), or another queuing mechanism, depending on the choice in the implementation. In the analysis, PQ is used for illustration; however, the same or comparable results would be obtained with WFQ or other queuing mechanisms.

In addition to the QoS bandwidth management procedure for bandwidth allocation requests, a QoS priority of service queuing capability is used during the time connections are established on each of the three VNETs. At each link, a queuing discipline is maintained such that the packets being served are given priority in the following order: key VNET services, normal VNET services, and best-effort VNET services. Following the MPLS CRLSP bandwidth allocation setup and the application of QoS resource management rules, the priority of service parameter and label parameter needs to be sent in each IP packet, as illustrated in Figure 6.12. The priority of service parameter may be included in the type of service (ToS), or differentiated services (DiffServ), parameter already in the IP packet header. In the IP/MPLS case, the priority of service parameter is associated with the MPLS label appended to the IP packet. In either case, from the priority of service parameters, the IP node can determine the QoS treatment based on the QoS resource management (priority queuing) rules for key VNET packets, normal VNET packets, and best effort VNET packets. In the IP/MPLS case, the MPLS label allows the IP/MPLS node to determine the next node to route the IP packet to, as well as the QoS treatment for the packet, which achieves a straightforward implementation of QoS resource management and MPLS routing.

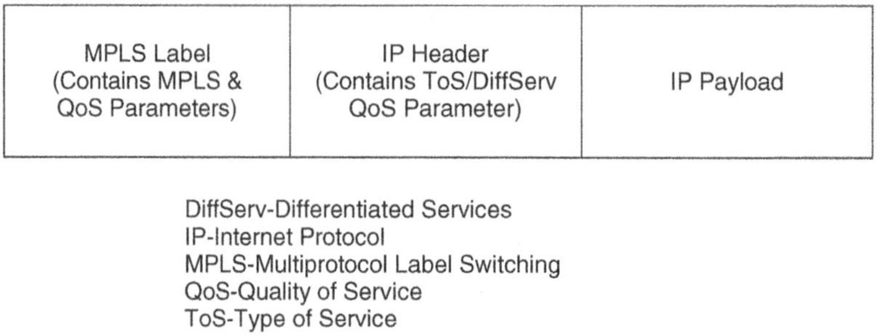

MPLS Label (Contains MPLS & QoS Parameters)	IP Header (Contains ToS/DiffServ QoS Parameter)	IP Payload

DiffServ-Differentiated Services
IP-Internet Protocol
MPLS-Multiprotocol Label Switching
QoS-Quality of Service
ToS-Type of Service

FIGURE 6.12

IP packet structure under MPLS packet switching.

6.7 INTERNET QOS RESOURCE MANAGEMENT

In current practice, internetwork routing protocols in packet networks generally do not incorporate standardized path selection or per class-of-service QoS resource management. For example, in IP-based networks, BGP is used for internetwork routing but does not incorporate per class-of-service resource allocation as described in this section. Also, MPLS techniques are still in progress for internetwork applications, such as path computation element (PCE) capability. In the PCE architecture, path computation does not occur on the head-end (ingress) LSR, but on some other path computation entity that may not be physically located on the head-end LSR. The PCE capability supports applications within a single domain or within a group of domains, where a domain is a layer, IGP area, or AS with limited visibility from the head-end LSR. The protocol for communication between LSRs and PCEs, and between cooperating PCEs, will enable requests for path computation, including a full set of constraints and the ability to return multiple paths, as well as security, authentication, and confidentiality mechanisms. This includes both intradomain and interdomain TE LSPs, the generation of primary, protection, and recovery paths, as well as computations for (local/global) reoptimization and load balancing.

Extensions to internetwork routing methods discussed in this section therefore can be considered to extend the call/session routing and connection routing concepts to routing between networks. Internetwork routing can also apply class-of-service routing concepts described in Section 6.4 and increased routing flexibility for internetwork routing. Principles discussed in Section 6.4 for class-of-service derivation and policy-based routing table derivation also apply in the case of internetwork QoS resource management. Internetwork routing works synergistically with multiple ingress/egress routing and alternate routing through transit networks. Internetwork routing can use link status information in combination with connection completion history to select paths and also use dynamic bandwidth reservation techniques.

Internetwork routing can use the virtual network concept that enables service integration by allocating bandwidth for services and using dynamic bandwidth reservation controls. These virtual network concepts have been described in this chapter and can be extended directly to internetwork routing. For example, links connected to the originating network border nodes can define VNET bandwidth allocation, protection, reservation, and routing methods. In that way, bandwidth can be fully shared among virtual networks in the absence of congestion. When a certain virtual network encounters congestion, bandwidth is reserved to ensure that the virtual network reaches its allocated bandwidth. Internetwork routing can employ class-of-service routing capabilities, including key service protection, directional flow control, link selection capability, automatically updated time-variable bandwidth allocation, and alternate routing capability through the use of overflow paths and control parameters such as internetwork routing load set periods. Link capability selection allows specific link characteristics, such as fiber transmission, to be preferentially selected. Thereby internetwork routing can improve performance and reduce the cost of the internetwork with flexible routing capabilities.

Similar to intranetwork routing, internetwork routing may include the following steps for connection establishment:

- At the originating border node (OBN), the destination border node (DBN), SI, VNET, and QoS resource management information are determined through the number/name translation database and other service information available at the OBN.
- The DBN and QoS resource management information are used to access the appropriate VNET and routing table between the OBN and the DBN.
- The connection request is set up over the first available path in the routing table with the required transmission resource selected based on the QoS resource management data.

The rules for selecting the internetwork primary path and alternate paths for a connection can be governed by the availability of primary path bandwidth, node-to-node congestion, and link capability. The path sequence consists of the primary shortest path, lightly loaded alternate paths, heavily loaded alternate paths, and reserved alternate paths, where these load states are refined further by combining link load state information with path congestion state information. Internetwork alternate paths, which include nodes in the originating network and terminating network, are selected before alternate paths that include via-network nodes are selected. Greater path selection depth is allowed if congestion is detected to the destination network because more alternate path choices serve to reduce the congestion. During periods of no congestion, capacity not needed by one virtual network is made available to other virtual networks that are experiencing loads above their allocation.

The border node, for example, automatically computes the bandwidth allocations once a week and uses a different allocation for various load set periods, for example, each of 36 two-hour load set periods: 12 weekday, 12 Saturday, and 12 Sunday. The allocation of the bandwidth can be based on a rolling average of the traffic load for each of the virtual networks, to each destination node, in each of the load set periods. Under normal no-congestion network conditions, all virtual networks fully share all available capacity, but under network congestion link bandwidth is reserved to ensure that each virtual network gets the amount of bandwidth allotted. This dynamic bandwidth reservation during times of congestion results in network performance that is analogous to having the link bandwidth allocation between the two nodes dedicated for each VNET.

Traffic Engineering and QoS Optimization of Integrated Voice & Data Networks by Ash provides an analysis of the TQO methods by modeling a full-scale 135-node network to study the TQO scenarios and trade-offs.

6.8 SUMMARY AND CONCLUSIONS

The conclusions reached in this chapter are as follows:

- Class-of-service routing is an important capability of converged TQO networks to define table-driven service elements and component application/network capabilities to avoid software development, network element development, and new network implementation for new service deployment.
- Bandwidth reservation is critical to the stable and efficient performance of TQO methods in a network and to ensure the proper operation of multiservice bandwidth allocation, protection, and priority treatment.
- Per-VNET bandwidth allocation is essentially equivalent to per-flow bandwidth allocation in network performance and efficiency. Because of the much lower routing table management overhead requirements, per-VNET bandwidth allocation is preferred to per-flow allocation.
- QoS resource management is shown to be effective in achieving key service, normal service, and best-effort service differentiation.

Both MPLS QoS and bandwidth management and DiffServ priority queuing management are important for ensuring that multiservice network performance objectives are met under a range of network conditions. Both mechanisms operate together to ensure that QoS resource allocation mechanisms (bandwidth allocation, protection, and priority queuing) are achieved.

6.9 APPLICABILITY OF REQUIREMENTS

Bandwidth reservation, per-VNET bandwidth allocation, and QoS resource management are already in widespread use in TDM-based dynamic routing networks. These methods are extensible to IP/MPLS networks, as demonstrated in this chapter.

Such methods are shown to provide robust and efficient networks and are applicable to both intranetwork and internetwork dynamic routing networks.

Based on these and other results presented in this book, we give service provider requirements for a standardized GTQO protocol, which includes generic service aspects, management aspects, and CAC aspects. These GTQO protocol requirements would then be used to drive the vendor implementations in the direction of network operator requirements and vendor interoperability. Service providers and their customers would benefit from these capabilities in terms of network performance and profitability, as demonstrated in this chapter and throughout this book. Service provider interest in adopting such TQO features then also leads to vendor profitability if their products support these features.

MPLS Traffic Engineering Recovery Mechanisms

Multi-Protocol Label Switching (MPLS) traffic engineering (TE) has encountered an ineluctable success during the past years, which led to the development of a rich set of MPLS TE recovery techniques.

This chapter, from *Network Recovery: Protection and Restoration of Optical, SONET-SDH, IP, and MPLS* by Vasseur, Pickavet, and Demeester, examines the MPLS recovery techniques with the objective to provide a detailed description of their mode of operation and their respective pros and cons, the type of the network design they preferably apply to, and aspects of design that operators find important for deployment in their network.

Furthermore, various properties of each recovery technique are analyzed. These properties are of the utmost importance when choosing a particular recovery technique in a network: the recovery time, the impact on scalability, the ability to provide some quality-of-service (QoS) guarantees along the alternate path, and the technique efficiency with respect to the amount of bandwidth dedicated to recovery path. These are just a subset of the aspects covered for each recovery technique.

This chapter covers the default restoration mode of operation of MPLS TE, as well as the global and local protection recovery schemes. A rich set of examples are provided throughout this chapter that illustrate the mode of operation and how those various recovery techniques can be deployed in a network. An entire section of this chapter in *Network Recovery: Protection and Restoration of Optical, SONET-SDH, IP, and MPLS* is devoted to a complete set of case studies that show how an operator can use those MPLS recovery techniques to satisfy a set of recovery objectives while respecting network constraints. This first part of this chapter includes the standardization aspects of the MPLS TE recovery techniques. Then, the second part of this chapter is devoted to some advanced topics of MPLS recovery. The aim of those two sections is to cover in detail the signaling aspects of MPLS local protection (Section 7.12) and the interesting topic of the backup path computation (Section 7.13).

7.1 MPLS TRAFFIC ENGINEERING TERMINOLOGY

Because there are several terms specific to MPLS TE recovery techniques, which are used throughout this chapter, we illustrate each of them via an example (Figure 7.1).   **157**

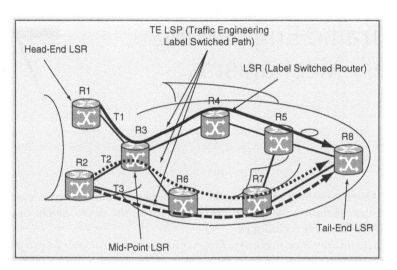

FIGURE 7.1

Illustration of MPLS traffic engineering recovery.

As depicted in Figure 7.1, three TE LSPs, called T1, T2, and T3, are signaled. For instance, the TE LSP T1 starts on R1 and terminates on R8. We say that R1 is the head-end label switched router (LSR) of T1 and R8 is its head-end LSR. Any other LSR traversed by T1 is a midpoint LSR (e.g., R3, R4, and R5 are all midpoint LSRs). Note that an LSR can play the role of a head-end LSR for an LSP while being a midpoint or a tail-end LSR for other TE LSPs.

Notion of Disjoint Paths

Two TE LSPs are said to be link disjoint if they do not have any link in common (e.g., T1 and T2 in Figure 7.1 are link disjoint). The terminology link diverse is also used. On the other hand, two TE LSPs are said to be node disjoint if they do not share any TE LSR (e.g., T1 and T3 are node disjoint), except potentially their head-end and tail-end LSRs. The term node diverse is also used.

The recovery-specific terminology aspects are covered in their respective sections. For instance, several terms are specific to the local protection techniques, and these are covered in the section devoted to local protection techniques.

Shared Risk Link Group

The notion of shared risk link group (SRLG) is crucial when studying network resiliency and specifically refers to the notion of simultaneous failures of multiple network elements that can be caused by the failure of a single element. Let us consider the network scenario in Figure 7.2.

Figure 7.2A shows a set of six optical cross-connect OXC1 through OXC6, which are interconnected by a set of fibers, which constitutes an optical layer

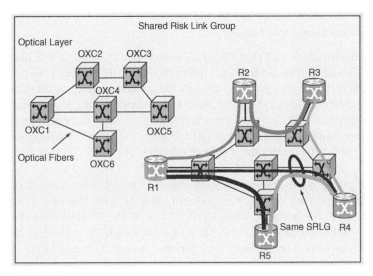

FIGURE 7.2

Shared risk link group.

used to interconnect the LSRs R1 through R5. More precisely, the various links are routed in the optical layer as follows:

- Link R1-R2 follows the optical path OXC1-OXC2.
- Link R1-R4 follows the optical path OXC1-OXC4-OXC5.
- Link R1-R5 follows the optical path OXC1-OXC6.
- Link R2-R3 follows the optical path OXC2-OXC3.
- Link R3-R4 follows the optical path OXC3-OXC5.
- Link R5-R4 follows the optical path OXC6-OXC4-OXC5.

In this scenario, the two optical paths followed by the links R1-R4 and R4-R5 share a common resource: the optical fiber interconnecting the OXC4 and OXC5. We say that the two links share a unique *SRLG* because the failure of a single resource (the optical fiber OXC4-OXC5) would provoke the simultaneous failure of the two links.

By default the IP/MPLS layer does not have any visibility of the optical layout, which may lead to an incorrect path selection for TE a LSP. To remedy to this problem, an Internet Gateway Protocol (IGP) extension has been defined. The TE-related information is flooded within an OSPF area using an opaque LSA type 10 (for IS-IS the TE-related information is flooded in a specific type-length value, TLV). This opaque LSA carries one top-level TLV, which can be one of the two following types: router address (type 1) or link (type 2). The link sub-TLV is made of several sub-TLVs. One of them is the SRLG sub-TLV (type 16); it has a variable length with 4 bytes per SRLG value.

Important notes:
- A link may belong to multiple SRLGs.

- The IGP extensions allow carrying the SRLG values. On the other hand, having the knowledge of the underlying optical/SONET-SDH topology is not always possible. Indeed, an operator may rely on another carrier to provide optical lambda, and in that case, the SP does not always have the knowledge of the actual physical path and the potential SRLG. Moreover, an optical path may be dynamic and so its path may change over the time. This requires updating the SRLG value each time a change occurs if the SRLG changes also.

Notion of SRLG disjoint: A TE LSP is said to be *SRLG disjoint* from a link L or a node R if and only if its path does not include any link or node that is part of the SRLG of that L or R. For instance, back Figure 7.2, a TE LSP T1 following the path R1-R2-R3-R4 is SRLG disjoint from the link R1-R4. Two TE LSPs are said to be SRLG disjoint if the respective set of links they traverse do not have any SRLG in common.

7.1.1 MPLS Traffic Engineering Components

The aim of this section is to review the main components of MPLS TE:

1. *Configuration of TE LSP on head-end LSR:* The first step consists of configuring the TE LSPs' attributes on the head-end LSR. Various attributes can be configured like the destination (address of the tail-end LSR), the required bandwidth, the required protection/restoration, the affinities, and others.

2. *Topology and resource information distribution:* To compute a path obeying the set of specified constraint(s), the head-end LSR needs to gather topology and resource information. Note that this applies only to situations in which the TE LSPs path is dynamically computed by each LSR (also referred to as *distributed* or *on-line* path computation) by contrast with *centralized* or *off-line* path computation in which the LSPs' path is computed by an off-line tool. In such a case, the topology and resource information is distributed by a link state routing protocol (OSPF or IS-IS) with TE extensions that reflect links characteristics and reservation states. TE TLVs have been defined and are carried within an LSP for IS-IS and TE opaque LSA type 10 for OSPF to flood the reservation states and other parameters.

3. *TE LSP computation:* As already stated, the computation of a TE LSP path can either be performed by an off-line tool or on-line. In the former case, an external tool simultaneously computes all the TE LSPs paths according to the network resources. In the latter case, every router (LSR) uses its resource and topology database (IS-IS or OSPF), takes into account the set of requirements of the TE LSP, and computes the shortest path satisfying the

set of constraints usually using a constraint shortest path first (CSPF) algorithm. Various types of CSPFs can be used.

4. *TE LSP setup:* Once the path of a TE LSP has been computed, the head-end LSR signals the TE LSP by means of the Resource Reservation Protocol (RSVP) signaling protocol with the corresponding set of extensions defined as RSVP-TE. For instance, in Figure 7.1, R1 computes a path for the LSP T1: R1-R3-R4-R5-R8 based on T1's attributes and the network and resources topology information disseminated by the routing protocol. Once T1's path is computed, T1 is signaled by RSVP-TE. TE LSPs are then signaled, maintained (refreshed) and potentially torn down using various RSVP messages: Path, Resv, Path Error, Path Tear, Reservation Error, Resv Confirmation, and Resv Tear. Also, various new objects have been defined in RSVP-TE for the purpose of MPLS TE, for example, to allocate labels to TE LSPs that will then be used in the MPLS data plane. Note that labels are assigned in the upstream direction using RSVP messages (Resv message) and intermediate LSRs are programmed accordingly. For instance, when the TE LSP T1 is signaled, labels are assigned by LSRs in the upstream direction: R8 provides a label to R5, R5 provides a label to R4, and so on.

Note: It is worth mentioning that RSVP has often been criticized for its scalability, in particular the number of states required in the network. As a matter of fact, currently deployed networks can handle thousands of RSVP TE reservations (TE LSPs) on a single router without any problem. Moreover, various protocol enhancements have been defined to further increase the scalability, if needed. Finally, MPLS TE can be deployed with multiple levels of hierarchies, if required, in very large networks.

5. *Packet forwarding:* Once a TE LSP is set up, the head-end LSR can update its routing table and start using TE LSP to forward IP packets. A label of 32 bits is pushed onto the IP packet, which is then label switched across the network (intermediate routers do not make any routing decision).

7.1.2 Notion of Preemption in MPLS Traffic Engineering

There is one interesting property called "preemption" defined in MPLS TE, which deserves to be slightly elaborated in the chapter because upon network element failure, preemption mechanisms may be triggered. RSVP-TE defines the notion of preemption or priority for a TE LSP. This parameter is signaled in the SESSION-ATTRIBUTE object of the RSVP TE Path message (more precisely, the RFC defines two priorities known as the "setup" and "holding" priorities, which define the priority of a TE LSP with respect to taking and holding resources, respectively).

When a new TE LSP is signaled, an LSR considers the admission of this newly signaled TE LSP by comparing the requested bandwidth with the bandwidth available at the priority specified in the setup priority. If the requested bandwidth is available but this requires preempting other TE LSPs having a lower priority, then the newly signaled TE LSP is admitted and one or more TE LSPs with a lower priority are preempted. Note that the selection of the set of lower priority TE LSPs to be preempted is a local decision and is generally implementation specific.

The preemption process implies the set of following actions for each preempted TE LSP:

- The corresponding local RSVP states are cleared and the traffic is no longer forwarded.

- Messages are sent both upstream (RSVP Path Error message) and downstream (RSVP Resv Error) so all the states corresponding to the preempted TE LSP are cleared along its path. Then the head-LSR LSR of a preempted TE LSP initiates a TE reroute procedure as detailed earlier to reroute the TE LSP along another path.

This means that hard preemption is by nature a *disruptive* mode. So the concept of soft preemption has been introduced and proposes a different mode of preemption. If a TE LSP must be preempted to accommodate a higher priority TE LSP requests, the preempting LSR performs the following actions:

- The preempting LSP signals to the respective head-end LSR the need to reroute the TE LSP in a nondisruptive fashion (so-called "make before break" procedure).

- The local states of the soft preempted TE LSP are not cleared and no RSVP Path Error/RSVP Error messages are sent.

Hence, the preempting node keeps forwarding the traffic of a soft preempted TE LSP for a certain period. This gives a chance for the soft preempted TE LSPs head-end LSR to reroute their TE LSPs along an alternate path without disrupting traffic flow.

It is worth pointing out that this implies to temporary provoke reservation overbooking on some links because until the soft preempted TE LSPs are rerouted by their respective head-end LSR, the sum of admitted bandwidth is higher than the maximum allowed. Note that some algorithms can be carefully designed to preempt hard preemptable[62] TE LSPs first. Moreover, appropriate MPLS Diffserv mechanisms can be used to make sure that high-priority traffic is served adequately.

7.2 ANALYSIS OF THE RECOVERY CYCLE

Before studying the various recovery techniques used in IP/MPLS networks, it is worth spending some time on the recovery cycle analysis depicted in Figure 7.3.

---

[62] The hard/soft preemptable property of a TE LSP is explicitly signaled in RSVP Path message.

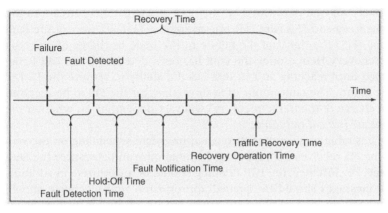

FIGURE 7.3

Recovery cycle.

7.2.1 **Fault Detection Time**

As with any other recovery techniques at any layer, the fault detection time is a key component of the total recovery time and highly varies depending on the fault detection mechanism in use and the underlying layer 1 and layer 2. For instance, the fault detection time can vary from a few tens of milliseconds when two LSRs are interconnected via a SONET/SDH VC or an optical lightpath to a few hundreds of milliseconds or seconds when *hello* mechanisms are required.

7.2.2 **Hold-Off Timer**

A hold-off timer can be very useful if the underlying layer has a recovery scheme. In a nutshell, consider, for instance, a multilayer network where fast recovery mechanisms are implemented both at the optical layer and at the MPLS layer. Then, when the failure occurs, one should generally avoid any racing conditions where both recovery mechanisms simultaneously try to perform a reroute along an alternate path. In that case, a bottom-up timer-based approach can be adopted, in which the MPLS layer will wait for a hold-off timer to expire before trying to perform a reroute, to give the optical layer a chance to restore the failed resources. If the optical layer does not succeed in restoring the failed resource before the hold-off timer expires, the MPLS recovery mechanism will be triggered to restore the failed resource at the MPLS layer.

7.2.3 **Fault Notification Time**

To perform traffic recovery, an LSR must first be informed of the failure. As we will see in this chapter, depending on the MPLS TE recovery mechanism used, the traffic recovery may be performed on the node immediately upstream to the failure or on the head-end LSR (the LSR originating the TE LSP); we call the fault indication signal (FIS) the signal of the failure to the node in charge of performing the traffic recovery. Hence, once the fault has been detected by an LSR R, the FIS is propagated until reaching an LSR that has the ability to reroute the TE LSP affected by the failure. The fault notification time (time for the FIS to be received by the node in charge of the traffic recovery) will vary depending on whether the recovery technique is *local* or *global*.

It is usually desirable to guarantee through appropriate scheduling on the various LSRs that the FIS receives the proper QoS, to minimize and guarantee the fault notification time. For instance, the IGP flooding should be prioritized. In addition, IGP and RSVP messages should be queued appropriately and of course should never be dropped in the case of congestion. Refer to Chapter 6 for further details on QoS mechanisms.

RSVP Reliable Messaging

IGP updates are always sent in reliable mode; this is inherent to link state routing protocols. By contrast, RSVP messages are sent by default in nonreliable mode. So a loss of a Path Error message (which is used to report an LSP failure to upstream nodes) may significantly increase the fault notification time, especially if the IGP has not been tuned to provide fast notification. Refresh reduction proposes a mechanism to send RSVP messages in reliable mode.

Two additional RSVP objects are defined: the MESSAGE-ID and the MESSAGE-ID-ACK objects. Each RSVP message sent in reliable mode contains a unique MESSAGE-ID object and is acknowledged by a MESSAGE-ID-ACK object (note that it may be piggybacked to any other RSVP messages or to an RSVP acknowledgment message). The retransmission of a nonacknowledged message for which an explicit acknowledgment had been requested is based on an exponential back-off procedure; when an LSR has to send a message in reliable mode, it inserts a MESSAGE-ID object in the RSVP message and sets a particular flag in the MESSAGE-ID header called the *ACK-Desired* flag. Upon receiving the RSVP message, a neighboring LSR will send back an RSVP message containing a MESSAGE-ID-ACK object. When the message is acknowledged, the transmission procedure is terminated. If the sending LSR does not receive any acknowledgment before a dynamic timer has elapsed, the message is retransmitted. The dynamic timer Tk is exponentially increased until a maximum value is reached. Tk is first set to an initial retransmission value (generally a short value).

For example, let us suppose that a message is sent for the first time, and Tk = T1 is set to initial timer (the recommended value is 500 ms).

- If the message is not acknowledged after T1, then it is retransmitted. Otherwise the procedure is stopped.
- Then T_k is set to $T_{k-1} * (1 + delta)$ (the recommended value for delta is 1).
- The maximum value for k is set to a fixed value (k = 3 is recommended).

Table 7.1 Categories of MPLS Recovery Mechanisms.

	Protection	Restoration
Local recovery	Local protection (Section 75.5)	
Global recovery	Global protection (Section 57.4)	Global default restoration (Section 57.3)

In summary, the sending LSR waits 500 ms and then retransmits the message, then waits for the 500 ms*2, then 500 ms*4 with exponential increased waiting times. If the maximum retransmission value is set to 3, the message is no longer retransmitted after three trials.

7.2.4 Recovery Operation Time

Any recovery technique involves a set of actions to be completed. This includes potential synchronization between network elements to coordinate.

7.2.5 Traffic Recovery Time

The traffic recovery time represents the time between the last recovery action and the time the traffic is completely recovered. Each component described earlier is analyzed for the various recovery techniques described in this chapter. We just saw a brief description of each phase of the recovery cycle.

There are multiple types of MPLS TE recovery techniques (Table 7.1):

- MPLS TE *global default restoration* (Section 7.3). This is the default mode of recovery of MPLS TE, whereby the failure is notified to the head-end LSR by means of RSVP and the routing protocol, which in turn recomputes a new path and finally resignals the TE LSP along that new path.

- MPLS TE *global protection* (Section 7.4): The basic principle is that two TE LSPs are set up by the head-end LSR: a primary LSP and a backup. Once the head-end LSR is notified of a failure along the LSP path, it starts using the backup LSP.

- MPLS TE *local protection* (Fast Reroute; Section 7.5) is a *local* repair recovery scheme in which upon failure detection the LSPs affected by the failure are locally rerouted by the node immediately upstream to the failure.

7.3 MPLS TRAFFIC ENGINEERING GLOBAL DEFAULT RESTORATION

MPLS TE global default restoration is the default recovery technique. Once a failure is detected by some downstream node, the head-end LSR is notified by means of RSVP and the routing protocol (FIS). Upon receiving the notification, the head-end LSR recomputes the path and signals the LSP along an alternate path.

7.3.1 Fault Signal Indication

It is probably worth elaborating on the nature of the FIS in the context of MPLS TE because this aspect might be a source of confusion. In the context of an IP/MPLS TE network, the FIS is either an IGP update[63] or an RSVP Path Error message. Actually, both will be generated independently. In the case of the IGP, a node detecting a loss of routing adjacency will generate an LSA/LSP update. When a link fails between two nodes, the nodes attached to the failed link will send an IGP update. In the case of a node failure, all the neighbors of the failed node will send an IGP update. The timing sequence will highly depend on the failure detection time and IGP parameter tuning. Moreover, every node detecting a failure will also generate an RSVP Path Error message sent to each head-end LSR having a TE LSP traversing the failed resource. For instance, in Figure 7.1, if the link R3-R4 fails, as soon as the node R3 detects the link failure, it sends a notification (RSVP Path Error message) to R1, the head-end LSR of T1 because T1 traverses the failed link. In addition, an IGP update will be sent by both the nodes R3 and R4 to reflect the new topology. Again, the timing sequence depends on the IGP tuning. Usually, the RSVP Path Error message is received by the head-end LSRs within a few tens of milliseconds so generally before the IGP update, but regardless of which FIS is first received, the head-end LSR will get notified. As pointed out in Section 7.2, the FIS delivery is of the utmost importance with MPLS global default restoration, because it triggers the rerouting of the affected LSPs by the head-end LSR.

7.3.2 Mode of Operation

When a TE LSP is configured on a head-end LSR, its set of attributes is specified: destination (IP address of the tail-end LSR), bandwidth, priority, protection/restoration requirements, and other MPLS TE parameters. As far as the recovery is concerned, an important parameter is the TE LSP path. As mentioned in Section 7.1, the path of a TE LSP can be computed in either a distributed or a centralized fashion. In the former case, the configuration does not specify any particular path and the head-end LSR dynamically computes the LSP path, taking into account the constraints and available resources in the network. In the latter case, the path for the TE LSP is statically configured on the head-end LSR. Some MPLS TE implementations allow the configuration of both options with an order of preference.

In Table 7.2, a TE LSP is defined, with its corresponding parameters/constraints: destination address (10.0.1.100), bandwidth (10000), and priority (1). In addition,

---

[63] In the rest of this chapter, the term *IGP* will be used in place of *routing protocol*.

Table 7.2 An example of MPLS Traffic Engineering TE LSP Configuration.

---

interface Tunnel1
ip unnumbered Loopback0
no ip directed-broadcast
tunnel destination 10.0.1.100
tunnel mode mpls traffic-eng
tunnel mpls traffic-eng priority 1 1
tunnel mpls traffic-eng bandwidth 10000
tunnel mpls traffic-eng record-route
tunnel mpls traffic-eng path-option 1 explicit name path1
tunnel mpls traffic-eng path-option 2 explicit name path2
tunnel mpls traffic-eng path-option 3 dynamic

Path1 = {192.170.14.2, 192.170.10.1, 192.170.4.5}
Path2 = {192.170.13.2, 192.170.17.1, 192.170.20.5}

---

the notion of path-option allows specifying in order of preference the list of paths that the LSP should follow. In this example, the preferred path is a static path (path 1) for which the set of hops is statically configured on the head-end LSR. If path 1 is not available (path broken, not all the required constraints can be satisfied along this path), path 2 is the second preferred path. Note that this corresponds to the off-line path computation method already mentioned for MPLS TE where the LSP path is computed by some other tool (not by the head-end LSR itself). Then, if none of the static paths is available, the head-end LSR will try to find a path that complies with the requested constraints using the CSPF algorithm (this is the path option 3). Note that in addition, it might be possible to have different sets of constraints for different path options. For example, suppose that no path satisfying the bandwidth constraint (10000) can be found. Then one solution could be to try a lower value. Of course, that example of configuration shows a combination of static and dynamic paths for the sake of illustration. Just one dynamic path could have been configured or one or more static paths.

Recovery Cycle with Global Default Restoration

The mode of operation of global default restoration is relatively simple: When the head-end LSR is informed of the link/node failure, if an alternate path is specified, the head-end LSR will check to see whether the configured path satisfies the constraints for the TE LSP. If so, the TE LSP is reestablished along that path. If no preconfigured path is specified on the head-end router and if configured as such, then it triggers a new path computation for the set of affected TE LSPs, calling the CSPF process (this exactly corresponds to the example in Table 7.2: If a notification is received reporting that path 1 is unavailable, the head-end LSR tries to determine whether it can use path 2, and if path 2 is not valid for some reason, it tries to compute a path itself).

> *Note 1:* Various existing MPLS TE implementations allow relaxing constraint(s) upon failure, which might sometimes be necessary. A slightly more complicated example could be given in which for each path option, a set of different constraints is specified. For instance, consider a network with relatively high link utilization in terms of bandwidth reservation; a major node failure may cause the inability for several TE LSPs to find an alternative path. In this case, one of the options is to relax some constraints, like the bandwidth constraint so the TE LSP can be routed. There is one undesirable side effect though: Allowing a TE LSP to be rerouted as a 0 bandwidth TE LSP implies that traffic will flow over this tunnel without any CAC. Thus, no bandwidth can be guaranteed in this case. There are also various constraints a TE LSP can be configured to support. Bandwidth is just one of them. Another example is affinities. This allows, for instance, to ensure some TE LSPs will avoid particular network resources, using some bit masks. This can be seen as color. As an example, some network links might be colored in red (with red meaning "high propagation delay" or "poor quality"). This affinity link property is propagated through IGP TE extensions (OSPF-TE and IS-IS-TE). This way, a TE LSP carrying very sensitive traffic like voice-over-IP (VoIP) will be configured so red links are excluded from the path selection. In such a case, a major network failure may imply for the affected TE LSP to be non-reroutable without crossing one or several red links. In this case, it might be desirable to relax the affinity constraint.

> *Note 2:* A large proportion of deployed MPLS TE networks rely on distributed computation in which no static path is configured; in this case, just a dynamic path is configured and the head-end just recomputes a new path based on the LSP constraints its knowledge of the network and resource topology information provided by the IGP.

A usual question is: *What is the CSPF duration time?* And the systematic answer is: *That depends.* Indeed, the CSPF duration time is a function of the network size and the CSPF algorithm in use. Finding the shortest constraint path in a very large network obviously requires more time than in a small network. Furthermore, the CSPF complexity may be variable depending on the algorithm in use. Finally, the router CPU should also be taken into account. That said, in an order of magnitude, an average CSPF computation time using a classic CSPF algorithm on a network with hundreds of nodes rarely exceeds a few milliseconds. It is worth noting that one CSPF must be triggered per affected TE LSP. Indeed, if N LSPs starting on a head-end LSR R1 traverse a failed link, R1 will have to compute a new path for each of them.

Once a new path has been found and computed, the TE LSP is signaled along the new path. The final operation before any traffic can be routed over the newly

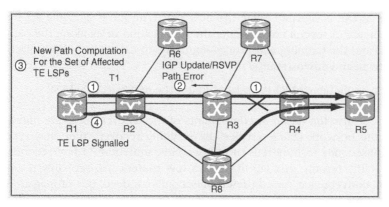

FIGURE 7.4

Event scheduling in the case of link/node failure with MPLS TE reroute.

signaled TE LSP consists of updating the routing table for the destinations that can be reached via the TE LSP.

7.3.3 Recovery Time

Providing hard numbers is not a realistic exercise because a significant number of factors influence the rerouting time, but we describe the different components of the recovery cycle with global default restoration through an example. Figure 7.4 shows the different steps of the recovery cycle with MPLS TE global default restoration.

Step 1: The link R3-R4 fails, and an FIS (RSVP and IGP update) is sent to the head-end LSR. As already pointed out, the sequence timing of IGP update and the RSVP Path Error depends of many factors. The receipt of one of them is sufficient for the head-end LSR to be notified of the failure.

Step 2: The FIS is sent to the head-end LSR. Note that the propagation delay might be nonnegligible and is made up of two components: the *propagation delay* (on wide area networks; this can be on the order of tens of milliseconds and can become as large as 100 ms between two continents where the optical path can be very long) and the *queuing and processing delays* for the FIS to reach the head-end router. As mentioned in Section 7.2, an appropriate marking and scheduling in the forwarding path is highly recommended to ensure that the queuing and processing delays are both minimized.

Step 3: Upon receiving the failure notification, the head-end LSR (R1 in this example) tries to find an alternate path satisfying the set of constraints for each TE LSP affected by the failure.

Step 4: The TE LSP is signaled along the new path. The RSVP signaling set up time is also made of several components: the propagation delay along the path (round trip) and the queuing and processing delays at each hop in both directions (upstream and downstream).

Step 5: The routing table of R1 is updated to use the newly signaled LSP.

In conclusion, because the different components of the recovery time are highly dependent of the network characteristics, the resulting recovery time may vary from a few milliseconds to hundreds of milliseconds, sometimes a few seconds. Testing MPLS traffic reroute in a lab made of a few routers will probably result in a very short convergence time (a few milliseconds); indeed, the propagation delays are negligible, as is the FIS processing delay. The CSPF computation is also very short because the network size is limited, and finally the set up time will also be negligible. In contrast, a network with 1000 nodes, links with high propagation delays, and hundreds of TE LSPs to reroute will require a much more significant amount of time to converge.

7.4 MPLS TRAFFIC ENGINEERING GLOBAL PATH PROTECTION

MPLS TE global path protection (also usually referred to as *path protection*) is a *global 1:1 protection* recovery mechanism. This implies that the head-end LSR performs the rerouting *(global recovery)* and a presignaled backup LSP is used *(protection)* if the protected LSP fails.

7.4.1 Mode of Operation

Figure 7.5 describes the mode of operation of global path protection. In this figure, there are two primary TE LSPs, T1 (which follows the path R2-R3-R4-R5-R6) and T2 (which follows the path R7-R8-R9-R6). For each primary TE LSP, a dedicated backup LSP is set up, before any failure occurs. It is worth noting that a backup TE LSP (also called *secondary TE LSP*) must be link diverse or node diverse from the primary TE LSP. In this example, the backup LSP of T1 follows the path R2-R1-R10-R11-R5-R12-R6, which is *link diverse*[64] from T1. By contrast, the backup LSP of T2 follows the path R7-R2-R3-R4-R5-R6 and is *node diverse* from T2. The aspects related to the backup path computation are covered in Section 7.13. A backup (secondary) TE LSP is a regular TE LSP; that is, as far as RSVP signaling is concerned, a backup TE LSP is signaled as any other TE LSP and the backup TE LSP can be configured with either the same attributes as the primary TE LSP (in

---

[64] The terms *disjoint* and *diverse* are used interchangeably.

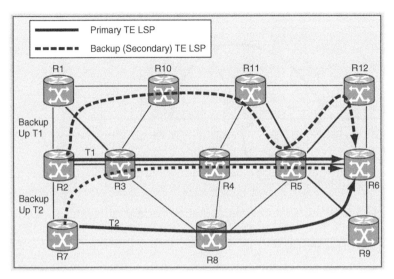

FIGURE 7.5

MPLS traffic engineering path protection.

this case, the backup TE LSP satisfies the same set of constraints as the primary TE LSP) or with different constraints (e.g., no affinities, less bandwidth [say, 50% of the primary TE LSP]). For instance, if the backup TE LSP is configured with 50% of the primary TE LSP bandwidth, when used, the traffic will be forwarded along a path where 50% of the bandwidth has been reserved. This does not mean that the traffic will suffer from QoS degradation, depending on the actual use of the other LSPs sharing the same network resources along its backup path.

The mode of operation is quite straightforward: Once the failure is detected by some downstream node, an FIS is sent to the head-end LSR of each affected LSP (by *affected LSP,* we mean each LSP traversing the failed resource).

Note that all the aspects related to the FIS delivery described in Section 7.3 identically apply here because both the global default restoration and the global path protection rely on the FIS delivery to trigger an LSP recovery.

Then upon receiving the FIS, the head-end LSR immediately switches the traffic onto the backup TE LSP and updates its routing table accordingly.

7.4.2 **Recovery Time**

Compared to global default restoration, no routing computation has to be done "on the fly" to find an alternate route for the failed TE LSP. Moreover, with global path protection, the backup tunnel is already signaled, so no signaling round is required to set up the backup TE LSP. It is important to note that the saving in convergence time is predominately provided by the presignaling of the TE LSP.

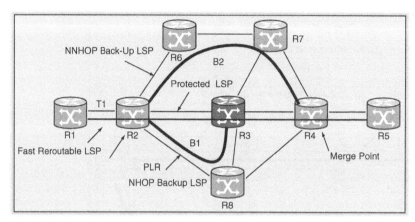

FIGURE 7.6

Terminology (MPLS local protection).

7.5 MPLS TRAFFIC ENGINEERING LOCAL PROTECTION

After a brief section introduction to the specific terminology used for MPLS TE local protection, we describe the principle and mode of operation of two local protection techniques called *MPLS TE Fast Reroute*. The last section describes two deployment strategies of local protection recovery techniques. Note that the terms *MPLS TE local protection* and *Fast Reroute* are used interchangeably throughout this chapter.

7.5.1 Terminology

We begin this section by defining the terminology specific to MPLS TE Fast Reroute through an example (Figure 7.6).

As shown in Figure 7.6, an LSP T1 is signaled that follows the path R1-R2-R3-R4-R5. T1 is said to be "fast reroutable" if it is signaled with a specific attribute set in the RSVP Path message that indicates its desire to benefit from local recovery in the case of a failure.[65] As shown in further subsections, Fast Reroute is a local protection recovery scheme; hence, the LSPs affected by a failure are locally rerouted by the node immediately upstream to the failure. This node is called the *point of local repair* (PLR). For instance, the node R2 is a PLR if the link R2-R3 or the node R3 fails. Fast Reroute uses backup tunnels to reroute affected LSPs. When a backup tunnel terminates to PLR's next hop (direct adjacent neighbor), it is an *NHOP backup tunnel*. When the backup tunnel terminates on the neighbor of the PLR's neighbor, the backup tunnel is an *NNHOP backup tunnel*. Back to

---

[65] See Section 5.14 for the details on RSVP signaling for Fast Reroute.

our example, B1 is an NHOP backup tunnel of the PLR R2 and B2 is an NNHOP backup tunnel of R2. The node where the backup tunnel terminates is called the *merge point* (MP); hence, R4 is the MP of B2. Finally, a fast-reroutable LSP is said to be protected at a node R if there exists a backup tunnel that can be used in the case of a failure. T1 is protected at R2 by B1 and B2.

The terminology of detour merge point used in one Fast Reroute technique (one-to-one protection) is discussed in Section 7.12.

7.5.2 **Principles of Local Protection Recovery Techniques**

We use the generic term *MPLS TE Fast Reroute* or *Fast Reroute* to describe local protection techniques. There are two techniques of Fast Reroute (both are local protection techniques) that are described in this chapter:

- *Facility backup* (also referred to as *bypass*)
- *One-to-one backup* (also referred to as *detour*)

Although the terminology might appear difficult to understand, the terminology used in this section is in line with the corresponding standardized documents.

Both methods described are local repair techniques using *local protection*:

- *Local:* In the case of a link or node failure, a TE LSP is rerouted by the node that is immediately upstream to the failed link or node. Compared to the global default restoration and global path protection where the TE LSP is rerouted by the head-end LSR, in the case of local protection, the protected LSP is rerouted at the closest location upstream to the failure. This presents the very significant advantage of eliminating the need for the FIS to be received by the head-end LSR to reroute the affected TE LSP along an alternate path.

- *Protection:* With protection recovery mechanisms, a backup resource is pre-allocated and signaled before the failure. With both local protection recovery methods (facility backup and one-to-one backup), the backup LSPs are established before the failure occurs. When a failure occurs and is detected, every protected TE LSP traversing the failed resource (usually referred to as *affected TE LSP*) is rerouted over a backup TE LSP without having to compute a backup path "on the fly."

Although both methods are local repair techniques, they significantly differ in terms of backup LSPs. With facility backup, a single (or a very limited number of) backup LSP(s) is used to protect all the fast-reroutable TE LSPs from the failure of a link or node, which is a major benefit of the MPLS label stacking property. By contrast, the one-to-one backup creates a separate backup LSP for each protected TE LSP at each hop. More details about their respective scalability are provided in Section 7.5.8.

To ease the understanding on each local protection technique, the following approach is followed: First, a quick overview of each local protection method is provided via an example. Then each method is described in detail in subsequent subsections.

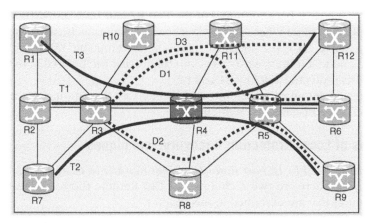

FIGURE 7.7

Illustration of the Detour LSP with one-to-one backup.

7.5.3 **Local Protection: One-to-One Backup**

As depicted in Figure 7.7, with one-to-one backup, at each hop, one backup LSP (called a *Detour LSP*) is created for each fast-reroutable TE LSP. So, for instance, at the node R3, to protect the set of fast-reroutable TE LSPs T1, T2, and T3, the following set of backup TE LSPs are set up:

- One Detour LSP D1 for the protected TE LSP T1, following the path R3-R10-R11-R5-R6
- One Detour LSP D2 for the protected TE LSP T2, following the path R3-R8-R5-R9
- One Detour LSP D3 for the protected TE LSP T3, following the path R3-R10-R11-R12

Note that this only protects the fast-reroutable TE LSPs T1, T2, and T3 against a failure of the link R3-R4 and the node R4. Similarly, each node along the fast-reroutable TE LSP paths will perform the same operation.

At each PLR along the fast-reroutable TE LSP path, a local backup tunnel called *Detour LSP* that avoids the protected resource and terminates on the tail-end LSR for the fast-reroutable TE LSP is set up. In the previous example, for the fast-reroutable TE LSP T1, R3 sets up a Detour LSP D1 originated at R3 and terminated at R6 that avoids both the link R3-R4 and the node R4.

Figure 7.8 shows the label allocation for both the primary TE LSP T1 and the Detour TE LSP D1 protecting T1 against a failure of either the link R3-R4 or the node R4. The respective labels of the protected TE LSP T1 and the Detour LSP D1 originated on R3 are shown in Figure 7.8.

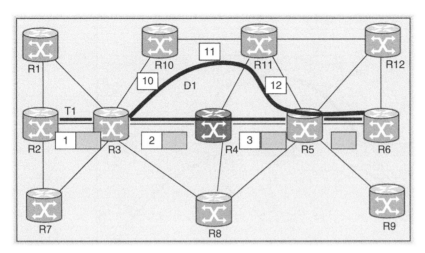

FIGURE 7.8

Mode of operation of one-to-one backup.

Detour LSP merging: Various merging rules allow for the reduction of the number of Detour LSPs and are described in Section 7.12.

7.5.4 Local Protection: "Facility Backup"

By contrast with one-to-one backup, with facility backup, just one backup tunnel per NHOP is required to protect against a link failure and one NNHOP backup tunnel is required to protect against a node failure. Of course, an NNHOP protects against not only a node failure (the bypassed node) but also the link between the immediately upstream node and the bypassed node. As discussed later, there are some benefits in setting up both NHOP and NNHOP backup tunnels. More accurately, a small set of backup tunnels may be required if bandwidth protection must be guaranteed (see Section 7.13 for more details on bandwidth protection), but the key point is that the number of required backup tunnels is not a function of the number of TE LSPs in the MPLS network, which is a crucial property to preserve scalability.

In Figure 7.9, a single NNHOP backup tunnel (bypass) is configured on R3 (PLR) to protect any fast reroutable TE LSP traversing the node R3 and following the R3-R4-R5 path against a failure of the link R3-R4 or the node R4 (indeed, the same NNHOP backup tunnel can be used in both failure scenarios). R5 is the merge point. Hence, for instance, the two fast-reroutable TE LSPs T1 and T2 are protected by the NNHOP bypass tunnel B1 that follows the path R3-R10-R11-R5.

Let us now consider a fast-reroutable TE LSP T1 that follows the path R2-R3-R4-R5-R6. As shown in Figure 7.9, the corresponding labels are distributed in RSVP

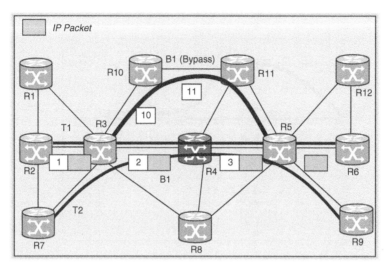

FIGURE 7.9

Facility backup operation.

Resv messages (R5 distributes the label "3" to R4, R4 distributes the label "2" to R3, R3 distributes the label "1" to R2). In this example, a bypass tunnel B1 starting at the PLR R3 is also set up to protect against a link failure of the link R3-R4 and a node failure of R4. The corresponding labels are depicted in Figure 7.9.

Note: In the case of an NHOP backup tunnel, this is often referred to as *MPLS TE Fast Reroute link protection*. When the backup tunnel is an NNHOP backup tunnel, this is usually called *MPLS TE Fast Reroute node protection*.

A PLR can have NHOP and NNHOP backup tunnels. Furthermore, a PLR can have multiple NHOP backup tunnels and multiple NNHOP backup tunnels between a pair of LSRs to guarantee the bandwidth to the protected LSPs. This is discussed in detail in Section 7.13.

Let us now consider a node failure and see the mode of operation of facility backup (Figure 7.10). As shown in Figure 7.10, in the case of a node failure of R4, as soon as the failure is detected by the PLR (R3), each protected TE LSP following the path R3-R4-R5 will be rerouted onto the bypass tunnel B1. The rerouting operation consists of swapping the incoming label to the appropriate outgoing label, pushing an additional label corresponding to the backup tunnel label, and redirecting the traffic onto the outgoing interface of the backup tunnel. The "appropriate" label is the label expected at the MP for the protected TE LSP.

It is worth elaborating on what the expected label is. So let us consider the two following situations:

Situation 1: The backup tunnel is an NHOP backup tunnel, in which case, the MP is also the PLR's NHOP for the protected LSP before failure occurs. Upon link

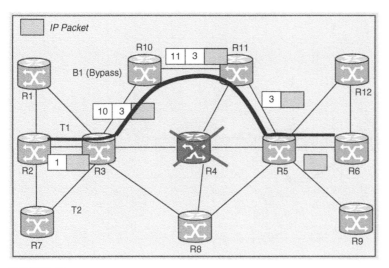

FIGURE 7.10

Facility backup: Example of the mode of operation when the node R4 fails and the protected TE LSP T1 is locally rerouted by the PLR R3 onto the NNHOP backup tunnel B1.

failure, the PLR must perform a similar swap (no label change) as before the failure occurs; then the MP will receive the same label as before the failure but from a different interface.

This is illustrated in Figure 7.11.

In Figure 7.11, an NHOP backup tunnel B1 is set up from R3 to R4, which follows the path R3-R8-R4, protecting against a failure of the link R3-R4. The backup label distributed by R8 to R3 is 10 and a PHP (penultimate hop popping, PHP) operation is performed between R8 and R4. Once the link failure is detected by the PLR (R3 in this example), for all the protected TE LSPs traversing the link R3-R4, the PLR R3 performs the following operations:

- Label swap of the protected TE LSP using the same label as before the failure
- Push of the label corresponding to the NHOP backup tunnel
- Redirect the traffic onto the backup tunnel outgoing interface

Figure 7.12 shows the situation after the link R3-R4 has failed and the PLR R3 has locally rerouted the protected TE LSP T1 onto the NHOP backup tunnel B1.

The PLR R3 performs the following operations to locally reroute the protected TE LSP T1 onto the NHOP backup tunnel B1: R3 swaps 1 to 2 (as before), pushes the label 10 and redirects the traffic onto B1's outgoing interface (R3-R8). R4 (the MP) receives a label-switched packet containing the same label as before the failure but from a different interface.

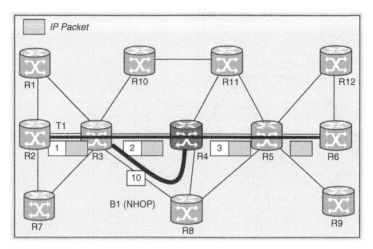

FIGURE 7.11

Facility backup: Example of the mode of operation when the node R4 fails and the protected
TE LSP T1 is locally rerouted by the PLR R3 onto the NHOP backup tunnel B1.

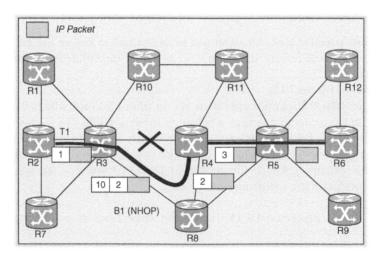

FIGURE 7.12

Situation after the failure of the link R3-R4 and the PLR R3 has locally rerouted the protected
TE LSP T1 onto the NHOP backup tunnel B1.

Situation 2: With an NNHOP backup tunnel, the MP is now the PLR's next-
next hop of the protected LSP before the failure. So the PLR must perform a swap
so the MP receives a label switched packet with the expected label (but from a
different interface).

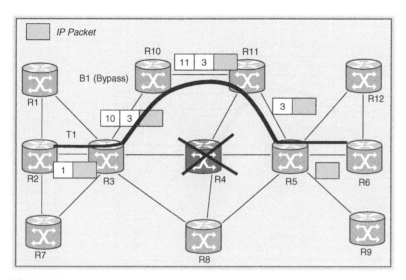

FIGURE 7.13

Situation after the failure of the link R3-R4 and the PLR R3 has locally rerouted the protected TE LSP T1 onto the NNHOP backup tunnel B1.

To highlight this mechanism, let us consider the example depicted in Figure 7.13. Remember, at steady state (without any failure) the label swapping operation performed by R3 for the fast-reroutable TE LSP T1 is 1 to 2. In the case depicted in Figure 7.13, the MP R5 expects to receive a label 3 (label distributed by R5 to R4 for T1). So when the failure of the link R3-R4 or the node R4 occurs, R3 must swap 1 to 3 (instead of 2 before the failure), push the label 10, and redirect the traffic onto B1's outgoing interface (R3-R10). This way, R5 (the MP) receives an identical packet as before the failure but from a different interface. By default, the PLR does *not* have the knowledge of the label used between its NHOP LSR and NNHOP LSR; it just learns from its direct downstream neighbor the label it must use for the TE LSP. An extension to an existing RSVP object (RRO object) is used to learn the label used between the NHOP and the NNHOP LSR (that signaling extension is described in Section 7.12).

Important notes:

Note 1: An identical operation is performed for every protected LSP rerouted onto the *same* backup tunnel; indeed, with facility backup, the same backup LSP is used for all the rerouted TE LSPs that intersect the backup tunnel on both the PLR and the MP.

This is illustrated in Figure 7.14. This figure shows two primary tunnels T1 and T2 that used to follow the paths R1-R3-R4-R5-R6 and R7-R3-R4-R5-R6 before the failure. The labels in use are 100 (between R1 and R3), 101 (between R3 and R4), 102 (between R4 and R5) and PHP (between R5 and R6) for T1 and

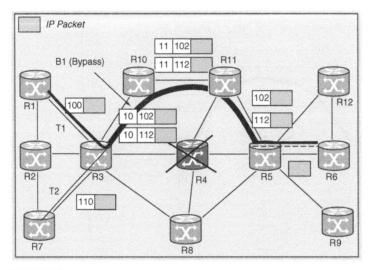

FIGURE 7.14

Illustration of the use of the MPLS stacking property by facility backup: Several protected TE LSPs are rerouted onto a single NNHOP backup tunnel B1 upon R4 node failure.

110 (between R7 and R3), 111 (between R3 and R4), 112 (between R4 and R5) and PHP between R5 and R6. Because both T1 and T2 intersect at R3 and R5, the same NNHOP backup tunnel B1 can be used in the case of failure of the link R3-R4 or node R4. This is of course a very important scaling property of facility backup that uses MPLS stacking. Note also that the same property applies to NHOP backup tunnels.

Note 2: In both cases (NHOP and NHOP bypass tunnels), no additional RSVP states are created along the backup paths for the rerouted TE LSPs. In other words, the LSRs along the backup path do not "see" the rerouted TE LSPs as far as the control plane is concerned. This is also a crucial property for the scalability properties of this solution.

7.5.5 Properties of a Traffic Engineering LSP

When using MPLS TE local protection, there are three properties a TE LSP can have:

1. Fast Reroute desired
2. Bandwidth protection desired
3. Node protection desired

Fast Reroute desired TE LSP: Fast Reroute is a technology that can be used for some TE LSPs only (as already stated, such TE LSPs are called fast-reroutable TE LSPs), so if a backup tunnel has been configured on a PLR, just the TE LSP signaled as "fast reroutable" will be fast rerouted in the case of a failure. Typically, this provides fast recovery using local protection to a subset of TE LSPs having stringent recovery requirements (e.g., the TE LSPs carrying sensitive traffic like VoIP or ATM-over-MPLS), whereas other TE LSPs carrying less sensitive traffic (e.g., Internet traffic) will be rerouted using TE LSP reroute. This obviously requires the ability to explicitly signal this fast-reroutable property of a TE LSP. The details of the signaling aspects are covered in Section 7.13.

Bandwidth protection desired: The notion of bandwidth protection is extensively covered in Section 7.13, but here is a high-level description of this important notion. The previous section described the mode of operation of Fast Reroute for both the facility backup and the one-to-one backup method. When a TE LSP is signaled, one of the TE LSP attributes of the TE LSP is the bandwidth. A TE LSP is said to be *bandwidth protected* at a node R only if it can be fast rerouted and the selected backup tunnel offers an equivalent bandwidth as the primary TE LSP used to receive along the primary path (before the failure). In other words, the TE LSP does not suffer any QoS degradation along the alternate path. Note that the QoS may be a function not just of the bandwidth but also of the propagation delay or jitter. Section 7.13 details how backup paths can be computed to provide such guarantees. When signaled, a protected TE LSP can explicitly request bandwidth protection.

Node protection desired: In some cases, also further discussed in Section 7.13, it might not be possible for a PLR to find both an NHOP and an NNHOP backup tunnel offering full bandwidth protection. For example, let us consider the simple case of three routers R1, R2, and R3 connected in a row, and the R1-R2 link bandwidth is 20 Mbps and the R2-R3 link is 10 Mbps. Then the PLR may try to find an NHOP backup tunnel with 20 Mbps worth of bandwidth and an NNHOP backup tunnel with min(20,10) = 10 Mbps worth of bandwidth. Suppose that no such NNHOP backup tunnel can be found but just an NNHOP backup tunnel of 5 Mbps. Then as new TE LSPs requesting for bandwidth protection are signaled, it may happen that no NNHOP backup tunnel offering bandwidth protection can be found. In this case, having an additional signaled parameter explicitly requesting node protection is desirable and can be used as a tie break. So if the PLR has two requests for bandwidth protection and cannot select an NNHOP backup tunnel for both of them because of insufficient bandwidth on the NNHOP backup tunnel, it can preferably select the NNHOP backup tunnel for the TE LSP having expressed a desire to get node protection in addition to bandwidth protection. Such a parameter has been standardized and is described in Section 7.13.

Notion of Class of Recovery

The various TE LSP recovery requirements mentioned earlier allow an operator to define multiple CoRs and assign a different CoR to each TE LSP according to its recovery requirements. For instance, very sensitive traffic like voice-over-IP/MPLS or ATM-over-MPLS could be routed over protected TE LSPs with bandwidth and node protection. In the case of a link or node failure, those TE LSPs would be very quickly rerouted, while maintaining an equivalent QoS. On the other hand, MPLS VPNs traffic could be routed onto protected TE LSPs without bandwidth protection. Finally the less sensitive traffic could be routed over nonprotected TE LSPs.

Defining multiple classes of recovery provides the two following benefits:

- The set of rerouting operations can be prioritized. Indeed, every LSR will preferably start to recover the TE LSPs that belong to the highest CoR.

- When bandwidth protection is required, this implies reserving some backup capacity in the network. With multiple CoRs, the amount of backup capacity is limited to the set of TE LSPs that belong to the CoR for which bandwidth protection is required. This allows to significantly optimize the required backup capacity.

7.5.6 Notification of Tunnel Locally Repaired

As described earlier, upon detection of a link/node failure, the PLR immediately starts rerouting the set of protected TE LSPs over their respective backup tunnels (bypass tunnels or Detour LSPs). This may result in following a suboptimal end-to-end path. Consequently, in addition to performing the local reroute, the PLR sends a specific RSVP Path Error message for each rerouted TE LSP to their respective head-end LSR to indicate that a local reroute has occurred. This type of RSVP Path Error is sometimes qualified as nondisruptive because no RSVP states are cleared; it serves as a pure indication to the head-end LSR. The receipt of such of message will then trigger a reoptimization on the head-end LSR for the affected TE LSP. Indeed, as previously mentioned MPLS TE Fast Reroute is a temporary network recovery mechanism; the protected TE LSPs are quickly and locally rerouted onto backup tunnels using a local protection technique, but the path followed by the rerouted flows might no longer be optimal. This is illustrated in Figure 7.15.

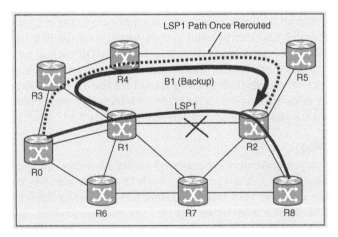

FIGURE 7.15

Notification of local repair followed by head-end reoptimization.

In Figure 7.15, a protected TE LSP, T1, following the path R0-R1-R2-R8 is set up. At router R1 (PLR), T1 is protected by an NHOP backup tunnel B1 against a failure of the link R1-R2 (B1 follows the path R1-R3-R4-R5-R2). When the link R1-R2 fails, upon detecting the link failure, the PLR (R1) reroutes the LSP T1 onto B1 and sends a Path Error "tunnel locally repaired" to T1's head-end LSR (R0). As you can see in Figure 7.15, the path followed by T1 is not optimal (R0-R1-R3-R4-R5-R2-R8). The receipt of the Path Error triggers a reoptimization on R0, which in turn reroutes the TE LSP T1 along the path R0-R3-R4-R5-R2-R8, which is more optimal than the path followed by the rerouted flows during failure (R0-R1-R3-R4-R5-R2-R8). In this example, we assume that all the links have the same metric. Of course, the TE LSP reoptimization should always be performed using the "make before break" procedure, avoiding any traffic disruption.

The head-end will also be informed of the link failure via the receipt of an IGP update from one of the routers adjacent to the failed link. Either upon the receipt of an RSVP Path Error notify message "tunnel locally repaired" or an IGP update, the head-end triggers a TE LSP reoptimization.

Case of a Multiarea (OSPF) or Multilevel (IS-IS) Network

In the case of a multiarea (OSPF), multilevel (IS-IS), or multiautonomous systems network, if the failure does not occur in the head-end LSR area/level, no IGP notification will be received by the head-end LSR. This means that the head-end LSR exclusively relies on the receipt of the RSVP Path Error message to be informed that a local repair has been performed on a downstream node. Consider the network depicted in Figure 7.16.

In Figure 7.16, a fast-reroutable interarea TE LSP (T1) is routed from R0 to R4 and spans multiple areas. On R2, a NHOP backup tunnel that follows the path R2-R5-R6-R7-R3 protects any fast-reroutable TE LSPs traversing the link R2-R3

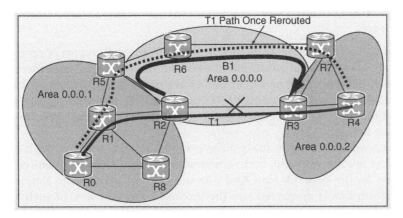

FIGURE 7.16

Notification of local repair followed by head-end reoptimization in a multiarea routing domain.

from a failure. When the link R2-R3 fails, the TE LSP T1 is rerouted onto the backup tunnel B1, but in this case the head-end LSR R0 does not receive any IGP update. Indeed, the failure occurred in the backbone area, so R0 does not have any visibility of the backbone area topology. A failure in the backbone area is invisible to R0 (R2 might send a new summary LSA if some addresses are no longer reachable, but generally the address aggregation scheme will be such that no summary LSA will be flooded into the area 0.0.0.1). Because the RSVP Path Error notify message is the only mechanism allowing the head-end LSR to be informed of a local repair that occurred on a downstream node that does not reside in the head-end area, a best common practice consists of sending the RSVP Path Error message in reliable mode.

7.5.7 Signaling Extensions for MPLS Traffic Engineering Local Protection

By contrast with MPLS global default protection and MPLS TE global protection, which do not require any signaling protocol extensions beyond those of RSVP TE for the signaling of MPLS TE LSP, MPLS TE local protection (Fast Reroute) requires several signaling extensions. Although they are undoubtedly important, their detailed understanding is not a prerequisite to grasp how local protection works. Consequently, the signaling aspects of Fast Reroute are covered in detail in Section 7.12.

7.5.8 Two Strategies for Deploying MPLS Traffic Engineering for Fast Recovery

As mentioned in Section 7.1, there might be several motivations for deploying MPLS TE:

- *Bandwidth optimization:* So that the network resources are used in a more efficient way. This also helps in providing better QoS.
- *Providing strict QoS guaranties* to some specific traffic flows.
- *Fast recovery.*

In some networks, there might be an interest in MPLS TE for its fast recovery property only. In other words, bandwidth optimization and/or strict QoS guarantees are not required, but the operator would like to benefit from the fast recovery property of Fast Reroute without tuning its IGP parameters. This section proposes two strategies for deploying MPLS TE when the only objective is to get fast recovery by using Fast Reroute.

For instance, consider an underutilized (or overprovisioned) network. Such a network does not require any bandwidth optimization because it is not congested. Also, depending on the network load, QoS guarantees could rely on the simple assumption that no link is congested and the link loads are very low. In such a situation, MPLS TE is not required, and paths computed by the routing protocol are perfectly satisfactory. However, such a network may require fast recovery of link or node failures, making Fast Reroute a good candidate. Because Fast Reroute requires TE LSPs, the solution includes deploying TE LSPs but in a quite specific way, which we describe in this section.

There are two strategies for deploying MPLS TE when the sole objective of the operator is to use Fast Reroute:

1. With a full mesh of unconstrained TE LSPs
2. With one-hop unconstrained TE LSPs

Network Design with a Full Mesh of Unconstrained TE LSPs

A simple and efficient strategy is to deploy a full mesh of unconstrained TE LSPs. An unconstrained TE LSP is an LSP without any constraint. For instance, the required bandwidth is 0, and no affinities are defined. The only property of such a TE LSP is to be fast reroutable. Indeed, the objective is not to use the traffic engineering property of MPLS TE (in the sense of "traffic engineer" the flows across the network). So the available bandwidth and other TE link-related information are still flooded by the IGP TE extensions but will never change. When a head-end LSR computes a path for an unconstrained TE LSP, the same CSPF algorithm is used as with any other TE LSP, but the obvious outcome is that the TE LSP will follow the IGP shortest path. In other words, the traffic routed onto unconstrained TE LSPs will follow the same paths as IP routed traffic, but in the case of link and/or node failures, fast-reroutable TE LSPs will be rerouted by MPLS TE Fast Reroute, which was the initial objective.

Network Design with Unconstrained One-Hop TE LSPs

If the requirement is to use Fast Reroute for link protection only, then exactly one primary unconstrained TE LSP plus one single NHOP backup tunnel are required for every link to protect.

The idea is to set up a one-hop tunnel following the same path as the link to protect. One way of achieving this is to set up an unconstrained TE LSP. This way the CSPF algorithm will just follow the most direct path between the head-end LSR and the tail-end LSR (the next hop of the head-end LSR in this case). Note that in this case the PLR node is also the head-end LSR. Then the one hop primary TE LSP must be configured so that all the traffic follows the TE LSP.

It is important to note that because the TE LSP is a one-hop LSP, if PHP is used, no label is added once the traffic is routed over the primary TE LSP. Such a strategy is depicted in Figure 7.17.

In the example shown in Figure 7.17, the objective is to protect the link R2-R3. So a single-hop tunnel (T1) is configured from R2 to R3 and all the traffic is routed onto this one-hop primary TE LSP through this link. T1 has no constraint, so this TE LSP follows the path R2-R3. An NHOP backup tunnel B1 is configured between R2-R3 with the constraint of being diversely routed from the protected link and follows the path R2-R8-R3. As discussed in Section 7.13, additional constraints may be added to also provide bandwidth protection. In the case of failure of the link R2-R3, the PLR (R2) will trigger Fast Reroute and all the traffic that

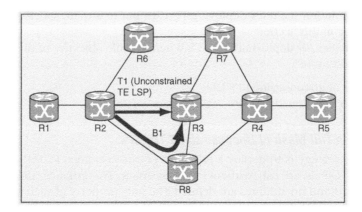

FIGURE 7.17

Deploying MPLS TE Fast Reroute with one-hop tunnel to protect against link failure.

used to be routed over the link R2-R3 will be rerouted over B1, following the path R2-R8-R3. Then the primary TE LSP T1 will be rerouted (reoptimized) and will follow the new shortest path between R2 and R3. Finally, the routing protocol will be informed of the link failure and will recompute a new path, which may or not follow B1's path.

The same configuration has to be repeated for each link to protect using Fast Reroute. Note that if the link R2-R3 is protected using a SONET/SDH protected VCs, Fast Reroute may also be used to protect against a router interface failure on the R2 or R3 side. In that case, one must ensure that both mechanisms are not simultaneously triggered. Existing implementations support mechanisms to automate the creation of both the primary and the backup TE LSP, because in this case their set of attributes is known in advance to alleviate the configuration burden. The only constraint of the backup tunnel is to be diversely routed from the link to protect (some implementations support the computation of SRLG-diverse paths).

Protection against link and node failures: To guard against both link and node failures, a similar approach is followed, with the only difference that at each hop, both one unconstrained TE LSP and one NNHOP backup tunnel per next-next hop must be configured.

Why are one primary and one NNHOP backup tunnel required per NNHOP?

Let us consider the example in Figure 7.18. As shown in Figure 7.18, in the case of a node failure of R3, all the traffic traversing the protected LSR needs to be rerouted onto some appropriate backup tunnels. That requires setting up one primary TE LSP for each possible traffic path traversing the protected node. In Figure 7.18, there are three paths leaving R2 that traverse the node R3 to consider: R2-R3-R4, R2-R3-R7 and R2-R3-R8. So three unconstrained TE LSPs are configured and set up on R2: T1, T2, and T3. Because each of these tunnels needs to

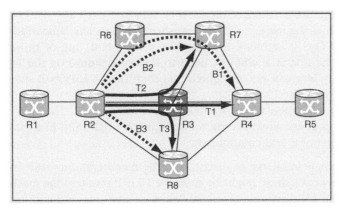

FIGURE 7.18

Deploying MPLS TE Fast Reroute with two-hop tunnel to protect against both link and node failures.

be rerouted over a diversely routed backup tunnel, three NNHOP backup tunnels are configured: B1 protecting the traffic following the path R2-R3-R4 and routed onto the tunnel T1, B2 protecting T2, and finally B3 protecting T3. As in the case of link protection, the protected TE LSPs are unconstrained and follow the shortest IGP path.

This explains the requirement for one unconstrained TE LSP and one backup tunnel per NNHOP. In the previous example, the number of NNHOPs of R2 is equal to 3: R7, R3, and R8.

Important note:
> Conversely to the previous case of link protection, the traffic must start flowing onto the primary 2-hops tunnels only when the failure occurs.

Comparison of Both Approaches

Both the "unconstrained full mesh TE LSPs" and the "unconstrained approach" can be used and have their respective pros and cons. Indeed, the unconstrained approach clearly has the advantage to require the configuration and set up of a very limited number of TE LSPs. If just link protection is required, for every link to protect with Fast Reroute, just two TE LSPs are required: the primary one-hop TE LSP and an NHOP backup tunnel diversely routed from the link to protect. If node protection is required, one pair of TE LSPs (primary and backup) is needed for every next-next hop, as described earlier, which is still a very reasonable number. Note that at the time of publication, commercial implementations support only the 1-hop unconstrained approach. Moreover, some implementations ease the configuration process with the use of very few commands to automate the configuration of such primary and backup TE LSPs.

On the other hand, the unconstrained full mesh TE LSPs approach also offers a very easy migration path to the use of MPLS TE for other purposes like bandwidth optimization and strict QoS guarantees. Indeed, if at some point, one of those requirements appears, the operator will just need to set constraint(s) on the TE LSPs. For instance, bandwidth can be configured and then the TE LSPs will start using alternate path(s), if required.

In terms of existing implementations, some solutions are available that automate the configuration process when setting up a full mesh of TE LSPs. In a nutshell, those solutions rely on several components:

- A discovery process is in charge of discovering the members of a mesh. In some MPLS TE networks, there might be multiple TE LSP meshes: one mesh of TE LSPs between LSRs acting as VoIP gateways, for instance, and another full mesh of TE LSPs between routers carrying the Internet traffic. Each TE mesh has its own set of characteristics in terms of bandwidth, priority, and protection/restoration, to mention just a few requirements. Then each router uses an IGP extension (OSPF or IS-IS) to advertise that it is a member of one or multiple TE meshes. This mechanism allows every router to discover all the other routers that belong to the same TE mesh.

- Then, once a router has discovered all the routers that belong to the same mesh, it can use a "template" (where the constraints specific to that particular mesh are locally specified) to set up the mesh of TE LSPs. Note that in this particular context of using MPLS TE for fast recovery only, the template is very restricted because the primary TE LSPs are unconstrained.

In terms of IGP, both methods are equivalent. The TE-related information is flooded by the IGP but will never changed because the TE LSPs are unconstrained and never reserve bandwidth.

7.6 ANOTHER MPLS TRAFFIC ENGINEERING RECOVERY ALTERNATIVE

Another MPLS TE recovery alternative has been proposed but never got any traction in the industry because of severe limitations: 1+1 packet protection whose principle is to permanently bridge the IP/MPLS traffic over two diversely routed TE LSPs. The traffic bridging is made on the head-end LSR, and the decision to switch the traffic is performed by the tail-end LSR, which permanently compares the two identical received flows from the primary and secondary TE LSPs. When a failure occurs in the network, the traffic received from one of the TE LSPs is affected. Once the tail-end LSR detects the failure, it switches to the secondary TE LSP. Note that such a mechanism is also called a *single-ended protocol* because the switching decision process is made by a single entity (the tail-end LSR in this case) without requiring any signaling exchange between the nodes. A failure may be a traffic interruption, an unacceptable error rate, or any other kind of defects.

Once the tail-end LSR has performed the switch, it can either decide to stay indefinitely on this TE LSP and start using the other TE LSP (once restored) in the case of failure of the currently selected TE LSP or decide to switch back to the original TE LSP, once restored.

Although this mechanism is simple and efficient in terms of recovery time, it has two major drawbacks that drastically limit its applicability:

- The amount of traffic forwarded in the network is doubled for each TE LSP protected with this 1+1 mechanism. This is a serious issue because it basically implies at least[66] a bandwidth wastage of 50%.
- The failure discovery at the tail-end LSR usually requires some hardware changes and thus equipment replacement, which can also be expensive.

For those reasons, such a mechanism has never been implemented or deployed but is just mentioned here for the sake of completeness in describing MPLS TE recovery techniques.

7.7 COMPARISON OF GLOBAL AND LOCAL PROTECTION

The evaluation of a recovery mechanism requires the consideration of several parameters: scope of recovery (link, node, SRLG), recovery time, guaranteed bandwidth, backup capacity requirements, state overhead, scalability, reordering, additive latency and jitter, signaling requirements, stability, and others. Throughout this chapter, we saw several MPLS TE recovery techniques, so the natural question that comes to mind is, which one to use. Although there is no unique answer because each network has its own constraint and requirements, the aim of this section is to provide a comparison of the global protection and local protection techniques with a particular focus on three key performance aspects:

- The recovery time
- The state overhead, which is directly correlated to the scalability
- The ability to perform bandwidth sharing when bandwidth protection is required

7.7.1 Recovery Time

With global protection, rerouting is performed by the head-end LSR, which means that this requires for the head-end LSR to receive the failure notification to reroute the affected traffic onto their respective backup paths (whose paths have been precomputed and signaled). So in terms of recovery time, the delta between global and

---

[66] This technique implies at least a bandwidth wastage of 50% because one of the constraints of the backup TE LSP is to be disjoint from the protected TE LSP, which usually means that it will follow a longer path.

local protection is the failure indication signal propagation time to the head-end LSR. How large this delta is highly depends on the network characteristics. Thus, for instance, a network confined to a small country generally implies short propagation delays (less than 10 ms); on the other hand, an international network may easily experience much longer propagation delays...up to a few hundreds of milliseconds. In that case, convergence of a few tens of milliseconds requires the use of local protection techniques. Furthermore, queuing delays to process the control plane notification (RSVP and/or IGP) messages can be reduced via the use of QoS mechanisms.

Note that in terms of recovery time, the two local protection schemes described earlier (i.e., "one-to-one" and "facility backup") are equivalent; they both rely on local protection where fast-reroutable TE LSPs are locally rerouted on pre-signaled backup tunnels and then reoptimized by their respective head-end LSR.

In summary, as far as the recovery time is concerned, the key difference between local and global protection is in the failure propagation notification time to the head-end LSR which, in the case of global protection is made of incompressible propagation delays and queuing delays that can be reduced by means of QoS mechanisms.

7.7.2 Scalability

Scalability is undoubtedly one of the major aspects to consider when evaluating a recovery mechanism, and to that respect, global path protection, one-to-one backup, and facility backup local protection differ very significantly.

Scalability is a relatively generic term that requires clarification in this context. Protection mechanisms require setting up backup tunnels before any failure to provide fast convergence (by contrast with global default restoration, the backup path is already computed and signaled). The configuration of backup tunnels can be facilitated via an automatic process, but setting up backup tunnels in a network is not entirely cost free. Although the scalability of RSVP is very high, in large networks, the number of backup tunnels can be significant as shown below, which requires to potentially handle a large number of states on routers. Moreover, the troubleshooting task is even more complicated for the team in charge of operating the network. So scalability is considered in terms of number of required backup tunnels in this context.

Let us evaluate the number of required backup tunnels with global path protection, Fast Reroute facility backup, and one-to-one, based on the following assumptions:

D: network diameter (average number of hops between a head-end LSR and a tail-end LSR)

C: degree of connectivity (average number of neighbors)

L: total number of links to be protected with Fast Reroute[67]

---

[67] Some links may be protected via other means like SONET/SDH and optical protection/restoration.

N: total number of nodes (LSRs)

T: total number of protected TE LSPs in the MPLS network

Bu: number of backup tunnels required

K: number of class of recovery (as mentioned in Section 7.5.5, there might be several classes of TE LSPs, each requiring different CoR. In this case, each CoR has a dedicated set of backup tunnels)

S: average number of splits (as discussed in Section 7.13, in some cases where bandwidth protection is required and backup bandwidth is a very scarce resource, more than one backup tunnel per protected link/node may be required if a single backup tunnel with enough bandwidth cannot be found)

Note: Realistic assumptions for S and K are as follows:

- $S < 4$: Generally S will very rarely exceed 3. In a network where bandwidth protection is required but backup capacity is not a very scarce resource $S = 1$. If bandwidth protection is not required, then $S = 1$.
- Also $K < 3$.

M: number of meshes in the network (e.g., there may be multiple meshes of TE LSPs in a network serving different purposes: one mesh for the voice traffic and one mesh for the data traffic).

It follows that

$\rightarrow$ $L < N * C$ (because some links may not be protected by Fast Reroute)

$\rightarrow$ $T = M * N * (N - 1)$ (assuming a full mesh TE deployment)

Let us now compute the total number of required backup tunnels Bu with global path protection, Fast Reroute one-to-one, and facility backup.

1. Computation of Bu with global path protection

The number of backup tunnels is equal to the number of primary TE LSPs:

$$Bu = M * T = M * N * (N - 1)$$

One has to keep in mind that the number of backup TE LSP grows proportionally with the number of primary TE LSPs and as the square of the number of LSRs in a full mesh scenario. This can have a nonnegligible impact on the overall network scalability. Consider a full mesh of 200 LSRs: The total number of primary TE LSPs in the network will be $199 * 200 = 39,800$. Using path protection in this context doubles the number of TE LSPs, which gives a total number of TE LSPs equal to 79,800.

This basically has nonnegligible consequences on *state overhead:* Every head-end LSR will see its number of TE LSPs to manage doubled. However, one must admit that this is not a major concern because the total number of TE LSPs on every head-end LSR is generally limited (equal to the number of LSRs in every mesh to which the head-end LSR belongs). On the other hand, especially in

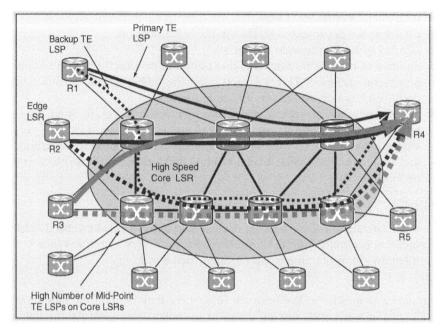

FIGURE 7.19

State overhead with MPLS traffic engineering path protection.

networks sparsely interconnected from a layer 1/layer 2 perspective, the total number of TE LSPs per midpoint LSR can be substantially large.

Consider the example of the network depicted in Figure 7.19. This simple network is made of two levels of hierarchy:

- A high-speed core backbone with high-capacity LSRs interconnected by high-speed links (OC48, OC192)
- An edge layer with a large number of smaller LSRs connected (or dual connected to the high speed core) via medium speed links

The edge LSRs are fully meshed with each other (for the sake of readability, just the TE LSPs from R1, R2, and R3, to R4 are represented). Observe the number of TE LSPs traversing the high-speed core LSRs. This example shows that the number of TE LSPs per midpoint LSR can be quite high in such a network and the proportion of TE LSPs passing through those high-speed nodes can be substantial in comparison to the total amount of TE LSPs in the network. In typical existing networks, this can be as high as 20% to 30%, at steady state. In the case of failure of a high-speed core link or LSR, this number would be even more increased.

The scalability impact can be characterized through various aspects:

- *Memory impact* on the midpoint LSR: Each TE LSP requires some memory to handle the RSVP states.

- *States refresh:* RSVP is a soft-state protocol. This requires for each TE LSP to refresh the RSVP states, exchanging RSVP Path and Resv messages at regular intervals between neighbors. Note that the impact of TE LSP refresh can be drastically reduced, using two methods:
- *Refresh reduction:* this mechanism consists of using specific messages (SREFRESH) so that an LSR sends a unique message to its neighbor to refresh a large set of TE LSPs, instead of sending an individual RSVP Path message per TE LSP.
- *Refresh interval:* Moreover, the RSVP refresh frequency can be decreased; in this case, other liveness mechanisms like RSVP hellos (see Section 7.9) can be used.
- *Recovery time* on the midpoint LSR: When local recovery mechanisms are used on the midpoint LSRs, the number of TE LSPs to reroute may have an impact on the recovery time.

2. Computation of Bu with local protection: *facility backup*
Situation 1: If just links are protected with Fast Reroute, then $Bu = L * K * S$
Situation 2: If both links and nodes are protected with Fast Reroute then:

$$Bu = L * K * S + N * C * (C - 1) * K * S$$
$$Bu = (L + N * C * (C - 1)) * K * S$$

3. Computation of Bu with local protection: *one-to-one backup*
Without merging, $Bu - T * D = M * N * (N - 1) * D$

Because we have now computed the theoretical formulas, let us make a few (realistic) assumptions that will help figure out the scalability impact.

We consider a fully meshed network with the following characteristics:

- D (diameter) = 5
- C (degree of connectivity) = 4
- M (number of meshes) = 2 (one mesh for voice and one mesh for data traffic)
- K = 2 (two classes of recovery: one for voice with bandwidth protection and one for data without bandwidth protection)
- S = 2 (on the average, two backup tunnels are necessary to get the required backup bandwidth between a PLR and a MP)
- All links must be protected by Fast Reroute: $L = N * C$

Let us now compare Bu for global path protection, Fast Reroute one-to-one, and facility backup, using the previous formulas:

Global path protection: $Bu = M * N * (N - 1) = 2 * N * (N - 1)$

Local protection-facility backup (node protection):

$$Bu = (N * C + N * C * (C - 1)) * K * S = N * C^2 * K * S = 64 * N$$

Local protection-one-to-one backup:

$$Bu = M * N * (N - 1) * D = 10 * N * N(N - 1)$$

Figure 7.20 shows the value of Bu for the three MPLS recovery methods as a function of the number of nodes in the network (from 10 to 50 nodes and from 10 to 150 nodes).

Figure 7.20 clearly shows that both global path protection and Fast Reroute one-to-one backup scale poorly in large environments. The number of backup tunnel per midpoint LSR can rapidly cause some scalability issues. Indeed, in a full mesh network of very reasonable size (50 nodes), with the assumption made above, the total number of primary TE LSPs is 4900 and the number of backup tunnels with each MPLS TE recovery techniques is as follows:

- With global path protection: 4900
- With local protection facility backup: 3200
- With local protection one-to-one backup: 24,500

Although merging of Detour LSPs can help reduce the number of backup tunnels, their number stays very high in large networks.

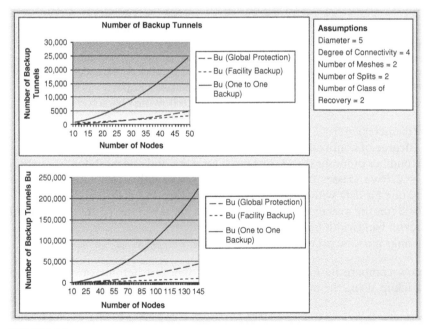

FIGURE 7.20

Comparison of the set of required backup tunnel with global protection, local protection "facility backup and one to one."

7.7.3 **Bandwidth Sharing Capability**

The last criteria we want to evaluate in this comparison is the ability to perform bandwidth sharing with both global and local protection. To be cost-effective, the backup capacity (bandwidth reserved for backup tunnels) should of course be minimized. Section 7.13 will show that this goal can be efficiently met thanks to the interesting property of bandwidth sharing under the single failure assumption. Trying to conclude on the respective efficiency of global and local protection as far as bandwidth sharing is concerned is almost impossible because their relative performance is highly driven by the algorithms in place and even more importantly by the network topology. So the objective of this section is to provide some general facts about each of them with respect to the bandwidth sharing capability.

Global Path Protection

Performing bandwidth sharing between backup path protecting independent resources is of course possible. By contrast with local protection, a path completely diverse/disjoint from the primary TE LSP must be found as opposed to protecting a single local resource; on the other hand, the level of granularity is higher (protect a TE LSP instead of a link or a node) and the backup capacity can be spread through the entire network.

One of the major constraints with global path protection is that it requires an off-line computation for both the primary and the backup TE LSP when the objective is to achieve optimal bandwidth sharing.

As already pointed out, with MPLS TE, the TE LSP path computation can be performed either by an off-line tool or in a distributed fashion. If TE LSP primary path computation is done off-line, the tool can find a TE LSP placement satisfying the set of constraints while trying to compute their respective backup path whose placement maximize the degree of bandwidth sharing. Although this problem is clearly NP complete, sophisticated algorithms have been proposed along with a large set of heuristics to achieve that goal. On the other hand, if primary TE LSP path computation is done in a distributed fashion, trying to achieve bandwidth sharing between backup paths protecting independent resources would require some synchronization between every head-end LSR, which is by default not the case with a distributed computation. This would require very extensive signaling extensions and overhead of the control plane (signaling and routing), which makes this option virtually impossible and certainly not desirable.

The bottom line is that if one decides to use global path protection with bandwidth guarantee and requires minimizing the backup capacity via bandwidth sharing, the only possible option is to perform the path computation of both the primary and the backup path by using an external off-line tool. Also, as the set of constraints is quite strict (compute primary and backup path simultaneously), this sort of solution is generally not very flexible. Indeed, a change in bandwidth requirement for a specific subset of TE LSPs may end up in a relatively important set of changes on other primary and backup TE LSPs. Algorithms may try to minimize the set of changes (this is known as the *minimal perturbation problem,* but this is not always possible). For instance, suppose a set of 5000 TE LSPs with their corresponding backup tunnels, so a total of 10,000 TE LSPs. All the TE LSPs are up and running in the network. After some time, the operator requests for more bandwidth for a few TE LSPs (because of traffic growth in a specific region of the network). The bandwidth increase of those few TE LSPs may require displacing a significant number of other TE LSPs, especially if the bandwidth is scarce. Moreover, the other constraint added by path protection is that diverse paths must be found while achieving optimal bandwidth sharing; those additional constraints certainly amplify the phenomena and the risk to end up with significant changes, which represents a nonnegligible constraint in terms of network operations.

Local Protection: "Facility Backup" and "One-to-One Backup"

As shown in Section 7.13, bandwidth sharing is perfectly achievable with local protection facility backup using either a centralized or a distributed backup path computation model. Also, the performance in terms of bandwidth sharing depends on the path computation algorithm efficiency. To give some rough estimates, the numbers obtained on several large networks using some off-line backup tunnel path computation tools showed a degree of bandwidth sharing up to 5; in other words, the sum of bandwidth of the backup tunnels on the links was on average five times more than the actual backup capacity, thanks to the single failure assumption, which allows a high degree of bandwidth sharing. This means that the use of the independent CSPF-based model described in Section 7.13 would have required five times more backup bandwidth on each link. This degree of efficiency is of course a function of various aspects; the network topology (degree of connectivity, number of SRLGs, elements to protect, and their protected bandwidth to mention a few of them), backup bandwidth capacity, and in particular the efficiency of the backup tunnel path computation algorithm.

By contrast, performing bandwidth sharing is very difficult with one-to-one backup. Indeed, an individual backup tunnel is set up for each individual protected TE LSP. Bandwidth can be shared via merging but not between backup tunnels protecting independent resources. This would require very extensive signaling and routing overhead, as well as synchronization between various PLRs, which would increase the scalability impact even more. With facility backup, when backup tunnel path computation is performed, a new backup tunnel path computation does not need to be triggered (if a bandwidth pool is protected) each time a new TE LSP is set up or torn down; a facility (like a link or a node) can be protected by a set of backup tunnels regardless of the set of TE LSPs actually traversing the protected resource.

7.7.4 Summary

In the previous sections of this chapter, we saw various MPLS TE recovery techniques in detail from various angles; the protocol extensions, the mode of operations, the capability of each technique, along with several other aspects. The aim of this section is to highlight the main advantages and disadvantages of each of them with the objective of providing some guidance of where each recovery mechanism preferably applies.

MPLS Traffic Engineering Default Global Restoration

Quick Summary

Global default restoration is the default mode of MPLS TE. When a failure is detected by the head-end LSR of one or several TE LSPs, for each affected TE LSP, a new path is computed "on the fly" (using CSPF to find a path that obeys the constraints or using some preconfigured alternate paths), and if a new path can be found, the TE LSP is signaled along that path. The traffic is then restored using the new TE LSP.

Advantages and Drawbacks

Advantages

- Global default restoration does not require any additional configuration of backup path (unless the network administrator decides to explicitly configure the backup path). So, for instance, if a TE LSP is configured as dynamic (the path is computed using a CSPF algorithm), no other configuration is required.

Drawbacks

- Global default restoration is the slowest recovery mechanism compared to the other protection mechanisms, because it implies the FIS propagation to be received by the head-end LSR, a dynamic path computation (which grows with the number of TE LSPs to reroute and the network complexity) and TE LSP signaling. It cannot be used to provide recovery times on the order of tens of milliseconds. Note that a separate CSPF must be computed per TE LSP to reroute.

- Lack of predictability. In some cases, there is no guarantee that the TE LSP could be rerouted upon failure. A last-resort option is to relax all the TE LSP constraints, which guarantees that CSPF will always find a path for the TE LSP (which will be the IGP shortest path) and so the TE LSP will stay "up" (provided that there exists a path between the TE LSP's head-end and tail-end LSRs).

MPLS Traffic Engineering Global Path Protection

Quick Summary

With MPLS TE global path protection, a diversely[68] routed backup TE LSP is computed and signaled for each primary TE LSP before any failure. The constraint for the backup TE LSP can be identical or different from the primary TE LSP.

---

[68] *Diversely routed* means link, node, or SRLG disjoint.

In the case of a failure along the path, once the failure notification is received by the head-end LSR, it switches the traffic over the backup TE LSP and the traffic is recovered.

Advantages and Drawbacks

Advantages

- In networks with many links and nodes and a limited number of TE LSPs to protect, this mechanism is easy to deploy and requires a limited amount of provisioning. For instance, suppose a very large network, where just a limited number of TE LSPs must be protected. With global path protection, just a few diversely routed TE LSPs must be configured and set up. On the contrary, the use of local protection would require the protection of every network element with backup tunnels along any potential primary path.

- Because the backup tunnel is signaled before the failure, the path is deterministic and this provides a strict control of the backup tunnel path.

Drawbacks

- Global path protection requires doubling the number of TE LSPs, which has a significant scalability impact in full mesh networks, as shown earlier.

- Global path protection cannot in most cases (especially in international networks), provides tens of milliseconds of recovery time, which might be an issue to protect very sensitive traffic like voice or ATM/frame relay over IP/MPLS networks. This is due to the need for the failure notification to be received by the head-end LSR before switching the traffic over the backup path.

- If bandwidth guarantee is required, to provide bandwidth sharing, path protection requires the use of an external off-line tool for the computation of both the primary and secondary TE LSPs.

- The requirement for an end-to-end diversely routed path may imply in some cases to select a nonoptimal path for the primary TE LSPs.

MPLS Traffic Engineering Local Protection

Quick Summary

MPLS TE Fast Reroute is a local protection recovery mechanism. There are two flavors of Fast Reroute:

- *Facility backup:* For each protected network element, a backup tunnel is set up, before any failure. The number of backup tunnels is equal to 1 for link protection (potentially more if bandwidth protection is required, and a single backup tunnel with the required capacity cannot be found) and to N for node protection (where N is the number of next-next-hops for each

LSR). This applies to each LSR in the network where protection is required. Potentially, as in the link protection case, more than one backup tunnel might be required per next-next hop if a single backup tunnel with the required capacity cannot be found. When the link or node fails, upon failure detection, the node immediately upstream to the failure switches all the fast-reroutable TE LSPs onto their appropriate backup TE LSP (using the MPLS label stacking property).

■ *One-to-one backup:* For each fast-reroutable TE LSP using the one-to-one backup method, a separate diversely routed TE LSP is set up at each hop that terminates at the tail-end LSR. The number of backup TE LSPs (called *Detour LSP*) is a function of the number of fast-reroutable TE LSPs and the network diameter. Merging rules can help reduce the number of Detour LSPs in the network. When a link or a node fails, upon failure detection, the node immediately upstream to the failure switches all the fast-reroutable TE LSPs onto their Detour LSP.

With both methods, once the PLR (node immediately upstream to the failure) has locally rerouted the protected TE LSPs affected by the failure onto their respective backup tunnel, it sends a notification to every head-end LSR of the fast rerouted TE LSPs, so that the head-end LSR(s) can potentially trigger a reoptimization and reroute the TE LSPs over a more optimal path in a nondisruptive fashion.

Advantages and Drawbacks

Advantages

■ MPLS TE Fast Reroute is a local protection mechanism and can provide very fast recovery time, equivalent to SONET-SDH/optical protection. This is particularly important to protect TE LSP carrying very sensitive traffic. Facility backup and one-to-one backup are equivalent in terms of recovery time.

■ Fast Reroute can provide bandwidth, propagation delay, and jitter guarantees in the case of link/SRLG/node failure. In the case of facility backup, the required backup capacity can be drastically reduced thanks to the notion of bandwidth sharing between backup tunnels protecting independent resources.

■ High granularity: The concept of CoR allows to offer a wide range of protection coverage with a high granularity because the CoR is a per-TE LSP property.

■ The facility backup method has a high scalability because the number of backup tunnels is a function of the number of network elements to protect and does not grow with the number of fast reroutable TE LSPs.

■ Can easily be used even in networks where full mesh of TE LSPs are not deployed.

Drawbacks

- Requires configuring and setting up a number of backup TE LSPs, which can be nonnegligible in large networks.

- Might be more complex to troubleshoot.

- The Fast Reroute one-to-one backup method has a limited scalability in large networks.

7.8 REVERTIVE VERSUS NONREVERTIVE MODES

There is another important aspect that we have not discussed so far in the context of MPLS TE recovery: the notion of *revertive* versus *non-revertive* mode. Indeed, once a network element failure occurs, recovery mechanisms are responsible for finding an alternate path. *But once the resource is restored, how is the traffic rerouted onto that resource?* This depends on whether the recovery mechanism is revertive or non-revertive and this is the subject of this section (Section 7.8).

7.8.1 MPLS Traffic Engineering Global Default Restoration

With MPLS TE global default restoration, when a link, an SRLG, or a node fails, each TE LSP affected by the failure is rerouted over an alternative path determined by its head-end LSR. When the failed resource is restored, any head-end LSR has the possibility to reuse the restored resource. This relies on the reoptimization process by which a head-end LSR tries to evaluate for each of its TE LSPs whether a better path exists.

There are several possible configurations for a TE LSP.

- *Several static paths are configured:* The head-end LSR reevaluates whether a preferred path (different than the path in use) is available.
- *The TE LSP is configured as purely dynamic (no static path is specified):* The head-end LSR reevaluates whether a more optimal path exists (*more optimal* usually means "shorter" path using either the IGP or the TE metric).

When is the reoptimization task performed?
Several existing implementations support multiple reoptimization triggers:

- *Event driven:* A new IGP OSPF LSA or IS-IS LSP has been received and the head-end LSR determines that triggering a reoptimization may be appropriate because a better path may have appeared.
- *Timer driven:* Each x seconds, the head-end LSR reevaluates whether a more optimal path can be found.

7.8.2 MPLS Traffic Engineering Global Path Protection

With MPLS TE global path protection, upon link or node failure notification, the head-end LSR switches the traffic onto the backup LSP. When the link/node recovers, the head-end LSR can trigger either a revertive or a non-revertive action. In the former mode, the traffic is immediately switched back to the primary TE LSP once the primary TE LSP is restored (successfully resignaled). This should be done without traffic disruption but may provoke some packets reordering. In the latter mode, the traffic keeps flowing over the backup TE LSP. This option might be avoided if the backup TE LSP is less constrained than the primary TE LSP (i.e., has less bandwidth or follows a longer path). In the revertive mode, the switch-back action can be either event driven or timer driven.

Important note:

A side effect of trying to reuse a restored resource is the risk of multiple traffic disruption in case of resource flapping.

7.8.3 **MPLS Traffic Engineering Local Protection**

There are actually two kinds of revertive modes with MPLS TE Fast Reroute, which are both specified in the Internet Engineering Task Force (IETF) specification:

1. The *globally revertive mode:* In this case, the decision to reuse a restored resource is left to the head-end TE LSP upon reoptimization (which can be event or timer driven, as previously mentioned).

2. The *locally revertive mode:* When the PLR detects that the link/node is restored, it tries to resignal all the TE LSPs that are currently rerouted over a backup tunnel along the restored resources. If the resignaling attempt fails, the fast-rerouted TE LSPs keep using the backup TE LSP; if the attempt succeeds, the TE LSPs are switched back to their original path. Note that the locally revertive mode tries to switch back all the TE LSPs along the restored path contrary to the globally revertive mode where the head-end LSR can decide to reuse the restored resource on a per-TE LSP basis, depending on the TE LSP attributes.

It is worth noting that the locally revertive mode may have undesirable effects:

■ In case of resource flapping, the revertive mode would potentially cause multiple traffic disruptions; consequently, a locally revertive mode should implement some dampening revertive mechanism. Otherwise, if the resource flaps, the PLR constantly switches the TE LSP between the primary link and the backup tunnels, which results in multiple traffic disruptions.

■ Limited TE LSP attributes view: Contrary to the globally revertive mode, the PLR makes the switch-back operation without a complete knowledge of the TE LSP attributes. Suppose the following situation: A TE LSP T1 is signaled along a path P1. A link along P1 fails and Fast Reroute is triggered. A new link along another (shorter) path between T1's head-end and tail-end LSR goes up. The failed link L1 is restored. A locally revertive mode would switch the traffic back to the restored link even if a better path exists between T1's head-end and tail-end LSR. The globally revertive mode would have been more efficient in this case.

That said, there are some circumstances in which a locally revertive mode might be useful though.

For the reasons mentioned earlier, the MPLS TE Fast Reroute specification recommends the globally revertive mode, whereas the locally revertive mode is optional.

7.9 FAILURE PROFILE AND FAULT DETECTION

This section covers the MPLS-specific aspects of failure profile and fault detection.

7.9.1 MPLS-Specific Failure Detection Hello-Based Protocols

In the context of MPLS TE, another hello-based protocol has been defined, called "RSVP hello protocol extension." The basic mode of operation is similar to any other hello mechanism. RSVP hello messages are sent at a certain frequency, and if no RSVP hello messages have been received during a configurable amount of time (usually some number of times of the hello frequency), the RSVP hello adjacency is considered down. It is worthwhile noting that RSVP hello is a TE LSP property, but a proper implementation needs ensure that just one RSVP hello adjacency is activated per set of TE LSPs traversing the same interface. To illustrate that statement, let us consider the case of two routers R1 and R2 interconnected via n links L1, L2,..., Ln and where several sets Si of TE LSPs traverse each link L1, L2,..., Ln. A very poorly scalable solution is to activate one RSVP hello adjacency per TE LSP. Instead, for each set Si, the routers R1 and R2 should select one TE LSP for which the RSVP hello adjacency will be activated. If the link Li fails, the RSVP hello adjacency of the selected TE LSP will go down and the router will declare all the TE LSPs traversing the link Li as impacted by the failure. So the total number of RSVP hello adjacencies will be n in this case.

As with any other hello-based protocol, the important question of the scalability impact arises and there is no exception with RSVP hellos; sending RSVP hello messages requires some processing treatment by an LSR, which might not be an inexpensive operation. This explains why running fast hellos at very high frequency like 5 ms must be avoided. Moreover, a large number of neighbors also has an impact on the scalability of such a solution.

Hence, if the number of neighbors is not too high and the RSPV hello frequency is reasonable, RSVP hellos may be a candidate for failure detection when lower layer fast detection mechanisms are not available.

Of course, those numbers are highly dependent on the platform, but to give some rough numbers, at the time of writing, some routers can currently support

20 neighbors with RSVP hello messages sent every 100 to 200 ms without any problem.

Note that the potential issue of platforms not being able to sustain RSVP hello is the potential triggering of *false-positive alarms*. A false-positive alarm occurs when Fast Reroute is inappropriately triggered by a loss of RSVP adjacency not because of a failure but just because the neighboring router is too busy to echo the RSVP hello message. This would not create any traffic black-holing, but the protected TE LSPs would be rerouted on their backup tunnel, although this was not required. Moreover, if the backup tunnel does not offer an equivalent QoS, the rerouted traffic may experience some performance degradation. Then they would very likely be eventually reoptimized by their respective head-end LSR along the initial path, but clearly this is not very desirable and should not happen too frequently.

7.9.2 **Requirements for an Accurate Failure Type Characterization**

In the context of MPLS TE local protection, being able to differentiate a link from a node failure may be particularly useful. Such a differentiation is not always obvious. In this section we will see why such a capability can be very useful and we will describe some potential solutions.

Let us now analyze the situations where being able to differentiate a link from a node failure may be desirable:

Situation 1: Optimal Backup Path Selection

Let us consider the network depicted in Figure 7.21 where two backup tunnels are configured on the PLR R0: the NHOP backup tunnel B1 and the NNHOP backup tunnel B2. A conservative approach might be to systematically select B2

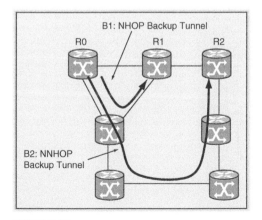

FIGURE 7.21

Optimal backup tunnel selection.

upon link failure detection because the PLR cannot tell a link from a node failure upon detecting the link failure. This way, if the failure was a node failure, the decision was correct. On the other hand, if the failure was a link failure, a better choice would have been to reroute the set of protected TE LSPs traversing the failed link onto B1. The fast rerouted TE LSPs (onto B2) could have followed a shorter path if B1 had been selected in this case. This is mainly due to the additional constraints imposed for the NNHOP backup tunnel path computation. It is worth highlighting that this drawback might be relevant only in some networks; typically, in a non-heavily loaded national network where the propagation delays are not significant, choosing a slightly longer path for a short period (until the TE LSPs are rerouted by their respective HE LSRs) is not necessarily an issue. On the other hand, in a poorly connected network with international links (having significant propagation delays), rerouting along a longer path is not desirable. This is even more true if the network is congested because the temporary rerouting along the B2 backup tunnel is likely to increase the level of congestion over a larger number of links.

Situation 2: Bandwidth Protection Violation

As we will see Section 7.13, one can benefit from the single failure assumption to achieve bandwidth sharing between backup tunnels protecting independent resources. Unfortunately, the inability to differentiate a link from a node failure can lead to situations where backup tunnels protecting independent resources are simultaneously used, resulting in bandwidth protection violation.

Let us consider the example in Figure 7.22. In the network depicted in Figure 7.22, B1 is a NNHOP backup tunnel originating on R1 and terminating on R3 protecting against a node failure (R2) and B2 is a NNHOP backup tunnel originating on R2 and terminating on R0 protecting against a node failure (R1). Because those two backup tunnels protect independent resources (R1 and R2),

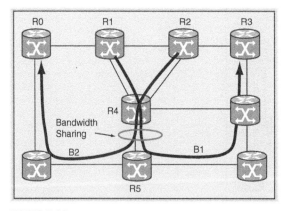

FIGURE 7.22

Bandwidth protection violation.

by virtue of the single failure assumption, they can share bandwidth because they are never simultaneously active (see Section 7.13 for further details). This is true in particular on the link R4-R5. Adopting the same backup tunnel selection strategy as in situation 1, as soon as the link failure is detected by the PLRs R1 and R2, they will both start rerouting protected TE LSPs on both B1 and B2, which would result in a bandwidth protection violation.

This example clearly illustrates the need for some mechanism allowing to unambiguously differentiate a link from a node failure. An alternative (only available if the set of backup tunnel paths are computed by a central entity) is to make sure when computing NNHOP backup tunnels that two NNHOPs backup tunnels protecting adjacent nodes never collide (i.e., never share bandwidth on their common section). The counterpart of such an additional constraint is the increase of the path computation algorithm complexity and a lower bandwidth sharing efficiency.

So the two examples clearly highlight the benefits of a solution that would allow a PLR to differentiate a link from a node failure.

A solution has been proposed which relies on sending hello messages along a link diverse path upon link failure detection; typically, an obvious candidate for the alternate path is the NHOP backup tunnel itself. In the example in Figure 7.23, several backup tunnels are configured: On R1, there is one NNHOP backup tunnel B1 protecting against a failure of the node R2 and one NHOP backup tunnel B3 protecting against a failure of the link R1-R2. Likewise, on R2, there is one NNHOP backup tunnel B2 protecting against a failure of the node R1 and one NHOP backup tunnel B4 protecting against a failure of the link R2-R1.

Mode of operation: Upon link failure detection (by means of layer 2 link failure notification or RSVP/IGP hellos time out), R1[69] starts sending some hello

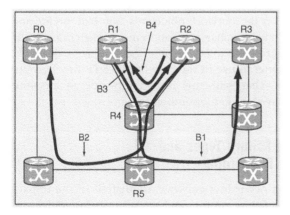

FIGURE 7.23

Mechanism allowing to differentiate a link from a node failure.

[69] R2 performs the same set of operations.

message to R2 via the NHOP backup tunnel B3. If a response is received from the adjacent node (R2), R1 can conclude that the failure is just a link failure and not a node failure. On the contrary, if no response is received from R2, the failure is a node failure.

If we assume that such a failure characterization scheme is available, there are two strategies that can be put in place in terms of MPLS TE Fast Reroute decision:

Option 1: Start using the NNHOP backup tunnel and switch back if required: In this option, as soon as the link failure is detected by the PLR (R1), all the protected TE LSPs traversing the failed link are rerouted onto the NNHOP backup tunnel. Then the failure characterization mechanism mentioned earlier is activated. If it turns out that the failure is a link failure, the rerouted TE LSPs are switched from their NNHOP back up tunnel to their NHOP backup tunnel. If the failure is characterized as a *node* failure, no particular action is required.

Option 2: Start using the NHOP backup tunnel and switch back if required: This option basically does the opposite: Upon detecting the link failure, the PLR starts rerouting the protected TE LSPs traversing the failed link onto the NHOP backup tunnel. Then the failure characterization mechanism is activated; if it turns out that the failure is a link failure, no particular action is required. On the other hand, if the failure is characterized as a *node* failure, the rerouted TE LSPs are switched from their NHOP back up tunnel to their NNHOP backup tunnel.

Pros and cons of each approach: The failure characterization process takes some time Tc (this amount of time depends on the protocol and timers used). With option 1, in the case of link failure, this might cause temporary bandwidth protection violation and/or nonoptimal backup path selection for the reasons mentioned earlier, but this option always minimizes the packet loss. With option 2, in the case of node failure, the duration of traffic loss is increased by Tc, but bandwidth protection is always preserved and a more optimal backup path is selected in the case of link failure. Hence, depending on the network objectives, one may prefer one option or the other, provided that a failure characterization mechanism is available.

In summary, being able to differentiate a link from a node failure is desirable to optimally select the backup tunnel to use in the case of MPLS TE Fast Reroute local protection "facility backup." That said, this is certainly not an absolute requirement and should just be considered an optimization.

7.9.3 Analysis of the Various Failure Types and Their Impact on Traffic Forwarding

A large set of possible failures can occur in a network. An analysis of the impact on the forwarded traffic of various failure profiles and the set of failure detection mechanisms that can be used to detect those failures. We will just focus on the MPLS TE specific aspects here:

1. *Link failure:* Link failures always affect the data traffic until an alternate path is found and data traffic is rerouted over some backup paths. Various

mechanisms have been described in this chapter to handle link failures and find an alternate path.

2. *Node failure:* There are multiple possible causes of node failures, and their nature has a different impact on the forwarded traffic.

■ *Power supply outage:* The traffic is black-holed until it is rerouted over a backup path.

■ *Route processor failure:* In centralized platform architectures, a route processor failure usually implies that packets forwarded to the failing routers are dropped. On the other hand, on distributed platform architectures this type of failure usually does not affect the data plane, and packets are still forwarded by the router, but just the control plane fails. The expected behavior in this case is that after some period,[70] either the IGP or the RSVP hello adjacency will go down. In the former case (IGP adjacencies go down), the IGP neighbors of the failing routers will flood an updated LSA (router link LSA for OSPF) or LSP (for IS-IS). Every head-end LSR will detect that one or more of their TE LSPs traverse a failed LSR and should take the appropriate action (usually a graceful TE LSP reroute will be triggered in a nondisruptive fashion). In the latter case (the RSVP hello adjacency goes down), the node immediately upstream to the failed node will issue an RSVP notification (an RSVP Path Error message) to every head-end LSR having one or more TE LSPs passing through the failed node. Every head-end LSR should then in turn take an appropriate action. This description does not apply to the case of graceful restart procedures.

■ *Software failure:* The impact of a software failure on forwarded traffic is highly coupled to the nature of the software failure, which can vary from the simple generation of a warning message followed by an automatic recovery (via restorable module) handled by the operating system to a situation where the router is completely hosed and can no longer recover from the failure, which might require a complete reinitialization. In the latter case, the traffic is black-holed until the control plane detects the node failure.

■ *Planned node failure:* Because the failure is "planned," various actions can be taken before performing the upgrade. The traffic may be gracefully rerouted around the node. Various methods can be used to meet that goal: For instance, the link costs of every adjacent node can be manually increased or an updated IGP LSA for OSPF or IS-IS LSP can be flooded by the node to be upgraded. The consequences will be that the IGP will smoothly reroute the traffic around this node and every head-end LSR upon triggering a TE LSP reoptimization will likely reroute its TE LSPs along some other path in a nondisruptive fashion. The node to be upgraded will no longer carry any transiting traffic and could be safely upgraded without risking any traffic disruption.

---

[70] This period depends on the IGP or RSVP timer's configuration.

Important note:
Some software and hardware architectures support "hitless" software and hardware upgrades without requiring any of the actions mentioned above.

7.10 STANDARDIZATION

Before we elaborate on the standardization aspects of the MPLS traffic recovery mechanisms described in this chapter, it is worth highlighting one important comment: You might have noticed that several references are provided, which refer to IETF *drafts* that are not RFC (Request For Comment) yet. Strictly speaking, even if an IETF draft is not a standard yet, this does not preclude from being a technology already, available in commercial products and deployed in existing networks. A good illustration of this statement is MPLS TE local protection (Fast Reroute). At the time of writing, this is still an IETF draft: draft-ietf-mpls-rsvp-lsp-fastreroute, which will likely become an RFC soon. For some other drafts, there might still be individual submission that will potentially never become RFCs. Note that the IP and MPLS standards are specified by the IETF.

The aim of this section is not to provide an exhaustive list of all the standards related to MPLS TE recovery but to highlight the most important ones. Several IETF drafts have been listed throughout the chapter in the related sections. The ultimate web site where all the related IETF drafts and RFCs can be consulted is the IETF web site, at *www.ietf.org*.

We first saw MPLS TE global default restoration: By definition this does not imply any standards other than the RFC that defines the signaling extension for MPLS TE.

Then, the next MPLS TE recovery mechanism covered in this chapter was MPLS TE global path protection. Because it simply relies on the set up of diversely routed TE LSPs, there is no specific standard in addition to MPLS TE. Indeed, the path computation of diversely routed TE LSPs does not need to be standardized.

Finally, the last MPLS TE recovery mechanism that has been studied in detail is MPLS TE local protection (Fast Reroute): The main IETF draft specifying both the facility backup and the one-to-one backup local protection recovery techniques is RFC 4090.

Usually, the question that immediately arises is: *Does a protocol specification have to be a standard to be implemented in commercial product?* This answer is a definite no, and we saw several examples in this chapter. Indeed, vendors may decide to implement a protocol that is not yet an RFC based on customers' demands or its confidence in the fact that the IETF draft will become an RFC.

7.11 SUMMARY

This first part of this chapter is devoted to the study of the MPLS TE protection and restoration mechanisms: Global default restoration, the default rerouting mode of

MPLS TE, was first introduced. Then various protection mechanisms were covered: global path protection, which provides a substantially faster convergence time than global default restoration but adds a significant amount of backup states, which may be a limitation in large network. Moreover, in networks where the propagation delay can be significant, convergence time of a few tens of milliseconds is not achievable. Then a large part of this section was dedicated to Fast Reroute, which allows not only a fast convergence time (tens of milliseconds) upon a link or node failure but also with strict QoS during failure in terms of bandwidth and propagation guarantees. Furthermore, MPLS TE allows the use of different classes of recovery assigned on a per TE LSP basis, with a high degree of granularity. As mentioned in this chapter, strict QoS during failure is required neither in every network (but just where bandwidth is very scarce) nor for every traffic type. Finally, for the sake of reference, another last recovery mechanism (not really pursued in the industry) has been briefly presented: the 1+1 protection. Then a comparison of the different sets of mechanisms has been provided with their respective advantages and drawbacks.

Strictly speaking, load balancing cannot be considered a recovery technique. That said, it has been shown that load balancing can contribute to reducing the impact of a network failure on the traffic flow between two points, with some drawbacks though.

An entire section dealt in detail with the delicate problem of failure detection and characterization and the impact of each failure profile on the forwarded traffic.

The three case studies proposed in *Network Recovery: Protection and Restoration of Optical, SONET-SDH, IP, and MPLS* have different sets of assumptions and objectives: from a simple objective of fast convergence upon link failure in an IP network to a more complex network with a wide set of objectives including fast convergence upon link or node failures with different classes of recovery where network backup bandwidth has to be minimized.

In the second part of this chapter (Sections 7.12 and 7.13), we explore some specifics advanced topics, which are not required to understand the MPLS recovery mechanisms but might be interesting if you want to read advanced material on the subject. First, we investigate in detail the signaling extensions that have been specified for MPLS TE Fast Reroute. The reader interested by the mechanisms of Fast Reroute but not in the detailed signaling aspect may want to skip that section.

In the first part of this chapter, we saw that both MPLS TE global path protection and local protection use preestablished backup tunnels; we will see that there are several techniques to compute the path of those backup tunnels depending on the set of recovery objectives and network constraints.

7.12 RSVP SIGNALING EXTENSIONS FOR MPLS TE LOCAL PROTECTION

This section defines the set of RSVP signaling extensions for the two local repair techniques: facility backup and one-to-one backup. Note that some RSVP

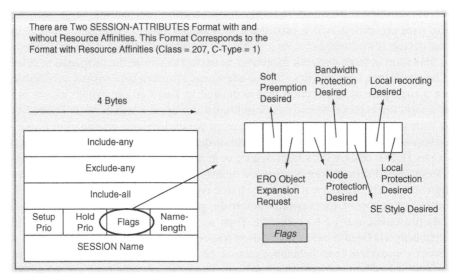

There are Two SESSION-ATTRIBUTES Format with and without Resource Affinities. This Format Corresponds to the Format with Resource Affinities (Class = 207, C-Type = 1)

FIGURE 7.24

RSVP SESSION-ATTRIBUTE object.

extensions are common to both techniques, whereas others are specific to either facility backup or one-to-one backup.

7.12.1 SESSION-ATTRIBUTE Object

The format of the RSVP SESSION-ATTRIBUTE object carried in an RSVP Path message is depicted in Figure 7.24. Let us detail the various flags defined in the RSVP SESSION-ATTRIBUTE object:

1. *Setup and holding priority flag:* These flags are not specific to Fast Reroute. The setup priority characterizes the ability of a TE LSP to get resources, potentially preempting existing TE LSPs with lower priority. The holding priority defines the priority of a TE LSP once set up (used to decide whether the TE LSP can be preempted by another TE LSP).

2. *Flags field.*

   Local protection desired: 0x01
   When set, this flag signals a fast-reroutable TE LSP

   Label recording desired: 0x02
   This flag indicates that the labels used for this TE LSP must be recorded in the RSVP RRO object carried in the RSVP Resv message. The RRO object is described in Section 7.12.4. The label recording flag must be set for a fast-reroutable TE LSP. As mentioned earlier, label recording is necessary to

discover the label used between the NHOP and NNHOP LSR in the case of facility backup with NNHOP backup tunnels. So when this flag is set, every node along the TE LSP path will insert an IPv4 subobject in the RRO object carried in the RSVP Resv message which travels in the upstream direction (from the tail-end LSR to the head-end LSR). This provides the required information about the label used by downstream nodes.

SE (Shared Explicit) Style desired: 0x04

The "Shared Explicit" flag allows two TE LSPs to share some reservation and is used when a TE LSP is rerouted (e.g., when a TE LSP is reoptimized along a shorter path, the new TE LSPs share its reservation with the "old one" before this "old" reservation is torn down: This is known as the *make before break* procedure). When requesting Fast Reroute, the head-end LSR should set this flag.

Bandwidth protection desired: 0x08

When set, this flag indicates that the TE LSP requests bandwidth guarantees during failure (period during which the fast-reroutable TE LSP is rerouted onto its backup tunnel) and so should not suffer from QoS degradation during failure. If a different value for the bandwidth is requested during failure (less than the original bandwidth), then the bandwidth (in case of failure) is specified in the FAST-REROUTE object defined below.

Node protection desired: 0x10

When set, this signals to the LSRs along the path that a NNHOP backup tunnel should preferably be selected over a NHOP backup tunnel.

Soft preemption desired: 0x40

The soft preemption flag is used to indicate that soft preemption is desired (as opposed to "hard" preemption).

Important note:

It is important to underscore the term *desired*. If the request cannot be satisfied, the PLR can decide either not to set up the TE LSP or to select a backup tunnel not satisfying the request. This is a local decision. For instance, suppose a TE LSP carrying voice traffic requesting both Fast Reroute and bandwidth protection. If a PLR along the path cannot find a backup tunnel with the requested amount of bandwidth, the PLR may select a backup tunnel to fast reroute the TE LSP in the case of failure, even if the bandwidth request in the case of failure is not satisfied. Note that additional mechanisms should be used to ensure that this decision will preserve the bandwidth guarantees that might have been provided to other TE LSPs.

Another object, the RRO object, described later in this section, is used by each PLR to indicate whether the request is satisfied. In other words, whether a backup tunnel has been selected, the nature of the selected backup tunnel (NHOP or NNHOP backup tunnel), and finally whether the bandwidth protection request could be satisfied.

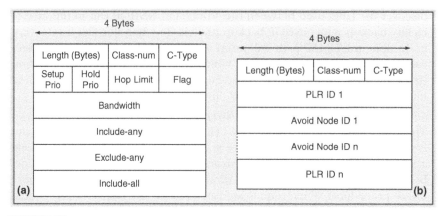

FIGURE 7.25

FAST-REROUTE and DETOUR objects.

7.12.2 **FAST-REROUTE Object**

The purpose of the FAST-REROUTE object is to signal the requirements of the backup tunnel to use for a fast reroutable TE LSP. The FAST-REROUTE object is carried in RSVP Path messages and its format is described in Figure 7.25.

Each RSVP object has a class and a C-type. The class of the FAST-REROUTE object was not determined at the time of writing but will use the form 11bbbbbb for compatibility (this allows an RSVP implementation that does not recognize this object to just ignore it and forward it unchanged to the downstream nodes). The C-type value is 1. Let us now detail the different fields of the FAST-REROUTE object depicted in Figure 7.25A).

Setup and holding priorities: Both the setup and the holding priorities are used to specify the priorities of the backup tunnel. They have an identical usage as any other TE LSP as defined in RSVP-TE.

Hop-limit: The hop-limit field specifies the maximum number of hops between a PLR and an MP (a value of 0 means that just direct links can be used).

Flags: Two methods for Fast Reroute local repair have been presented in the first part of this chapter: facility backup and one-to-one backup. This flag allows specifying the requested method at each PLR along the path:

One-to-one Backup Desired: 0x01

Facility Backup Desired: 0x02

Bandwidth: This field indicates the required bandwidth to protect the TE LSP. This field is a 32-bit IEEE floating point integer, in bytes-per-second.

Exclude-any: 32-bit vector representing a set of attribute filters associated with a backup path any of which renders a link unacceptable.

Include-any: 32-bit vector representing a set of attribute filters associated with a backup path any of which renders a link acceptable (with respect to this test). A null set (all bits set to zero) automatically passes.

Include-all: 32-bit vector representing a set of attribute filters associated with a backup path all of which must be present for a link to be acceptable (with respect to this test). A null set (all bits set to zero) automatically passes.

Note:

Using attributes filters can be very useful. Indeed, MPLS TE allows to use colors (also called *affinities*). Affinities can be used during path computation to include or exclude some particular links. For instance, let us suppose that links with long propagation delays are marked with the color red (this would correspond to a particular bit of the resource class affinity vector). This property is carried within IGP TE extensions. Then one of the attributes of a primary TE LSP carrying voice traffic will be to exclude from its path all the red links (links with long propagation delays). The same set of rules applies to the backup tunnel. If the PLR requires setting up a backup tunnel to protect fast-reroutable TE LSPs requesting for bandwidth protection, for instance, it can use affinities to avoid red links. Note that the affinity constraint of the fast reroutable TE LSP may be different than the ones of the corresponding backup tunnel.

When used, the FAST-REROUTE object can only be inserted by the head-end of a TE LSP and cannot be changed by any other LSR along the TE LSP path.

7.12.3 **DETOUR Object**

The RSVP DETOUR object (whose format is depicted in Figure 7.25B) is specific to the one-to-one backup method and is used to identify Detour LSPs. The DETOUR object does not have a class-num normalized at the time of writing, but it will have the form: 0bbbbbbb. It is worth noticing at this point that the high order bit of the class-num is 0, which implies that a node receiving a path message with a DETOUR object must reject the path message *if it does not support that object,* and it must send an RSVP Path Error message to the PLR. The C-type is 7. Let us now describe the different fields of the DETOUR object.

PLR ID and Avoid Node ID: The PLR ID is an IPv4 address of the PLR and the "Avoid Node ID" contains an IPv4 address of the immediate downstream neighbor (preferably its router-ID) that the PLR wants to avoid. The reason for multiple possible (PLR ID, Avoid Node ID) pairs is that Detour LSPs might be merged to reduce the total number of Detour LSPs in a network. In that case, when multiple Detour LSPs are merged by the Detour Merge Point (DMP), the DETOUR object of the merged Detour LSP contains all the pairs of (PLR ID, Avoid Node ID) of the merged Detour LSPs. An example will be provided later in this section that illustrates the use of the PLR ID and Avoid Node ID.

7.12.4 **Route Record Object**

Another important object to describe is the RRO object (Figure 7.26). This object has not been explicitly defined for Fast Reroute, but several new flags have been

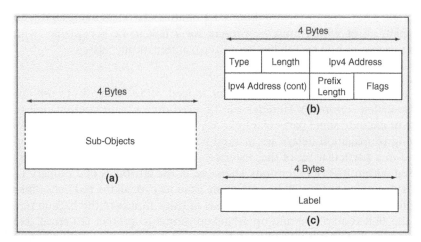

FIGURE 7.26

RRO object and subobject.

added which are required for Fast Reroute. The RSVP RRO object has a Class-num = 21 and a C-Type = 1:

The RRO object is used to record route, labels, and other useful information detailed hereafter along a TE LSP path and is made of variable length subobjects:

IPv4 address subobject is quite simple: The type 0x01 defines an IPv4 address and the IPv4 address specifies a regular IPv4 address of the recording node.

Then several important flags for Fast Reroute are defined:

0x01 Local protection available: This flag indicates that a backup tunnel is available at the PLR adding the subobject.

0x02 Local protection in use: When Fast Reroute is triggered on a PLR, because of a link or node failure, the PLR sets this flag in the corresponding IPv4 subobject. This indicates that Fast Reroute is in use and that the protected TE LSP is rerouted over a backup tunnel at this node. Before any failure occurs, this flag must be cleared.

0x04 Bandwidth protection: As mentioned above a TE LSP has the option to signal its desire to be protected with a backup tunnel offering an equivalent bandwidth (the TE LSP is said "bandwidth protected"), either by setting the "bandwidth protection desired" bit in the SESSION-ATTRIBUTE object or by including a FAST-REROUTE object in the RSVP Path message. When the bandwidth protection request can be satisfied (a backup tunnel offering an equivalent bandwidth can be selected by the PLR), the "bandwidth protection" flag of the IPv4 subobject is set. If bandwidth protection is requested, then each PLR must set this flag appropriately. If bandwidth protection is not explicitly requested, the PLR has the choice to set the bit or not.

0x08 Node protection: Desired protection from node failure can be explicitly requested for a particular TE LSP by setting the "node protection desired" bit in the SESSION-ATTRIBUTE object. If the PLR can find an NNHOP backup tunnel, then the "node protection" bit is set; otherwise (an NHOP backup tunnel has been selected), this bit is cleared; in this case, just the "Local protection available" bit is set. Similar to the previous case, if "Node protection" is requested, each PLR must set this flag appropriately. If node protection is not explicitly requested, the PLR has the possibility to set the bit or not.

As already mentioned, there may be some situations where a request cannot be fully satisfied. Suppose, for instance, that a TE LSP requests local protection (setting the "Local protection desired" bit of its SESSION-ATTRIBUTE object or using the FAST-REROUTE object) along a path R1-R2-R3-R4-R5. If all the nodes can select a backup tunnel in case of link/node failure except the node R3 (because its backup tunnel is down or just not configured), the RRO object carried in the RSVP Resv message sent from R5 to R1 (in the upstream direction) will contain a set of IPv4 subobjects listing all the nodes from R5 to R1 with the Ipv4 subobject of R3 having its "Local protection desired" bit cleared. Another example is if the TE LSP has requested bandwidth protection and the node R2 can find a backup tunnel but not offering an equivalent bandwidth. In that case, the "Bandwidth protection desired" bit of the IPv4 subobject of R2 will be cleared. The RRO object is a very efficient way of signaling the protection status at each hop. This can be used for troubleshooting on the head-end LSR or to take some appropriate actions at the head-end LSR.

Label subobject: This field contains a 32-bit label and is used to learn downstream labels and must be included by each node if the "label recording desired" bit of the SESSION-ATTRIBUTE object carried in the RSVP Path message has been set. Note that the presence of this subobject is of the utmost importance for Fast Reroute facility backup so the PLR learns the label to use when rerouting some protected TE LSPs onto an NNHOP backup tunnel, as previously explained in detail.

7.12.5 Signaling a Protected Traffic Engineering LSP with a Set of Constraints

As already mentioned, a head-end LSR can either use the "Local protection desired" of the SESSION-ATTRIBUTE object or the FAST-REROUTE object to signal the fast reroutable property of a TE LSP. Note that even if the FAST-REROUTE object is used, it is recommended to also set the "Local protection desired" bit of the SESSION-ATTRIBUTE object.

Some other parameters/constraints pertaining to the protected TE LSP can also be signaled: the request for bandwidth protection and/or node protection. This just requires to set the "bandwidth protection desired" and "node protection desired" bit, respectively, in the SESSION-ATTRIBUTE object of the RSVP Path message. If additional control over the backup tunnel is required, the head-end can also include a FAST-REROUTE object in the path message, specifying the bandwidth, attributes filters, hop limit, and priorities that apply to the backup tunnel.

If the head-end requires the PLR along the TE LSP path to use a particular local repair technique (facility backup or one-to-one backup), the corresponding flag should be set in the FAST-REROUTE object.

An example of the mode of operation for facility backup with node protection has been provided in Section 7.5.4. It was mentioned that in this case, a discovery label process is required so the PLR can discover the label used between the NHOP and NNHOP to perform the appropriate label operation when Fast Reroute is activated. The complete backup label discovery process is described below. At this point, one just needs to mention that the "Label recording desired" bit must be set in the SESSION-ATTRIBUTE of the RSVP Path message. This will trigger the label recording process at each hop from the TE LSP tail-end LSR to the head-end LSR.

7.12.6 Identification of a Signaled TE LSP

A TE LSP is uniquely identified by two objects carried in the RSVP Path message: the SESSION and the SESSION-ATTRIBUTE objects. More precisely, the following fields present in those two objects uniquely identify the TE LSP:

- The *IPv4 (or IPv6) tunnel endpoint address* (IPv4 [or IPv6] address of the egress node for the tunnel).
- The *Tunnel ID* (a 16-bit identifier used in the SESSION object that remains constant over the life of the tunnel).
- The *Extended Tunnel ID* (a 32-bit [IPv4] or 128-bit [IPv6] identifier used in the session object that remains constant over the life of the tunnel). Normally set to all zeros. Ingress nodes that wish to narrow the scope of a SESSION to the ingress-egress pair may place their IP address here as a globally unique identifier.
- The *IPv4 (or IPv6) tunnel sender address* (IPv4 [or IPv6] address for a sender node).
- The *LSP ID* (a 16-bit identifier used in the SENDER_TEMPLATE and the FILTER_SPEC that can be changed to allow a sender to share resources with itself).

With one-to-one backup, the backup LSP (also called *Detour LSP*) must be differentiated from the protected LSP. Likewise, when a protected TE LSP is fast rerouted using the facility backup method, the signaling must be updated so one can differentiate the fast rerouted TE LSP from the original one. This differentiation is necessary for merging and to perform appropriate states treatment.

Two methods have been defined to achieve this objective:

Method 1: The Sender-Template-Specific method (referred to as *STS*): With this method, when the RSVP Path message of the rerouted TE LSP is sent along the backup path, the five attributes mentioned above are unmodified, except the "IPv4 tunnel sender address," which is set by the PLR to one of its local address (if the PLR is also the head-end LSR this address must be different from the original one).

Method 2: The Path-Specific method (referred to as PS): With that second method, both the SESSION and the SESSION-ATTRIBUTE object are unchanged, but an additional object (the DETOUR object) is added. This way the PLR can differentiate the protected TE LSP (also called the fast-reroutable TE LSP) because it contains a FAST-REROUTE object or the "Local protection desired" bit of its SESSION-ATTRIBUTE is set from the backup LSP that contains a DETOUR object.

Facility backup always uses the STS method, whereas the one-to-one backup may use either the STS or the PS method.

7.12.7 Signaling with Facility Backup

Earlier in this chapter, we described the mode of operation of Fast Reroute facility backup: In a nutshell, to protect a facility like a link or a node, one or more backup tunnels are preestablished and maintained by a PLR. When a TE LSP is first signaled, a PLR analyzes the signaled parameters and selects the appropriate backup to use in case of a failure. All those operations are performed before any failure and upon a link or a node failure, the set of protected TE LSPs are rerouted onto their backup tunnel. This section details the signaling operations performed by the PLR and the MP at each step of the rerouting procedure.

Point of Local Repair Behavior before the Failure

To select a backup tunnel for a TE LSP, when the TE LSP is first set up, any PLR along the path first determines the TE LSP properties and requested attributes explicitly signaled through RSVP:

1. *Label recording desired (mandatory with facility backup):* If set, the PLR must insert a label subobject in the RRO object carried in the RSVP Resv message sent upstream.

2. *Local protection desired:* If the "Local protection desired" bit of the SESSION-ATTRIBUTE object of the corresponding RSVP path message is set and/or a FAST-REROUTE object is present in the RSVP Path message (in this latter case, an optional preference for the facility backup or one-to-one local protection technique may be signaled), then the TE LSP is said "fast reroutable" and a backup tunnel must be selected. If the PLR can successfully select a backup tunnel for the TE LSP, then it must reflect it in the RRO object carried in the corresponding RSVP Resv message forwarded upstream (the "Local protection available" bit of the RRO IPv4 object is set; otherwise, the bit must be cleared). For example, if a backup tunnel is selected for a protected TE LSP and goes down, the bit must be cleared in the subsequent Resv messages sent upstream.

3. *Bandwidth protection desired:* If the "Bandwidth protection desired" bit of the SESSION-ATTRIBUTE object is set and/or a FAST-REROUTE object

is present in the RSVP Path message with a "bandwidth" field set to the required bandwidth during failure, then a backup tunnel guaranteeing an equivalent QoS during failure should be selected. If the request can be satisfied, then the "Bandwidth protection" bit of the IPv4 RRO subobject carried in the corresponding RSVP Resv messages forward upstream must be set.

4. *Node protection desired:* If the "Node protection desired" bit of the SESSION-ATTRIBUTE object is set and/or a FAST-REROUTE object is present (with hop limit > 0), the PLR should try to find a backup tunnel that does not terminate to the NHOP (i.e., a backup tunnel that does not just protect against a link failure). If this is not possible, the "Node protection" bit of the IPv4 RRO subobject carried in the RSVP Resv message forwarded upstream must be cleared.

It is worth reemphasizing that the backup tunnel selection is a local decision and different implementations may make different choices; the bits defined above express a "desire." So for instance, an implementation may decide to provide bandwidth guarantees to a fast-reroutable TE LSP if such a service can be offered even if bandwidth protection has not been explicitly desired, provided that other requests for TE LSPs that have explicitly requested bandwidth protection can also be satisfied.

As already mentioned, if facility backup is in use, another task that the PLR must perform is to identify the label used between the NHOP and the NNHOP LSR for the protected TE LSPs for which an NNHOP backup tunnel has been selected. Let us consider Figure 7.27.

As illustrated in Figure 7.27, when the TE LSP T1 is first signaled, because the "label recording desired" of the SESSION-ATTRIBUTE object carried in RSVP Path message is set, each node includes in the RSVP Resv message traveling in the upstream direction (from R6 to R2 in the example) both an IPv4 subobject and a label. This way, the PLR R3, for instance, will learn the label used between R4 (NHOP) and R5 (NNHOP). Note that this is just required with facility backup if the selected backup tunnel is an NNHOP backup tunnel. Indeed, in the case of an NHOP backup tunnel, the label used is the same as the fast-reroutable TE LSP.

There is just one exception to this discovery procedure, which is related to the per-interface label space platform. By contrast with global label space platforms where the label space is shared between all interfaces, some platforms (e.g., the ATM LSR platforms) have different label spaces per interface. Consequently, an MP may use different labels for a TE LSP for different interfaces. With a global label space platform, for a given incoming label, an MPLS packet will be identically switched regardless of the incoming interface. For instance, in Figure 7.27, when T1 is fast rerouted by the PLR R3, the traffic from T1 will be received either from the link R4-R5 (prior to failure) or from the link R11-R5 (during failure) but always with the same incoming label. Hence, it will be forwarded to the link R5-R6 in both cases. With a per-interface label space platform, the PLR will have to perform a specific procedure consisting in sending, before any failure, a path message onto the backup tunnel (as if the protected LSP was fast rerouted) to discover the label

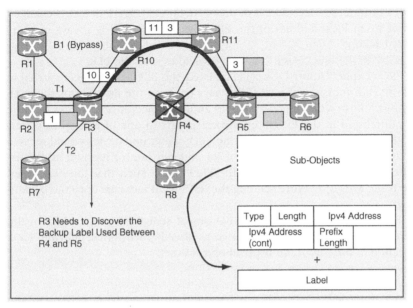

FIGURE 7.27

Illustration of the label discovery process with Fast Reroute facility backup.

that the MP (R5) expects to receive for T1 when Fast Reroute is triggered. Note that the vast majority of packet LSRs use a global label space.

Point of Local Repair Behavior during Failure

Upon failure detection, the PLR triggers Fast Reroute and the protected TE LSPs are rerouted onto their respective backup tunnels. Besides the traffic rerouting, the PLR must also perform a set of control plane operations.

Because RSVP is a soft state protocol, the RSVP Path messages for the rerouted TE LSP(s) must be sent onto the backup tunnel to refresh the TE LSP states on downstream nodes. Indeed, without any specific action, the RSVP states for the rerouted TE LSP would not be refreshed and would time out; after a certain period, downstream nodes would tear down the TE LSPs. In the previous example, after Fast Reroute has been triggered, the PLR (R3) sends the RSVP messages of T1 onto the backup tunnel. Note that intermediate nodes (R10 and R11) do not see those control messages because they are label switched. Then the MP (R5 in this example) continues to receive RSVP Path messages and can refresh the corresponding RSVP states. Compared to the original RSVP Path message that used to be forwarded before the failure on the R3-R4 link, the RSVP Path message sent onto the backup tunnels contains the following changes:

- The "local protection desired," "Bandwidth protection," and "Node protection desired" bits are cleared.

- The IPv4 tunnel sender address of the SENDER-TEMPLATE object is changed and set to an local address of the PLR (the STS method is always used by facility backup).
- The RSVP-HOP object is set to a local IPv4 address of the PLR.
- The ERO (Explicit Route Object) is updated: the RSVP ERO object carried in an RSVP Path message of a TE LSP always contains the list of hops that a TE LSP must follow. When a node receives an ERO object it first checks that the first node listed in the ERO object corresponds to one of is local interface. So in Figure 7.27, without any specific ERO object update, R5 would receive an ERO object listing an address of R4 and not one of its own addresses. So the PLR (R3) needs to update the ERO object such that the next listed node is the MP (R5) before sending the RSVP Path message onto the backup tunnel.
- The RRO object is updated: The RRO object sent in Resv messages in the upstream direction (to R2) is updated as already mentioned, and the "local protection in use" bit of the IPv4 subobject is set.

Note:
The RSVP messages sent onto the backup tunnel are path, path tear, and ResvConf messages.

Merge Point Behavior during Failure

Once Fast Reroute becomes active, the PLR starts sending path messages onto the backup tunnel for every rerouted TE LSP that will be received by the MP, which in turn refreshes the corresponding states.

7.12.8 Signaling with One-to-One Backup

With one-to-one backup the procedure is significantly different. Indeed, with facility backup, no signaling occurs for the protected TE LSP before the failure; the backup tunnel is maintained as any other TE LSP and there is no signaling for the set of protected TE LSP that may use this backup tunnel. By contrast, with one-to-one backup, each protected has a Detour LSP originated at the PLR and terminating at the tail-end LSR, which must be set up and maintained. In this section we describe the signaling operation to set up and maintain those Detour TE LSPs.

1. Remember, the one-to-one backup technique may either use the sender-template specific or the path specific method to identify a protected TE LSP and its Detour LSP:
   - If the sender-template specific method is used, then when signaling the Detour LSP, the PLR replaces the IPv4 (IPv6) address present in the SENDER-TEMPLATE object by one of its local address (which must be different from the one used in the protected TE LSP). A DETOUR object *may* also be added, but this is not mandatory because the new address

in the SENDER-TEMPLATE object is sufficient to differentiate it from the protected TE LSP.

- ■ If the path specific method is used, the PLR adds a DETOUR object in the path message of the Detour LSP.

2. The "local protection desired," "Bandwidth protection," and "Node protection desired" bits are cleared.

3. The PLR also removes the FAST-REROUTE object that may have been present in the original protected TE LSP.

4. RSVP-HOP object is set to a local IPv4 address of the PLR.

5. The ERO object is updated; indeed, the ERO object of the protected TE LSP used to contain the list of hops to follow from the PLR to the tail-end LSR for the protected TE LSP.

Let us illustrate the ERO object update operation through the example shown in Figure 7.28.

In this example, the primary TE LSP T1 follows the path R2-R3-R4-R5-R6. When the PLR R3 signal its Detour LSP (called *D1* in the Figure 7.28), the ERO object is updated from R4-R5-R6 to R10-R11-R5-R6, which is the path computed by the PLR for the Detour LSP.

6. The bandwidth advertised in the Sender-TSPEC object reflects the bandwidth of the Detour LSP, which can be equal to either the bandwidth of the protected TE LSP if there was no FAST-REROUTE object and the "bandwidth protection desired" bit was set in the SESSION-ATTRIBUTE object of the RSVP Path message or the bandwidth explicitly specified in the FAST-REROUTE object signaled in the RSVP Path message of the protected TE LSP.

7. The RRO object is updated: The RRO object sent in Resv messages in the upstream direction (to R2) is updated, as already mentioned; the "local protection in use" bit of the Ipv4 subobject is set when Fast Reroute is triggered.

7.12.9 **Detour Merging**

As pointed out previously, MPLS TE Fast Reroute one-to-one backup has the drawback of generating a potentially considerable number of TE LSPs because the number of required backup tunnels (Detour LSPs) is a function of the number of protected TE LSPs and the network diameter (number of hops traversed by each protected TE LSP). One method helping in alleviating this concern is to proceed to LSP merging. Several rules are defined for fast reroute to handle Detour LSP merging, but the concept is quite simple and described in Figure 7.29.

Let us consider the network depicted in Figure 7.29, A protected TE LSP T1 is set up and follows the path R0-R1-R2-R3-R4-R5 and the local repair technique used in this network is one-to-one backup. So taking the PLR R0 as an example,

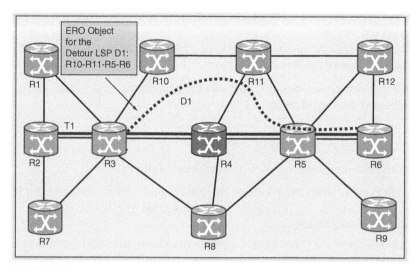

FIGURE 7.28

ERO object calculated for the detour LSP with Fast Reroute "one-to-one backup."

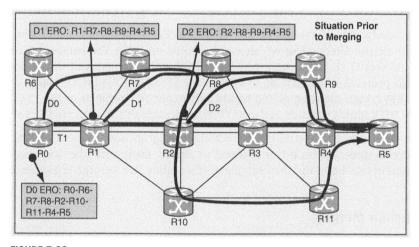

FIGURE 7.29

Backup tunnel (Detour LSP) path computation with MPLS TE Fast Reroute "one to one."

R0 computes a Detour LSP D0 following the path R0-R6-R7-R8-R2-R10-R11-R4-R5 according to the requirements for the protection of T1 and the topology and resource information flooded by the IGP. Likewise, R1 computes a Detour LSP D1 following the path R1-R7-R8-R9-R4-R5 and R2 computes a Detour LSP D2 following the path R2-R8-R9-R4-R5. For the sake of simplicity, both R3 and R4 will perform the same operation, but their respective Detour LSPs are not represented in the diagram.

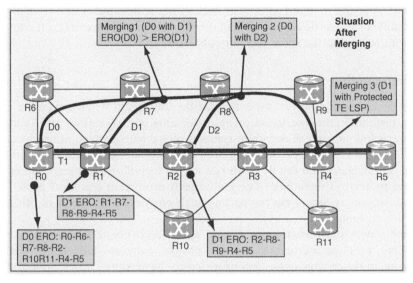

FIGURE 7.30

Illustration of the merging rules with Fast Reroute "one-to-one backup."

As shown on the Figure 7.30, it follows that R7 detects the presence of two detour LSPs D0 and D1 that both protect the same TE LSP: T1. So they can be merged. Because D1 has a shorter path than D0, the resulting merged Detour LSP will be D1 (note that when those Detour LSPs are merged, there are some additional rules to compute the resulting DETOUR object). Likewise, R8 can also perform a merging of D1 and D2. And finally, a third detour merging operation can be performed by R4, but in this latter case, the situation is slightly different. Indeed, when the LSR R7, for example, performs a detour merging operation, it merges two Detour LSPs, whereas in the case of the LSR R4, the merging of a Detour LSP and the primary TE LSP is performed. When an LSR merges the protected LSPs with a Detour LSP, the result is always the protected TE LSP. Figure 7.30 shows the result after merging.

7.13 BACKUP PATH COMPUTATION

In this section, we cover the aspects related to the backup path computation for each of the MPLS TE recovery techniques studied in this chapter. This section is quite dense because of the complexity of the problem to solve, which greatly varies with the set of objectives. Indeed, simple algorithms can be used to compute a diverse path for global path protection or local protection. By contrast, for example, the algorithms to find a set of backup tunnels for Fast Reroute to provide bandwidth guarantees and a bounded increase of the propagation delay while trying to minimize the required amount of backup network capacity can certainly be very complex. This section deals with all the issues of backup tunnel path computation with respect to the set of recovery objectives.

7.13.1 **Introduction**

As previously mentioned, several aspects must be considered when evaluating a protection/restoration scheme. In the previous sections, we saw various MPLS traffic recovery techniques: global default restoration, global path protection, and local protection. Each recovery technique requires the computation of backup path, which can be calculated "on the fly" with restoration techniques or precomputed when using protection techniques like global path protection and local protection. In this section, we focus on the backup path computation aspects of MPLS TE protection techniques.

The first aspect that crosses one's mind about recovery techniques is the recovery time, which is a crucial aspect but not the only one. Indeed, the QoS during failure, in other words, the QoS provided to the rerouted flows along the backup path is also a very important aspect that is directly correlated to the backup path computation.

The backup tunnel path computation complexity is essentially driven by the set of objectives and increases nonlinearly with the set of associated constraints. So for instance, in the case of Fast Reroute, if the only objective is to compute a diversely routed backup tunnel from the protected section (link, node, SRLG) to provide fast convergence in case of resource failure, then the path computation complexity is not very high (rerunning a regular CSPF on a subgraph is usually sufficient). On the other hand, if the objective is to provide a recovery mechanism offering fast convergence and strict QoS guarantees during failure (e.g., bandwidth guarantee and bounded increase of the propagation delay) while trying to minimize the required backup capacity, then this increases the backup tunnel path computation complexity by an order of magnitude.

This section explores those different requirements and details for each of them some possible backup tunnel path computation techniques.

7.13.2 **Requirements for Strict QoS Guarantees during Failure**

Typically, voice traffic does not tolerate QoS degradation for a long period without being perceptible by the users. So an operator may decide to provide QoS guarantees to the TE LSP carrying voice traffic, even during failure. The same reasoning is likely to apply to ATM CBR traffic carried over MPLS. On the other hand, some other TE LSPs carrying less sensitive traffic could tolerate a QoS degradation during failure (until they are reoptimized by their respective head-end LSR). This can be part of the service-level agreement (SLA) between an operator and its customers. This highlights the notion of CoR introduced earlier. As previously mentioned, in the case of Fast Reroute, the requirement for bandwidth guarantee during failure is explicitly signaled and so can be applied on a per TE LSP basis, providing a high granularity.

7.13.3 **Network Design Considerations**

Every network is different and the constraints on backup path computation are not just driven by the set of objectives but also by the network design considerations. The aim of this section is to describe several typical network designs to illustrate the network design implication on the backup path computation for a defined set of recovery objectives in term of QoS during failure.

QoS Considerations in Typical Backbone Network Profiles

We can list three typical networks designs:

1. *Overprovisioned networks:* A simple strategy to provide QoS is to put in place strict planning rules and make sure that the network has always enough bandwidth to accommodate the traffic demand while respecting the QoS objectives. For instance, if at any time the maximum utilization of any link is less than 20% (this is of course just an example for the sake of illustration), there is no need for any particular QoS mechanisms and/or TE mechanism in the network. Note that failure simulation should help figuring out whether the utilization rule mentioned above is still valid under various failure scenarios. In such a network, the backup tunnel path just needs to be diverse from the protected section (link, node, or SRLG). This approach is simple, efficient, but expensive (and requires some network planning tools and a reasonably accurate traffic matrix knowledge).

2. *MPLS Diffserv-aware networks:* In networks where multiple classes of service must be provided with different QoS objectives, one can use the Diffserv architecture where the traffic is marked (colored) based on its CoS and then queued appropriately in the data plane to reach the QoS objectives on a per-CoS basis. In addition to the queuing, congestion avoidance disciplines like WRED can be used. This ensures that delay-sensitive traffic is serviced appropriately while best-effort traffic gets a lower priority and can potentially suffer from some congestion (of course the number of CoS is not limited to two). A very well-known fact is that strict bounded delays and jitter can be provided to high-priority traffics (like voice) provided that some appropriate queuing mechanisms are deployed in the network and the proportion of high-priority traffic served by the high-priority queue (usually preemptive queue) is limited to a fixed percentage of the total amount of traffic forwarded on a specific link. So if the network is designed so the proportion of voice traffic on every link is bounded to, for instance, 30% in both steady state and under failure scenarios, then no particular constraint needs to be applied to the backup tunnel path computation; the

backup tunnel just needs to be diversely routed from the protected section (link, node, or SRLG).

3. *Traffic-engineered network:* In some other networks, there is clearly a need for traffic engineering (voice, ATM, IP, and MPLS) to optimize network resource utilization. Various studies have been conducted during the last 20 years to propose IGP metric computation algorithms so the traffic is routed in an "optimal" way to prevent situations where some links are heavily congested while some other links in the networks have some spare capacity; this refers to IP traffic engineering techniques. Another way of achieving traffic engineering in MPLS-enabled networks is to rely on MPLS TE where the traffic is routed on TE LSPs whose path computation is based on the network topology and available resources with call control admission schemes; in that case, one makes sure that a TE LSP is routed in the network so every traversed network link can accommodate the traffic demand.

Of course traffic-engineered networks can also be Diffserv aware. Diffserv mechanisms ensure that each traffic receives the level of required QoS, whereas traffic engineering is in charge of computing a path that can meet the bandwidth and other requirements. Furthermore, MPLS Diffserv aware TE allows to enforce different CAC schemes (and so underbooking/overbooking) on a per-class type basis, which provides a very high degree of granularity.

Guaranteeing QoS during Failure

Things get a bit more complicated when QoS objectives must also be met during non-steady state periods. *What if a link or a node fails?* An operator may simply decide that the QoS objectives may not be respected in the case of failure in its network. Let us first consider the simple case of an overprovisioned network (Figure 7.31).

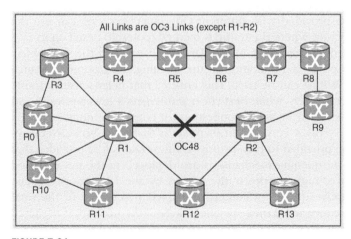

FIGURE 7.31

Bandwidth guarantee during failure in an overprovisioned network.

Although this chapter is dedicated to MPLS TE, let us consider the case of the pure IP (non-MPLS) overprovisioned network depicted in Figure 7.31. Clearly, in such a network, even if IP traffic engineering techniques are used (tuning of the IGP metrics) to avoid congestion on any link at steady state, a link failure is likely to provoke congestion on alternate paths. As depicted on Figure 7.31, all the IP flows destined to R2 and beyond and traversing the nodes R3, R0, and R10 will be rerouted along their next shortest path in case of the failure of the link R1-R2 (through the south path); a maximum of 30% worth of traffic at steady state could potentially result in a congestion of the links R10-R11, R11-R12, R12-R13, and R13-R2 in the case of failure of the link R1-R2. Some IGP metric optimization techniques try to solve that issue for both steady state and under single network failure scenarios. The result varies with the effectiveness of the algorithm in use and the network topology. Also, the degree of granularity is relatively poor because all the IP traffic must be rerouted along the same alternate path by contrast with MPLS TE where several backup paths (backup tunnels) can be computed to reroute a subset of the traffic.

Hence, MPLS TE provides a higher flexibility and granularity, which eases the finding of appropriate backup paths to provide QoS guarantees during failure. For instance, back to our previous example in Figure 7.31, in the case of failure of the link R1-R2, the TE LSPs originally routed through the link R1-R2 will be rerouted along alternate paths obeying the set of required constraints; so TE will play its role, trying to avoid congestion, and if necessary, multiple backup tunnels will be used to be able to reroute the TE LSPs requiring an equivalent QoS during failure.

During failure, protected TE LSPs are rerouted over their respective backup tunnel. As illustrated in Figure 7.32, in this particular example, if a single NHOP backup tunnel is provisioned to reroute all the protected TE LSPs traversing the

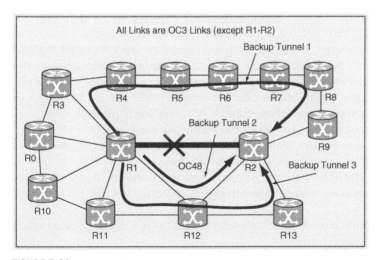

FIGURE 7.32

Bandwidth guarantee during failure with Fast Reroute, using multiple backup tunnels.

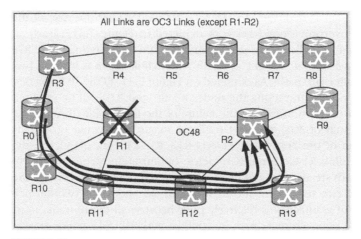

FIGURE 7.33

Bandwidth guarantee during failure.

link R1-R2, in case of failure of this link, fast recovery is certainly achieved, but without QoS guarantee.

Hence, the solution consists of provisioning multiple backup tunnels (Figure 7.32). As shown in Figure 7.32, in the case of failure of the link R1-R2, three backup tunnels are used to reroute the set of primary TE LSPs requiring fast recovery and bandwidth protection that traverse the link R1-R2. So this example illustrates the statement upon which the use of multiple backup tunnels can help achieving the goal of QoS guarantee during failure.

Let us now consider another example (Figure 7.33). Figure 7.33 shows the situation of an MPLS TE network using Fast Reroute. Let us suppose that the NNHOP backup tunnels originated at R3, R0, R10, R11, and R12 are computed without trying to ensure bandwidth guarantees. What could happen (as depicted on the Figure 7.33) is that those NNHOP backup tunnels may be routed over the same path (the IGP shortest path). In this case, the sum of traffic carried by the set of protected TE LSP rerouted onto those tunnels will very likely provoke some congestion along the south path. This example highlights the fact that node failures usually have a greater impact than link failures so the statements mentioned in the case of link failure are even more valid in this case.

The examples above brought out several important considerations, which are worth being summarized before considering in more details the backup path computation aspects.

Let us again briefly consider the following steps during a failure process when using a local protection recovery:

- *t0:* The network element (link, node or SRLG) failure occurs.
- *t1:* Protected TE LSPs are rerouted onto their respective backup tunnel.

- *t2:* TE LSPs are reoptimized by their respective head-end LSR along a new path satisfying their respective constraints (if such a path exists).
- *t3:* The failed resource is restored.
- *During t1-t0:* The traffic is dropped (t1-t0 is the recovery time).
- *During t2-t1* (also called *during failure*): Protected TE LSPs are rerouted onto their respective backup tunnel.
- *During t3-t2* (also called *after failure*): TE LSPs are rerouted over an alternate path (if such a path exists).
- *After t3:* The initial network capacity is restored.

Situation 1: The network is overprovisioned and QoS objectives can be met at steady state, during, and after the occurrence of a failure. For those networks, a perfectly reasonable approach consists in provisioning the backup tunnels without applying any constraint, except of course the one of being diversely routed from the link/SRLG/node that they protect. In the case of failure, the traffic is quickly rerouted and does not suffer from any QoS degradation.

Situation 2: The network is overprovisioned at steady state, but upon a link or a node failure, congestion may appear:

If QoS degradation during failure (t2-t1) is acceptable but not after failure (beyond t2), then a reasonable approach is to limit the backup path computation to a single constraint: being diversely routed. In this case, during failure, the rerouted TE LSPs may suffer from QoS degradation, but this is considered as acceptable. After a short period, they will be rerouted along an alternate path (if such a path exists) that offers the required QoS.

If QoS must be guaranteed also during failure, then the additional constraint is to compute backup tunnel paths such that the QoS is preserved along the backup path, at least for some Class of Recovery.

Situation 3: The network uses of MPLS TE for network resource optimization and/or strict QoS guarantees at steady state. The same conclusions as with situation 2 apply.

In summary, the previous discussion demonstrates that the constraints on the backup paths are driven by both the QoS objectives and the network design. In overprovisioned networks (at steady state and under failure) or in networks where QoS during failure is acceptable, then the constraint of the backup path is minimal; the backup tunnel path just needs to be diversely routed from the protected section, a problem whose complexity is not greater than computing a regular TE LSP path on a sub-graph. On the other hand, in non-overprovisioned networks where QoS guarantees must be ensured during failure for some traffic, backup paths must satisfy additional constraints. Undoubtedly, MPLS TE makes those objectives more likely achievable by allowing to restrict those requirements to a subset of the traffic and by using multiple backup paths for different TE LSPs to reroute.

Before covering in detail the backup path computation aspects, there is another important fact to notice. As already pointed out, in some networks, MPLS

TE is deployed for the sole interest of fast recovery and several deployment scenarios have been described in Section 7.5. Let us consider the very realistic scenario, where at steady state, no particular traffic engineering measures should be taken. The traffic load on every link is perfectly acceptable and the QoS objectives are met. This does not mean that under failure congestion does not appear in some regions in the network. For instance, a fiber cut of a core network router failure can sometimes result in severe congestion spots event though the network load at steady state was perfectly acceptable without any need for traffic engineering. Hence, an interesting strategy can consist of deploying MPLS TE where the TE LSPs are configured with their respective bandwidth but follow the IGP shortest path at steady state (because every IGP shortest path has enough capacity to accommodate the traffic demand). That said, as pointed out, this may no longer be true during failure. Then during failure, the TE LSP will be rerouted over non-IGP shortest paths and congestion will be avoided or at least reduced. This is another application of MPLS TE: bandwidth optimization after failure (until the resource is restored). Note that some failures may last several hours or even days before being fixed.

7.13.4 Notion of Bandwidth Sharing between Backup Paths

The previous section provided several examples where backup tunnels must follow a path offering QoS guarantees (in terms of bandwidth and sometimes propagation delay). Backup tunnels are regular TE LSP, so a simple approach consists of setting backup tunnels with bandwidth as any other primary TE LSP. But this may lead to a very inefficient backup bandwidth usage as shown in the Figure 7.33. So at this point, the very important and simple notion of bandwidth sharing is introduced: Two backup tunnels can share some bandwidth only if they cannot be simultaneously active. For instance, as depicted in Figure 7.33, if two backup tunnels T1 and T2 protect two independent resources R2 and R7 and one makes the assumption that R2 and R7 cannot simultaneously fail, then the total amount of bandwidth that must be reserved on the links they both traverse is the maximum of their bandwidths, not the sum, which highlights why simply setting up backup tunnels with the required bandwidth would be quite inefficient in term of network bandwidth usage (Figure 7.34).

In Figure 7.34, both T1 and T2 are backup tunnels used in the context of local protection to protect against a failure of the nodes R2 and R7, respectively. Suppose also that QoS guarantee during failure is required. If T1 and T2, respectively, require X and Y Mbps, at first sight, one might think that the amount of required bandwidth for both T1 and T2 on the link R4-R5 is X + Y. But if we assume that either R2 or R7 can fail (but they cannot simultaneously fail), then T1 and T2 are never simultaneously active; hence, the required bandwidth for T1 and T2 on the link R4-R5 is max(X,Y) instead of X + Y, which results in considerable bandwidth gain in terms of required network backup capacity.

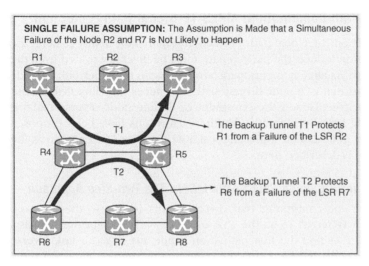

SINGLE FAILURE ASSUMPTION: The Assumption is Made that a Simultaneous Failure of the Node R2 and R7 is Not Likely to Happen

The Backup Tunnel T1 Protects R1 from a Failure of the LSR R2

The Backup Tunnel T2 Protects R6 from a Failure of the LSR R7

FIGURE 7.34

Notion of bandwidth sharing between two backup tunnels protecting independent resources.

It is probably worth defining more accurately what *simultaneously fail* means. When a link or a node fails (at time t0), the protected TE LSPs traversing the failed resources are rerouted onto their backup tunnel. Then those TE LSPs are rerouted by their respective head-end LSR along an alternate path (at time t2, according to the terminology previously introduced), if such a path exists. After a period of ta = t2 − t0, those TE LSPs are no longer rerouted over their backup tunnel. The single failure assumption assumes that a second failure will not happen during ta, so two backup tunnels protecting independent resources cannot be simultaneously active. Then if a second failure occurs after Ta, bandwidth protection can still be ensured (provided that the backup tunnels that used to be routed over the previous failed resources have been reestablished). Hence, the benefit of the single failure assumption is very straightforward; bandwidth sharing between backup tunnels protecting independent resource is possible and results in very significant bandwidth saving as the required amount of backup capacity in the network is drastically reduced. Moreover, the single failure assumption is considered perfectly realistic in many networks, especially because router node failure probability is generally very low.

Note also that the diagram depicted in Figure 7.34 is generic and equally applies to global or local protection (facility backup). In the former case, the backup TE LSP are end to end (between head-end LSR and tail-end LSR). In the latter case, those two backup tunnels are between a PLR and an MP.

Now that the general concepts of QoS guarantees and bandwidth sharing have been illustrated, it is time to describe how those concepts apply to the backup path computation in the context of global path protection and local protection.

7.13.5 Backup Path Computation: MPLS TE Global Path Protection

As described in Section 7.4, global path protection requires the ability to compute diversely routed paths. Indeed, the backup path must be diversely routed from the primary TE LSP path. As already mentioned, two paths can be either link or node disjoint; it is obvious that two node-diverse paths are necessarily link diverse, but the opposite is not true. Hence, the constraint of finding node diverse paths is stricter than finding link diverse paths. Multiple algorithms have been proposed to compute link- or node-diverse paths and a simple algorithm (referred to as the *two-step approach*) is described here.

A Simple Algorithm for Diverse Path Computation: The Two-Step Approach

A simple approach for computing two diverse paths is to use the two-step approach algorithm (referred to as the *2SA algorithm*). This algorithm consists of first running CSPF to find the first path, then prune any link (for link diverse paths) or node (for node diverse paths) traversed by this shortest path and run a second iteration of CSPF to find the second path.

Although very simple and fast, this algorithm has the following limitations:

- It may fail to find two link- or node-diverse paths for some pair of nodes even if such a solution actually exists.
- The resulting solution may be suboptimal in finding two diverse paths so the sum of their cost is minimal (Figure 7.35).

To illustrate this statement, let us consider the double-square network diagram depicted in Figure 7.35A) and the two pairs of LSRs (R1-R3) and (R4-R3). This network has links with costs 1 or 2 as shown on the figure.

Using the 2SA algorithm, two link- and node-diverse paths can easily be found between R1 and R3 (Figure 7.35A). On the other hand, the situation is different between the LSRS R4 and R3; the 2SA fails to find two link- or node-diverse paths (Figure 7.35B).

This raises another interesting question related to the objective the computation of two diverse paths has to meet: *How should one define the optimality criteria of the paths computation?* To illustrate this, let us go back to Figure 7.35, where it can be easily seen that two node-diverse paths can be found. They would follow the paths R4-R1-R2-R3 and R4-R5-R6-R3.

Remember, there may be two situations in which two diverse paths are required:

- *Situation 1:* MPLS TE global path protection is used (Section 7.4).
- *Situation 2:* The traffic between R4 and R3 is load balanced between two diverse paths.

In situation 1, this means that the traffic follows a nonoptimal path at steady state (with a cost of 5 instead of 3 for the shortest path between R4 and R3). This is clearly a trade-off that should be considered when evaluating MPLS TE global path protection because at steady state, traffic may not follow an optimal path to satisfy

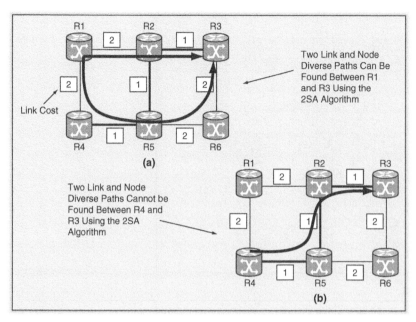

FIGURE 7.35

Computation of diversely routed paths using the 2SA algorithm.

the requirement of having a diverse path for the backup tunnel. Furthermore, the backup tunnel will just be used in the case of failure along the primary TE LSP path for a short period, *so is it worth following a nonoptimal path at steady state (during the vast majority of the cases) just to be able to get a diversely routed path under failure?* A possible compromise is to add a constraint to the diverse path computation: the cost increase of the primary TE LSP cost compared to the shortest path obeying the set of constraints. If no such paths can be computed, fall back to the global repair mechanism. For instance, if to satisfy the constraint of finding two diversely routed paths, this results in a path cost increase of 50% for the primary TE LSP (compared to the shortest possible path satisfying the set of constraints), then global default restoration should be used instead of global path protection.

In situation 2 (load balancing), it would then be interesting to find a solution where the sum of the costs of the two diverse paths is minimized, something that the 2SA algorithm cannot guarantee either. Let us consider Figure 7.36 and study the performance of the 2SA algorithm in trying to find two diverse paths so the sum of their costs is minimized.

Let us now run the 2SA algorithm and determine the sum of the costs of the two diverse paths between the node pair (R4,R3). Figure 7.37 shows the two diverse computed paths that would be obtained by running the 2SA algorithm described above. As shown in Figure 7.37, the two diverse paths obtained with the 2SA algorithm provide two paths so the sum of their cost is $4 + 13 = 17$, which

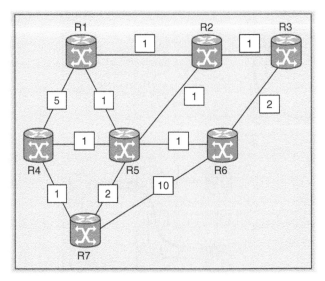

FIGURE 7.36

Optimization of the sum of the cost of two diversely routed paths.

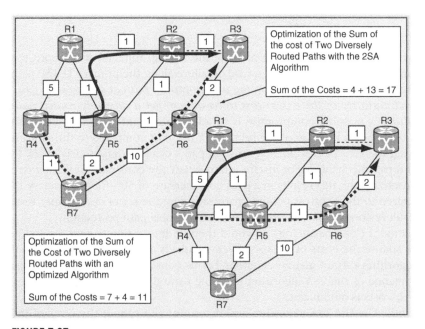

FIGURE 7.37

Sum of the cost of two diversely routed paths using the 2SA algorithm.

is clearly not the most optimal set of diverse paths that could have been obtained (here, the best set of diverse paths have a sum of costs of 11 instead of 17).

What does this highlight? The two examples depicted above show that the 2SA algorithm, though very simple, is not always very efficient because it sometimes fails to find two diverse paths even though such paths exist, and when an additional objective of minimizing the sum of costs of the two diverse paths is added, which can be useful in the case of load balancing, for example, this algorithm cannot meet that objective either.

Hence, more optimal diverse path computation algorithms have been proposed that can always find diverse paths if such paths exist and that can compute two diverse paths so the sum of their cost is minimized where, for instance, two runs of (modified) Dijkstra algorithms[71] allow for the computation of diverse optimal paths. Additional constraints like introducing a trade-off between path diversity and path cost increase can be added but at the cost of increasing the algorithm complexity.

7.13.6 Backup Tunnel Path Computation: MPLS TE Fast Reroute Facility Backup

Let us now describe the backup path computation in the context of MPLS TE local protection.

Backup Tunnel Path Computation without QoS Guarantee during Failure

The simpler case of backup tunnel computation without QoS guarantee during failure is first considered. As already discussed, in several deployment scenarios, the unique constraint that must be considered for the backup tunnels computation is to find a diversely routed path from the protected facility (link/node/SRLG).

This can be for one of the following reasons:

- *The network is overprovisioned:* In this case, regardless of the backup tunnel path, the rerouted TE LSPs will follow a noncongested path. This ensures QoS guarantees during failure.

- *QoS guarantee during failure is just not a requirement:* Fast recovery is the unique constraint and the flows rerouted over a backup path can suffer from QoS degradation during failure for a limited period (until they are rerouted along another path by their respective head-end LSRs, provided such a path can be found).

Because the backup path complexity is drastically reduced in those cases, there are just two aspects to discuss:

1. Manual configuration versus dynamic backup tunnel path computation
2. Backup tunnel path computation triggers

---

[71] Other algorithms can also be used.

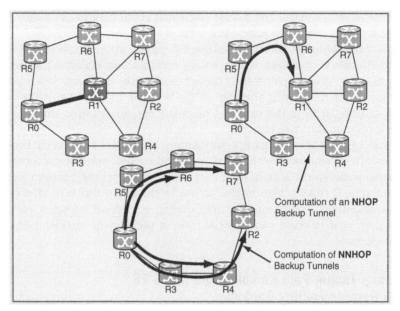

FIGURE 7.38

Backup path computation of NHOP and NNHOP backup tunnels without strict QoS guarantee.

Manual configuration versus dynamic backup tunnel path computation: As previously discussed, with MPLS TE Fast Reroute facility backup, the number of backup tunnels is a function of the number of protected resources, not the number of protected TE LSPs. Because the number of backup tunnels that must be configured is limited, the network administrator may just decide to manually configure the backup tunnels paths; in this case, no dynamic computation is performed by the LSRs.

On the other hand, as stated earlier, the backup tunnel path computation is, in this case, quite straightforward and not CPU intensive, so another option is to rely on some distributed path computation where each PLR computes its own set of backup tunnels:

Let us consider the example in Figure 7.38.

Figure 7.38 depicts a simple network where the PLR R0 requires setting up the following set of backup tunnels:

- An NHOP backup tunnel to protect against a failure of the link R0-R1 (no other constraint other than computing a diversely routed path).
- A set of NNHOP backup tunnels to protect against a failure of the node R1 (no other constraint other than computing a diversely routed path). Note that one NNHOP backup tunnel is required per NNHOP.

The LSR R0 needs to perform the following steps:

Step 1: Compute a NHOP backup tunnel path to protect the link R0-R1: Because no other constraint than the diverse route computation is required for the NHOP backup, a single algorithm consists of pruning the protected section (link R0-R1 in this case) and running CSPF over the remaining topology. The selected path will be the shortest path, taking into account either the IGP or the MPLS TE metric, because no bandwidth is required for the backup tunnel. The resulting NHOP backup tunnel is depicted in Figure 7.38.

Step 2: Compute a set of NNHOP backup tunnel paths, one for each NNHOP. In this particular example, R0 has 4 NNHOPs: R6, R7, R2, and R4. For each of them, the PLR R0 performs a CSPF computation over the remaining topology (after having pruned the protected resource R1).

Such a backup tunnel path computation is straightforward and several existing implementations support dynamic backup tunnel computation.

Important note:

So why not always adopting a dynamic backup tunnel path computation scheme?

Although such a backup path computation can easily be handled in a distributed fashion, there might be another reason why manual configuration is required: the nonsupport or configuration of the IGP TE extensions specifying the SRLG. In this case, the PLR does not have the required knowledge to compute an SRLG-diverse path. To illustrate this issue, let us consider Figure 7.39.

In the example depicted in Figure 7.39, the two lightpaths interconnecting the pair of LSRs (R1, R4) and (R4, R5) belong to the same SRLG. In other words, they have some equipment in common (at the optical layer in this case) whose failure would provoke the failure of both lightpaths. By default the IP/MPLS layer does not have such visibility and the topology seen by the IP/MPLS layer is reduced to the topology described in Figure 7.39B.

Computing the backup tunnel path to protect the link R1-R4 from a link failure would result (in this simple example) in selecting the shortest path diversely routed from the protected link, hence the path R1-R5-R4 (supposing that all the links have an equal metric and the path satisfies other constraints), as shown in Figure 7.40A.

Unfortunately, such a backup tunnel path would not be the right choice. Indeed, a failure of the SRLG shared by the links R1-R4 and R5-R4 would imply the failures of both the protected link R1-R4 and its associated backup tunnel because the link R5-R4 would also fail. This highlights the importance of being able to compute a SRLG diverse path for the backup tunnel by means of, for example, distributed CSPF SRLG-diverse backup path computation algorithms.

Backup path computation triggers: Now another interesting question arises. *When should a backup tunnel (with facility backup) path computation be triggered?*

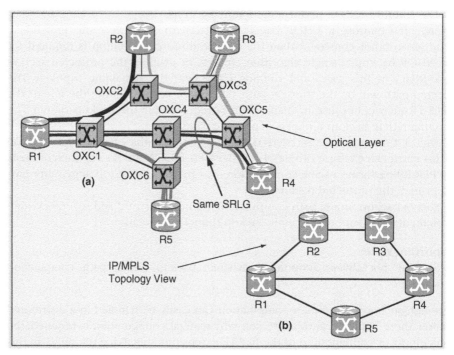

FIGURE 7.39

IP/MPLS logical view.

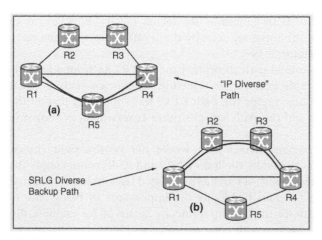

FIGURE 7.40

Computation of an SRLG diverse path.

The backup tunnel path computation and establishment can either be triggered when the link goes up (for an NHOP backup tunnel) or when the neighbors adjacency is first established (for an NNHOP backup tunnel). Another alternative is to set up a NHOP or NNHOP backup tunnel when the first protected TE LSP traversing the protected resource is signaled.

Furthermore, a PLR can trigger backup tunnel path reoptimization at regular intervals to determine whether a better path (shortest path) exists.

Backup Tunnels Path Computation with Strict QoS Guarantees during Failure

Undoubtedly, when QoS guarantees during failure are required, backup tunnel path computation is getting significantly more complicated because the requirement of ensuring that the backup tunnel paths offer QoS guarantees (at least for some CoRs) is added. This section explores the various aspects of the backup tunnel path computation to satisfy such a set of constraints. Strict QoS guarantees can be reduced to the ability to reroute TE LSPs over a backup tunnel providing an equivalent bandwidth and sometimes a bounded increase of the propagation delay. This is why the terms *QoS guarantee* and *bandwidth protection* are used interchangeably throughout this section.

It is worth reinforcing the fact that Fast Reroute is a temporary mechanism (i.e., a protected TE LSP is rerouted onto a backup tunnel until it gets reoptimized by its respective HE LSR). Therefore, while the protected TE LSPs are rerouted over their backup tunnel, the QoS provided to those TE LSPs is dictated by the amount of bandwidth of the backup tunnel and the propagation delay experienced along the backup tunnel path.

To compute a set of backup tunnels that satisfy such a set of requirements, one must follow several steps:

Step 1: First answer the following set of questions:

1. What is the amount of bandwidth to protect?
2. What is the network backup capacity?
3. What are the backup tunnel path computation triggers?

Step 2: Choose a backup tunnel path computation path model.

Step 1: Answer the Following Set of Questions
1. What is the Amount of bandwidth to protect?
When trying to achieve bandwidth protection with Fast Reroute, one must first determine the amount of bandwidth to protect (also called the *protected bandwidth*).

The protected bandwidth is the amount of bandwidth required for the backup tunnel(s) (i.e., amount of bandwidth that needs to be protected).

At first glance, this seems a quite obvious question. That said, there are two approaches that can be taken here, each having its respective pros and cons:

Approach 1: Protect the actual reserved bandwidth. To illustrate that first approach, let us consider the following example of an OC3 link where just 10 TE LSPs have been signaled that traverse this link and such that the sum of their bandwidth is 50 Mbps. Suppose also that just a subset of them requires bandwidth protection and the sum of their bandwidth is 30 Mbps. In this model, the idea consists of computing an NHOP or NNHOP backup tunnel having a capacity of 30 Mbps: The protected bandwidth is 30 Mbps. *Indeed, why try to protect the entire OC3 capacity if only 30 Mbps worth of traffic must be protected?*

The advantage of this approach is that just the amount of required bandwidth is reserved, not more, which thus allows optimal backup bandwidth usage in the network. The immediate counterpart is the requirement for more frequent backup tunnel path computations. Indeed, the protected bandwidth changes as new TE LSPs are signaled and torn down. If a new backup tunnel path computation is triggered each time the protected bandwidth changes in the network, this will generate the computation and signalling of new backup tunnels more frequently. One might try to limit this frequency by the introduction of a threshold mechanism—for instance, for an OC3 link, set a threshold every 20 Mbps (a more efficient mechanism would not adopt a nonlinear spacing of the thresholds though). When the protected bandwidth crosses a threshold a new backup tunnel path computation is triggered. Another set of thresholds is defined when the protected bandwidth decreases of course.

Approach 2: Protect a bandwidth pool regardless of the actual amount of reserved bandwidth. The protected bandwidth does not depend on the actual amount of reserved bandwidth by a set of protected TE LSPs requesting bandwidth protection that traverse a protected resource. So typically, if an OC3 link has a capacity of 155 Mbps, one tries to find a set of backup tunnels for 155 Mbps. Similarly, a protected SDH-SONET VC of 155 Mbps reserves 155 Mbps of backup capacity in the network, whether the protected VC carries some traffic or not.

Important notes:

- Because bandwidth protection can be requested on per-TE LSP basis, if the operator knows *a priori* that the proportion of TE LSP requesting bandwidth protection will never exceed x% of each link capacity, then the protected bandwidth can be limited to x% of each link capacity. For example, if bandwidth protection is just required for the voice traffic and the operator knows *a priori* that each link will never carry x% of voice traffic, then the required protected bandwidth for each facility to protect is limited to x% of the link capacity.

- When MPLS Diffserv aware TE is configured on the network, more than one pool of bandwidth can be configured. The aim of such a model is to allow different CACs for different classes of traffic. For instance, an OC3 link can be configured so the maximum amount of voice traffic does not exceed a fixed percentage of the link capacity, for instance, 50 Mbps and the maximum amount of data traffic does not exceed 200 Mbps. This interesting model can guarantee different overbooking/underbooking ratios per class of traffic. In the example mentioned above, the maximum amount of voice traffic admitted for the TE LSP carrying voice will never exceed 50 Mbps, whereas up to 200 Mbps of TE LSPs carrying data traffic can be admitted for this OC3 links. A proper scheduling mechanism then needs to be configured to guarantee that each class of traffic will be served appropriately. Hence, the network administrator may decide to protect the bandwidth of a certain pool, for instance, the bandwidth pool dedicated to the voice traffic. This allows guarantees fast recovery with Fast Reroute for the data traffic and fast recovery with bandwidth guarantee for the voice traffic. So the protected bandwidth is in this case limited to a specific bandwidth pool, which reduces the amount of required backup capacity.

Though a bit less optimal because it potentially required more protected bandwidth than necessary, this approach is more scalable than the previous one, as backup tunnel path computation is much less frequently triggered.

2. What is the network backup capacity?

The backup capacity is defined as the network capacity dedicated for backup tunnels requiring bandwidth and that cannot be used by primary TE LSPs. The ratio of the required backup capacity divided by the available bandwidth is an important efficiency factor of a recovery mechanism. Typically, if the required capacity to provide bandwidth protection is 20% of the total network capacity, the recovery mechanism can be defined as extremely efficient as far as the bandwidth usage is concerned. Indeed, this means that just 20% of the network capacity is dedicated to backup while being able to provide bandwidth protection when required, by contrast with SONET-SDH, for instance, where a protected VC requires to allocate twice the VC bandwidth: once for the primary VC and the same bandwidth for the backup.

Hence, for each link, the network administrator defines the following:

- *The primary bandwidth pool(s).*[72] This determines the maximum amount of bandwidth that can be admitted on the given resource for primary TE LSPs.
- *The backup pool:* Total amount of bandwidth that can be used by backup tunnels.

This is illustrated in Figure 7.41. In Figure 7.41, the network administrator configures the proportion of the link that can be used by regular TE LSPs and the amount of bandwidth reserved for the backup tunnels used by TE LSPs requiring bandwidth protection. The overlay backup network is the network with link capacity equal to the backup bandwidth pool on each link.

---

[72] Potentially multiple bandwidth pools will be defined on a per class type basis if MPLS Differsv aware TE is used. For the sake of simplicity, we consider that a single pool is defined.

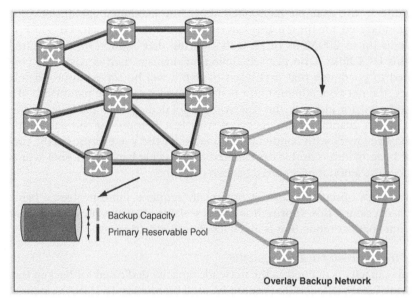

FIGURE 7.41

Illustration of the network backup capacity.

Important note:

An important aspect of the reserved backup capacity in an IP/MPLS network is that the bandwidth is unavailable in the control plane but still fully available in the data plane. So, for instance, if an OC3 link is configured with a backup pool of 30 Mbps and a reservable bandwidth pool for the primary TE LSPs of 125 Mbps, no more than 125 Mbps of bandwidth can be reserved by all the primary TE LSPs traversing the link (CAC function). That said, the bandwidth is still available in the data plane. In other words, the packets forwarded onto the link R0-R1 will be served at link speed rate. This offers a higher QoS at steady state (when the backup tunnels making use of the backup pool are not active), a major difference with other recovery mechanisms at lower layers where the backup capacity cannot be easily reduced by primary traffic. For instance, in the optical plane, the optical backup capacity cannot be used by the active primary optical paths. So to avoid some bandwidth waste, one technique consists of allocating the backup capacity to low-priority optical paths that are preempted in the case of failure by the high-priority rerouted optical paths.

Overlay backup capacity network discovery: We describe below a backup tunnel path computation model whereby the entity responsible for the backup tunnel path computation will first have to acquire the knowledge of the backup capacity on each link to perform the backup tunnel path computation (i.e., the backup network capacity). There are two ways by which the entity responsible for computing the backup tunnel paths can acquire the knowledge of the overlay backup network:

1. *Via a local static configuration:* The network administrator just manually configures the amount of backup capacity for each link in the network. An alternative would consist in using for the capacity the difference between the actual link speed and the maximum reservable bandwidth. Indeed, when a link is configured with MPLS TE, the network administrator configures the maximum reservable bandwidth, as already mentioned. Furthermore, the link speed is advertised by the IGP. So the entity could implicitly conclude that the backup capacity is equal to *link-speed-maximum reservable bandwidth*. For example, an OC3 link is configured with maximum reservable bandwidth of 120 Mbps; in this case, the entity in charge of the backup tunnel path computation could implicitly deduce that the backup capacity on this link is OC3-link-speed = 155 Mbps-120 Mbps = 33 Mbps. Unfortunately, this approach does not work with overbooking. Suppose that the network administrator decides to apply overbooking on some links. If the maximum reservable bandwidth is 200 Mbps to allow for an overbooking ratio, this strategy no longer works.

2. *Via an automatic IGP discovery:* This just requires a simple and straightforward IGP (OSPF or IS-IS) extension so every node can explicitly signal through its IGP the amount of backup capacity on each of its attached link(s). Such an extension has been proposed and a new sub-TLV (called *backup bandwidth pool sub-TLV*) has been defined. This IGP extension does not have any IGP scalability impact, which is an important aspect that must be highlighted. Indeed, every router advertises the backup bandwidth pool for each of its attached link. In the FACILITY-BACKUP model studied in this section, this value does not change as new backup tunnels are dynamically signaled.

3. What are the backup tunnels path computation triggers?

The same backup path computation triggers as in the previous case (backup tunnel computation without QoS) are valid here. In addition, a backup tunnel path computation is also triggered when there is a change in the protected bandwidth and/or the network backup capacity.

Step 2: Choose a Backup Tunnel Path Computation Path Model

Once the protected bandwidth on each link is determined and the network backup capacity is known, the next step is to choose a backup tunnel path computation model. Several models have been proposed and listing all of them is virtually impossible. Some of these models rely on distributed backup tunnel path computation (each PLR is responsible for computing its set of backup tunnels) and others explicitly rely on centralized backup tunnel path computation. They all differ by their degree of efficiency, required set of protocol signaling extensions, complexity, and scalability, along with other criteria.

Hence, two models, known as the *independent CSPF-based model* and the *facility backup model*, are described in detail in the rest of this section, but bear in mind that they are not the only backup tunnel path computation models available.

Model 1: the *independent CSPF-based model:* A simple approach to provide fast recovery and bandwidth guarantees during a failure is to simply set up a backup tunnel with a bandwidth equal to the protected bandwidth. In this model, each PLR simply executes the following set of tasks:

- The PLR first determines the amount of bandwidth required[73] for the NHOP or NNHOP backup tunnel (protected bandwidth).
- Compute a path for the backup tunnel applying the bandwidth constraint as for any regular TE LSP (could either use the regular reservable bandwidth or the backup bandwidth).
- Set up the backup tunnels with their associated bandwidth.

Although this approach is certainly simple and meets the requirements, it suffers from several limitations:

1. Bandwidth sharing between backup tunnels protecting independent resources cannot be performed, requiring much more backup bandwidth than necessary in the network.
2. Inability to find a placement of the backup tunnels even if a solution exists (in some cases).

Let us illustrate those limitations through two examples:

1. *Inability to perform bandwidth sharing:* Although the concept of bandwidth sharing has already been introduced, it is worth providing another example to highlight its benefits.

As explained previously, under the single failure assumption, two backup tunnels protecting independent resources can share bandwidth. By contrast, two backup tunnels originated by two LSRs that protect against the failure of the same resource (link or node) cannot share their bandwidth because upon failure of the resource they protect, they will be simultaneously active.

In Figure 7.42, B1 and B2 are NNHOP backup tunnels originated on the PLRs R8 and R0, respectively, to protect against a failure of the node R1, whereas B3 is an NNHOP backup tunnel originated at the PLR R5 to protect against a failure of the node R6. As mentioned in Figure 7.42, all links are OC3 except R0-R1 (10 Mbps), R8-R1 (15 Mbps), and R5-R6 (30 Mbps). In this example, we assume that the protected bandwidth is equal to the link bandwidth (e.g., a backup tunnel of 10 Mbps is required to protect from a failure of the link R0-R1 or the node R1). Moreover, the single failure assumption is made, which is that two LSRs cannot

---

[73] The determination of the required amount of bandwidth to be protected is discussed later in this chapter.

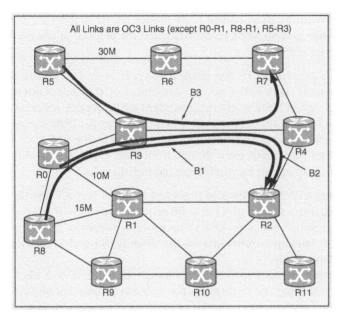

All Links are OC3 Links (except R0-R1, R8-R1, R5-R3)

FIGURE 7.42

Illustration of the inability to perform bandwidth sharing with the independent CSPF model.

simultaneously fail. In this example, B1 and B2 both protect against the failure of the same resource (node R1). This means that upon R1's failure, both B1 and B2 will be active so the required bandwidth on the link R3-R4, for instance, for both of them is 10 Mbps + 15 Mbps. On the other hand, because the backup tunnel B3 protects R5 from a failure of the node R6, the backup tunnel B3 can share the bandwidth with B1 and B2, so the required bandwidth on the link R3-R4 is max ((B1 + B2),B3) = 30 Mbps and not 10 Mbps + 15 Mbps + 30 Mbps = 55 Mbps. So the single failure assumption allows the use of bandwidth sharing and 25 Mbps of backup bandwidth is saved on the link R3-R4.

Another interesting fact is that in some scenarios, the actual amount of reserved bandwidth for B1 and B2 may not be the sum of their bandwidth. Suppose now that the bandwidth of the link R1-R2 (or bandwidth pool; see below) is now equal to 5 Mbps. The maximum amount of traffic originated by R0 and R8 that can traverse the link R1-R2 is bounded by the R1-R2 bandwidth pool: 5 Mbps. So in this case, the total amount of protected bandwidth for B1 and B2 on the link R3-R4 is indeed 5 Mbps not 10 Mbps + 15 Mbps = 25 Mbps.

Therefore, this example clearly highlights the benefit of bandwidth sharing under the assumption of a single failure. Unfortunately, with the independent CSPF model, each PLR determines the amount of bandwidth to be protected and sets up its own backup tunnel; there is no synchronization between PLRs. This is why no bandwidth sharing can be achieved. With the independent CSPF model, B1, B2, and B3 are signaled with 10 Mbps, 15 Mbps, and 30 Mbps, respectively, and the amount of reserved bandwidth on the link R3-R4 is 55 Mbps.

   2. *Inability to find a placement of the backup tunnels even if a solution exists (in some cases):* This is the second limitation of the independent CSPF-based model. By definition, the independent CSPF model relies on the uncoordinated backup tunnel path computation of various LSRs; consequently, the order of setting is arbitrary, which can result in the inability to find a backup tunnel placement even though a solution exists. Let us illustrate this statement through an example depicted in Figure 7.43.

In Figure 7.43, R0 requires an NNHOP backup tunnel of 10 Mbps (capacity of the link R0-R1) to protect against a failure of R1 and R8 requires an NNHOP backup tunnel of 20 Mbps (capacity of the link R8-R1) to protect against a failure of R1. Suppose also that the backup bandwidths on the links R3-R4 and R8-R9 are 20 Mbps and 10 Mbps, respectively.

If the first node starting its backup tunnel computation is R0, it will likely select the shortest path satisfying the constraints for its backup tunnel: R0-R3-R4-R2. Then no path obeying the required constraint of 20 Mbps of bandwidth can be found by R8, although a backup tunnel placement could be found as depicted in Figure 7.44.

Of course, a solution could have been found even with the first placement allowing for load balancing with two backup tunnels having 10 Mbps of bandwidth each and following the paths R8-R0-R3-R4 and R8-R9-R10-R11. But with the independent CSPF model, for a fixed number of backup tunnels (also called *splits*), a similar example could be found where potentially a solution cannot be found to satisfy the requirement of protecting X Mbps.

Model 2: The facility-based computation model provides strict QoS guarantees to a set of specific protected TE LSP requesting bandwidth protection with an efficient backup bandwidth usage. This aspect is indeed extremely important for cost effectiveness. The "facility-based computation" model is described as follows:

   1. *Centralized versus distributed path computation models:* The facility-based computation model specifies two possible methods for the computation of the set of required backup tunnel paths:
      a. The *centralized model,* in which a central server (also called a *path computation element, PCE*[74]) computes the paths for the set of backup tunnels that protect all the network resources
      b. The *distributed model,* in which each router (LSR) is responsible for the computation of a subset of backup tunnel paths

---

[74] There are several possible terms to refer to the capability of computing a TE LSP path for a client LSR: *path computation server, path computation element,* and *path computation router.*

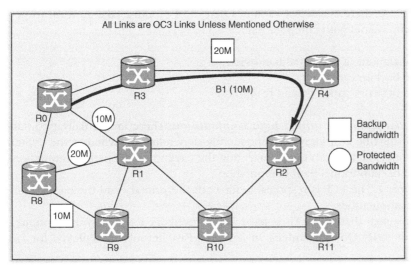

FIGURE 7.43

Illustration of the potential inability to find a placement of backup tunnel with independent CSPF model.

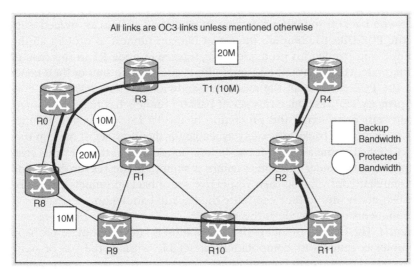

FIGURE 7.44

Illustration of the potential inability to find a placement of backup tunnels with the independent CSPF model, although a solution exists.

In any case, there is a set of variables that the PCE must take as input to perform backup tunnel path computation:

1. The amount of protected bandwidth
2. The backup capacity
3. The network topology and resources

Centralized backup tunnel path computation: There are actually two subcases that must be considered independently, depending on whether the central PCE is responsible for both the primary and the backup tunnel path computations or just the backup tunnel path computation.

Situation 1: The PCE is responsible for both the primary and the backup tunnel path computations.

This assumes that MPLS TE is used in the network for bandwidth optimization and/or strict QoS guarantees. In addition, Fast Reroute is deployed for fast recovery.

In this case, the PCE knows both the amount of protected bandwidth, which is equal to the actual reserved bandwidth (because it is also responsible for the primary tunnel placement) and the backup capacity, which is nothing but the remaining capacity once all the primary TE LSPs have been placed. So the PCE can protect one element at a time (an element being either a link, a node, or an SRLG), using all the network backup capacity. This will ensure that bandwidth is shared between backup tunnels protecting independent resources; indeed, suppose that the PCE tries to compute the set of backup tunnels to protect all the TE LSPs requesting bandwidth protection that traverse a node R1 in the case of failure of the node R1. The protected bandwidth is equal to the sum of their bandwidth and the PCE can use all the available bandwidth on every link not consumed by primary TE LSPs. Once this set of backup tunnels has been computed, the PCE can start considering the protection of the TE LSPs traversing another node R2. The amount of backup capacity available for that new set of backup tunnels is strictly equal to the amount of bandwidth considered in the previous case. *Why?* Simply because under the single failure assumption, the resources R1 and R2 cannot simultaneously fail so their respective set of backup tunnels cannot be simultaneously active and so they can share the backup bandwidth.

A few comments can be made at this point:

Comment 1: The backup tunnel path computation is an NP-complete problem whose complexity renders its computation intractable without the use of some heuristics to speed up the path computation.

Comment 2: Some complex algorithms can be used to find an optimal placement for the primary TE LSPs while trying to fully protect bandwidth and achieving an optimized bandwidth sharing, but this might not always be possible. For the sake of illustration, if the bandwidth is a scarce resource and the bandwidth cannot be fully protected if the primary TE LSPs are placed in an optimal fashion, then the PCE may decide (based on some preconfigured local policy) to displace some primary TE LSPs from their optimal path to free up some bandwidth on some path to get a complete bandwidth protection.

As far as the network topology is concerned, the PCE can acquire it either via routing or any connection to a seed router. In the first case, the PCE can be adjacent to any LSR in the network and run an IGP like IS-IS or OSPF. The only requirement is to make sure that the PCE set the "Overload bit" for IS-IS or "Max metric" for OSPF so that the PCE is not considered as a router by other routers and is never included in their SPT. Another possibility is for the PCE to acquire the network topology (IGP database) via a Telnet session or SNMP management information base. The PCE can collect the IGP database from any router in a routing area because all routers of the same routing area share an identical IGP database (which is a fundamental property of link state routing protocols). If the autonomous system is made of several areas, then the PCE needs to have at least one connection to a router in each area. It is worth pointing out that the acquisition of the network topology via routing offers a significant advantage: a real-time view of the network topology. As a reminder, bandwidth sharing relies on the single failure assumption (i.e., backup capacity cannot be shared by backup tunnels protecting nonindependent resources [resources that can fail simultaneously]). Thus, when a failure occurs, rapid backup tunnel recomputation makes the single failure assumption more reliable.

Situation 2: The PCE is responsible only for the backup tunnel path computation.

This case typically applies to two scenarios:

- *Scenario 1:* The primary TE LSPs paths are computed in a distributed fashion (by each head-end LSR using a CSPF algorithm), whereas the backup tunnel paths are computed by the (centralized) PCE.
- *Scenario 2:* Separate centralized PCEs are used to compute primary and backup tunnel paths.

Scenario 1: Because the PCE is responsible only for the backup tunnel path computation, it cannot use the unreserved bandwidth (not used by the primary TE LSPs) for the backup capacity. *Why?* Let us suppose that the PCE, in order to compute the backup tunnel paths, uses the unreserved bandwidth by the primary TE LSPs. It will be shown hereafter that the backup tunnels are signaled with 0 bandwidth; this is to avoid some extensions of the CAC process, but let us just make the assumption that backup tunnels are signaled with 0 bandwidth for the moment. So under the previous assumption, the PCE computes the set of backup tunnels (using the current available bandwidth). Because the LSRs compute the path for their primary TE LSP and do not have any knowledge about the backup tunnels in place and their respective computed bandwidth (backup tunnels are signaled with 0 bandwidth), this implies that they could at any time draw some bandwidth from the reservable bandwidth pool, outdating the backup tunnel path computation, which explains why, when the PCE is just responsible for the backup tunnel path computation, the PCE cannot consider the unreserved bandwidth as the backup capacity. The solution is to get non-overlapping pools for primary and backup tunnels (two pools are defined: one for the primary and one for the backup and they do not overlap). This way, an LSR could use the bandwidth pool reserved for primary tunnel and the PCE could use the backup pool reserved for backup tunnels; there is no overlap, so the set up of new primary TE LSP does not invalidate previously computed backup TE LSPs.

Scenario 2: Scenario 2 is somewhat similar to scenario 1 because the PCE in charge of computing the backup tunnels paths cannot use the unreserved bandwidth (known by the other PCE responsible for the primary TE LSPs path computation); hence, non-overlapping bandwidth pools are also required.

Distributed model: The aim of the distributed model is to distribute the backup tunnel path computation among several LSRs instead of relying on a central PCE to perform backup tunnel path computation. To avoid confusion, it is worth clarifying the notion of "distributed computation." In the computer science world, the notion of distributed computation usually refers to the ability to involve several processors in a computation task. In the distributed facility computation model, the computation of a set of TE LSPs to protect a particular resource is always performed by a unique entity (in this case an LSR). The notion of distributed computation refers to the fact that the set of backup tunnels to protect a set of N resources is shared among several entities but the set of backup LSPs required to protect a particular resource R is always computed by a unique PCE (an LSR in this case).

Let us now consider the situations in which a set of backup tunnels must be computed to protect a node, a link, and an SRLG:

Situation 1: protection against a node failure

As previously pointed out, the set of backup tunnels that needs to be computed by a unique entity (PCE) is the set of backup tunnels protecting against the failure of a resource R. In other words the set S of backup tunnels protecting against the failure of a resources R cannot be computed by different entities. *Why?* Because they cannot share bandwidth. Let us go back to the diagram depicted in Figure 7.42 for a moment. In the case of failure of the node R1, the backup tunnels B1 and B2 are simultaneously active. Moreover, backup tunnels are signaled with 0 bandwidth for a reason detailed later in this section. So the implication is that a unique entity must be responsible for the computation of all the backup tunnels that protect against the failure of R1 (this is required to make sure that the backup tunnel paths offer the required bandwidth). A very natural choice for this entity is the node R1 itself! In the distributed model, to protect against a node failure (the failure of R1), R1 will compute all the backup tunnels from every neighbor to their set of next-next hops: from R0 to R2, R0 to R8, R0 to R9, R0 to R10, R8 to R0, R8 to R2, R8 to R9, R8 to R10, R9 to R8, R9 to R0, R9 to R2, R9 to R10, R10 to R9, R10 to R8, R10 to R0, R10 to R2, R2 to R10, R2 to R9, R2 to R8, and R2 to R0. Likewise, R6 performs the computation of backup tunnels from each of its neighbors to their NNHOP in the case of its own failure (from R5 to R7 and R7 to R5). Neither synchronization nor communication is required between the two

PCEs R1 and R6 because they compute backup tunnels to protect independent resources (R1 and R6). Each of them may use the whole backup network capacity, which allows them to naturally perform bandwidth sharing.

As in the case of the centralized model with the PCE responsible for the backup tunnel path computation only, a separate backup bandwidth pool is required. Communication between a node acting as a PCE and its neighbors requires some communication protocol detailed later in this section.

Situation 2: protection against a link failure

To protect a link L, if unidirectional TE LSPs are used, two NHOP backup tunnels are required (one in each direction). If the link fails in one direction (e.g., a laser on the sender side or a photodiode on the receiver side fails), then one NHOP backup is used. On the other hand, in the case of a bidirectional link failure (e.g., fiber cut), both NHOP backup tunnels will be used. This requires for the two NHOP backup tunnels offering bandwidth protection to be computed by a single PCE to avoid bandwidth protection violation. This is illustrated in Figure 7.45.

So let us consider the network depicted in Figure 7.45: An NHOP backup tunnel B1 protects the fast-reroutable TE LSPs traversing the link R1-R2 against a failure of the link R1-R2. Another NHOP backup tunnel B2 protects the fast-reroutable TE LSPs traversing the link R2-R1 against a failure of the link R2-R1.

Let us now suppose that the two NHOP backup tunnels B1 and B2 are computed independently; they may share bandwidth! Indeed each NHOP backup tunnel path computation will be performed independently. But in the case of a bidirectional link failure, both NHOP backup tunnels will be active, which will result in bandwidth protection violation, hence the requirement for two NHOP backup tunnels to be computed by a single PCE. This can clearly be seen in Figure 7.45; in the case of a bidirectional failure of the link R1-R2, both B1 and B2 are simultaneously active on the link R4-R5, which results in a bandwidth protection

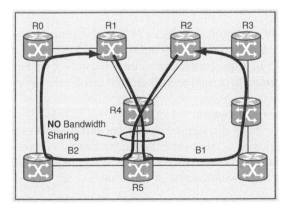

FIGURE 7.45

Computation of NHOP backup tunnels with bandwidth protection with the facility backup model.

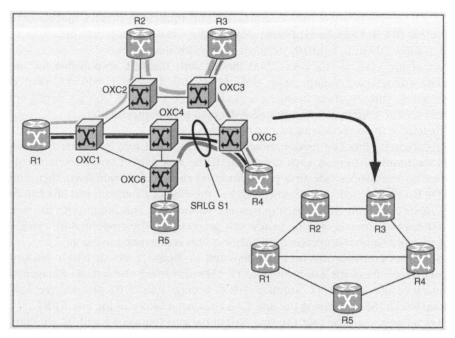

FIGURE 7.46

Protection of an SRLG with the facility backup model.

violation. A simple solution consists in electing one of the two ends of the link as the PCE for the computation of the set of NHOP backup tunnel paths protecting against a bidirectional link failure (e.g., the LSR with the smaller routed ID could be selected).

Situation 3: protection of an SRLG

Likewise, the protection of an SRLG requires to elect a PCE to compute the set of required backup tunnels in the case of failure of this SRLG (Figure 7.46).

As shown in Figure 7.46, the set of required backup tunnels to protect against a failure of SRLG S1 must be performed by a unique PCE elected among the set of LSRs: R1, R4, and R5.

Signaling of backup tunnel with 0 bandwidth.

Several times in this section, we made the statement that backup tunnels providing QoS guarantees are signaled with 0 bandwidth in the "facility-based computation" model. To illustrate why backup tunnels are signaled with 0 bandwidth (although their path is computed to provide bandwidth guarantees), let us consider Figure 7.47.

In Figure 7.47, a set of backup tunnels have been computed:

- *B1 (30 Mbps) and B2 (50 Mbps)* protect fast-reroutable TE LSPs traversing the path R8-R1-R2 against a node failure of R1.

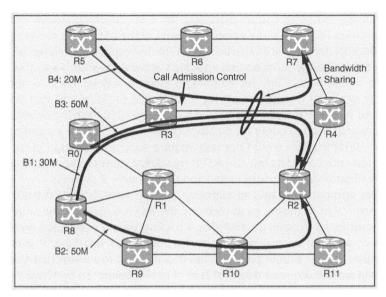

FIGURE 7.47

Signaling backup tunnels with 0 bandwidth with the facility backup model.

- *B3 (50Mbps)* protects fast-reroutable TE LSPs traversing the path R0-R1-R2 against a node failure of R1.
- *B4 (20Mbps)* protects fast-reroutable TE LSPs traversing the path R5-R3-R4-R7 against a node failure of R6.

For the sake of simplicity, just a few backup tunnels are shown in Figure 7.47 (e.g., there are other backup tunnels: B5, from R9 to protect the fast-reroutable TE LSPs traversing the path R9-R1-R2 against a failure of the node R1, to mention one of them).

B1, B2, and B3 cannot share the bandwidth because they protect different TE LSPs from the failure of the same resource (node R1 in this case). On the other hand, under the single failure assumption, they can share bandwidth with B4 because B4 protects from the failure of a different resource (node R6). The paths of B1, B2, B3, and B4 have been computed to ensure bandwidth protection.

Now, as far as the signaling is concerned, there are actually two options:

- *Option 1:* Signal backup tunnels with their bandwidth
- *Option 2:* Signal backup tunnels with 0 bandwidth

Let us now see each option and the respective pros and cons: First, it is worth reiterating here that a backup tunnel LSP is just a regular TE LSP.[75] In other words, when a backup tunnel is signaled, any LSR along its path performs the same

---

[75] This applies to the facility backup method of MPLS TE Fast Reroute.

operation as with any other TE LSP, in particular the CAC checking against the available bandwidth on the link for the priority signaled in the RSVP Path message.

Option 1: Backup tunnels are signaled with their respective bandwidth. Although this seems to be the most natural approach, it would require some CAC modifications on midpoint to allow for bandwidth sharing. Indeed, back to our previous example depicted in Figure 7.47, R3 would need to figure out that B4 protects a different resource than B1 and B3 and so they can share the bandwidth. Its CAC function would need to count for 80 Mbps (max((T1 + T3),T4)) instead of T1 + T3 + T4 = 100 Mbps. This would not only require some modification of the CAC module on the midpoint LSRs but also RSVP signaling extensions so a backup TE LSP should be identified as a backup tunnel and the resource it protects.

Option 2: This approach consists of signaling backup tunnels with 0 bandwidth, which prevents from having to implement any RSVP signaling extensions and CAC modifications. Of course, the fact that a backup tunnel is signaled with 0 bandwidth is completely decorrelated from the bandwidth this TE LSP gets. Remember that the backup tunnel path has been computed to ensure that the backup tunnel will get the required bandwidth in case of a failure. So by virtue of the backup tunnel computation, backup tunnels will have the required bandwidth along their respective path, but they are just signaled with 0 bandwidth.

The distributed backup tunnel path computation model presented here is just one model among others. At the time of publication, other distributed models under investigation could allow for some degree of bandwidth sharing with limited requirements in terms of extra routing and signaling extensions.

Backup tunnels selection: At this point, a set of backup tunnels have been computed to provide fast recovery and bandwidth protection. The next interesting question is: *How are those backup tunnels selected as primary TE LSPs requesting for Fast Reroute and bandwidth protection are signaled?*

When a new TE LSP explicitly requiring local protection and bandwidth protection is signaled, a backup tunnel satisfying the request must be selected by each PLR along the path. In the example of Figure 7.47, the paths of the backup tunnels B1 and B2 have been computed to provide 30 Mbps and 50 Mbps of bandwidth, respectively. Each time a fast reroutable TE LSP traversing the node R8 and requesting bandwidth protection is signaled, the PLR R8 has to select a backup tunnel (B1 or B2) satisfying the bandwidth constraint. So the PLR has to keep track of the total amount of available bandwidth per backup tunnel, which is equal to the backup tunnel bandwidth minus the sum of the bandwidths of all the protected LSPs that have selected the backup tunnel. A detailed example follows.

The algorithm in charge of the backup tunnel selection, called the *packing algorithm,* is usually implementation specific.

At this point, it is worth mentioning a few issues that the packing algorithm must resolve:

1. *Constraints prioritization:* When a protected TE LSP is signaled that explicitly requires bandwidth protection, its set of requirements must be taken

into account to proceed to the backup tunnel selection: amount of the requested bandwidth, link versus node protection and others. Furthermore, if several backup tunnels exist at the PLR, they may have different properties like NHOP versus NNHOP, different bandwidth available, or different path lengths. The set of required constraints with potentially some hierarchy between constraints) and the backup tunnel properties must be considered by the backup selection algorithm to perform an appropriate selection. For instance, suppose two backup tunnels: B1 is an NNHOP backup without enough bandwidth to satisfy the bandwidth requirement and B2 is an NHOP backup with enough bandwidth. If the protected TE LSP requires both bandwidth and node protection, a choice must be made about which constraint will be satisfied first.

2. *Bandwidth fragmentation:* Various algorithms can be designed for the backup tunnel selection. Here is just a subset of some possible implementations for the sake of illustration:
   - *A1:* always select the backup tunnel with the smallest available bandwidth that meets the bandwidth protection requirement
   - *A2:* "load balance"
   - *A3:* always select the backup tunnel with the highest bandwidth that meets the bandwidth protection requirement

Let us illustrate the challenge of the packing algorithm (which is also known as the "knapsack" problem) through an example. Consider a link R0-R1 with a protected bandwidth of 25 Mbps (i.e., R0 requires a set of backup tunnels such that the sum of their bandwidth is equal to 25 Mbps). Because no single backup tunnel having a 25 Mbps capacity can be found, the backup tunnel path computation algorithm has calculated two backup tunnels B1 and B2 having a capacity of 10 Mbps and 15 Mbps (B1 and B2 follow different paths), respectively. We note [X,Y] the remaining backup capacity (RBC) on the respective backup tunnels B1 and B2. In the example, we illustrate the resulting outputs of each packing algorithm described above upon a specific sequence of events. Note that the assumption is made in this example that all the signaled TE LSPs request for Fast Reroute and bandwidth protection.

Time t0: a first TE LSP 1 is signaled with a bandwidth requirement of 4 Mbps.
With A1: RBC = [6,15]
With A2: RBC = [6,15]
With A3: RBC = [10,11]
Time t1: TE LSP 2 is signaled with a bandwidth requirement of 4 Mbps.
With A1: RBC = [2,15]
With A2: RBC = [6,11]
With A3: RBC = [10,7]
Time t2: TE LSP (LSP 3) is signaled with a bandwidth of 12 Mbps.
With A1: RBC = [2,3]
With A2: FAILS, no backup tunnel can be selected
With A3: FAILS, no backup tunnel can be selected

This simple example shows that A1 proposes the best strategy in this example to avoid bandwidth fragmentation, but unfortunately, as shown below, this does not prevent from having to implement a bandwidth defragmentation strategy as new TE LSPs are signaled and torn down. An interesting analogy is the de-fragmentation of a hard disk, with a noticeable difference though: In the case of a file that must be stored on a hard disk, if no single contiguous set of blocks with the requested file size can be found, the operating system will store the file in multiple noncontiguous blocks whose addresses are stored in a file allocation table (FAT). By contrast, when the PLR has to select a backup tunnel, it must find a single backup tunnel with enough bandwidth to satisfy the requirement of the newly setup protected TE LSP. Using multiple backup tunnels to reroute a single protected TE LSP is not desirable (indeed, if multiple backup tunnels are used to reroute the same TE LSP and these backup tunnels have significantly different propagation delays, this may lead to undesirable out-of-order packet delivery).

Let us now continue the example with the assumption that the algorithm A1 is chosen.

Time t3: A new TE LSP (LSP 4) is signaled with a bandwidth requirement for the protection of 3 Mbps. RBC = [2,0].

Time t4: LSP 1 is torn down. RBC = [6,0].

Time t5: LSP 3 is torn down. RBC = [6,12].

Time t5: A new TE LSP 5 is signaled with a protection bandwidth requirement of 14 Mbps. The backup tunnel selection algorithm fails as no backup tunnels with 14 Mbps can be found. This shows that a bandwidth defragmentation procedure must be triggered at this point to satisfy the new request. The backup assignment must become:

B1: LSP1, LSP2, LSP4

B2: no TE LSP

So RBC = [3,15]. This allows accommodating the request of LSP5.

Note that the backup bandwidth defragmentation procedure may be triggered by a timer or a backup tunnel selection failure event. In the former case, the PLR performs a defragmentation when a timer expires, whereas in the latter case, the defragmentation is triggered when a new bandwidth protection request cannot be satisfied. Both approaches can also be combined.

Path computation client: PCE communication protocol.

As already mentioned, the PCE (in this case the entity in charge of the backup tunnels path computation) can be either a central PCE (in the centralized model) that performs the backup tunnels computation for all the protected resources in the network or an LSR (in the distributed model). In both cases, a communication protocol is required such that an LSR (a Path Computation Client, or PCC) can request the computation of a set of backup tunnels to protect its TE LSPs traversing a particular resource in the case of failure of this resource and the PCE can provide the set of computed backup tunnels.

Such a signaling protocol has been proposed and is being developed in the IETF. In the particular context of Fast Reroute, a specific protocol object has been defined that allows specifying the resource to protect, the destination of the set of backup tunnels, optional resource classes, as well as the maximum number of backup tunnels in the set and for each of them the minimum required bandwidth.

For instance, let us consider the computation of the set of NNHOP backup tunnels between two LSRs R0 and R2. Suppose that the protected bandwidth is 50 Mbps and that no single NNHOP backup tunnel of 50 Mbps can be found. Although 5000 TE LSPs of each 10 Kbps would give a total of 50 Mbps, this is certainly not a desirable scenario. Indeed, a protected TE LSP can just use a single backup tunnel at a time; furthermore, the number of backup tunnels would be considerably high. Another scenario would be to get three backup tunnels having the following bandwidths: 49 Mbps, 500 Kbps, and 500 Kbps. In some networks, the last two backup tunnels would be too small to be able to protect any protected LSP requesting bandwidth protection. This explains why being able to specify some constraints on both the number of backup tunnels and their minimum bandwidth in the path computation request is desirable.

7.13.7 Backup Tunnel Path Computation with MPLS TE Fast Reroute One-to-One Backup

As described previously, Fast Reroute one-to-one backup requires one backup tunnel (Detour LSP) per protected TE LSP at each hop acting as a PLR. In other words, each LSR along the protected TE LSP path, using one-to-one backup will have to compute a Detour LSP path originated at this node up to the egress LSR of the protected TE LSP (destination).

This requires collecting a set of information:

1. *The list of LSRs traversed by the protected TE LSP:* This information is available in the RSVP RRO object carried in the Resv message traveling in the upstream direction (from the tail-end LSR to the head-end LSR). One may think that the ERO object always contain the complete list of downstream nodes, but this is not always the case, for instance, if the ERO object contains some loose hop(s). A loose hop address is a nondirectly connected address. This is illustrated in the Figure 7.48.

The example depicted in Figure 7.48 shows the situation where a TE LSP path is specified as a mix of strict and loose hops. In that example, a TE LSP T1 is set up from the LSR R2 to R6 with the following ERO object: R3(strict)-R5(loose)-R6(strict). Typical use of loose hops is when the head-end LSR cannot compute the whole path of a TE LSP, as it lacks topology and resources information—for example, when the TE LSP spans multiple routing areas. In this case, one solution is to specify a list of strict hops in the head-end area followed by a list of loose hops (the area border routers, ABRs). Each ABR is then responsible for a partial route computation, up to the next loose hop (in general another ABR connected to the next hop routing area). Back to our example of Figure 7.48, the PLR R2, for example, does not compute the path between the LSR R3 and R5 (R5 is specified

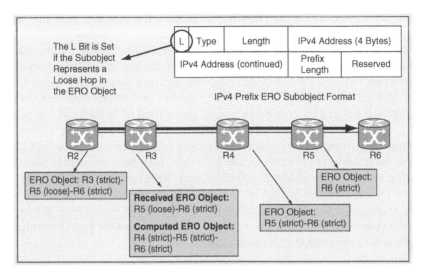

FIGURE 7.48

Illustration of an ERO object specified as a mix of strict and loose hops, which shows why the RRO object must be used in some cases to learn the TE LSP path on downstream nodes.

as a loose hop); the path between the nodes R3 and R5 is computed by R3. This highlights an example where the PLR (R2 in this example) may not have the full list of hops traversed by the protected TE LSP by observing the ERO object; in this case, the information would be obtained via the RRO object carried in the RSVP Resv message. More details on the signaling can be found in Section 7.12.

2. *The list of downstream links and nodes that the PLR wants to protect.* This information is also available in the RRO object carried in the RSVP Resv message forwarded in the upstream direction.

3. In addition, the PLR must learn *the list of upstream links that the protected TE LSP traverses.* Likewise, this information is available in the RRO object. The Detour LSP and the protected TE LSP should not share a common next hop upstream of the failure:
   - With the *path-specific method,* the Detour LSP must not pass through the same links as the protected TE LSP to avoid an early LSP merging.
   - With the *sender template-specific method,* the reason is that the Detour LSP and the protected TE LSP would share the bandwidth, although in case of failure they would be simultaneously active, resulting in bandwidth violation.

4. *The required protected bandwidth* (i.e., the amount of bandwidth required for the protected TE LSP, which will be the bandwidth of the Detour LSP). The head-end LSR of a protected TE LSP has the ability to request a backup

tunnel with an equivalent bandwidth or a percentage of the primary TE LSP bandwidth.[76]

5. *The maximum number of hops the backup tunnel path can have between the PLR and the MP if a FAST-REROUTE object is present.* A value of 0 indicates that the backup tunnel protects against link failure only.

6. *Finally, some link attribute filters that may be applied to the backup tunnel path if, for instance, some links should be avoided* (e.g., long propagation delay links).

Once all that information is gathered by the PLR, it tries to find the shortest path (running a CSPF on the remaining topology, once the protected section have been pruned) for the backup tunnel taking into account the constraints mentioned earlier. Note that the destination address of the backup tunnel in the context of Fast Reroute one-to-one backup is the egress LSR (destination of the protected TE LSP).

Note that the PLR may or may not succeed in finding a path for the backup tunnel that satisfies the set of requirements. In such a case, the PLR can start a timer and retry when the timer expires. Furthermore, a PLR can trigger a backup tunnel path reoptimization at regular intervals to determine whether a better path (i.e., the shortest path) exists.

7.13.8 Summary

In Sections 7.12 and 7.13, we saw the signaling aspects of MPLS TE local protection, which include several RSVP TE extensions. This also included the Fast Reroute mode of operation as far as the signaling aspects are concerned. Another key aspect covered in detailed is the backup path computation for the MPLS TE protection techniques (global and local). Although many algorithms and modes have been proposed for the computation of the backup path, a few of them have been presented that can both be implemented on a central server (usually referred to as the off-line approach) or LSRs (distributed computation). The choice between centralized and distributed backup tunnel path computations is, as usual, driven by the tradeoff between optimality (centralized computation) and flexibility and reactiveness (distributed computation). That said, the relative degree of optimality of both approaches is really a function of the algorithms in use and the network topology. This area is constantly evolving, and undoubtedly, new algorithms will be designed that will allow taking into account new constraints with a increasingly higher efficiency; however, it has been shown that the level of complexity grows nonlinearly with the number of required constraints.

---

[76] This information can either be derived from the SESSION-ATTRIBUTE object ("Bandwidth protection desired" bit) or the FAST-REROUTE object, if present. In the former case, if the bandwidth protection desired bit is set, the requirement is for full protection; in other words, the bandwidth requirement for the backup tunnel is identical.

GMPLS and Service Recovery

GMPLS introduces a host of new functions that are applicable to packet and non-packet technologies. Because many of the networks for which GMPLS was designed are transport networks, GMPLS comes with a set of high-function recovery mechanisms, and these can be successfully applied in MPLS networks. Additionally, GMPLS introduces new techniques for discovering and repairing control plane faults without the need (present in the MPLS control plane) to disrupt data traffic when the control plane fails.

This chapter, from *GMPLS: Architecture and Applications* by Farrel and Bryskin, describes some of these protection techniques. Although some of them are presented in the context of non-packet technologies (such as TDM and WDM) they can be applied equally effectively in packet (i.e., MPLS) networks. They present alternatives to the Fast Reroute techniques discussed in the previous chapter, and show how the techniques may be more appropriate in core transport networks.

Transport network resources do fail. Fibers get cut, and cross-connects, amplifiers, DWDM devices, network controllers, and control channels go out of service unexpectedly. Considering the huge amounts of data carried over transport networks, a single such failure, even for a short period of time, can cause a lot of damage to users of services that happen to traverse the point of failure. Users do not generally tolerate losses of data or connectivity. Usually there is a very stringent requirement on the time within which a service must be recovered after its interruption. The only way for transport Service Providers to meet this requirement is to over-provision their networks so that, at any point in time, active services could be diverted from any potential point of failure onto some other network resources. But even this is not sufficient. There should also be an intelligence that can rapidly detect and localize failures as well as switch the services away from them. Likewise, there should be an intelligence capable of computing diverse primary and recovery paths, so that a single failure will not affect them both. Finally, there should be an intelligence that can place primary and recovery paths of multiple services in such a way that the same network resources could protect multiple services and could be used for so-called extra-traffic services while there are no failures in the network, thereby considerably lessening the cost of over-provisioning without providing a significantly reduced ability to protect against failures.

In this chapter we will discuss how GMPLS enables such intelligence. We will start with identifying failures that may happen in transport networks. We will describe responsibilities of different network elements in detecting and correlating them and sending failure notifications to the elements that are provisioned to perform recovery actions. We will discuss different recovery schemes that are used for link recovery, as well as those used for end-to-end path and segment recovery. At the end of the chapter we will analyze the consequences of control plane failures.

8.1 FAILURES IN TRANSPORT NETWORKS

There are numerous ways to classify failures within transport networks. Depending on the type of failed network element, the failures can be broken into two groups: control plane failures and data plane failures. The failures of the latter group (for example, fiber cuts, cross-connect failures) directly affect services using the failed elements, whereas the failures of the former group (for example, controller, control channel failures) make services unmanageable or only partially manageable.

Further, depending on the type of a failed component, the failure can be classified as a hardware (electronic or optical component defect), software (bug), or configuration (operator mistake) failure. Additionally, Service Providers distinguish failures caused by internal events (that is, some network imperfection), and by external events (for example, electricity breakdown, flood, digging accident, etc.).

Many failures can be prevented: Fiber-optic cables can be placed deeper in the ground within armored casings, hardware and software components can be tested more thoroughly, personnel can be better trained, high-quality security systems can be installed to protect against hacker attacks. However, it is well understood and widely accepted that failures cannot be completely eliminated. Therefore, transport networks must handle failures in such a way that they cause minimal disruption (if any) for affected services. In other words, networks must be able to survive any single failure or multiple simultaneous failures.

This is a very challenging task. First of all, networks are required to have enough resources to accommodate user traffic under conditions of one or more failures. Equally important is that there must be an intelligence that could support rapid failure detection and localization and that could switch the affected services onto alternative paths, so that that user traffic is not affected to an extent beyond the level that was agreed upon between users and Service Providers.

The next section provides some definitions that are necessary to quantify the network survivability.

8.2 NETWORK SURVIVABILITY DEFINITIONS

Let us make the following definitions.

- The *availability* of a network element is the probability that the element can deliver some specified Quality of Service (QoS) at some point of time.

- The *failure* of a network element is the moment when the element stops delivering the specified QoS.
- The *repair* of a network element is the moment when the element regains its ability to deliver the specified QoS.
- A *fault* (also known as an *outage*) is the period of time when a network element is not functional—that is, the period of time between a failure and subsequent repair.

Note that not every defect in a network element can be categorized as a failure. Some defects degrade the quality or level of services using the affected element, but do not fully disrupt them, which leaves their QoS parameters within an acceptable (agreed upon) range. Some defects do not have a notable impact on existing services, but might prevent further services from being established. In this chapter we will only consider those defects that fully disrupt services—that is, stop delivering the specified QoS—as failures.

Network element availability can be calculated according to the formula:

$$A = 1 - Tmr/Tmbf$$

where A is the network element's availability,
     Tmr is the element's mean time to repair,
     Tmbf is the element's mean time between failures.

For hardware elements the mean time to repair may typically be quite large because it will involve the dispatch of a service engineer (a truck-roll). Nevertheless, the mean time to repair is normally a considerable order of magnitude less than the mean time between failures. Any other state of affairs would require the service engineer to camp out on site with the equipment. For software components the mean time between failures is often considered to be quite short: Although a lot of effort is put into testing, software does not have a good reputation for reliability and stability. However, software repair is generally achieved simply by reloading the software so that the mean time to repair is very small. Thus, it is usually the case that Tmr $\ll$ Tmbf, and so A is some number very close to 1.

Suppose a network is built of *n* network elements. The network availability can be computed as the compound:

$$AN = A1 * A2 * \cdots * An$$

where AN is the network availability and A1, A2, …, An are the availabilities of each of the network constituents. Note that this formula is correct only if one assumes complete independence of failures of all network elements.

It is also worth mentioning that because Tmr $\ll$ Tmbf for each element, the probability of two or more simultaneous failures is often considered negligible, and many recovery schemes are provisioned for a single failure scenario.

8.3 SERVICE RECOVERY CYCLE

One can distinguish the following stages of a service recovery process.

- Fault detection
- Fault hold-off
- Fault localization
- Fault correlation
- Fault notification
- Recovery operation
- Traffic recovery

The five first stages are collectively called *fault management*. Fault detection is the only stage that cannot be accomplished without interaction with the data plane—all other stages can be realized by either the control plane or the data plane independently or by cooperation between the two planes.

When a fault occurs, the nodes adjacent to the failed link or node do not detect the fault instantly. It takes some time for the hardware dedicated to fault detection (for example, components monitoring signal overhead bytes, power level, and so forth) to identify the failed component, define the exact fault state, and notify the entity responsible for fault management (for example, the GMPLS control plane). The *fault detection time* may depend heavily on the data plane technology (for example, TDM or WDM), how intrusive each node is in the processing of signals (for example, whether electronic components are used for timing synchronization, signal regeneration, or signal monitoring), and whether the signal is normally expected to be continuous or only present when data is being transferred.

The fault management entity does not usually react to the fault notification right away. First, it moves the service into the *fault hold-off* state. This is necessary because a lower network layer may have a recovery scheme of its own, and it is highly undesirable to have multiple layers simultaneously trying to recover from the same fault, as that might actually lead to service disruption and would certainly result in inefficient use of network resources. It is also possible that the fault will self-heal very rapidly (or has even been misreported) and that the service will resume without any need for intervention. Hence, generally speaking, there is a need for some hold-off time to give a chance for other layer(s) to attempt to recover. If after the hold-off time the fault indication is still not removed, the service recovery is moved into the next—*fault localization*—stage. Note that in most cases the fault managing entity is collocated with a fault detecting entity; however, this is not always the case. When the two entities are physically separated an additional stage of the service recovery cycle—fault report—is required.

Multiple nodes may detect the same failure. For example, after a fiber cut, all downstream nodes are likely to detect a loss of signal (LOS), and all nodes downstream as far as the next point of regeneration will report a loss of light (LOL). The fault managing entity needs to understand where on the network the failure actually occurred through a process of *fault localization* in order to define proper recovery scope. For services that have only end-to-end protection fault localization is not urgent and can be performed after the traffic is switched onto recovery path (that is, after the recovery cycle is completed). On the other hand, if the recovery action will involve switching only a segment of the path to a recovery path, it is clearly important to determine where the failure is located. If the failure happened on the protected segment, local recovery is sufficient, but if the failure happened outside the protected segment, some upstream entity (perhaps the service head end) must be notified in order to take the necessary recovery action. Thus, failure localization is important. We will discuss end-to-end path and segment protection later in this chapter.

In some transport technologies (for example, SONET/SDH networks) failure localization is supported by the data plane. In others (for example, Optical Transport Networks) some other out-of-band means are needed, and the GMPLS control plane (more specifically the Link Management Protocol, LMP) provides such function. It is worth noting that there is no absolute need for an additional failure localization procedure in the control plane, even in the case of segment protection because all nodes that detect the failure can report it to a *deciding entity* (that is, a entity that controls the recovery procedures), which can perform the localization by examining the Traffic Engineering Database and/or analyzing the paths of the impacted services. However, specific failure localization procedures built into the control plane mean that faults can be localized more rapidly, services recovered more quickly, and recovery actions can be more precisely tuned to the specific failure.

With or without the failure localization stage, at least one of the failure-detecting nodes must play the role of reporting entity—sending the fault notification to the deciding entity. The dispatch of fault notifications may be delayed until the *fault correlation* stage is completed. To understand why this stage is desirable, keep in mind that a single failure may cause multiple fault indications. For instance, a fiber cut triggers fault indications for all services going through the affected link. It is possible (and very likely) that the same node performs the role of deciding entity for many or all of these services. For this case the GMPLS signaling protocol allows for the aggregation of fault indications and for sending the related notifications within a single message. Fault notifications must be delivered reliably (with possible re-transmission), and so, from the scalability point of view, such aggregation is a considerable improvement compared to delivering fault notifications for each service individually. Thus, during the fault correlation stage the fault-reporting node waits a certain amount of time to gather all fault indications, and groups them together according to the fault notification destination address.

During the *fault notification* stage a fault notification message arrives at the deciding entity from a fault-reporting node. The message can be delivered either via the data plane (for example, using the SDH overhead RDI signal) or via the control plane (for example, the GMPLS RSVP Notify message). In any case it is crucial that the message is delivered in a reliable manner. Note that when the control plane transports a fault notification message, the message does not necessarily follow the control plane path used to establish the service—the general flexibility of the network is used to deliver the message over the shortest available path.

On receipt of a fault notification message the deciding entity either relays it to another deciding entity or starts the *recovery operation* stage. Most of the remainder of this chapter is dedicated to an analysis of recovery operations. Depending on the type of recovery scheme provisioned for the service, the recovery operation on the deciding entity may range from doing nothing (for unprotected services, or for unidirectional 1+1 protection) to computing and setting up an alternative path and switching the traffic onto it (full re-routing).

Service recovery cycle is not completed by the recovery operation stage. It takes some non-negligible time for the traffic to settle down on the alternative path. This happens during the *traffic recovery* stage

The overall service recovery time T can be computed as:

$$T = Td + Th + Tl + Tc + Tn + Tr + Tt$$

where Td—fault detection time,
      Th—hold-off time,
      Tl—fault localization time,
      Tc—fault correlation time,
      Tn—fault notification time,
      Tr—recovery operation time,
      Tt—traffic recovery time.

Some services have very stringent requirements on the service recovery time (notoriously, 50 ms is often stated as an absolute maximum recovery time for voice traffic). In principle there are two fundamentally different approaches to meet these requirements.

In the first approach the traffic is permanently bridged (that is, cross-connected) onto two alternative paths and selected by the receiver from the path that has the better quality signal—this is called a 1+1 protection scheme. When a failure happens on one path, the receiver simply selects data from the healthy channel. The advantages of this approach are simplicity, best possible service recovery time, and independence from the recovery domain (see the definition in Section 8.7.1) size. The obvious disadvantage is that it is very expensive: One needs to allocate twice the network resources compared to the same unprotected service, and specialist equipment may be needed both to generate the signal on more than one path, and to monitor and select the received signals at the merge point (although the latter function can be controlled through the use of fault notifications).

The second approach is to use other protection schemes that are more efficient from the resource utilization point of view (for example, 1:N protection) and to provision multiple small, sometimes overlapping, protection domains, so that it is guaranteed that, no matter where on the protected path a failure occurs, the relevant deciding entity will always be near (one or two hops away from) the point of failure. Fast recovery is achieved in this case by minimizing the two most significant components of service recovery time—Tn and Tr—the fault notification, and recovery operation times. This approach is called *local repair*. Fast re-route and path segment recovery that will be discussed later in this chapter are two examples of the local repair.

8.4 SERVICE RECOVERY CLASSES

Depending on the way alternative service paths are provisioned, service recovery can be broken into two classes: service protection and service restoration. Because most of the control plane aspects—path computation and selection, advertising, signaling, and so forth—are identical for both classes, the common term *service recovery* is used most of the time. Only when there is a need to highlight peculiarities of one of the two classes are the terms *protection* or *restoration* used instead.

In the early days of GMPLS, when the work on service recovery had just begun, there was a very clear distinction between service protection and service restoration. The former was defined as a class of service recovery where one or more alternative paths were fully established (that is, computed and signaled, with resources reserved, selected, and committed on all links, cross-connects programmed and prepared to switch traffic on all nodes) *before* a failure was detected. Service restoration was defined as a class of service recovery where no control plane actions related to the provisioning of alternative path(s) occurred until after failure had been reported to the deciding entity. In other words, in the case of service restoration, only when the deciding entity receives a fault notification is it supposed to trigger an alternative path setup starting from the path computation function.

The definition of service protection remains unchanged. However, it turned out that there could be many other ways to provision alternative paths that were definitely not under the umbrella of service protection, and did not quite fit into the definition of service restoration. For example, one or more alternative paths could be computed in advance, so that the process of service restoration could be started from the point of path selection rather than requiring the path computation phase. This scheme potentially yields a better recovery time compared to one of full restoration, but at the cost of a possibility that at the moment of service restoration the pre-computed paths will not be available because they were not provisioned and, therefore, their resources could have been taken by other services. Furthermore, one or more of the pre-computed paths could be pre-selected and pre-signaled, so that only activation is required after failure detection and indication.

Thus, the definition of service restoration was changed. The difference between service protection and restoration is now much subtler. Essentially, a service recovery scheme that does not require any *provisioning* signaling for the alternative path after the failure indication is classified as service protection. Everything else is service restoration. Note that some service protection schemes (most, in fact) require some synchronization between nodes initiating and terminating the protecting path and, therefore, some switchover signaling, but this is not classified as signaling for the purpose of provisioning.

Both service recovery classes have their pros and cons. The obvious advantage of service protection is the significantly better recovery times. The important advantages of service restoration are efficiency and flexibility in the use of network resources. To understand this, keep in mind that in the service protection model it is not known in advance which of the nodes or links on a protected path will fail. Therefore, the protected and protecting paths must be provisioned to be as diverse as possible, so that a single failure will not take both paths out of service simultaneously. Two diverse paths use more network resources than the one (shortest) path needed by an unprotected service. In the service restoration model the alternative path does not have to be fully diverse from the primary path. The only requirement is for it to be disjoint from the links or nodes that actually failed. In fact, the alternative path will be likely to reuse those resources unaffected by the failure of the primary path. This is the first reason why service restoration is more efficient than service protection. The other reason is that, until the failure happens, the resources that will be required to support the alternative path can be used by any other services in the network in any way. Note that while it is true that some service protection schemes allow for the reuse of resources required to support the protecting paths in order to carry extra-traffic services, the possibilities for this reuse are limited. It is possible, for instance, to reuse the entire protecting path in a service protection scheme for a single extra traffic service, but it is not possible to reuse it partially for multiple services as in case of service restoration.

Service protection does not provide for recovery from unexpected failures. For instance, many protection schemes are designed on the assumption that there will not be simultaneous failures on a protected path. Such schemes protect against a single failure of any link or node on the path; however, they may not provide the ability to recover from simultaneous failures of two or more links, even when feasible alternative paths exist. Furthermore, it is not expected that both protecting and protected paths will fail simultaneously. There are situations, however, where a single failure takes both the protecting and the protected paths out of service. For instance, the two paths could be provisioned to be not completely diverse either willingly (fully diverse paths are too expensive), or unwillingly (the information about physical layout of the fibers was not available at the time of path computation). Again, service protection provides no recovery from such situations. On the other hand, service restoration (especially full re-routing) has no problem recovering from unexpected failures, provided, of course, that a suitable alternative path is available.

As was mentioned earlier, service restoration has several flavors. These flavors also have their relative pros and cons, but, as a general rule, more pre-planning yields a better recovery time but is more rigid and less efficient.

8.5 RECOVERY LEVELS AND SCOPES

Depending on the object of protection—TE link or service path—one can identify two different levels of recovery.

- Link level recovery (also referred to as span recovery)
- Path level recovery

In the context of this book we define a *span* as an abstraction associated with network resources that are necessary to deliver user traffic between a pair of nodes that are adjacent in the data plane. From the traffic engineering perspective, a span can be represented (and advertised) as a separate TE link. Alternatively, several spans interconnecting the same pair of nodes can be collectively represented as a single (bundled) TE link.

In the case of span recovery, all services traversing a particular span are protected against any failure detected on the span. Specifically, when the span fails, *all* span-protected services are switched simultaneously onto some other parallel span (that is, a span interconnecting the same pair of nodes as the failed one). It is worth emphasizing that not all protected services are recovered through this operation—only those that are provisioned to be span-protected. In the span recovery model the deciding entities are located on the span's ends, and the recovery operation is triggered either by local failure detection or by a failure notification message received from the opposite end of the span. We will discuss span recovery in Section 8.6.

In the path level recovery model *each* protected service is recovered from a failure independently. It means that if some failure affects multiple services, the failure is indicated separately for each of them, and, generally speaking, multiple fault notification messages are sent to different deciding entities located on different nodes, which trigger independent recovery operations. One can distinguish different scopes of path level recovery, depending on which part of the path a particular recovery scheme is provisioned to protect. The scopes are:

- End-to-end recovery
- Local recovery

In the case of end-to-end recovery, an alternative path, starting and ending on the same pair of nodes as the protected path, provides recovery from a failure of any link or node on the protected path. In the case of the service *protection*, the alternative path is usually required to be fully disjoint from the protected path. This is because, at the time that the alternative path is provisioned, it is not known exactly where the failure will happen; hence care must be taken to avoid the situation where a single failure makes both protected and protecting paths unusable. In the case of service *restoration*, an alternative path needs to be disjoint from the protected path only at the point of failure. In the end-to-end path recovery model the deciding entities—called the point of local repair (PLR) and merge node (MN), see definitions in Section 8.7.1—are always located on the ends of the protected path. We will discuss end-to-end path recovery in Section 8.7.2.

Two methods of local recovery will be discussed in this chapter: fast re-route (FRR), and path segment recovery.

In the FRR model each resource of a protected path—link or node—is separately protected by an individual backup tunnel. The important feature of this model is that the point at which the paths diverge (the PLR) for each protection domain is guaranteed to be located within one data plane hop of any point of failure. The backup tunnels also merge with the protected path very close to the resource they protect. The point at which the paths re-merge (the MN) is immediately downstream, being either the next hop (in case of an NHOP tunnel) or the next-next hop (in case of an NNHOP tunnel). The close proximity of the PLR and MN to the point of failure makes the FRR recovery time the same as, or better than, in the span protection model, while retaining the granularity of path level recovery.

The FRR model makes use of two types of backup tunnel: *facility bypass tunnels*, and *detour tunnels*. The former protects all paths that traverse the protected resource (that is, only one facility bypass tunnel per resource is needed). The latter protects each path individually (that is, one detour tunnel is required per resource per path).

A major problem with FRR is its poor applicability for non-packet switched networks. Facility bypass tunnels cannot be applied even conceptually because they require the notion of a label stack, and there is no such thing within a single switching capability in circuit-switched networks. In theory the FRR detour model could be used for local protection of transport network services. However, making it feasible requires a certain level of network density, which is not the case in currently deployed transport networks built of ring interconnections. Furthermore, an LSP protected in this way requires a lot of protection resources for the detours, which can neither be used in failure-free conditions to support extra traffic nor be shared with other LSPs, because resource sharing and over-subscription have very restricted applicability in non-packet environments. This fact makes FRR even less attractive and less likely to be deployed in transport networks, especially considering the cost of transport network resources. FRR has already been discussed at length in the previous chapter.

The path segment recovery model is similar to the end-to-end path recovery model. The difference is that in the case of path segment recovery the alternative path protects some segment (or sub-network connection, to use the ITU-T term) of a protected path rather than the entire path. One may see end-to-end path recovery as a special case of path segment recovery with a single recovery domain covering the whole path. In general, though, multiple concatenated, overlapping, and/or nested recovery domains are provisioned for a segment protected path, each of them separately protecting a path segment from failures, and each possibly doing so in a different way. In the case of path segment recovery, the deciding entities (the relevant PLR and MN) are likely to be closer to the point of failure, so the overall recovery time of a segment protected path is likely to be better than that of an end-to-end protected path. On the other hand, unlike FRR, the path segment recovery model is not limited to protecting one resource at a time, and thus it works well on both dense and sparse topologies. Even more importantly, it requires many fewer protection resources, which, with careful network planning, could be shared between several protected paths and could also be used for carrying extra traffic if there are no failures in the network. Hence the model is very applicable for transport networks. We will discuss segment recovery in detail in Section 8.7.3.

It is important to note that the flexibility provided by the GMPLS control plane is such that all of the recovery models mentioned above are completely independent and can be provisioned for the same service in any combination. For instance, it is possible to require end-to-end recovery in addition to span protection for a path (recall that in MPLS/GMPLS a path onto which a service is mapped is called a Label Switched Path or LSP). Likewise, it is possible for packet switched LSPs to combine the FRR technique with path segment recovery to get the optimal trade-off between recovery time, resource utilization efficiency, and level of control of the backup LSP topology.

8.6 **SPAN RECOVERY**

In the context of this chapter, the term *recovery* usually means both protection and restoration. However, at the time this book was written, link-level (span) restoration was neither standardized nor deployed. Therefore, in this section the terms *span recovery* and *span protection* are used interchangeably.

A service that takes path A-B-D-E-F in the network depicted in Figure 8.1 can be provisioned as span protected. This is because each pair of adjacent nodes

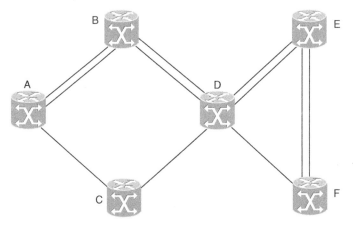

FIGURE 8.1

Span protection.

along the path is interconnected with two parallel links, so that one of them can protect the other. The following schemes of span protection are defined.

- Dedicated unidirectional 1+1
- Dedicated bidirectional 1+1
- Dedicated 1:1 with extra traffic
- Shared M:N
- Enhanced

Each span protection scheme requires a consistent view of the association of protected and protecting spans for every link. The GMPLS Link Management Protocol (LMP) and/or local configuration should satisfy this requirement.

8.6.1 Dedicated Unidirectional 1+1 Span Protection

In this scheme a TE link contains at least two parallel spans, and for every working span there is a dedicated protecting span. All traffic traversing the link is permanently bridged onto both spans on one side of the link, and is selected from one of the spans on the other side (usually from one that has a better quality signal). When the selection function detects a failure, it autonomously starts receiving data from the other span. Similarly, when the failure is restored, the failure-detecting node may switch back (also autonomously) to receiving data from the restored span. Note that in this model there could be periods of time when traffic in one direction is received from one span, while in the opposite direction it is received from the other.

From the Traffic Engineering point of view the combination of protected and protecting spans is advertised as a single TE link. The Link Protection Type attribute is specified as "Dedicated 1+1," and the Interface Switching Capability (ISC) Descriptor attribute is defined only by the protected span. The bandwidth parameters of the protecting span are not advertised.

If an LSP is required to take advantage of 1+1 span protection, its path must be computed with the constraint of the Link Protection Type attribute to be no worse than (that is, numerically greater or equal to) Dedicated 1+1. Furthermore, the LSP should be signaled with the Dedicated 1+1 link protection flag set in the GMPLS Protection object so that each hop knows that it must utilize 1+1 span protection. As was pointed out earlier, no signaling happens after a span failure is detected—in 1+1 protection, the failure-detecting node simply starts receiving data from the protecting span.

Dedicated unidirectional 1+1 span protection guarantees the best possible recovery time for all LSPs protected in this way. However, the scheme is also the most expensive: It requires double the resources for protection purposes.

8.6.2 Dedicated Bidirectional 1+1 Span Protection

This scheme is very similar to the previous one. The only difference is that when one of the nodes terminating a link detects a link failure, *both* nodes switch to receive data from the protecting span. Likewise, when the failure is restored and reversion mode operation is locally configured, both nodes switch back to receiving data from the restored span. This is in contrast with the unidirectional 1+1 span protection model (see the previous section), where only the failure-detecting node switches to receive data from the other span during protection switchover and reversion switchback operations. In both schemes both nodes never stop bridging data onto both spans.

It is worth noting that whether the protection is unidirectional or bidirectional is a local matter for a particular link. There are no differences in link advertisement for unidirectional and bidirectional 1+1 span-protected links. Likewise, there are no differences in path computation and signaling of LSPs willing to take advantage of link protection of either type.

The required switchover synchronization is performed according to the following rules.

- When one of the link-terminating nodes detects the link failure, it switches to receive data from the protecting span and sends a Switchover Request to the node at the opposite end of the link (the message is sent only if the sending node has not already received a Switchover Request from the other end; otherwise, Switchover Response is sent instead).

- When one of the link-terminating nodes receives a Switchover Request, it switches to receive data from the protecting span (if it has not already done this due to a locally detected failure) and sends a Switchover Response.

Similarly, when the failure is restored and the reversion mode is configured, switchback synchronization is performed according to the following rules.

- When one of the link-terminating nodes that has previously detected link failure (or acted on a Switchover Request) realizes that the failure is restored, it switches back to receive data from the restored span and sends a Switchback Request to the node at the opposite end of the link (again, the message is sent only if the node has not itself received a Switchback Request from the other end; otherwise, a Switchback Response is sent instead).

- When one of the link-terminating nodes receives a Switchback Request, it switches to receive data from the protected span (again, if it has not already done this yet because of locally detected failure restoration) and sends a Switchback Response.

Special care must be taken to handle span *flapping*—the situation where the span failure indication/restoration sequence happens many times in quick succession. The switchback procedure is not usually started immediately on the failure restoration event. Rather, it is triggered on the expiration of the so-called Wait-to-Restore Timer (WRT) started by the failure restoration event and cancelled by a new failure indication event. This mechanism guarantees that switchback happens only after the restored span has been functional for some time.

There is a need for signaling to synchronize the switchover and switchback—Switchover/Switchback Request/Response messages. This signaling can be provided by the GMPLS Control Plane (via LMP or GMPLS RSVP Notify messages), or by the data plane (for example, SONET/SDH APS signaling).

8.6.3 Dedicated 1:1 Span Protection with Extra Traffic

Under this scheme, there is a dedicated protecting span for every working (protected) span. Traffic is always sent over only one of the spans. This is in contrast with the 1+1 span protection schemes where traffic is always bridged onto both spans. Normally (that is, before link failure is detected), the data is sent over and received from the protected span in both directions, while the protecting span is either idle or carries some extra traffic. Note that the ability to handle extra traffic requires support of resource preemption by the control plane. The GMPLS control plane provides such support.

When a failure is detected on the protected span, the span-protected LSPs are moved onto the protecting span: Both link-terminating nodes switch to send and receive their traffic over the protecting span. In case of resource contention, the resources allocated for any extra traffic LSPs are preempted by the span-protected LSPs causing the interruption of the extra traffic. When a failure of the protected span is restored and the reversion mode is locally configured, the span-protected LSPs are switched back onto the protected span, thus releasing the protecting span, so that it can start carrying extra traffic again.

During the protection switchover procedure, special care should be taken to avoid misconnection—the situation where traffic is sent to an unintended receiver. Under 1:1 span protection a misconnection may occur; for instance, when a node switches to receive normal traffic over to the protecting span before the node on the other end of the link stops sending extra traffic over the protecting span.

A 1:1 span-protected link is advertised to the TE network domain as a single TE link. The Link Protection Type attribute is specified as "Dedicated 1:1" and the ISC Descriptor attribute is built as a combination of the attributes of the protected and protecting spans according to the following rules.

- For priorities higher (that is, numerically lower) than the priority configured for extra traffic LSPs, the advertised attribute matches the attribute of the protected span. Thus, bandwidth parameters of the protecting span are not advertised.

- For priorities lower than or equal to those of the extra traffic LSPs, the advertised unreserved bandwidth is computed as the sum of the unreserved bandwidth of both protecting and protected spans, and the Maximal LSP Bandwidth value is set equal to the greater of MaxLSPBandWork and MaxLSPBandProtect, where MaxLSPBandWork is the Maximal LSP Bandwidth available on the protected span, and MaxLSPBandProtect is the Maximal LSP Bandwidth available on the protecting span.

In this way, every TE domain controller can always tell which resources are available on the link for normal and extra traffic.

If there is the need to establish a 1:1 span-protected LSP, its path must be computed with the constraint of the Link Protection Type attribute to be no worse than (numerically greater or equal to) Dedicated 1:1. Furthermore, the LSP should be signaled with the Dedicated 1:1 link protection flag set in the GMPLS Protection object.

When one of the link-terminating nodes detects a failure on the protected span, it initiates protection switchover, which is performed according to the following rules.

- The failure-detecting node immediately stops using the protecting span for sending/receiving data of those extra traffic LSPs whose resources need to be preempted by the span-protected LSPs. Head ends of such extra traffic LSPs are notified about resource preemption (via GMPLS RSVP Notify or PathErr messages). If a Switchover Request from the opposite side of the link has not been received yet, such a request is sent to the node at the remote end of the link; otherwise, a Switchover Response is sent.

- On receipt of a Switchover Request the receiving node immediately stops using the protecting span for sending/receiving data of the extra traffic LSPs that are about to be preempted. It also stops using the protected span and starts using the protecting span for sending/receiving traffic of the span-protected LSPs. After that, a Switchover Response is sent to the opposite side of the link.

- On receipt of a Switchover Response the receiving node stops using the protected span and starts using the protecting span for sending/receiving traffic of the span-protected LSPs.

When the failure is restored and the reversion mode is configured, switchback synchronization is performed, but only after the WRT interval has passed without further failures. Under the dedicated 1:1 with extra traffic span-protection scheme, the switchback procedure is carried out according to the following rules.

- When one of the link-terminating nodes that has previously detected a link failure realizes that the failure is restored and the restored span is failure-free for some (WRT) time, it starts sending data on and selecting data from the span-protected LSPs on both the protecting and protected spans. After that it sends a Switchback Request to the node at the opposite end of the link.

- On receipt of a Switchback Request the receiving node stops using the protecting span and starts using the restored protected span for sending/receiving data of the span-protected LSPs. It also sends a Switchback Response to the opposite end of the link.

- On receipt of a Switchback Response the receiving node stops sending/ selecting data onto/from the protecting span.

Note that these switchback procedures involve a short period of time where the sending node that originates the procedure bridges the traffic onto both spans (as in 1+1 protection). This is necessary to ensure that the switchback procedure does not cause significant disruption to the traffic flow. Once the switchback procedures are completed, the released resources become available again for extra traffic LSPs.

As in the case of the bidirectional dedicated 1+1 span protection model, the switchover/switchback synchronization signaling can be provided either by the GMPLS Control Plane (via LMP or GMPLS RSVP Notify messages) or by the data plane (for example, SONET/SDH APS signaling).

Dedicated 1:1 span protection with extra traffic is more complex than 1+1 span protection schemes and yields worse recovery times. However, it is more efficient from the bandwidth utilization point of view because it allows the use of protection bandwidth for extra traffic in the steady state.

8.6.4 Shared M:N Span Protection

In the case of shared M:N (M < N) span protection there are two sets of spans interconnecting a pair of adjacent nodes. The first set contains N (working) spans that carry normal traffic and are protected by the second set of M (protecting) spans. The spans from the second set do not carry normal traffic but may carry extra (preemptable) traffic. M and N are configurable values (for example 1:5, meaning 1 protecting span protects 5 working spans). The fact that M < N makes this scheme even more efficient than the dedicated 1:1 span protection—the same number of protecting spans protects more working spans—but it is clearly more vulnerable to multiple simultaneous failures.

When a failure affects one or more working spans, both span-terminating nodes switch onto one or more protecting spans. Because the amount of protection resources is less than the amount of protected resources (M < N), it is possible that not all span-protected LSPs can be recovered. Which LSPs are actually recovered is a matter of local policies (for instance, those that have higher holding priorities). When the failure is restored, the traffic affected by the failure may be switched back onto the restored working span(s), releasing the protecting span(s) back to the protecting pool, and thus making it/them available for extra traffic again.

In contrast to all previously described span protection schemes, where link-terminating nodes play the same role in the switchover and switchback procedures, this scheme is not symmetrical. This is because, generally speaking, it is not known prior to the detection of a failure which of the protecting spans will be switched onto when a particular working span fails. Therefore, it is necessary that one of the nodes (playing the *master* role) is responsible for the allocation of a protecting span and for letting the other node (playing the *slave* role) know about its choice. Which of the nodes plays which role is either configured, based on the results of some neighbor discovery procedures (for example, via LMP), or algorithmically determined. In the latter case, for instance, the node with the larger node ID could be determined as the master, with the other node as the slave.

Both sets of spans are advertised to the TE network domain as a single TE link. The Link Protection Type attribute is specified as "Shared M:N" and the ISC Descriptor attribute is built as a combination of the attributes of the protected and protecting spans according to the following rules.

- For priorities higher (that is, numerically lower) than the priority configured for the extra traffic, the advertised attribute is compiled as the union of the ISC Descriptors of *only* the working spans. The procedures are described in an Internet-Draft that documents link bundling.

- For priorities lower than or equal to the priority of the extra traffic, the advertised attribute is compiled as the union of the ISC Descriptors of *all* spans (both working and protecting).

If there is a need to establish an M:N shared span-protected LSP, its path must be computed with the constraint of the Link Protection Type attribute to be no worse than (numerically greater or equal to) Shared M:N. Furthermore, the LSP should be signaled with the Shared M:N link protection flag set in the GMPLS Protection object.

When the master node detects a failure on one of the working spans it initiates the protection switchover procedure, which is performed according to the following rules.

- The master node allocates a protection span from the pool of available protecting spans. It immediately stops using the allocated span for sending/receiving data of those extra traffic LSPs whose resources need to be preempted by the span protected LSPs. Head ends of such extra traffic LSPs are notified about the preemption (via GMPLS RSVP Notify or PathErr messages). After that, the master node sends a Switchover Request to the slave. The message contains the IDs of the failed (working) and selected (protecting) spans.

- On receipt of a Switchover Request the slave immediately stops using the specified protecting span for sending/receiving data of the extra traffic LSPs that are about to be preempted. It also stops using the specified (failed) working span and starts using the protecting span for sending/receiving traffic of the span-protected LSPs. The slave also sends a Switchover Response back to the master. The message contains the IDs of working and protecting spans.

- On receipt of a Switchover Response the master completes the switchover procedure. Specifically, it stops using the failed working span and starts using the protecting span for sending/receiving traffic of the span-protected LSPs.

When the slave node detects a failure on one of the working spans, it sends a fault indication message specifying, among other things, the ID of the failed span. On receipt of the message the master node performs the exact same actions (described above) as if it had detected the failure itself.

As was mentioned before, the master may discover that not all span-protected LSPs can be recovered via shared M:N span protection. Those that cannot be recovered (usually, ones provisioned with lower holding priority values) are individually notified with a failure indication event, which is likely to trigger some path level recovery scheme.

When the master node detects that a previously indicated span failure is restored, it may (depending on whether the reversion mode is locally configured or not) start switchback synchronization.

- The master node starts the WRT. If during the life of the WRT it neither detects a failure of the restored span nor receives a fault indication message from the slave regarding the restored span, it starts sending and selecting data for the span-protected LSPs onto/from both protecting and restored spans. It also sends a Switchback Request to the slave. The message includes the IDs of the restored and protecting spans.

- On receipt of a Switchback Request the slave stops using the protecting span and starts using the working span for sending/receiving data for the span-protected LSPs. It also sends a Switchback Response to the master.

- On receipt of a Switchback Response the master stops sending/selecting data onto/from the protecting span and releases the span back to the pool, thus making it available again for protecting the working spans and for carrying extra traffic.

When the slave node discovers that a failure that it previously indicated to the master node has been restored, it sends a fault restoration message specifying the IDs of the restored and protecting spans. On receipt of the message the master performs the same actions (described above) as if it had detected the failure restoration itself.

The necessary fault notification and switchover/switchback synchronization signaling can be provided either by the GMPLS Control Plane (via LMP or GMPLS RSVP Notify messages) or by the data plane (for example, SONET/SDH RDI/APS signaling).

8.6.5 Enhanced Span Protection

Enhanced span protection is defined as any protection scheme that provides better (more reliable) span protection than dedicated 1+1 span protection. A good example of enhanced span protection is the four-fiber SONET BLSR ring, which is discussed later in this section.

Every TE link that participates in such a span protection scheme is advertised with the Link Protection Type attribute set to the "Enhanced" value. Path computation for an LSP that needs to use enhanced span protection should be constrained to selecting TE links advertising the Enhanced link protection type. The LSP should be signaled with the Enhanced link protection bit set in the GMPLS Protection object.

Four-Fiber SONET BLSR Rings

The SONET BLSR ring (Figure 8.2) is a popular way to interconnect SONET digital cross-connects. Each node on the ring is connected to each of its neighbors

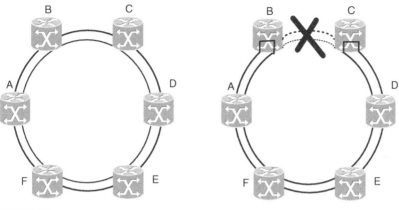

FIGURE 8.2

Four-fiber SONET BLSR.

by two pairs of fibers. In the steady state, one pair of fibers carries traffic in both directions (in the diagram on the left of Figure 8.2, the working fiber pair constitutes the outer ring), whereas the other fiber pair is reserved for protection purposes. In the event of a failure, the fault-detecting nodes (nodes B and C in our example) loop the traffic back onto the protecting fiber pair.

Suppose there is a bidirectional service provisioned between nodes A and D. Before the failure, the service was using the path A-B-C-D with reverse path traffic using D-C-B-A. In both cases, the outer fiber ring is used. After the failure the service path is A-B-A-F-E-D-C-D with reverse path traffic using D-C-D-E-F-A-B-A. Where the same traffic appears to flow in both directions between a pair of nodes (such as between C and D in this example) it is using both rings. Thus, no matter which link or node on the ring fails, the traffic of all services going over the ring is rapidly recovered, provided that there is no more than one fault per ring at any moment.

Note that, from a GMPLS point of view, we are still talking about a single span. That is, the BLSR ring provides support for a single hop in the GMPLS network. Thus the paths A-B-C-D and A-B-A-F-E-D-C-D in this example provide a single TE link between A and D which are GMPLS nodes. The nodes B, C, E, and F are part of the lower-layer transport system that provides connectivity for the GMPLS network.

8.7 PATH RECOVERY

In this section we will discuss service recovery on the path level—that is, recovery of entire LSPs (end-to-end recovery) or individual segments of LSPs (segment recovery and fast re-route). We will start by introducing the notion of the *path recovery domain*, because it is important for all types of path level recovery. After that we will discuss in detail end-to-end path recovery, segment recovery, and the fast re-route technique.

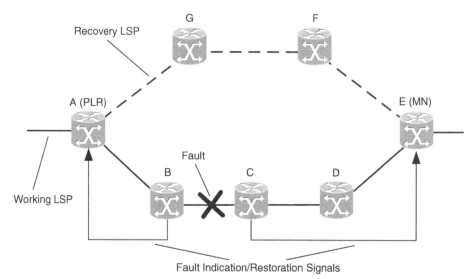

FIGURE 8.3

Path recovery domain.

8.7.1 Path Recovery Domain

Consider the fragment of a network depicted in Figure 8.3. Assume that a working LSP of some protected service goes through nodes A-B-C-D-E. A path recovery domain for the service could be defined as a part of the network where some scheme is provisioned to recover the service from failures of a segment of one of the service's LSPs (normally a working LSP, but protecting LSPs can also be protected). In the end-to-end path recovery model, the recovery domain covers the entire protected LSP. In case of path segment recovery, the protected LSP spans multiple recovery domains, which, generally speaking, may overlap, nest one within another, and so forth. It is reasonable to think of end-to-end path recovery as a special case of path segment recovery, where the protected segment is the entire LSP.

Figure 8.3 shows a recovery domain. It provides recovery from any fault that might happen on the segment A-B-C-D-E. The LSP going through nodes A-G-F-E is called a recovery LSP. This is the LSP that carries traffic for the service after a failure on the protected segment has been detected.

The timing of when a recovery LSP is established relative to the moment of failure detection distinguishes the notions of path protection and path restoration. If the recovery LSP is fully pre-established—no provisioning signaling is necessary after the detection of a failure—then the recovery domain provides *path protection*. In all other cases:

- Recovery path was not pre-computed; or
- Recovery path was pre-computed but not pre-selected; or

- Recovery path was pre-computed and pre-selected but not pre-signaled; or
- Recovery path was pre-signaled, resources were pre-allocated but not pre-selected; or
- Recovery path was pre-signaled and resources were pre-allocated and pre-selected but not activated.

These are all different types of *path restoration*.

The node originating the recovery LSP (node A) is the PLR, and the node terminating the recovery LSP (node E) is the MN. Both nodes have special but similar roles as deciding entities in the path recovery cycle. In the data plane they are responsible for bridging traffic onto protected or protecting LSPs. They are also responsible for selecting incoming data from one of the LSPs. In the control plane they are expected to receive fault indication/restoration signals, and trigger and coordinate the switchover/switchback processes. Additionally, the PLR is, on many occasions, responsible for path computation/selection/re-optimization of the restoration LSP.

8.7.2 End-to-End Path Recovery

Each LSP can have an end-to-end path recovery scheme of one of the following types provisioned for it.

- Unidirectional 1+1 protection
- Bidirectional 1+1 protection
- 1:N protection with extra traffic
- Pre-planned re-routing without extra traffic
- Full re-routing
- Unprotected

The type of required end-to-end path recovery is signaled using the LSP flags in the GMPLS Protection object. There is another section of the Protection object—LSP status—that is important in the context of end-to-end path recovery. It is used to distinguish a protected LSP from the associated protecting LSP, an LSP that is fully established from one that needs some further activation signaling before it can carry traffic, and an LSP that actually carries traffic from one that is idle.

An end-to-end path protected LSP has a single PLR (its head end) and a single MN (tail end).

Unidirectional 1+1 Protection

In this scheme a protected LSP head end computes two link-, node-, or SRLG-disjoint paths—one for the protected LSP (for example, A-G-F-E in Figure 8.4) and another for the protecting LSP (for example, A-B-C-D-E). The protecting LSP is fully established at the same time as the protected LSP. In the data plane both head and tail ends (nodes A and E, respectively) bridge outgoing traffic onto both LSPs and select incoming traffic from one of the two (for example, from the one that

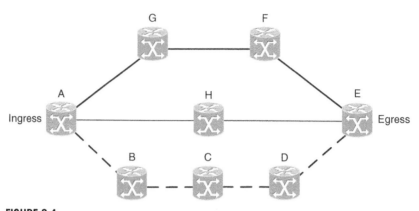

FIGURE 8.4

End-to-end 1+1 protection.

provides a better quality signal). When a failure is detected anywhere on the protected LSP, selectors on one or both ends autonomously switch to receive traffic from the fault-free channel. Neither fault notification nor synchronization of any sort is required. Because the protecting LSP is permanently used for carrying traffic, its resources cannot be shared with LSPs that protect other LSPs. Neither can it be used to carry extra traffic. Thus, the scheme is not efficient, although it is simple and guarantees the best possible service recovery time.

The notion of the *Shared Risk Link Group* (*SRLG*) has been discussed in other chapters. Here it is sufficient to know that sometimes TE links cannot be considered independent in the sense that a single failure may affect two or more links at the same time. For example, multiple fibers may be carried within a single conduit: If the conduit is cut it would make all these fibers (and hence the associated TE links) unusable. Such TE links are said to belong to a particular SRLG. Part of TE link advertisement supplies a list of SRLGs to which the link belongs. This makes it possible for any path computing entity in the network to select protected and protecting paths in such a way that the paths have non-overlapping unions of SRLGs of the links that constitute the paths. Such paths are referred to as *SRLG-disjoint*.

Bidirectional 1+1 Protection

This protection scheme works like the previous one with one exception: The selectors on both ends always select data from the same channel. This means that after fault detection the selectors switch to receive data from the second channel even if the fault affected only one direction of the protected channel. This synchronization requires signaling, which is performed according to the following rules.

- A node on the protected LSP detects a failure and reliably sends a Fault Indication Signal (FIS) to the PLR and MN, identifying the point of failure.

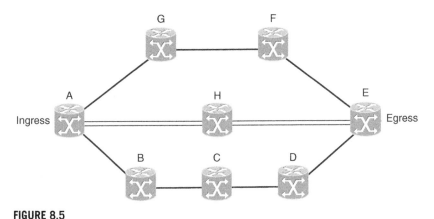

FIGURE 8.5

End-to-end 1:N protection with extra traffic.

- When the PLR receives either an FIS or Switchover Request, or locally detects the failure, it immediately stops receiving data from the channel that was affected by the failure, and starts receiving data from the alternative channel. After that, it sends a Switchover Request to the MN, unless by that time it has already received such a request from the MN. In the latter case the PLR sends a Switchover Response to the MN.

- Likewise, when the MN receives either an FIS or Switchover Request, or locally detects the failure, it immediately switches to receiving data from the alternative channel. It also sends a Switchover Request to the PLR, if by that time such a request has not yet been received. In the latter case a Switchover Response is sent instead.

GMPLS provides a convenient mechanism—the GMPLS RSVP Notify message—for fault notification and switchover synchronization signaling. Note that the messages do not need to follow either the working or protected LSP, they can take advantage of the general flexibility of the control plane network. However, it is imperative that the messages are delivered reliably. Fortunately, the GMPLS signaling protocol has a mechanism that guarantees reliable message delivery.

1:N Protection with Extra Traffic

In this model an end-to-end protecting LSP is signaled over a path that is link-, node-, or SRLG-disjoint from several protected LSPs. Suppose we have a couple of services carrying normal traffic over paths A-B-C-D-E and A-G-F-E (Figure 8.5), which require protection. The LSP, protecting both of them, can be provisioned over the path A-H-E, which is disjoint from the paths taken by both protected LSPs. Note that the protected LSPs are also mutually disjoint to avoid possible contention between them for the shared protection resources (something that might happen if the protected LSPs shared a link and it was that link that failed). As in the schemes described earlier, the protecting LSP is fully pre-established; however, normal traffic is not bridged onto it in the steady state because that would result in a mix of traffic from both protected LSPs. This means that the protecting LSP could be used to carry extra traffic. To make the mapping of extra traffic services onto the shared 1:N protecting LSPs possible, it is necessary that the advertising of the TE links taken by the LSPs should count resources allocated for the LSPs as unreserved on priorities lower than or equal to the priority of the extra traffic.

When a failure occurs on one of the protected LSPs, both of its ends switch sending and receiving traffic onto/from the protecting LSP, if necessary preempting its resources from carrying extra traffic. As in all other cases, when resource preemption is involved, special care must be taken to avoid misconnections. In this particular model, a misconnection may happen if the selector on one of the ends switches to receiving data from the protecting channel before the opposite end stops sending extra traffic. Such misconnection, even if lasts for a very short period of time, can cause serious damage to the service user, and is considered as a confidentiality breach.

It is possible that more than one protected LSP will attempt to claim resources of the protecting LSP. This could be triggered even by a single failure if the protected LSPs were not sufficiently disjoint. It may also happen because of multiple simultaneous failures (for example, if links GF and CD fail). If such a situation arises, only one of the protected LSPs (the one with the highest provisioned holding priority, or simply the one that makes the request first) will actually be recovered. The other affected LSPs must try some different recovery scheme(s). For instance, they could be fully re-routed (as described later in this section).

The fault notification and switchover synchronization signaling has the following sequence.

- A node on one of the protected LSPs detects a failure and sends an FIS to both ends of the LSP (that is, to the PLR and MN).

- When the PLR receives an FIS or locally detects the failure, it immediately stops using the protecting LSP for sending/receiving extra traffic. If by that time it has also received a Switchover Request from the MN, it switches to transfer normal traffic from the LSP affected by the failure to the protecting LSP, and also sends a Switchover Response to the MN. Otherwise, the PLR sends a Switchover Request to the MN.

- When the MN receives an FIS or locally detects the failure, it immediately stops using the protecting LSP for sending/receiving extra traffic. If by that time it has also received a Switchover Request from the PLR, it switches normal traffic from the protected LSP to the protecting LSP and sends a Switchover Response to the PLR. Otherwise, it sends a Switchover Request to the PLR.

- When either the PLR or MN receives a Switchover Response, the receiving node switches to sending/receiving normal traffic using the protecting LSP, if this has not been done yet.

As in the case of bidirectional 1+1 protection, the fault notification and switchover synchronization (GMPLS RSVP Notify) messages need not follow the path of either of the LSPs.

The protection scheme described here is more complex than the earlier schemes. It also yields a worse recovery time due to the fact that normal traffic starts to be carried over the protecting LSP only after failure detection. However, for the same reason, the scheme is more efficient, because the protection resources are provided at a favorable ratio and can be used in steady state for carrying extra traffic. It is important to keep in mind that this reuse of the protection resources is limited only to extra traffic services that happen to coincide with the full path of the protecting LSP by passing through the ingress and egress of the protection LSP (usually, this is restricted to extra traffic services that originate and terminate on the same nodes as the protected/protecting LSPs). It is not possible, for example, to partially share resources of the protecting LSP with other protecting LSPs as in the case of the pre-planned re-routing model (see Figure 8.6).

Pre-Planned Re-Routing Without Extra Traffic

This scheme assumes that a protecting LSP is pre-signaled to be disjoint from a protected LSP or from several mutually disjoint protected LSPs. In contrast with all of the path protection schemes described earlier, the resources on the links of the protecting LSP are allocated but are *not* bound into cross-connects. Thus, the protecting LSP cannot be used to carry extra traffic. More than that, after failure detection the protecting LSP must be activated (that is, signaled to bind the cross-connects) before the normal traffic can be switched onto it. Hence the scheme yields worse recovery times compared to the 1:N path protection model with extra traffic. The legitimate question is, what is this scheme good for?

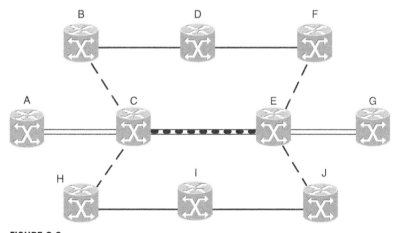

FIGURE 8.6

Pre-planned re-routing.

The scheme is useful because all resources pre-planned for use by each of the protecting LSP links can also be pre-planned for use to protect some other protected LSPs, not necessarily originated/terminated on the same nodes. This enables far wider protection at the cost of fewer protection resources, provided that all LSPs protected in this way are unlikely to fail simultaneously. More than that, the fact that resources are pre-planned for the protecting LSP does not mean that they cannot be fully activated for some other LSPs carrying extra traffic (which makes the name of this scheme confusing!). The distinction is that the protecting LSP cannot carry extra traffic, but the protection resources can be assigned to some other preemptable LSP that *does* carry extra traffic.

Thus, the model provides the most flexible way of sharing protection resources, where *arbitrary* segments of protecting and extra traffic LSPs are shared. In other words the sharing is partial and is not limited to end-to-end sharing as in the case of the 1:N protection model with extra traffic.

Consider the segment of a network depicted in Figure 8.6. Suppose that there are two end-to-end protected LSPs established—B-D-F and H-I-J. The first one is protected by an LSP going through B-C-E-F, and the second by an LSP going through H-C-E-J. Assuming that the protected LSPs cannot fail simultaneously, resources on link CE can be shared between the two protecting LSPs. Furthermore, suppose there is a preemptable extra traffic LSP going through A-C-E-G. In the steady state the same resources on link CE that are pre-planned for the protection of both protected LSPs can also be allocated and fully activated for the extra traffic LSP.

This recovery scheme falls under the definition of path restoration rather than path protection because some provisioning signaling is needed after fault detection (to activate the resources of the protecting LSP that is about to start carrying normal traffic). With careful placing of protected LSPs and pre-planning of protecting LSPs it is possible to achieve *full mesh restoration*, where a relatively small amount of resources, allocated for protection purposes, covers a relatively large amount of resources carrying normal traffic. Additionally, the pre-planned protection resources are available for carrying extra traffic. For path computing entities to take advantage of such resource sharing, each TE link should advertise the shared protection resources as unreserved on priorities equal to or lower than the extra traffic priority. And, of course, the control plane must support resource preemption, so that normal traffic can bump out extra traffic when a protected LSP fails.

The fact that the protecting LSP resources must be allocated but not activated during LSP setup is signaled using the LSP Status section of the GMPLS Protection object (the LSP is signaled as "Secondary," not as "Primary" as in all other recovery schemes). The resource activation signaling can be piggy-backed on the Switchover Request. In this case the message should be delivered hop by hop along the protecting LSP from the PLR to the MN, so that controllers along the path have a chance to stop using the resources for extra traffic and bind them into the LSP cross-connects. It is also important to bear in mind that the scheme's switchover paradigm is asymmetrical, meaning that FISs should be delivered to the master (the role normally assumed by the PLR, but sometimes by the MN), which controls the switchover procedures as follows.

■ The master unbinds the resources of the protecting LSP from the cross-connect to which they are currently bound and stops using them for sending/receiving extra traffic. It also sends a notification to the head end of the extra traffic LSP about the resource preemption. Then it activates the resources by binding them into the protecting LSP cross-connect and, after that, sends a Switchover Request (GMPLS RSVP Notify message) along the protecting LSP to the next controller.

■ Every controller along the Switchover Request path (including the slave) performs the same operations as the master, although some optimizations may be made to reduce the number of preemption notifications sent. Additionally, the slave immediately starts to send/receive traffic for the LSP affected by the failure using the protecting LSP, and sends a Switchover Reply direct to the master.

■ On receipt of a Switchover Reply the master starts sending and receiving the normal traffic over the protecting LSP.

Full Re-Routing

This path restoration scheme assumes no pre-provisioning of a recovery LSP before the actual failure of the LSP that carries normal (that is, subject for recovery) traffic. Consider the network shown in Figure 8.7.

Assume that there is an unprotected LSP going through nodes A, B, D, and E and carrying normal traffic. At some point in time a failure is detected on the link BD. The end-to-end full re-routing scheme works as follows.

■ A failure-detecting node (node B and/or node D) sends an FIS message to the LSP's head end (node A).

■ The head end computes an alternative path or selects a pre-computed alternative path. The alternative path must be divergent from the point of failure (say, path A-C-D-E).

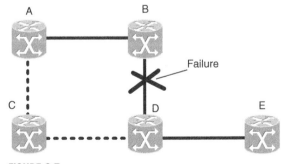

FIGURE 8.7

Full re-routing.

- The head end re-routes the LSP onto the new path, using the make-before-break procedure to take share resources already reserved on any parts of the path that are common.

- If the re-route fails for any reason, a new attempt is made to compute or select an alternative path divergent from the point of original failure and the point at which the re-route failed.

This procedure repeats itself until the LSP is successfully re-routed, or the head end fails to determine an alternative path divergent from all points of failure.

Compared to all of the recovery schemes described previously, this scheme yields the worst service recovery time. This is because of the extra time required for path computation and the establishment through signaling of the recovery path after the service head end receives the FIS. Note that establishment of the recovery LSP might fail several times before it is eventually set up and can be used for normal traffic delivery, which makes things even worse.

However, the full re-routing model also has some great qualities. First, it is the most efficient scheme from the resource utilization point of view. This is because it does not claim resources for recovery purposes until an actual failure occurs, hence the resources are fully available for other services (not limited to extra traffic services). Also, if full re-routing is provisioned for the service, it is likely that the re-routed LSP will take the shortest path which may be congruent with the original LSP for most of its path, whereas a protected LSP must take a fully diverse path which is usually longer (and so requires more network resources).

Secondly, the scheme can handle all failures, including unexpected and multiple simultaneous failures, provided that a feasible, fault-free path still exists in the network. On the other hand, all protection schemes recover only from failures that they are provisioned to protect against, and do not "like" any surprises. For example, it is normally assumed that a working LSP and its protecting LSPs cannot fail at the same time. But if they do (perhaps because they take paths that are not sufficiently disjoint), the service will not be recovered. Likewise, if several failures happen at the same time in a network where the full mesh restoration scheme was pre-provisioned on the assumption that no more than one failure could happen, only some of the services will be able to recover, while the rest (the lower priority ones) will not. There is no such problem with the full re-routing approach.

Thirdly, the scheme can recover services on topologies where path protection simply is not feasible. This is because, when a protection scheme is provisioned, it is not known *a priori* exactly where a failure will occur. Therefore, path protection requires at least two maximally disjoint paths to avoid the situation where a single failure breaks both working and protecting LSPs. In the full re-routing case, however, by the time a recovery path is selected it is already known which elements of the LSP have failed. Thus, the recovery path does not have to be fully disjoint from the original path: The only requirement is that it must avoid the point(s) of failure. In our example (Figure 8.7), a service going from node A to node E cannot be fully protected in principle, because two fully disjoint paths between the service source and destination cannot be found, but, as we see, it can be re-routed.

Considering the qualities of the full re-routing approach, it makes good sense to provision a hybrid recovery scheme, so that a segment and/or end-to-end protection scheme(s) could be engaged, with the full re-routing scheme available as a last resort if all of the protection schemes fail to recover the service.

Reversion

After protection switchover happens, normal traffic is delivered over the protecting LSP rather than over the failed working LSP. There are numerous reasons why this situation is not meant to persist. First of all, the protecting LSP is usually longer than the LSP it protects and hence is more expensive and may provide a lower quality service. More important the traffic is no longer protected and, if the protecting LSP fails, the service will be disrupted. The protection resources could also be shared between multiple services (for example, under the shared 1:N with extra traffic model), and so all other services that used to be protected are no longer protected, and the extra traffic, which used to be delivered over the protecting LSP, has been disrupted and must now be mapped onto some other LSP. Finally, the resources of the failed working LSP are locked (still allocated for the LSP) and cannot be used for any other purposes.

There are two ways that the service could be handled after its working LSP fails and protection switchover occurs. In the first approach (called the *non-revertive* mode) the service head end attempts to redirect the service LSPs onto new path(s), which may or may not use links and nodes of the previous path(s) that were not affected by the failure. Once the operation succeeds the unused resources of the previous working and protecting LSPs are released. In the case of shared protection, the protecting LSP is released to perform its steady state functions; that is, to protect other services and carry extra traffic.

Note that the non-revertive mode is not always possible—there might simply be no available or feasible alternative paths, divergent from the point of failure. In this case the second approach, the *revertive* mode, is a better choice. Reversion (also referred as *protection switchback*) happens in the following way: The control plane simply waits until the fault conditions are removed, and then has the service head and tail ends synchronously switch to sending/receiving traffic onto/from the restored working LSP.

The reversion procedures are similar to the switchover procedures described earlier. The fault-detecting/reporting node receives an indication from the data plane that the fault conditions have been cleared, and sends a Fault Restoration Signal (FRS) message to the PLR and/or MN (service head and tail ends, respectively, in case the of end-to-end protection). These nodes use switchback synchronization signaling and re-program the data plane to move normal traffic back onto the restored LSP.

Note that despite the similarity of the reversion and switchover procedures, their goals and the conditions under which they happen are fundamentally different. Switchover occurs because one or more failures have just been detected. This means that the traffic has already been disrupted; hence it is crucial for the operation to be started and completed as fast as possible. Reversion, on the other hand, happens when the traffic is stable and properly delivered over the protecting LSP. There is no rush either to start reversion or complete it; the goal is to make the switchback as smooth as possible in order to minimize any second traffic hit. Note also that during reversion there is no extra traffic involved, hence there is no danger of misconnection. Therefore, no constraints on the sequence in which the PLR and MN re-program their data planes are imposed.

Let us consider the sequence of events that happen during reversion within, say, the shared 1:N protection scheme.

- Each node that previously detected the failure receives an indication from the data plane about the fault restoration, and sends FRS messages to the PLR and/or MN.

- On receipt of an FRS or Switchback Request, or if the fault restoration is locally detected, the PLR/MN immediately starts bridging outgoing traffic onto both working and protecting LSPs, and begins to select incoming data from the LSP with a better signal. It also sends a Switchback Request to the opposite end of the LSP unless the request has already been received. In the latter case a Switchback Response is sent instead.

- On receipt of a Switchback Response the receiving node stops using the protecting LSP for sending/receiving data. The LSP is marked as available for protection and extra traffic delivery.

Recall the discussion of "flapping" in Section 8.6.2, and how the problem is handled in the span protection model. A similar issue needs to be addressed in path-level protection schemes as well. Consider, for example, the situation where the power level of an optical signal on a particular frequency is jittering around the "Signal Degrade" threshold. In this case, the local control plane might receive multiple sequences of failure detection/failure restoration indications in quick succession, which, in turn, could repeatedly trigger switchover and switchback procedures. This is a highly undesirable situation for any service because each switchover involves a traffic hit. To avoid such a condition the failure restoration-detecting node does not generate the FRS right away. Rather, the failure restoration event starts the Wait-to-Restore Timer (WRT), which is cancelled by any further failure indication received before the timer expires, and the timer is started again upon a subsequent failure restoration event. Only if no further failure indications are received during the life of the WRT is the FRS sent to the PLR and/or MN. This mechanism guarantees that the switchback happens only after the restored resource is functional for some time and may be judged to be stable. A smart implementation does not use a permanent WRT interval. Rather it uses exponentially increasing values to mitigate the resource flapping effect even more.

Pre-Planned Failures

Routine maintenance and periodic testing are always required for network resources. This is true even if the resources are engaged in carrying live traffic. The only way to conduct such maintenance without disrupting the services mapped onto the resources is to re-route the traffic onto some other path, complete all maintenance and testing operations, and then return the traffic back to its original path. Note that this is exactly the sequence of events that happens during automatic fault protection switchover and switchback procedures, which means that the necessary control plane infrastructure is in place already. All that is needed is the introduction of some external commands (typically issued by a network operator through the NMS or EMS or CLI) to simulate the failure indication/restoration events that are normally generated by the data plane. For example, one such command may be called "Forced Switch for Normal Traffic." It causes the unconditional switchover of the normal traffic onto the protecting LSP. A similar command, "Manual Switch for Normal Traffic," causes the same switchover, but only on the following conditions.

- No fault conditions are known to exist on the protecting LSP (that is, no failures were reported by the data plane).

- No management commands of a higher priority than the Manual Switch For Normal Traffic command are in effect blocking the execution of the command. The examples of such commands are: "Lockout of Recovery LSP" and "Lockout of Normal Traffic." The first command locks access to the protecting LSP for any traffic (normal or extra), while the second one disallows only normal traffic.

A further command, "Manual Switch for Recovery LSP," causes switchback of the normal traffic onto the working LSP unless the latter has active fault conditions or was locked via the 'Lockout of Working LSP' command.

8.7.3 Path Segment Recovery

In the path segment recovery model separate recovery schemes are provisioned to protect individual path segments rather than an entire path. Each of the schemes used can be of any of the types that are defined for end-to-end path recovery (see the previous section). All failures are handled just as in the case of end-to-end path recovery with two caveats.

- In the case of path segment recovery any node on a protected LSP (that is, not necessarily the LSP ends as in the case of end-to-end path recovery) may play the role of PLR and/or MN.

- A node on a protected LSP may belong to more than one (overlapping, nested) segment recovery domain and thus may use more than one pair of PLRs/MNs to trigger the recovery from a locally detected failure. This is a useful feature in situations when some PLRs/MNs fail to provide the expected recovery for some reason. This is in sharp contrast to the end-to-end path recovery model, where LSP ends are the only PLR/MN, and a failure of the control plane on either of them makes the LSP unrecoverable in many recovery schemes.

Consider the network presented in Figure 8.8. Suppose that an LSP going through nodes A-B-D-E is a path segment protected LSP: Segment A-B-D is protected by the recovery LSP A-C-D, and segment D-E is protected by the recovery LSP A-F-E. Thus, we have two recovery domains: one starting on PLR A and terminating on MN D, and the other starting on PLR D and terminating on MN E. Note that node D performs the role of MN in one domain and of PLR in the other.

The question is, why not use an end-to-end recovery LSP taking the path A-C-D-F-E instead, since this is link-disjoint from the working path? After all, it would be simpler and require fewer control plane states. But there are numerous advantages in using the segment recovery as follows.

One can see that each recovery domain used in segment recovery is smaller, compared to the end-to-end recovery domain, in the sense that for any possible failure the PLR and MN that are supposed to handle the failure are closer to each other and also to the point of failure. This is important for any recovery scheme that requires fault notification and switchover synchronization signaling simply because there are fewer hops for a signaling message to travel. This usually results in a significant decrease in the overall recovery time.

Segment recovery may provide better protection than end-to-end recovery. In our example, end-to-end recovery could be achieved using an LSP A-C-D-F-E, which uses the same resources as were proposed for the segment protection LSPs. But suppose that two failures—one on link BD, and one on link DF—happen simultaneously, as shown in Figure 8.8. These failures would disrupt the end-to-end protected service since both the protected and recovery LSPs would be affected. The segment-protected LSP, on the other hand, would be recovered in this case as long as a fault-free segment either on the protected LSP or the associated recovery LSP exists in each domain. That is, the traffic in our example would follow the path A-G-D-E.

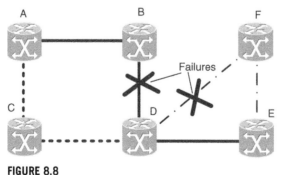

FIGURE 8.8

Path segment recovery.

In some network topologies a service may take a path, for which it is only possible to protect some segment(s), but not the entire path. Consider, for example, a service delivered by the network presented in Figure 8.7 traversing nodes A-B-D-E. There is no alternative path for the service that is fully disjoint from its working path; hence end-to-end protection is not feasible. However, an LSP going through nodes A, C, and D can protect the segment A-B-D. Such protection, albeit imperfect, is still better than no protection at all.

In other cases, alternative end-to-end paths may exist, but could be difficult to compute. Consider, for example, a service traversing multiple TE domains. Computing end-to-end alternative paths in this case is a challenge, especially if the paths may go through separate Service Providers' networks. It is much simpler to compute a single path for the working LSP in a distributed way with each domain border node on the path expanding the path segment within its TE visibility. While doing so, the border nodes can, at the same time, compute paths to be used for recovery of the segments. They have no problem performing such computations because all the recovery paths are located within their TE visibility.

There may be cases when it would make sense to protect a service in different ways on different network fragments. Some of the fragments may be underused, and provisioning dedicated 1+1 protection of the working LSP segments traversing them is reasonable. On the heavily used network fragments, on the other hand, allocating an extra 100% of network resources for protection purposes may prove to be too expensive, and shared protection or pre-planned re-routing could be a better choice.

It may seem that the path segment recovery method always leaves some LSP nodes unprotected as single points of failure: By definition a segment recovery domain must start and stop on some intermediate nodes, leaving them unprotected (for example, node D in Figure 8.8). Fortunately this need not be the case. Suppose that there is an additional sequence of links interconnecting nodes B and H (see Figure 8.9). The link(s) can be used for a recovery LSP specifically dedicated to protect against node D failures.

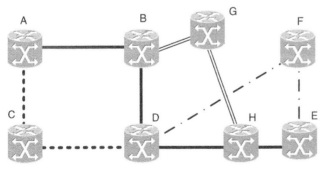

FIGURE 8.9

Overlapping segment recovery.

This is *overlapping segment recovery*, where a new recovery domain starts before some other recovery domain (that started somewhere upstream) is terminated. Generally speaking, GMPLS path segment recovery is very powerful as a concept. It support numerous complex path recovery topologies, and the overlapping path segment recovery scheme is just one example (see Figure 8.10). GMPLS signaling has a remarkably simple and efficient way (via a stack of GMPLS RSVP NotifyRequest objects—see the more detailed description below) of advertising the PLRs and MNs along the path of a protected LSP, so that each node on the path has a prioritized list of relevant PLRs/MNs it can notify to trigger the LSP recovery from a failure detected by the node. For example, a node located somewhere between MN3 and MN1 (Figure 8.10c) knows that only PLR1 and MN1 can take care of locally detected failures, while all other PLRs/MNs are of no use. Likewise, a node located upstream of MN2 knows that in case of a failure it needs to notify PLR2 and MN2 first, and only if they fail to provide the recovery should it try PLR1/MN1. Note that the node would know nothing about the PLR3/MN3 pair.

One may wonder why anybody would need such a complex recovery scheme. The main reason for this is the ability to recover from multiple simultaneous failures. Imagine, for example, that the control plane on the PLR of a 1:1 protection domain fails. If, before it is restored, some node along the protected LSP detects

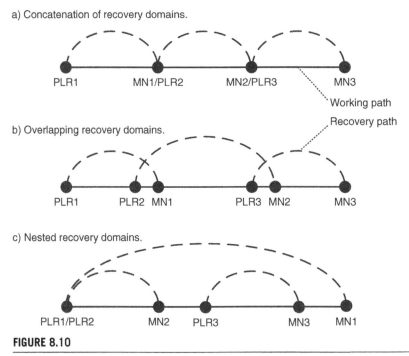

a) Concatenation of recovery domains.

PLR1   MN1/PLR2   MN2/PLR3   MN3

Working path
Recovery path

b) Overlapping recovery domains.

PLR1   PLR2 MN1   PLR3 MN2   MN3

c) Nested recovery domains.

PLR1/PLR2   MN2   PLR3   MN3   MN1

FIGURE 8.10

Segment recovery domains may be concatenated, overlapping, or nested.

a failure and sends an FIS to the PLR, the protection switchover will not happen, and service will be disrupted, possibly for a significant period of time. However, if the fault-detecting node is aware of some other PLR, it will send the FIS notification to it as soon as it realizes that the first choice PLR has failed to provide the required recovery, and so the service could still be recovered. There may also be a case where both protected and protecting LSPs fail simultaneously. When a PLR receives the FIS notification and realizes that the locally originated protecting LSP is, for some reason, not available, it may relay the FIS to some upstream PLR that starts an overlapping or nesting recovery domain. Consider the case where a node located between PL3 and MN3 (Figure 8.10c) detects a failure and sends the FIS to PL3. The latter may realize that the protecting LSP interconnecting PL3 and MN3 is also not available because of the same or an unrelated failure. In this case the PL3 simply forwards the FIS to PLR1/MN1, which will switch the traffic onto the outer protecting LSP.

The rest of this section analyzes two ways that path segment recovery for a particular service can be provisioned. The first approach assumes explicit provisioning of recovery domain types, boundaries, and possibly recovery paths using the GMPLS RSVP Secondary Explicit Route objects (SEROs). The second approach relies on the dynamic computation of recovery domains by the network. The hybrid approach—when the management controls certain recovery domains, while others are dynamically established—is also possible and sometimes very useful.

Explicit Provisioning of Segment Recovery

Recall that RSVP-TE includes a way to control the path taken by the LSP that supports a particular service. Specifically, the entire path or some parts of the path can be encoded within the Explicit Route object (ERO), and the signaling infrastructure makes sure that the LSP follows the specified path even if routing protocols would define a different one. A similar approach is taken to support segment recovery in an Internet-Draft that describes the technique: Parameters of all or some recovery domains (the identities of the PLR and MN, the type of recovery, strict or loose recovery path, and so forth) can be explicitly signaled within SEROs—one SERO per domain.

Each SERO should contain at least three sub-objects. The first sub-object is of type Protection. This type was introduced specifically for SEROs and identifies the type of recovery scheme to be provisioned within the domain, and the signaling parameters to be used while provisioning the recovery LSP in case they are different from the parameters used for signaling the protected LSP. The other two objects are of type IP. They identify the domain's PLR and MN, respectively. An SERO may optionally include any number of further sub-objects of any type as defined for EROs. They should be located within the SERO between sub-objects associated with the PLR and MN and specify (strictly or loosely) a recovery path.

Every node, while processing the protected LSP Setup message (RSVP Path), analyzes the set of SEROs within the message. If it discovers that the first IP sub-object of one of the SEROs is associated with one of the locally assigned IP addresses, it realizes that it needs to start a new recovery domain—that is, perform the PLR function. In this case, it extracts the SERO from the message and uses the information encoded within the object to trigger the setup of an appropriate protecting LSP, or stores the encoded route for the purpose of LSP restoration. Furthermore, it adds a new object to the stack of NotifyRequest objects in the LSP Setup message of the protected LSP to specify a new recipient of Notify messages by supplying a local IP address on which the PLR is willing to receive fault notifications. This makes sure that nodes within the domain learn about the PLR address.

The node where a recovery LSP converges with the protected LSP assumes the MN role. Specifically, it terminates the recovery LSP and removes the associated PLR's NotifyRequest object from the LSP Setup message. This prevents nodes located downstream from the MN from learning about the PLRs that *cannot* handle failures that they detect—that is, PLRs that control recovery domains to which the downstream nodes do not belong. The MN also adds a new NotifyRequest object to the protected LSP Accept message (RSVP Resv) to specify a local IP address. This ensures that nodes within the domain learn the identity of the MN.

These manipulations of the NotifyRequest objects guarantee that no matter how complex the topology of the recovery domains (nested, overlapped, and so forth), each node on the protected path will have a sorted list of valid PLRs (that is, a stack of NotifyRequest objects in the RSVP Path message) and MNs (a stack of NotifyRequest objects in the RSVP Resv message), which the node can alert if it detects a failure.

There is another signaling object, the Secondary Record Route Object (SRRO), which was introduced specifically for the purpose of the path segment recovery signaling. Before sending the protected LSP Setup message, the MN, in addition to updating the protected LSP Record Route Object (RRO), also adds to the message the entire path taken by the locally terminated recovery LSP encoded as an SRRO. Likewise, before sending out the protected LSP Accept message, the PLR, in addition to updating the protected LSP RRO, also adds to the message the entire path taken by the locally originated recovery LSP encoded as an SRRO. Thus, both ends of the service have access to the entire topology of network resources consumed by all protected (mainly, working) and all recovery LSPs.

Let us see how explicit provisioning of path segment recovery works in an example. Suppose that we need to provision 1+1 segment protection for the service whose working LSP traverses the nodes A, B, D, and E, as shown in Figure 8.8. In this case, the LSP Setup message for the working LSP will contain an ERO = {A-B-D-E} and two SEROs: $SERO_1$ = {A-C-D} and $SERO_2$ = {D-F-E}. Nodes A and D, while processing the message, will realize that each is instructed to set up one 1+1 protecting LSP and they will trigger the establishment of these LSPs. Node A will also remove $SERO_1$ from the outgoing working LSP Setup message and add to the message a NotifyRequest object indicating its local IP address. Likewise, node D will remove $SERO_2$ from the outgoing working LSP Setup message and add to the stack of NotifyRequest objects another one indicating its local IP address.

When the first protecting LSP Setup message arrives at node D, the node will realize that it needs to perform MN function for the first recovery domain. Hence it will perform the following actions.

- Remove from the stack of NotifyRequest objects in the outgoing working LSP Setup message (RSVP Path) the object that indicates the originator of the terminated recovery LSP (that is, node A). This may require the modification of an LSP Setup message that was sent previously.
- Insert into the working LSP Setup message the entire path of the recovery LSP (that is, the received RRO) encoded as an SRRO.
- Add to the stack of NotifyRequest objects in the LSP Accept message (RSVP Resv) for the working LSP an object that indicates its local IP address. Again, this may require that an update of a message that was sent previously is generated.

Node E performs similar operations while terminating the second recovery LSP.

Note that node D in our example performs the MN role for the first recovery domain and the PLR role for the second one. When the second recovery LSP Accept message arrives at node D, the latter as a PLR will conduct the following actions.

- Remove from the stack of NotifyRequest objects in the outgoing working LSP Accept message (RSVP Resv) the object associated with the terminator of the second recovery LSP (that is, node E). Again, this may require the modification of an LSP Accept message that was sent previously.
- Insert into the accept message the entire path of the locally originated recovery LSP encoded as an SRRO.

Node A performs similar operations while processing the accept message of the first recovery LSP.

By the time the setup of the working LSP is complete, the service head and tail ends will know about all links onto which the service is mapped. Note that node B will be aware of only one PLR (node A), and only one MN (node D). Likewise, the only PLR that node E will know about is node D. It is also important to note that node E will not know that node A is also a PLR, which is good because node A cannot help to recover from the faults detected by node E.

Note that a node on a protected LSP may know about more than one PLR/MN pair. This would be the case if the node belongs to more than one overlapping domain and/or to a domain nested entirely within some other domain. For example, node E in Figure 8.9 will be aware of two PLRs—D and B. Thus, when the node detects a failure it will first send the fault notification to node D. However, if the notification is not acknowledged (perhaps because the control plane of node D is not functional), the fault notification will be sent to the other PLR—node B.

Dynamic Provisioning of Segment Recovery

Explicit provisioning of segment recovery is convenient, but it assumes that some entity on the service head end is capable of identifying recovery domains and producing the SEROs. This is a big assumption because the head end may not have adequate computation capabilities to do the job. Furthermore, it may not have access to all of the necessary information. This is especially true if the service needs to traverse several TE domains.

One way of solving this problem is to have a remote Path Computation Element (PCE) generate the SEROs. However, this approach has its own issues, especially in the standardization of the very complex semantics of path computation requests.

An alternative is to put the task of determining recovery domains in the network. Currently, the Internet-Draft that describes segment recovery defines the following procedures for the dynamic provisioning of segment recovery.

- The desired recovery type for all service recovery domains is provisioned in a separate section of the Protection object of the LSP Setup message for the working LSP. Thus, in contrast to recovery domains that are provisioned via SEROs, dynamic recovery domains are limited to having the same recovery type.

- Every node on the working path may assume the role of PLR. If the node decides to do so, it attempts to compute a recovery path. Different policies may be applied when computing the path. For instance, an objective could be to determine the path that most rapidly converges with the working path. Alternatively, an attempt may be made to determine the path protecting the largest segment of the working path starting from the computing node.

- If the recovery path is successfully computed, it is either stored for service restoration purposes or the setup of the protecting LSP is triggered. In the latter case the Protection object of the outgoing LSP Setup message for the working LSP contains the "Segment recovery is in place" flag set to let downstream nodes know that they should not also attempt to establish more recovery LSPs—this avoids unnecessary allocation of protection resources.

- When a node on the working LSP terminates a protecting LSP (that is, realizes that it should perform the MN role), it resets the Segment recovery in place flag in the Protection object of the outgoing LSP Setup message for the working LSP, so that the node itself or some downstream node can attempt to start a new recovery domain.

It is important to mention that the dynamic provisioning of recovery domains is different from explicit provisioning only in the area of defining boundaries of the domains and computing recovery paths. All other aspects, such as advertising of identities of PLRs/MNs via NotifyRequest Objects, collecting RROs/SRROs, and so forth, are the same. Furthermore, explicit and dynamic methods of path segment recovery provisioning are not mutually exclusive. It is quite possible for an operator to provision one or more recovery domains via strict or loose SEROs, and to let the network figure out how to protect the other segments of the working LSP for which the operator has not specified any protection LSPs. In such a case, explicit provisioning always takes precedence, and a node on the working path will not attempt to compute a dynamic recovery path if it detects a "local" SERO in the LSP Setup message (that is, an SERO with the first IP sub-object indicating a locally assigned IP address).

Let us go back to our example presented in Figure 8.8 and see how the dynamic provisioning of path segment recovery works. Suppose 1+1 dynamic segment protection is requested for a service going from node A to node E. Suppose also that no SEROs are specified, and the service working path is provisioned to traverse nodes A-B-D-E. Before sending out the LSP Setup message for the working LSP, the service head end (node A) notices that dynamic 1+1 protection is required and realizes that no protecting LSPs are under construction yet (that is, the Segment recovery in place flag is not set). Therefore, it computes a recovery path (A-C-D) and triggers the setup of the 1+1 protecting LSP. After that, the node sets the Segment recovery in place flag in the Protection object and sends the LSP Setup message for the working LSP downstream. The flag will prevent all other nodes on the path from originating additional segment-protecting LSPs. Note that even node D, which will eventually need to establish the second protecting LSP, will likely not to do this immediately on the receipt of the working LSP Setup message. This is because by the time the LSP Setup message for the working LSP arrives at node D, the LSP Setup message for the first protecting LSP (A-C-D) may still be on its way, and hence node D cannot know that it is the MN for the first recovery domain. However, when it receives the first protecting LSP Setup message, it will realize that the first recovery domain ends and a new one is needed. Hence at the time node D receives the second of the two LSP Setup messages regardless of the order of their arrival, it will compute a new recovery path (D-F-E) and trigger the establishment of the second 1+1 segment-protecting LSP. As was mentioned earlier, the way nodes on the working path learn about identities of relevant PLRs/MNs, as well as how the service head and tail ends learn about the segment recovery topology, is identical to the method described for when the segment protection was provisioned via SEROs.

The procedures here for dynamic path segment recovery have some serious flaws. Notice that the service in the example is left unprotected against the failure of node D—the node that terminates one protection domain and starts another. This is not just because of the topological constraints; the same protection topology would be dynamically installed for the service in the network presented in Figure 8.9, despite the fact that an additional network segment (B-G-E) can protect against node D failures. This happens because during the establishment of the services, node B would realize by examining the Segment recovery in place flag that some upstream node (specifically node A) has started the establishment of a protecting LSP, which is not terminated on node B. Hence node B would never attempt to compute and establish an additional protecting LSP going over B-G-E. In general the scheme described here does not produce overlapping protection domains— the only way to avoid single points of failure in the path segment recovery model.

Furthermore, if the service needs to traverse multiple TE domains, it could easily be the case that a PLR will not be capable of identifying an existing recovery path due to limitations in the TE visibility. Consider, for instance, the situation when the working LSP (Figure 8.9) goes through two domains with node D as a boundary node between the two (that is, nodes B and E are in different TE domains). In this case, even if we somehow force node B to try to compute a recovery path, it will not be able to accomplish this because it does not have visibility into the neighboring TE domain. Note that node D could do the necessary path computation, because as a border node it has visibility into both TE domains. However, it needs a way to signal the resulting path to node B so that the latter can originate the protecting LSP establishment. This mechanism does not form part of the current dynamic path segment recovery method.

Finally, the dynamic segment recovery scheme gives no solution for how segment recovery resources could be shared between several services. This is because PLRs that compute dynamic recovery paths do not know anything about LSPs that do not go through themselves. In particular, they do not know which protecting LSPs are established in the network and what working LSPs they protect (a useful piece of information when deciding if resources protecting some LSP could be also used to protect other LSPs). In the model, where a node computes recovery paths protecting against its own failures and failures of its links, the computing node does not know about all LSPs on the network. However, it does know about LSPs that traverse it and that need to be segment protected, so it can keep track of the recovery paths that have been computed for their protection and use this knowledge when computing a recovery path for a new service. Obviously, a node computing a recovery path protecting against its own failures cannot originate the recovery LSP following the computed path. Hence, again, there is a need to signal the computed path to the PLR somehow.

Currently, the authors of the GMPLS segment recovery architecture (among them the authors of this book) are discussing an alternative solution for dynamic path segment recovery to address the issues just described. In a nutshell, every node on the protected LSP may try to compute one or more paths protecting against the node's failure and/or the failures of its links. The computed paths are signaled along the protected path in the upstream direction in the LSP Accept message (RSVP Resv) for the working LSP, and are encoded in objects specifically introduced for this purpose—Dynamic SEROs (DSEROs). The semantics of the DSERO are identical to that of the SERO. When a node, while processing the accept message for the protected LSP, discovers that one or more of the DSEROs have a first IP sub-object that indicates a locally assigned IP address, the node may attempt to originate one or more recovery LSPs. If more than one such DSERO is detected, the processing node may choose to set up a single recovery LSP (for example, the one covering the longest segment of the protected LSP). To see how this approach works, let us consider once again the establishment of a segment protected LSP as shown in Figure 8.9. Following the logic described in this paragraph, the LSP nodes produce the DSEROs as shown in Table 8.1.

By the time the establishment of the protected LSP is complete, three recovery LSPs (A-C-D, B-G-E, and D-F-E) are installed. Note that node D has produced a path

Table 8.1 DSEROs for Dynamic Segment Protection

Node	DSERO	PLR	MN
A	None		
B	A-C-D	A	D
D	B-G-E	B	E
E	D-F-E	D	E
	B-G-E	B	E

identical to one of the paths computed by node E. Obviously in this case node D does not need to add the locally computed path to the LSP Accept message—the proper DSERO has already been inserted into the message by node E.

Path Segment Recovery Operations

In many ways, path segment recovery is very similar to end-to-end path recovery described earlier in this chapter. Generally speaking, a node of a segment protected LSP, when detecting a failure, sends an FIS message to a PLR and/or MN, which triggers the switchover synchronization procedures. Likewise, when a previously reported failure is restored and the reversion mode has been provisioned for the service, the node that detects the failure restoration sends an FRS message to the PLR and/or MN, which synchronously switch traffic back onto the restored segment.

However, there are a couple of important differences between the two models of path recovery. First, in the case of end-to-end recovery there is only one PLR and only one MN—the service head and tail ends, respectively—whereas in the case of segment recovery any transient node of the protected LSP may play PLR or MN roles, or both roles at the same time. More than that, in the case of nested recovery domains the same node may act as multiple PLRs and/or MNs for the same protected LSP.

Secondly, every node located on an end-to-end protected LSP belongs to a single recovery domain, while a node on a segment protected LSP may belong to zero, one, or several (overlapping, nested, and so forth) recovery domains. As was pointed out earlier, segment recovery signaling guarantees that by the time a segment protected LSP is established, each node on its path is aware not only about all PLRs/MNs that can help to recover from locally detected failures, but also of the order in which the PLRs/MNs should be alerted so that fault-related notifications will be sent to the closest ones first. Only if this closest pair of PLR/MNs fails to provide the expected recovery (perhaps because the control plane on, say, the PLR is out of service at the time), should the FIS message be sent to the next best (closest) PLR/MN and so forth until the fault reporting node realizes that service is recovered or it runs out of PLRs/MNs to notify. Obviously, during the reversion process, only those PLRs/MNs that previously managed the service recovery (that is, not necessarily the closest ones) should be notified about the fault restoration.

8.7.4 Combining Segment and End-to-End Recovery

One might get the impression that path segment and end-to-end recovery methods are alternative solutions for service recovery. They are not! It makes perfect sense to provision both end-to-end and segment recovery for the same service at the same time. In fact it is valid to see end-to-end recovery as a simple case of segment recovery, where the entire working path of a service constitutes a single segment protected within a single recovery domain. Likewise, the combination of end-to-end and segment recovery could be seen as a special case of nested segment recovery where the end-to-end recovery domain nests all other (segment recovery) domains provisioned for the service.

Consider a service going from node A to node E in the network presented in Figure 8.11.

Suppose the working path is A-B-D-E. There are several options to protect the service.

Option 1: end-to-end protection using the protecting LSP A-I-H-G-E. The problem with this scheme is that the recovery time of any recovery type apart from 1+1 protection is unlikely to be good enough because the PLR (node A) and MN (node E) are likely to be too far away from a point of failure. Yet using 1+1 protection makes the service 100% more expensive because the protection resources cannot be shared with any other service.

Option 2: shared segment protection using A-C-D and D-F-E protecting LSPs. This looks better than option 1, because the protection is shared (hence less

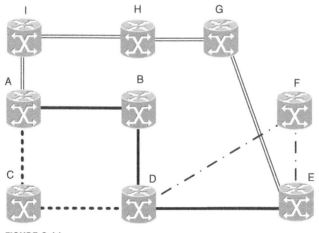

FIGURE 8.11

Combining end-to-end and segment recovery.

expensive) and the PLRs/MNs are closer to any point of failure (hence recovery time is better). But what if node D or any other resource not covered by the segment recovery (perhaps because of topological constraints) fails? In such a case the service could not be recovered.

Option 3: shared end-to-end protection with shared segment protection. This option seems to work the best. When a resource covered by segment protection fails (for example, node B and/or link DE), the service will be recovered very rapidly. If node D fails the end-to-end protection will be engaged. The recovery time will not be as good, but at least the service will be recovered. Furthermore, suppose something unexpected happened. For example, links BD and AC fail at the same time, or node E detects a failure on node DE but the control plane on node D, which is supposed to manage the switchover procedures, is out of service at the moment. Again, thanks to the end-to-end protection, the service will still be recovered. The only issue here is that once we consider multiple simultaneous failures, one of them can affect the end-to-end protecting LSP as well; the service will not be recovered in this case.

Option 4: end-to-end full re-routing with shared segment protection. This combination handles multiple simultaneous failures even better. Initially, recovery uses the shared segment protection LSPs, but, no matter what goes wrong, the service head end may always take into account all failures, compute a new recovery path (provided, of course, that such a path still exists), set up the restoration LSP, and switch traffic onto it. Understandably, the recovery time would be the worst in this case, especially because of potential crankbacks and retries needed to set up the restoration LSP. But such recomputation is only invoked when the segment protection has failed to deliver the required recovery. Note also that the recovery and working paths do not need to be fully diverse. The only requirement for the recovery path is to be disjoint from all points of failure; all healthy links can be shared. This is good, because a fully disjoint end-to-end path is not always available.

8.7.5 **Fast Re-Route**

Fast Re-Route (FRR) is a local recovery technique introduced in MPLS for the protection of packet switching network services. It is described more fully in the previous chapter. In this model every node, while processing an LSP Setup (RSVP Path) message, may realize that the LSP is requested to be FRR protected. The indication of such a requirement is the presence of an object (Fast-Re-Route), specifically introduced for this purpose, and/or the fact that certain flags in the Session-Attributes object are set.

In the steady state, FRR protection resources are not used for service traffic delivery. The good thing about FRR (possibly the only good thing!) is that it guarantees that, no matter where a failure is detected, a suitable PLR/MN pair will always be found within a single IP hop of the point of failure, and hence a recovery time close to that provided by 1+1 protection can be achieved without the permanent bridging of traffic onto the working and protecting LSPs.

An FRR-style local recovery model is not appealing for transport network services for several reasons. The facility bypass tunnel approach requires the use of the label stack construct, which is not necessarily applicable in transport networks (or generally speaking, any kind of circuit switching networks).

Using the detour approach to protect transport network services makes better sense, but realistically the approach is not feasible either. First, it requires an alternative path for every link or node of a protected LSP. This is possible only in a dense mesh network topology where each node has high degree; that is, where many network arcs (links) meet at each vertex (node). This is not the case in currently deployed transport networks, which are usually built as the interconnection of rings. Secondly, each transport network detour would require the allocation of an expensive resource (for example, timeslot, wavelength channel) on every link taken by the detour. In a packet switching environment it is realistic to set up detours wherever possible (especially if bandwidth protection is not required) for the cost of only extra control plane states. This is not the case on transport networks: Resources allocations are very "real," and the allocated resources cannot be used in the steady (fault-free) state, neither can they be shared with other services. Not good!

Note that hierarchies are not always as freely available as they are in a TDM network. For example, in a lambda switching network, the only realistic hierarchy that is available is to nest lambdas within a fiber. The use of an entire fiber to provide a facility bypass tunnel is equivalent to 1:1 span protection and is a highly resource intensive way to use the available resources.

Fortunately the path segment recovery model (described in Section 8.7.3) works very well for transport services. In fact we strongly believe that it is a much better solution for the local recovery of PSC network services as well. With the exception of facility bypass tunnels (which can be easily introduced to the segment recovery if needed) there is nothing in FRR that path segment recovery cannot provide and, at the same time, the latter has some serious advantages.

- The path segment recovery approach is not limited to protecting one resource at a time: A protected segment may contain an arbitrary number of LSP links. Hence, there is not such a stringent requirement for network topology density. Path segment recovery works equally well for mesh and ring topologies. It also provides more efficient utilization of protection resources, because, by protecting 2, 3, ..., n links rather than one link or node at a time, it is possible to achieve acceptable service recovery times while spending many fewer network resources compared to FRR with bandwidth protection guarantees.

- In FRR all protecting detours and facility bypass tunnels are dynamically computed. In segment recovery some or all recovery domains may be fully or partially provisioned by making use of SEROs. This means that Service Providers may take complete or partial control of the layout of resources allocated for protection of services they sell. This is a very valuable quality: Service Providers appreciate predictability very much and do not like surprises.

- In FRR it may also be the case that a PLR is not in a position to determine a path for a detour or bypass tunnel it is supposed to originate. A good example is defining an NNHOP detour protecting against ABR failures: As was discussed earlier, the ABR itself is in a better position to compute such a path because it has the TE visibility into both neighboring domains. Therefore, there is a need to signal such a path back upstream to the PLR. Segment recovery has a very lightweight naturally integrated mechanism for such signaling (DSEROs), whereas FRR does not have one and has to depend on some form of remote PCE protocol.

- FRR does not provide information about the exact topology of local recovery tunnels established for a particular service. The only information available is the flags in the RRO of the LSP Accept message that declare whether local protection is available or not on particular nodes along the protected path. This is in contrast with the path segment recovery approach, where the SRROs of an accept message for a protected LSP describe all resources committed or pre-planned to protect the service. It is possible, for example, to convert SRROs into SEROs and use them in an LSP Setup message with the guarantee that the exact same local protection layout will be installed for the service the next time it is provisioned.

- FRR relies on the fact that backup paths are computed after a protected LSP is established. It is a well-known fact that because of the greedy nature of path computation algorithms it could easily be the case that a primary path yields no diverse backup paths to protect one or more resources. In the path segment recovery model primary and backup paths may be computed and provisioned simultaneously; thus, the described situation can be avoided.

- Path segment recovery is not limited to protection: An SERO can identify either a protection or a restoration domain. FRR describes only how protection tunnels can be provisioned. It is not clear how FRR can guarantee bandwidth protection and have the protection bandwidth usable in the steady state at the same time. The path segment recovery approach, on the other hand, fits nicely into the full mesh restoration model.

- FRR provides no solution for unexpected events such as the situation where a single failure affects both protected resource and protecting tunnel, or where there are multiple failures (simultaneous, or in quick succession). Segment recovery provides a way to provision complex recovery schemes (for example, nested and/or overlapped recovery domains), so that a service can withstand multiple failures.

8.8 CONTROL PLANE RECOVERY

Control and data planes in transport networks are separated so that control plane messages do not necessarily flow along the links they control. One of the consequences of this is that the two can fail independently. Let us consider the following cases in respect to the relationship between control and data plane failures of a particular LSP.

1. Control plane is functional on all nodes; data plane failures are detected on one or more nodes.
2. Control and data planes fail at the same time on one or more nodes.
3. No data plane failures are detected (that is, user traffic is not affected); control plane fails on one or more nodes.
4. Control and data planes fail on different nodes.

So far in this chapter we have considered only case 1. We implicitly assumed that once a failure is locally detected, the FIS message is delivered to the appropriate PLR/MN, which uses the synchronizing signaling to perform the protection switchover operation, computes and signals a new path disjoint from the point of failure, or tears down the affected LSP. These assumptions require the control plane to function on all nodes of the protected and protecting LSPs.

Case 2 might seem a difficult one, but in fact it is not. If the data plane on a node fails, traffic of a service traversing the node is affected. Hopefully, the neighboring nodes detect the failure and the traffic is switched away from the failed node. Note that the failed node itself does not need to be involved in the recovery process, so it is not very important whether the control plane on the node is healthy or not. But the shortest path for propagation of the FIS or switchover signals might be through the control plane of the failed node/link. In this case, the fact that the fault-related messages are targeted at the PLM/MN and may be delivered by any route (not just hop-by-hop along the path of the failed LSP) is particularly important.

Having said that, it is fair to point out that for the purpose of reversion after the data plane restoration the control plane on the node must be recovered as well. Anyway, this case is not any different from the case of a failure of a packet switch (for example, an IP router, or Ethernet switch), where the data and control planes are inseparable. Therefore, the rest of this chapter is dedicated to cases 3 and 4.

Case 3 is a peculiar one. From the user's perspective the service looks perfectly healthy. However, if the control plane on even a single node of the working LSP fails, the LSP (and hence the service) becomes unmanageable. Imagine, for instance, that the data plane on a node with the failed controller detects a traffic-affecting failure. Unless 1+1 protection is provisioned or unless the failure is more widely detectable, the service might not be recoverable, because the PLR/MN responsible for the recovery might never learn about the fault. Likewise, if the control plane fails on the PLR or MN, there would be no entity to manage the switchover process unless there are nested recovery domains. Finally, if even one controller along the path of an LSP fails, it is impossible to modify the LSP in any way, and it is even awkward to just tear the LSP down. This is because the GMPLS signaling protocols use a hop-by-hop signaling paradigm and cannot tolerate gaps in the signaling message path.

Thus, it is very important to recover from control plane failures as soon as possible, and to re-synchronize the control plane state with the data plane state even for LSPs that have no failures in the data plane. This, however, is not always easy to accomplish, and the period of time when the user traffic is delivered over an LSP with a broken control plane might not be negligible.

In the rest of this section we will discuss failures of the control plane elements and the events that might cause them. After that, we will provide a brief analysis of different techniques for re-synchronization of the control plane states.

8.8.1 Control Plane Failures

It is convenient to represent the control plane of an intelligent transport network as a set of network controllers interconnected via control channels, where a *network controller* (or simply *controller*) is an entity realizing the control plane intelligence (for example, routing and signaling protocol speakers, path computer, traffic engineering applications), and a *control channel* is an abstraction that characterizes the network resources necessary to deliver control plane messages between adjacent controllers. An important difference between a transport and a packet switching network is that transport network control channels are conceptually separate from the TE links they manage, even if they share the same optical fibers. Likewise, transport network controllers are logically separate from the data switches they manage, even when the controllers and associated switches are collocated on the same physical devices.

The control plane learns about data plane failures only through failure indication events generated by the data plane. Control plane failures, on the other hand, are detected by controllers themselves (for example, by detecting a loss of the signaling adjacency with one of its neighbors). Control and data plane failures may coincide in some cases. For example, a fiber cut may bring the *Optical Supervisory Channel (OSC)* out of service and may also disrupt all data channels between two adjacent nodes. However, generally speaking, control and data plane failures are separate.

A *control plane failure* is a failure of a controller or a control channel. Numerous events may cause control plane failures: configuration errors (for example, a control interface was removed, or an important protocol was not enabled), software bugs (a controller software component was upgraded to a new release that had been insufficiently tested), hardware failures (failures of a shelf processor, Ethernet card, OSC controller), and so forth.

A special case of a control plane failure is the *controlled failure* caused by a software upgrade. To take advantage of new features, bug fixes, the software on a network controller must be upgraded to a new release from time to time. There are usually some active services currently mapped to LSPs on links and data switches managed by the controller to be upgraded. Obviously, the upgrade is not a reason to interrupt the services; the upgrade must be conducted with minimal (if any) effect on the user traffic. During the upgrade, new software is downloaded onto the controller and the controller is rebooted, making the controller's behavior very similar to recovery from any other nodal fault (for example, a software crash). The controller attempts to reconnect to the network and to re-synchronize the states of the LSPs with which it was involved in provisioning during its previous "life." In a way it is simpler to handle a software update than a crash because the former is predictable and can be planned in advance. The upgrade, however, has challenges of its own. For instance, the new release may not be 100% backward-compatible with the old one, and because it is impossible to carry out the upgrade on all controllers simultaneously, there is always a chance that additional (real) control plane failures could happen when some controllers already have the new software activated and some do not.

It was mentioned earlier that control plane recovery is not just the removal of the conditions that have caused the failures. It also includes a process of the re-synchronization of control plane state for all LSPs that continue to exist in the data plane. What exactly do we mean by an LSP control plane state? It is simply a record of the LSP. It contains provisioning parameters (for example, preferred and alternative paths, bandwidth, recovery requirements) as received/sent from/to upstream/downstream neighboring controllers. It also contains information dynamically learned about the LSP (for example, the actual path taken by the LSP, alarms detected on local and remote TE links). The LSP state may also point to the states of other related or co-dependent LSPs. For instance, if a controller happens to be a PLR for the LSP, the LSP state might include a pointer to the state of the associated protecting LSP. Finally, the LSP state also contains a record of the identity and status of all local network resources allocated for the LSP, and the identity of a management entity owning the LSP (that is, the entity that triggered the LSP Setup and is responsible for its teardown). That is all very important information for the correct operation and management of the LSPs; once it is lost it is difficult (if not impossible) to dynamically modify or even tear down the LSP, let alone to conduct protection switchover procedures. Hence it is crucially important that once the control plane failure is restored and the affected controller is restarted and reconnected to the network, the allocated resources are reclaimed and the states are restored for all LSPs (certainly for all active LSPs, and preferably also for the LSPs in setting up and tearing down state as well).

8.8.2 Control Plane Re-Synchronization via Signaling

The GMPLS RSVP-TE signaling protocol is very versatile. One of its remarkable features is that it allows a controller recovering from a control plane failure to take full advantage of cooperation with other controllers in the network, while re-synchronizing the states of the LSPs with which the controller was involved before the failure. Specifically, during the re-establishment of signaling adjacencies with its neighbors (via the GMPLS RSVP Hello message exchange), the recovering controller may signal its willingness to re-synchronize the states for such LSPs.

For each such LSP, the neighbors signal back to the recovering controller to provide all information that has been sent to and received from the controller during its pre-failure (that is, pre-reboot) life. The information includes the LSP provisioning parameters (bandwidth, recovery requirements, and so on), primary and recovery paths (which may have been previously computed dynamically by the recovering controller), locally detected data plane alarms, and so forth. Once it has this information available, it is quite straightforward for the controller to check it against the local data plane records, re-allocate resources used by the active LSPs, recreate relevant LSP states, and release any resources whose allocation is not known to the network.

Due to the adjacent (that is, hop-by-hop) nature of RSVP-TE, the recovery synchronization procedures described here only work if both neighbors of the recovering controller are fully active. If one neighbor also has a failed control plane, the recovering controller must wait until its neighbors have recovered before it can complete the full re-synchronization of all LSPs.

8.8.3 Control Plane Restoration using Local Databases

Another way to restore the "pre-failure" control plane states is by storing them into local database(s) that can survive reboots. Control plane implementations adopting this approach might save all significant state changes for every LSP, so that after reboot the controller could restore the states by simply reading them from the database(s). Such implementations have major problems for two reasons: It can never be known in advance when a failure will happen, and for each state there is always some piece of information that may be lost simply due to the timing of the failure. These two reasons make re-synchronization using a full-state database virtually impossible to test because of the tremendous number of different test cases.

A simpler and more predictable approach stores a compressed copy of every message that is sent or received by the controller in the database(s). After reboot the controller simply replays the stored messages as they were received from the network. One good thing about this approach is that a message is either available or lost, and RSVP-TE is very good at recovering from message losses. There is much less effort required to sufficiently test this technique in order to make sure it is reliable. The other good quality of this approach is that it can be easily integrated with signaled re-synchronization (see Section 8.8.2): It makes no difference whether a re-synchronization message is received from a neighbor or replayed from the database. Whenever a discrepancy between the stored and network state is detected, the network state always "wins."

The disadvantage of methods based on database re-synchronization is that they include additional processing in the normal steps of LSP management. This may include writes to non-volatile memory which are comparatively slow, and so this form of protection against control plane failure can significantly slow down the LSP setup process.

8.8.4 **Control Plane Restoration Using Data Plane State**

It could be that neither of the methods described in Sections 8.8.2 and 8.8.3 is an option for the restoration of control plane state. Consider, for example, the case where the network controllers must go through a major software upgrade, and the new software is significantly incompatible with the previous version. Usually in this case, the new software is downloaded onto the controllers, all of them are taken out of service, and after that one by one they are rebooted with the local databases removed (this is necessary because the old local databases would be unintelligible to the new version of the software).

The only way to restore the control plane states in such cases is by making use of the LSP information provided by the local data plane. A controller may query local cross-connects, line cards, and customer-facing ports, and so on, and realize that it used to manage the head end of a particular LSP. Using this information about the LSP bandwidth, data encoding type, available from the data plane state, it can start to build the LSP Setup message (RSVP Path) using the information. Note that there is no way for the controller to identify the LSP destination or the path taken by the LSP, but it does not have to. All it needs to do is to determine the outgoing link ID and the identity of the controller managing the remote end of the link. This information can be provided by LMP or can be deduced from the TE database. Having identified the next hop controller, the head end can send the LSP Setup message to the downstream neighbor, which will realize (perhaps, by looking into the Session object and detecting a special value in place of the LSP destination) that this is not an ordinary LSP Setup message. The neighbor controller verifies the information encoded within the message for consistency with the information provided by its local data plane, and identifies the next downstream controller and forwards the message to it. The process repeats itself on all controllers along the path until the LSP Setup message reaches the controller managing the LSP tail end. The latter triggers the LSP Accept message in the upstream direction. Note that the accept message contains the proper LSP destination address, so that all controllers along the path can complete the LSP control plane state restoration.

Clearly, not all details of the previous state can be restored this way. Things like relationships between LSPs may be hard to recover, although where 1+1 protection is in place, the data plane may be able to provide sufficient information. Full recovery of all relationships between LSPs may require additional manual intervention.

Operations, Management, and Security

The successful deployment of any networking technology relies on its operational utility in the field. It must be possible to install, configure, operate, and diagnose the equipment and services, and it must be possible to secure the technology against interference by outside parties. Thus the three elements of Operations, Management, and Security of MPLS networks, protocols, and equipment have become fundamental to the take-up of MPLS.

This section contains chapters that examine three key elements. Chapter 9 looks at how MPLS equipment and protocols can be inspected, configured, and controlled through the use of standardized management information interfaces. Chapter 10 introduces the latest techniques for detecting and diagnosing faults within MPLS networks. And Chapter 11 discusses issues of security as they apply to MPLS.

Management Techniques

The Simple Network Management Protocol (SNMP) is *the* management protocol of choice within the IETF. This does not mean that MPLS-conformant devices
are restricted to SNMP or are forced to implement SNMP. Indeed, most MPLS and
GMPLS-capable network elements have a variety of management interfaces.

However, it is an IETF requirement that all IETF protocols have Management
Interface Base (MIB) modules defined to allow implementations to be modeled
and managed. The MIB is the global distributed database for management and
control of SNMP capable devices, and a MIB module is a collection of individual
objects and tables of objects, each of which contains a value that describes the
configuration or status of a manageable entity or logical entity of the same type.

This chapter draws on material from *MPLS Network Management* by Nadeau,
and *GMPLS: Architecture and Applications* by Farrel and Bryskin, to briefly
describes the MIB modules that exist for MPLS and MPLS traffic engineering, and
then describes how those modules are extended for GMPLS.

9.1 KEY ASPECTS OF MPLS NETWORK MANAGEMENT

Networks need to be managed for several reasons. First, from an entirely practical perspective, devices need to be monitored to ensure that they are functioning
properly. Devices may also alert the operator to fault conditions, but if no corrective action is taken by the operator, then the device may continue to malfunction.
For example, if a router's routing table has grown to a size that will soon exceed its
available memory, it may be beneficial for the device to inform the operator of this
condition. Services that are offered by a network also need to be managed, particularly when they are provisioned. In these cases, devices are contacted and configured. Managed services also require monitoring and maintenance. For example, if a
service provider offers a virtual private network service to end users, it may be necessary to monitor the health and performance of the network paths that carry that
customer's traffic to ensure that they are getting the network services that they
paid for. In fact, this monitoring arrangement is sometimes a contractual necessity.

In all of these scenarios, it is either extremely difficult or nearly impossible for
operators of medium to large networks to monitor every device in their networks   **313**

by hand; instead, most prefer to do this in an automated manner. Some accomplish their management using a centralized approach at sophisticated operations centers. However, others may choose to have several smaller operations centers that are distributed. In either case, it is extremely time-consuming, and hence costly, for an operator to manually connect to each device's console in order to monitor its status, isolate faults, or configure the device. This becomes more obvious when you consider those provider networks where the network devices are located over a wide range of geographic areas. In this case, it becomes even more costly to travel to a remote location or hire additional staff to be on site where those additional devices are located.

Second, to make a sound business case for deploying MPLS, it must be made fully manageable so that the operational aspects of the network can scale up to numbers of devices, services, and customers that will make the network profitable. For example, the money spent debugging a problem by sending an operator into the field or by having the same operator go from router/switch to router/switch scratching their head might be better spent in building an automated system that can listen for alarms that the router/switch can emit when in distress. These alarms can then be used to pinpoint and isolate the scope of the problem. Once isolated, a management system can even take automated actions to correct the situation or simply alert an operator. An automated system can even be smart enough to not bother an operator if it deems a problem insignificant. Furthermore, management of the MPLS network becomes paramount when placed within the context of service level agreements and MPLS VPN services. When service level agreements are made between customers and providers, the service provider will not earn any money from that customer unless the services provided meet the agreement. The monitoring of the agreed-upon terms such as bandwidth, latency, delay, or service availability can be best accomplished using a network management system.

9.1.1 Origins of Network Management for MPLS

Once MPLS began to become mature and operational experience began to be gained by service providers deploying the technology, it was clear that MPLS was not very manageable given the lack of standard tools and management interfaces available at the time. In particular, the majority of MPLS vendors including Juniper and Cisco had only provided proprietary command-line interface extensions for the configuration and monitoring of MPLS features. When MPLS deployments were in early stages, it was acceptable for these and other vendors to provide minimal management capabilities for the MPLS features since operators were largely interested in simply having the protocol function up to specifications. However, as deployments became more mature and providers were more comfortable with the notion of using this protocol, it was clear that management of the protocol and its many features was now a priority. Furthermore, in heterogeneous networks where devices from multiple vendors had to coexist, an even larger problem existed. Since vendors had only deployed proprietary command-line interfaces, providers deploying devices from more than one vendor had to contend with more than one management interface for MPLS. This approach is expensive because it requires duplication of effort to manage the configuration and monitoring of the same features. The duplication of resources often ultimately translates into lost revenues for service providers. It was these requirements that began the push for standard interfaces for MPLS. In particular, the work on the IETF MIBs began in earnest during this time.

9.1.2 Configuration

One sore point for many operators is how to configure each one of the potentially hundreds of devices in their network. Further complicating the picture of configuration is the fact that many, if not most, provider networks are not comprised of devices made by a single vendor. This results in the service provider having to learn at least one different configuration language for each vendor from which it purchases equipment. Even further compounding this situation is that, through the magic of mergers and acquisitions, many vendors actually supply devices that have different configuration languages depending on which product line of theirs you choose to deploy.

It should be obvious from this description of the problems inherent in configuring a network of devices that it is a difficult situation at best. What would alleviate this situation would be the use of a common language and associated interfaces that can be used for the configuration of devices. There are many such languages available, yet no single one is used ubiquitously. Perhaps the closest contenders are SNMP—that is, SNMPvl (RFCs 1155, 1157, and 1213), SNMPv2c (RFCs 1901–1906), and SNMPv3 (RFCs 2571–2575)—CORBA, and XML. Unfortunately, today the clear winner, at least for configuration, is the proprietary command-line interface (CLI), although SNMP is generally regarded as the best option for monitoring. The difficulty with a proprietary CLI is that it is generally accessible only via telnet or hardwired connections and generally has no standards-based schema. This results in every vendor implementation having a different management interface, which is clearly not something that excites a provider deploying a multivendor network. Although the CLI represents a majority of management interfaces, at least in the configuration area, the fide is turning toward standardized interfaces as networks grow ever more complex. These interfaces are commonly used for monitoring, and in many cases for provisioning as well. We will delve into the details of these various standard mechanisms for configuration in the pages to come.

9.1.3 Service Level Agreements

Typically, when a user signs up for access service (e.g., DSL, cable modem, dial-up), the service provider only agrees to provide that user with access to their network, and sometimes eventual access to the Internet. This agreement typically only specifies a minimum amount of bandwidth and provides no specifics about the average delay between access points and any other point in the network, or generally any other guarantees of service. Furthermore, there is typically no minimum response time during which outages in the network will be corrected by the service provider. This generally means that the user of a service is out of luck if their service does not function as advertised.

Some operators take their level of service a step further. These operators choose to monitor and maintain what some refer to as the "user experience." Although many operators strive to have networks simply function (i.e., route and switch a lot of traffic), others wish to ensure that their network is performing at levels acceptable to its customers. For example, this can mean that if user access to the Internet is unacceptably slow, the service provider will take some action to correct the situation—sometimes automatically. This approach is in direct contrast to other providers who would be content with end users just having access to the Internet at any speed.

The notion of service assurance and verification can be taken a step further beyond a provider assuring that they will monitor the health of user services. Frequently, end users and service providers will enter a formal contract called a *service level guarantee* or *agreement* (SLA). This agreement is an official agreement or contract between the service provider and a customer that specifies that the provider will sell a certain service to an end user for a certain price. If this service is provided as agreed upon, the end user must pay a certain fee for the service. However, if the service is not provided, typical recourses for the user are a reduction or refund of the fee they pay for the service during that period. Often the amount of additional work that a provider must perform to ensure that a service is functioning according to the service level agreement is significant. This elevated cost is precisely why SLAs are typically only signed between service providers and higher-paying customers such as large corporations or other service providers.

For example, in the United States, the service provider market is largely focused on selling bandwidth. This bandwidth is sometimes sold with guarantees of quality such as minimum delay and jitter. In other parts of the world, service providers concentrate instead on selling VPN services where site-to-site access quality is most important. All of these deployments typically contain SLA agreements with guarantees on the components of the service that the customers find most important, as well as the things a provider is willing to assure.

Given the motivation and elevated revenues from SLA agreements, providers are motivated to offer these premium services. However, these services do not come without additional effort on their part to verify the service quality and take corrective action when it does not meet the specified quality. In this regard, manual verification of SLAs is highly undesirable from a provider's perspective. This is simply because of its repetitive and frequent nature, especially when performed on a large scale. SLA agreements may also require that the operator take corrective action within some short period of time after a fault is detected. It is for these reasons that SLA monitoring and verification can be cumbersome or impossible if done manually, and therefore is a driver for the task to be performed by a fully or semiautomated network management system. In order to realize a management system that can verify SLAs in an automated fashion, network management functions must be integrated into devices that must be monitored. In particular, common management interfaces allow a provider to effectively monitor the data points of a service. This is especially important for heterogeneous networks and is also important in cases where customers insist on having independent third parties verify the SLA, since these companies often prefer not to build SLA verification software that is customized to a particular provider's network. Instead, they prefer to build software that is able to talk to a large set of devices in order to service many different service provider networks.

9.1.4 Service Level Agreement Verification

One often-overlooked aspect of service level agreement contracts is called service level agreement verification. The agreement of services between the end user and provider can be verified in several ways. The simplest form might be to issue Internet Protocol (IP) "pings" that emanate from the customer access points to other points in their networks or to locations within the Internet. This simulates user traffic traveling along the data path that all traffic takes through the network. If this traffic takes too long to traverse the network, or worse, is not getting to certain points within or external to the service provider's network—then the user experience suffers. Monitoring of the user experience might also be as sophisticated as monitoring the performance of many key network devices, collecting this information at a central location, and then making dynamic adjustments to the network using this information.

More sophisticated SLA verification is typically accomplished using network management tools that are specifically designed for the task. These tools include remote monitoring (RMON) or simply monitoring various counters on the network devices. SLA monitoring and verification may be accomplished within an MPLS VPN deployment. A network management system (NMS) is positioned at key points, monitors certain traffic and quality of service (QoS) statistics, and reports them to the operator and customer. SLA verification can be done by the service provider, the customer, or by an unbiased third party. Use of standard network management interfaces to expose variables within the often-diverse population of network devices present in service provider networks is critical, especially when a third party is contracted to do the verification. The reason for this is simple: interoperability. SLA verification becomes quite cumbersome and costly if the party performing the verification is required to customize the verification suite for every device in a network. This is important if a third-party SLA verification company either sells software/hardware to service providers or performs the SLA verification service directly.

9.1.5 Fault Isolation

Fault isolation and detection are simply a means by which operators can detect, isolate, and report on defects discovered within their networks. The operator can use the information to repair the defect(s) found manually or automatically. When a device detects a problem, it will emit one or more messages as an alarm to alert the operator of the fault condition. These messages can be emitted under many conditions, including loss of service, device in distress (e.g., low on memory), or when the device has rebooted. Fault isolation is usually accomplished in modern networks in a three-part process that includes devices emitting asynchronous alarms, operators receiving those alarms, and then taking possible action because of those alarms. When a network device such as a router or switch discovers that an event of interest has occurred, it may issue an alarm. This alarm can be of the form of a system console message or an SNMP notification, which can be transmitted to the operators as an inform or notification. The reason for raising the alarms can include a configured threshold being exceeded, an internal fault condition such as low memory, or a system reboot. Although other forms of alarms do exist, including audible buzzers or flashing notifications on the command terminal, SNMP notifications are used in the majority of deployments. Depending on the size and structure of the service provider's network, the operator may place one or more listening probes (i.e., workstations) around their network to listen and collect these messages. An NMS may be deployed within an MPLS network to listen for notifications emitted from the LSRs in that network. The NMS would catch such notifications and possibly alert the operator to the situation or trigger an automated procedure for possible corrective action.

Sometimes, when the networks are large and/or multi-tiered, the operator will even have notifications aggregated and perhaps even summarized if processing power permits, and then relayed to a central alarm-processing center. This center will then decide whether or not to issue a trouble ticket for an alarm and dispatch personnel to address the situation. It should be obvious that the activities just described would be next to impossible to achieve if done manually in any practical network deployed today. It should be clear that in order for MPLS to be deployed successfully on a large scale, network nodes must be capable of issuing the necessary alarms (i.e., SNMP notifications) that are specific to not only MPLS functions, but also the other functions in the devices being deployed.

9.2 MANAGEMENT INFORMATION BASE MODULES FOR MPLS

The IETF, ITU, ATM Forum, and other standards bodies define documents called Management Information Base (MIB) modules that provide an external management interface for protocols and other features that are standardized within those organizations. Each MIB module can be thought of as a form of a data model used

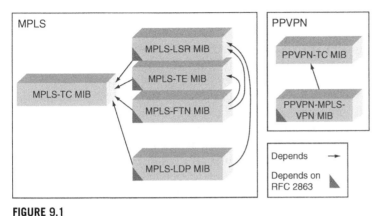

FIGURE 9.1

MIBs for MPLS network management discussed in this text.

to manage the protocol or feature. The MIB module also defines the syntax, maximum access levels, and object interactions between those objects defined in that and other MIBs. The collection of MIB modules comprises the conceptual MIB that defines the entirety of MIB modules. We should also note that a MIB module is sometimes referred to as "a MIB" within certain contexts; thus care should be taken to discern when you mean a single MIB module or a collection of MIB modules that comprise a MIB.

The remainder of this text will focus on SNMP MIB-based solutions for managing MPLS networks. To that end, Figure 9.1 illustrates how each MIB fits in with the others as well as how each one depends on the others.

The MIBs are organized as follows. The MPLS-TC MIB describes textual conventions that are used by all MPLS-related MIBs (even ones too new to be covered at this time).

The MPLS-LSR MIB (see Section 9.3) describes the basic label forwarding operations of an LSR. The MPLS-LSR MIB also exposes which interfaces the LSR has MPLS enabled on by cross-referencing each MPLS-enabled interface that appears in the interface MIB (the IF-MIB). This MIB presents a foundation of actual objects (as opposed to TCs in the MPLS-TC MIB) that are used in many other MIBs; thus it is viewed by many as the base MPLS MIB.

The MPLS-TE MIB provides the operator with a view of which traffic engineering tunnels are configured, signaled, or presignaled (for backup). If a runnel is also represented as an interface in the IF-MIB, an entry will exist there as well. The MPLS-TE MIB (see Section 9.6) depends on the MPLS-LSR MIB in that the system software in a device can be programmed to associate the active LSP with a runnel when such a relationship exists.

Next, the MPLS-LDP MIB (see Section 9.4) provides insight into what the LDP protocol is doing on an LSR, assuming that LDP is enabled and in use. The MPLS-LDP MIB depends on the MPLS-LSR MIB for its mapping tables that are used to associate LDP sessions with active LSPs. The MPLS-LDP MIB also depends on the IF-MIB in that it exposes which label ranges are configured on an MPLS-enabled interface. Finally, the MPLS-FTN MIB (see Section 9.5) presents the operator with a view of how IP traffic is entering the MPLS network and how that IP traffic is being mapped onto MPLS LSPs or traffic-engineered tunnel interfaces.

The MPLS-FTN MIB depends on the MPLS-LSR and MPLS-TE MIBs because the way that it associates incoming IP traffic is to point at the associated LSP or traffic engineering runnel head as represented in the MPLS-LSR and MPLS-TE MIBs, respectively. The MPLS-FTN MIB depends on the IF-MIB because it allows an operator to configure FEC-to-NHLFE mapping rules on a per-interface basis.

The PPVPN-MPLS-VPN MIB possesses only dependencies on the PPVPN-TC MIB. This MIB contains common textual conventions used by the PPVPN-MPLS-VPN MIB as well as other MIBs defined by the IETF PPVPN Working Group. The PPVPN-MPLS-VPN MIB provides an operator with a view of which VPN instances are configured on a specific PE, as well as related statistics, BGP, and interface information. The interface information extends those interfaces that are already represented in the IF-MIB; thus yet another dependency on the IF-MIB exists.

9.3 MPLS-LSR MIB AT A GLANCE

The basic function of the MPLS-LSR MIB is to expose the active MPLS label switching of an LSR, as well as to allow for the configuration of some things such as static label mappings. Thus, all network managers wishing to monitor the basic label forwarding activities of a label switching router should monitor the tables provided in this MIB. Similarly, device vendors whose products are required to provide such information should implement this MIB. In doing so, both devices and network managers will have a common understanding of what should be provided by devices as well as what management stations should expect to manage.

Management stations wishing to monitor the behavior of other MPLS applications such as traffic engineering (see Section 9.4) or virtual private networks should utilize the objects provided by this MIB in conjunction with the MIBs designed specifically for those applications. In this way, the basic label switching can be managed using the objects defined in this MIB, since they apply to all MPLS applications, and additional functions can be built around the MPLS-LSR MIB and/or separately. We should point out that although the MPLS-LSR MIB is not necessarily required to manage the other applications of MPLS (e.g., traffic engineering), it is certainly useful if a complete management picture of a label switching router is desired.

The MPLS-LSR MIB contains several tables, including the MPLS Interface Configuration Table (mplsInterfaceConfTable), Interface Performance Table (mplsInterfacePerfTable), InSegment Table (mplsInSegmentTable), InSegmentPerformance Table (mplsInSegmentPerfTable), OutSegment Table (mplsOut-SegmentTable), OutSegment Performance Table (mplsOutSegmentPerfTable), Cross-Connect Table (mplsXCTable), Label Stack Table (mplsLabelStackTable), and the Traffic Parameter

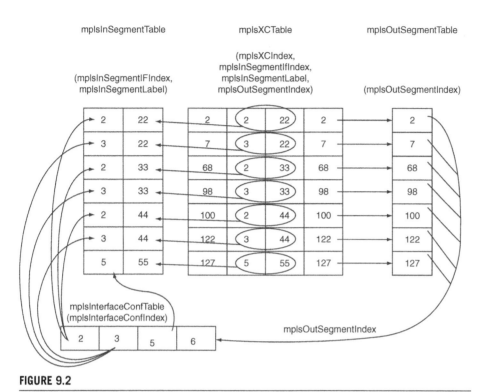

mplsInSegmentTable　　　　mplsXCTable　　　　mplsOutSegmentTable

FIGURE 9.2

Relationship between major tables in the MPLS-LSR MIB. The indexes for each table are shown to indicate the relationships clearly.

Table (mplsTrafficParamTable).These tables interact together in a manner that provides a coherent view of the MPLS label switching router's label switching activity.

As is the case with many of the MIBs that you will encounter, it is often useful to first sit down at a board and illustrate each table contained in that MIB at a high level to show how each interacts with the others. It may also be useful to include the indexing of each of the tables.This may sometimes make some sense of how each table fits with the others in the MIB, as well as what the MIB's designers had in mind (or didn't!).

Figure 9.2 illustrates, at a high level, the interaction of the major tables found in the MPLS-LSR MIB, including the mplsInSegmentTable, mplsOutSegmentTable, mplsXCTable, and mplsInterfaceConfFable. The indexing of each table is shown with each table, as well as how this indexing relates to that of the other tables. In particular, the example shows how a fictitious LSR that has four interfaces (2, 3, 5, 6) is actively swapping labels from incoming interfaces 2, 3, and 5 to outgoing interface 6. Note that the relationship between the mplsOutSegmentTable entries and the outgoing interfaces as found in the mplsInterfaceConfFable are not explicitly implemented as indexes in the mplsOutSegmentTable; rather, they are referenced using that table's mplsOutSegmentIfIndex object. The pointers from the entries in the mplsOutSegmentTable in the figure have this relationship set up implicitly. Also, note that the label assignment shown here is arbitrary and only for the purposes of the example.

The following list is a summary of tables contained in the MPLS-LSR MIB.

- *MPLS Interface Configuration Table:* The MPLS Interface Configuration Table (mplsInterfaceConfFable) contains the interfaces that are enabled to support MPLS on the LSR where the MIB is queried. LSRs must create entries in this table for every MPLS-capable interface and indicate other interface-specific parameters. This entry also corresponds to an entry in the IF-MIB.

- *Interface Performance Table:* The Interface Performance Table (mplsInterface-Per~able) contains objects used to reflect MPLS-related performance characteristics of MPLS-enabled interfaces supported by the LSR where the MIB is queried. Note that this table is not supposed to replace the performance counters in the IF-MIB; rather, it adds to the information found there.

- *InSegment Table:* The MPLS InSegment Table (mplsInSegmentTable) contains the MPLS insegments (i.e., incoming labels) and their associated parameters.

- *InSegment Performance Table:* This table contains objects used to measure the performance ofMPLS insegments (i.e., incoming labels).

- *OutSegment Table:* The MPLS OutSegment Table (mplsOutSegmentTable) contains the MPLS outsegment entries (i.e., outgoing labels) and their associated parameters.

- *OutSegment Performance Table:* The MPLS OutSegment Performance Table (mplsOutSegmentPer~able) contains objects used to measure the performance of MPLS outsegments (i.e., outgoing labels).

- *Cross-Connect Table:* The MPLS Cross-Connect Table (mplsXCTable) contains associations between in- and outsegments. When one or more insegments is combined with one or more outsegments, this notes that the LSR on which the MIB is viewed has been instructed to switch between the specified segments. This also indicates that an LSP has been constructed to support this configuration. Cross-connects may be administratively disabled using the associated administrative status (if supported). The associated operational status object indicates the actual status of the LSP at this LSR.

- *Label Stack Table:* This table contains a representation of the additional label stack imposed at the LSR where the MIB is queried. Specifically, this table contains the additional label stack entries that are replaced just under the topmost label on any labeled packet received on the associated LSP. Note that the topmost label is not found in this table.

- *Traffic Parameter Table:* The Traffic Parameter Table represents some traffic parameters that are commonly associated with an LSP.

9.4 MANAGING LDP

The MPLS-LDP MIB can be used to effectively manage an LDP deployment. LDP provides objects to configure potential, or monitor existing, LDP sessions on a specific LSR. The MPLS LDP Entity Table can be used to configure potential LDP sessions, where each row in the table represents an LDP session using a particular label space. This entry can be inserted by the LDP software or configured by the operator as a session the operator would like established in the future. For example, the operator may wish to configure targeted LDP sessions this way. Other entries in this table are added dynamically by the autodiscovery mechanism built into LDP. The MPLS LDP Peer Table is a read-only table that contains information learned from LDP peers via LDP discovery and the LDP session initialization message. Each row in the Peer Table represents an LDP peer relative to the LSR running the MIB. This table does not contain information about the local LDP entities per se. This is sometimes a subtle point made in the MIB that we would like to emphasize here for clarity. This table contains information that is specific to the peerentity relationships that exist between the LSR running the MIB and those to which it has established LDP sessions, but which are not appropriate for the MPLS LDP Session Table. The MPLS LDP Session Table is used to represent the actual LDP sessions that are established between the LSR in question and its LDP peers. It is also particularly useful for monitoring those sessions that are in the process of being established, and of course, those specific sessions between an entity and a peer that already are established.

9.5 THE MPLS FTN MIB

The MPLS Forwarding Equivalence Class (FEC) to Next-Hop table (FTN table) describes the forwarding decisions taken in an LSR when it receives an MPLS labeled packet, or when the LSR receives an unlabeled packet (that is an IP packet) and assigns it to an LSP. The MPLS FTN MIB encodes the FTN table for inspection and control by a management station

All management stations wishing to monitor or configure the basic label forwarding capabilities of a label edge router should monitor the tables provided in this MIB. This MIB is of particular interest to those who wish to understand the ingress prefix-to-label mapping being performed by the LER at any given time. Management stations wishing to monitor the core behavior of MPLS while monitoring other MPLS applications such as traffic engineering or virtual private networks should also utilize the objects provided by this MIB for a clearer picture of what a particular LSR is doing.

Let us begin the discussion of the FTN MIB with a simple explanation of the Label Forwarding Information Base (LFIB) that is present at MPLS label edge routers (LERs). Put simply, an MPLS LER has one basic function: to accept IP packets on non-MPLS interfaces, determine if there is an appropriate label switched path that will eventually reach the destination desired by the packet, impose the appropriate MPLS shim header, and forward that packet into the MPLS domain. The latter would be either an LSP or a traffic-engineered tunnel head interface. Thus, the basic function of an LSR is to accept unlabeled packets and to forward them onto an LSP or TE tunnel. These activities describe the operations of the Forward Equivalency Class to Next-Hop Label Forwarding Entry (FEC-to-NHLFE) mapping.

The forwarding function of a router is responsible for forwarding traffic toward its ultimate destination. The information in the forwarding table is programmed based on information from the control plane. If a packet is not delivered via a local interface directly to the destination, the router must forward the packet toward the ultimate destination using a port that will steer that traffic on a path considered most optimal by the routing function. For this reason, a router must forward traffic toward its destination via a next-hop router. This next-hop router may be the nexthop along the most optimal path for more than one destination subnetwork, so many packets with different network layer headers may be forwarded to the same next-hop router via the same output port. The packets traversing that router can then be organized into sets based on equivalent next-hop network nodes. We call such a set a Forward Equivalency Class (FEC). Thus, any packet that is forwarded to a particular next-hop is considered part of the FEC and can thus be forwarded to the same next-hop.

One important feature of the FEC is the granularity of the classification of traffic it can encompass. Since the FEC is based on a routing next-hop, it can include different classifications of packets. For example, since the routing information for a particular next-hop classification can be based on a destination prefix, it might include every packet traveling toward that destination. In this way, the granularity of packets classified by that FEC is quite coarse. However, if the routing database has programmed some next-hops for some traffic based on an application layer, for example, the traffic granularity might be much finer.

Each FEC is assigned an MPLS Next-Hop Forwarding Entry. This is fancy jargon for an MPLS label. The label assigned to a FEC is used to carry the FEC's traffic to the next-hop LSR, where it may continue along the label switched path. What this does is in effect forward all of the traffic from a FEC along the same LSP. When a FEC is mapped to a label, this represents the FEC-to-NHLFE (FTN). The basic FEC-to-NHLFE operation is demonstrated in Figure 9.3.

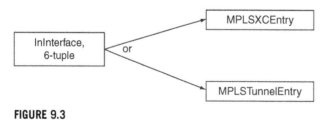

FIGURE 9.3

The basic functionality of the MPLS-FTN MIB: 6-tuple in, cross-connect/tunnels out.

The FEC-to-NHLFE operation is critical to the behavior of a correctly functioning LER, In some cases, this relationship is established manually, but more often it is established automatically by the LSR's control plane. It is for this reason and the important nature of the FEC-to-NHLFE relationship that this relationship needs to be exposed to network managers. Incorrect behavior of this function can result in misrouting or discarding of traffic. This is the basic premise behind the MPLSFTN MIB.

As was noted earlier, the MPLS-LSR MIB provides the user with a clear picture of what the label forwarding (switching) database (LFIB) looks like at any moment in time. It is thus possible to map incoming traffic to the LSPs that are modeled in this MIB. Figure 9.3 illustrates this. In Figure 9.3, traffic from a certain interface matching a 6-tuple used to uniquely describe an incoming packet is mapped to either an MPLS LSP or TE runnel interface. The 6-tuple consists of the IP source and destination addresses, the source and destination ports, the layer-4 protocol identifier, and the EXP bits. Once a match is found within one of the 6-mples, the traffic is then mapped to an MPLS LSR or TE runnel interface present in the MPLS-LSR MIB or MPLS-TE MIB, respectively.

9.6 THE MPLS-TE MIB OVERVIEW

Let us now focus on the MPLS-TE MIB and how it can be used to manage the traffic-engineered tunnels. The MIB allows a user to configure MPLS tunnels. These tunnels may be static (configured manually or through SNMP at each node) or signaled by any signaling protocol. The MIB is structured to contain enough information for signaling using RSVP-TE. Additionally, the MIB allows a user to configure a subset of the full route and apply a traffic engineering algorithm (such as CSPF), either at the head end or within the network, to compute the explicit route.

The MPLS-TE MIB fits into the larger picture of the MPLS-related MIBs in that it depends on both the MPLS-LSR and MPLS-TC MIBs. In the case of the MPLS-LSRMIB, each TE tunnel represented in the MPLS-TE MIB can optionally point (through the use of an SNMP RowPointer object) to the associated MPLSLSR MIB cross-connect entry. This can be useful for debugging a tunnel, since the actual LSP used to route the tunnel can be followed across the network. The dependency on the MPLS-TC MIB is for a few common SNMP textual conventions that are shared among the MPLS-related MIBs. Figure 9.1 shows where this MIB fits into the larger picture of the MPLS-related MIBs.

The MPLS-TE MIB is composed of several tables that are all designed to coordinate together to facilitate traffic engineering tunnel creation, deletion, modification, and monitoring. These tables include the Tunnel Table, Tunnel Resource Table, Tunnel Hop Table, Tunnel Actual Routed Hop Table, Tunnel Computed Hop Table, and Tunnel Performance Table. Figure 9.4 presents a high-level view of how the MIB is organized and how its tables interact.

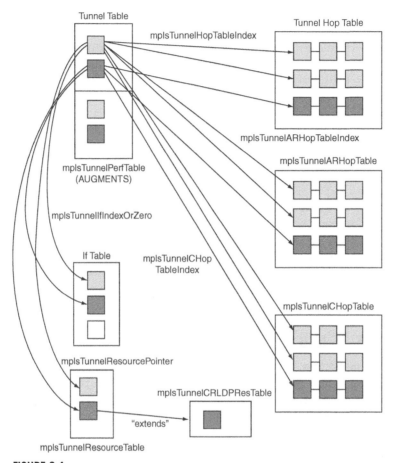

FIGURE 9.4

MPLS-TE MIB table relationships

9.7 MIB EXTENSIONS FOR ADVANCED MPLS-TE FUNCTION AND GMPLS

Three MIB modules are of particular relevance to the management of devices in an MPLS traffic engineered network: the MPLS Textual Conventions MIB module, the MPLS LSR MIB module, and the MPLS traffic engineering MIB module.

The MPLS Textual Conventions MIB module (MPLS-TC-STD-MIB) contains an assortment of general definitions for use in other MIB modules. In a sense it is a little like a header file that defines types and structures for use in other files. It includes definitions of things like bit rates, but more important, it defines textual conventions (that is, types) for use when representing tunnel IDs, extended tunnel IDs, LSP IDs, and MPLS labels.

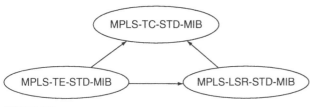

FIGURE 9.5

The relationship between the MPLS TE MIB modules.

The MPLS LSR MIB module (MPLS-LSR-STD-MIB) is used to model and control an individual MPLS LSR. This MIB module concerns itself with the core function of an LSR (that is, forwarding of labeled packets), so it is as applicable to LDP as it is to RSVP-TE. In fact, the LSR MIB module could be used in the absence of any signaling protocol to manually configure LSPs through the LSR.

There are four basic units to the LSR MIB module. There is a table of MPLS-capable interfaces on which labeled packets can be sent and received. There is a table of "in-segments" corresponding to labels received on interfaces, or upstream legs of LSPs; there is a table of "out-segments" modeling downstream legs of LSPs identified with a stack of one or more labels to be pushed onto a packet and indicating the interface out of which to send the packet. The fourth unit is a table of "cross-connects" that shows the relationships (which may be more complex than one-to-one) between in- and out-segments.

A third MIB module, the MPLS traffic engineering MIB module (MPLS-TE-STD-MIB), is used to model and control MPLS TE LSPs. The primary purpose of the module is to allow an operator to configure and activate a TE LSP at an ingress LSR, but the module is equally valid for examining the LSP at any LSR along its path.

The MPLS TE MIB module contains tables to configure multiple instances of an LSP tunnel for simultaneous activation (such as for load-sharing or protection), or for sequential activation (such as for recovery). Thus a tunnel, which is an end-to-end traffic trunk or service, has a common root in the mplsTunnelTable and may be supported by one or more LSPs either at the same time or at different times. Each LSP is represented in the mplsTunnelTable as an "instance" of the tunnel.

Other tables allow the configuration and inspection of resource usage for the LSP, and the request, computed, and actual routes of the LSP.

The dependencies between the MPLS TE MIB modules can be seen in Figure 9.5. The arrows indicate the relationship, "depends on."

9.7.1 **GMPLS MIB Modules**

GMPLS MIB management is built upon MPLS TE management. Nearly every aspect of the MPLS TE MIB modules is reused, but a fair amount of new objects are needed to handle the extra complexity and function of a GMPLS system.

Figure 9.6 shows the new MIB modules (in white) and their relationship to the MPLS TE MIB modules (in gray). As can be seen, there are four new modules

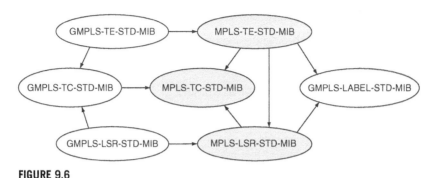

FIGURE 9.6

The relationship between the GMPLS MIB modules.

for GMPLS. The GMPLS-TC-STD-MIB provides some additional textual conventions specific to GMPLS. The GMPLS-LSR-STD-MIB and the GMPLS-TE-STD-MIB are mainly used to "extend" tables in the MPLS TE MIB modules; that is, they effectively provide additional objects for inclusion in the tables defined in the MPLS TE MIB modules.

The GMPLS Label Management MIB module (GMPLS-LABEL-STD-MIB) is a new module designed to handle the fact that GMPLS labels may be considerably more complex than the 23-bit numbers used as labels in MPLS. It contains a table of labels that have simple indexes, but may have complex form, and that may be referenced from the other MIB modules.

9.7.2 GMPLS LSR Management

The GMPLS LSR is managed using all of the tables in the MPLS LSR MIB with extensions to handle the additional function for GMPLS.

The table of MPLS-capable interfaces (mplsInterfaceTable) is extended by the gmplsInterfaceTable. An entry in the former means that the interface uses RSVP-TE for MPLS unless there is also an entry in the GMPLS table. In this case there is an object in the gmplsInterfaceTable that defines the GMPLS signaling protocol in use, and another that defines the signaling Hello period to use on the interface.

The performance of label switching on the interface is recorded in the mplsInterfacePerfTable, and no extensions are made for GMPLS. In fact, two of the counters are specific to packet processing and are consequently only valid when GMPLS is used in a packet-capable environment.

Inward segments in MPLS are tracked in the mplsInSegmentTable. For GMPLS, where bidirectional LSPs are permitted, this might appear confusing; however, the table is well named and the entries refer to the direction of data flow and have no bearing on the signaling used to establish the LSP. Thus, a bidirectional LSP would have one in-segment on the upstream interface (for the forward direction) and one in-segment on the downstream interface (for the reverse direction). The in-segment table is extended for GMPLS by the gmplsInSegmentTable, which tells us whether the segment is used on the forward or reverse direction of a bidirectional LSP, and provides a pointer to an external table (perhaps of a proprietary MIB module) that can contain additional parameters to support technology-specific transports (for example, SONET resource usage). The mplsInSegmentTable may contain a pointer into the gmplsLabelTable to handle the encoding of complex labels.

The performance of in-segments is tracked in the mplsInSegmentPerfTable. Most of the objects in this table are specific to bytes and packets and would only be used when GMPLS is running in a packet-capable environment.

The mplsInSegmentMapTable allows an operator to make a reverse lookup from {interface, label} to find the relevant in-segment in the mplsInSegmentTable. This useful function is preserved for GMPLS, but is slightly complicated by the fact that the label may be found by an indirection to the gmplsLabelTable.

Similar extensions are made for the mplsOutSegmentTable that contains the details of LSP legs that carry data out of the device. The top label to impose on the outgoing traffic may now be found, through indirection, in the gmplsLabelTable. The gmplsOutSegmentTable extends the MPLS table to say whether the segment is in use on the forward or reverse path of the LSP. There is also a pointer to an external table to encode additional parameters if appropriate. Finally, the gmplsOutSegmentTable contains an object to specify by how much to decrement the TTL of any payload packets forwarded on the segment if per-hop decrementing is done; this is clearly also only relevant in packet switching environments.

The performance of out-segments is tracked in the mplsOutSegmentPerfTable. in the same way as for in-segments, most of the objects in this table are specific to bytes and packets and would only be used when GMPLS is running in a packet-capable environment.

The mplsLabelStackTable is preserved for GMPLS, but also only applies in packet environments because this is the only time that label stacking is relevant. This table lists the additional label stack to be applied to outgoing packets beneath the topmost label. These labels may also be found through indirection to the gmplsLabelTable (although this particular usage is unlikely because the stack will be made up from simple 20-bit labels).

Both the in- and out-segment tables may contain pointers to an external table that contains parameters that describe the traffic on this LSP. The pointer may indicate an entry in the mplsTunnelResourceTable in the MPLS TE MIB module, or it may point to an entry in a proprietary MIB module.

This leaves just the mplsXCTable which is unchanged in usage from MPLS. That is, it ties together in- and out-segments to provide LSPs through the device.

Figure 9.7 shows all of the MIB tables used for managing a GMPLS LSR with their relationships indicated by arrows. Gray boxes denote tables in the MPLS LSR MIB module, ovals are tables in external MIB modules, and white boxes are tables in the GMPLS LSR MIB module.

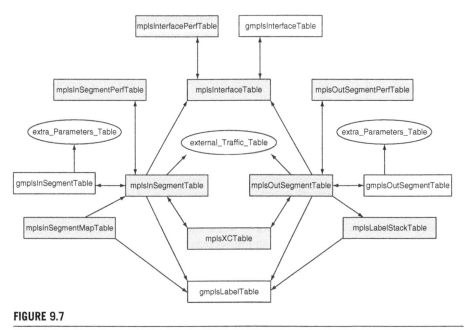

FIGURE 9.7

The relationship between MIB tables in GMPLS LSR management.

9.7.3 **GMPLS Traffic Engineering LSP Management**

Management of individual TE LSPs is slightly simpler and requires fewer tables than the management of the LSR described above. The basis of the management is the mplsTunnelTable, which contains active and configured LSP tunnels that start, end, or transit the device. Entries in the tunnel table are not indexed by the five-tuple that defines the LSP, as might seem natural, but by a slightly different set of parameters. That is, the normal group of identifiers of the LSP {source, destination, tunnel ID, extended tunnel ID, LSP ID} is replaced in this MIB table by {tunnel index, tunnel instance, ingress LSR ID, egress LSR ID}. The tunnel index maps to the tunnel ID that is signaled, while the tunnel instance disambiguates distinct LSPs that support the tunnel (either simultaneously or over time) and thus may be safely mapped to the LSP ID that is signaled. The MIB module assumes that the source and destination of the LSP will be expressed as LSR IDs (which might not be the case) and makes the false assumption that the extended tunnel ID will always be set equal to the ingress LSR ID and thus does not need to be configured. Having said this, the indexing scheme is actually quite acceptable for non-packet systems and, because it is now used for MPLS packet systems, it is clearly extensible for GMPLS packet LSPs.

The purpose of the GMPLS TE MIB module is both to allow LSPs to be configured and managed at their ingresses and to allow the LSPs to be inspected at any point within the network. To configure an LSP it must be possible to select parameters for any constraint or option that can be signaled. The core set of objects for this are found in the mplsTunnelTable, and this is extended by the gmplsTunnelTable to support the following additional features:

- Presentation of this tunnel within the LSR as an unnumbered interface
- Selection of label recording
- The encoding type requested for the LSP
- The switching type requested for the LSP
- The link protection requested for the LSP
- The payload (G-PID) carried by the LSP
- Whether the LSP is a secondary (that is, backup) LSP
- Whether the LSP is unidirectional or bidirectional
- The control of alarms and other LSP attributes
- What manner of path computation the ingress LSR is required to perform.

Some of these attributes are useful in MPLS as well as GMPLS and can be used by picking up the gmplsTunnelTable and setting the encoding type to zero to indicate an MPLS LSP. All of the objects listed above are also used when an LSP is examined at a transit or egress LSR. Additionally, it is possible to see the Notify recipients for forward and backward notification and the Admin Status flags. A pointer from the gmplsTunnelTable can be used to reference an additional external table (perhaps of a proprietary MIB module) that can contain additional parameters to support technology-specific transports (for example, SONET resource usage).

The MPLS TE MIB module contains the mplsTunnelPerfTable to record the performance of the LSP. However, because the MPLS tunnels are unidirectional, the GMPLS TE MIB module introduces the gmplsTunnelReversePerfTable to record the performance in the opposite direction. Both performance tables are primarily concerned with packets and bytes and may be largely inappropriate in non-packet environments.

The resource requirements/usage of each LSP are recorded in the mplsTunnelResourceTable. No changes are needed to this table for GMPLS.

A significant part of TE LSP management relates to the specification, computation, and recording of the path taken by the LSP. The MPLS TE MIB module provides three tables for this function: the mplsTunnelHopTable, the mplsTunnelCHopTable, and the mplsTunnelARHopTable, respectively. GMPLS increases the level of control that may be specified in a configured and signaled route (for example, by adding explicit control of labels) and also allows for this information to be recorded. Thus it is necessary to extend all three of the tables within the GMPLS TE MIB module. Further, because labels are now involved, the new tables include pointers into the gmplsLableTabel.

The final extension in the GMPLS TE MIB is the gmplsTunnelErrorTable. This table is not really specific to GMPLS because it records errors that occur when trying to establish an LSP or when the LSP fails at some later stage. Because

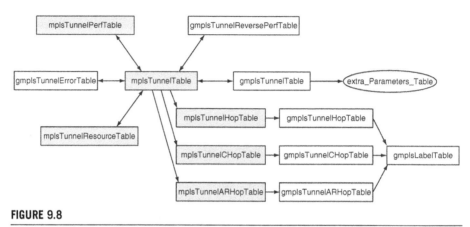

FIGURE 9.8

The relationship between MIB tables in GMPLS TE management.

it extends the mplsTunnelTable it may be used equally in MPLS and GMPLS systems.

Figure 9.8 shows all of the MIB tables used for managing GMPLS TE LSPs with their relationships indicated by arrows. Gray boxes denote tables in the MPLS TE MIB module, ovals are tables in external MIB modules, and white boxes are tables in the GMPLS TE MIB module.

9.7.4 The TE Link MIB Module

The Traffic Engineering (TE) Link MIB module is equally applicable to MPLS and GMPLS systems. It allows TE links to be configured and managed, in particular helping an operator to set up and use link bundles. Configuring a bundled link involves defining the bundled link and the TE links, assigning SRLGs to the TE link configuring the component links their bandwidth parameters, associating the component links with the appropriate TE link, and associating the TE links with the appropriate bundled link.

To this end, the TE Link MIB module includes seven tables.

- Entries in the teLinkTable represent the TE links, including bundled links, and their generic traffic engineering parameters.
- The teLinkDescriptorTable contains the TE link interface switching capabilities.
- The teLinkSrlgTable lists the shared risk link groups (SRLGs) that may be associated with the TE links.
- Priority-based bandwidth traffic engineering parameters for association with the TE links are placed in the teLinkBandwidthTable.
- Entries in the componentLinkTable represent the component links and show their generic traffic engineering parameters.

- The componentLinkDescriptorTable holds the switching capability descriptors for each component link.
- Priority-based bandwidth traffic engineering parameters for association with each component link are placed in the componentLinkBandwidthTable.

This MIB module contains the basic necessities for managing TE links, but is somewhat short of configurable constraints for links in optical networks. Further developments and extensions to this MIB are likely as traffic engineering becomes more established in photonic networks.

Monitoring and Maintenance

The management techniques described in the previous chapter provide some valuable diagnostic tools for an operator to inspect an MPLS network and determine that the LSPs are in place and are operating correctly. The control plane protocol state responsible for installing and maintaining LSPs can be examined at each LSR and compared with the label cross-connect and FTN table to trace the LSP in the data plane.

However, these mechanisms can be somewhat cumbersome, are hard to use to provide dynamic diagnostics, and are vulnerable to discrepancies between the control plane and forwarding plane state. A set of additional diagnostic tools has been developed to help monitor MPLS LSPs and to isolate any faults. This chapter introduces some of the more popular mechanisms.

10.1 LSP PING

RFC 4379 defines a diagnostic protocol for testing the continuity and connectivity of MPLS LSPs. This technique is commonly referred to as LSP Ping and provides a mechanism to trace the LSP in the forwarding plane under the control and coordination of the control plane.

The essence of LSP Ping is an Echo Request message that is sent as a UDP datagram encapsulated as an IP packet and then as an MPLS packet, and is forwarded along the path of the LSP. If the message is correctly received at the destination or is incorrectly received at some other LSR, it is responded to with an Echo Response that travels back as an IP datagram.

So the Echo Request can work correctly, it must appear and be treated exactly as any other data packet on the LSP. Thus, it is inserted into the LSP at the head end, and the identical labels that would be used for data are imposed on the packet. If the LSP is correctly connected and passing data, the Echo Request will be forwarded along the LSP and delivered to the egress LSR.

At the egress, the labels are stripped off all packets, and they are handled according to the payload type. That is, IP packets are forwarded based on the

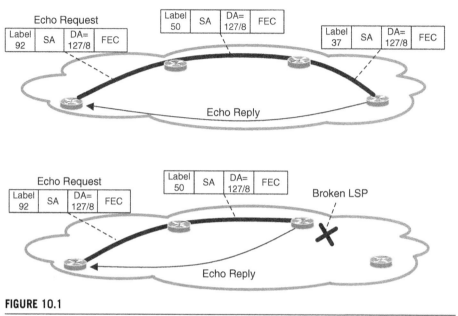

FIGURE 10.1

LSP Ping behavior for a normal and a broken LSP.

destination IP address that they carry. If the LSP has correctly delivered the Echo Request, it would be fine to use any address of the egress LSR to ensure that the Echo Request is delivered to the local system. However, if the LSP is misconnected or broken in such a way that packets "escape" from the LSP, we want the Echo Request to be processed at the LSR where the LSP is broken. The use of an IP address of the intended egress might cause the Echo Request to be forwarded as an ordinary IP packet. To avoid this, the IP destination address used is an internal host loopback address (some 127/8 address for IPv4), which means that any LSR that sees the Echo Request will deliver it to the local control plane for processing.

In addition, the Echo Request message carries an identifier of the LSP under test. This allows the receiver to cross-check the message against the LSP on which it was received and report any errors. It also means that the Echo Response has some information to return that can be correlated at the ingress so that the sender knows that the Echo Request was correctly received. The LSPs are identified by their FECs, which are copied direct from those used in LDP (if the LSPs were set up using LDP) or from the Session/Sender_Template identifiers used in RSVP-TE.

Figure 10.1 shows the LSP Ping behavior for a simple LSP when it is correctly connected to its destination and when it is broken. The Echo Request is sent as a UDP datagram bearing a source IP address that identifies the LSP head end and a destination address chosen from 127/8. The datagram is labeled, and the label changes as the packet flows through the network. The Echo Reply, generated at the egress or if the LSP is broken, is sent back to the initiator identified as the sender of the original Echo Request.

The echo request contains various timestamps and sequence numbers so that better correlation of responses can be made, and a very significant field, called the reply mode, describes what action the receiver should take when it sees an Echo Request.

- The normal response mode is "Reply via an IPv4/IPv6 UDP packet." This causes the Echo Reply to be sent back to the originator's IP address and confirms the receipt of the Echo Request.

- If the return path is considered by the initiator to be unreliable, it may specify the response mode as "Reply via an IPv4/IPv6 UDP packet using Router Alert." This enables the Echo Reply to be forwarded hop-by-hop toward the initiator.

- Some LSP Ping applications (such as VCCV, discussed in Section 10.4) have their own IP-based control channels through which they can send data (possibly with additional reliability features). If this is the case, the initiator can specify "Reply via application level control channel" to give the application freedom to use its own mechanisms.

- Lastly, a useful option is to set the reply mode to "Don't reply." It might seem that this makes LSP Ping useless, but that is far from the case. For example, the receiver can (under application or management control) monitor for received Echo Requests, and if none is received for a certain time period, if there are gaps in the sequence numbers, or if the timestamps indicate wildly varying propagation times, the receiver can raise alerts to the operator through the management system.

In using LSP Ping, it must be understood that the tool is good at determining the liveness of an LSP, but it is not good at determining or isolating faults. In particular, if there is a break in an LSP that causes packets to be discarded (as they should be if an LSP is broken) then LSP Ping will do no more than report that the LSP is not delivering packets. The only error that LSP Ping can diagnose successfully is when there is some misconnection that causes packets to be misdelivered to the egress of the wrong LSP—even then, LSP Ping cannot isolate where in the network the misconnection has arisen.

Further, it is not advisable to use LSP Ping as a continuous health monitoring system for LSPs, especially in a network where there are very many LSPs. Not only will the presence of Echo Requests in the LSPs detract from those LSPs' ability to deliver data, but the LSP egress can become swamped with the extra processing required to handle Echo Requests. Worse, an initiator that tests too many LSPs at the same time will be swamped with Echo Replies. In fact, this poses something of a security risk because an LSR could be the target of a large number of spurious Echo Replies, so LSRs are recommended to rate limit UDP packets received on the port number designated for LSP Ping.

This feature means that LSP Ping is not suitable for rapid detection of LSP failures, and that means that it is relegated to use for periodic continuity checks.

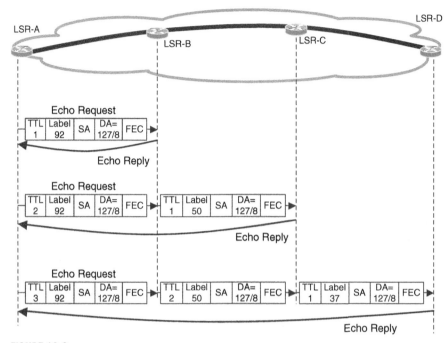

FIGURE 10.2

Simple example of LSP Traceroute.

10.2 LSP TRACEROUTE

As just described, LSP Ping can only be used to discover whether or not LSPs are working correctly. What is needed is a way of isolating faults by tracing the path of an LSP. This function is easily achieved by a simple modification to LSP Ping known as LSP Traceroute.

MPLS packets carry a time-to-live (TTL) field that is decremented hop-by-hop until the packet is discarded when the TTL reaches zero. By sending an Echo Request with MPLS TTL set to one, an initiator can ensure that it is delivered to the control plane of the downstream neighbor and not propagated further. Thus, by setting the TTL to any number, the initiator can cause the Echo Request to be delivered to any hop along the path. When an Echo Request is delivered to the control plane, it causes an Echo Reply to be sent back to the initiator. Figure 10.2 shows a simple example of how an ingress LSR can sequentially send Echo Requests to each hop of an LSP.

Some additions to the Echo Reply provide a little more information about the state of the LSP at each LSR that responds. TLVs are used to encode the downstream next hop information in terms of the label and interface that are used to forward data on the LSP.

Using LSP Traceroute, an operator at the ingress LSR of a working LSP can determine the full path and label swapping detail of the LSP. If the LSP is misconnected, this will provide all of the information necessary to locate the fault.

In the event that an LSP is broken and is dropping packets, LSP Traceroute also provides a good tool to determine the location of the fault. The process will return Echo Replies from each LSR up to the break but will then not produce any response. The final Echo Reply received will indicate the LSR immediately upstream of the problem and will indicate the outgoing interface toward the failure. This will give the operator enough information to isolate the fault.

10.3 BIDIRECTIONAL FORWARDING DETECTION

Bidirectional Forwarding Detection (BFD) is a protocol intended to provide a lightweight method to detect faults in the bidirectional paths between forwarding engines. It can be applied in IP or MPLS networks, and it can be used to detect faults between neighbors at the ends of interfaces, data links, or LSPs. Its function is independent of data plane technologies or protocols.

In essence, BFD is just a simple Hello protocol that operates in-band with the data and allows the ends of a connection to monitor the bidirectional connectivity of the link or LSP. Because MPLS LSPs are not bidirectional (although GMPLS LSPs can be), for the sake of this discussion we consider a "bidirectional LSP" to be either a GMPLS bidirectional LSP or a matched pair of MPLS LSPs in opposite directions. Each LSR periodically sends a BFD packet over the bidirectional LSP, and if one LSR stops receiving BFD packets for a certain period of time, it is assumed that some component of that particular bidirectional LSP has failed.

The LSRs at the ends of an LSP take either an active or a passive role. Active LSRs are responsible for generating BFD messages on a timer using a small amount of jittering to ensure that there is no convergence of messages used for several LSPs. A passive LSR only responds to BFD messages by sending an "echo" when it receives a message from its active neighbor. At least one LSR must take an active role, although it is possible for both to be active.

The BFD process is under configuration control in some sense. That is, the default is that BFD is not used, and some action is required to enable BFD. The protocol is capable of starting itself up with one active LSR beginning to send BFD messages using a slow timer. When the remote LSR responds, the BFD session is up, and the rate of transmission can be increased according to timer values carried on the BFD messages themselves. However, this initialization procedure might not be suitable in MPLS because it requires that the sender of the first BFD message knows the BFD identifier of the LSP in the sender and receiver context. To exchange this information and provide additional control of BFD, a simple bootstrap mechanism is needed, and in MPLS this is achieved by an extension to LSP Ping.

To provide a BFD bootstrap, the LSP Ping Echo Request message is enhanced to contain a sender's BFD identifier for the LSP. The receipt of the Echo Request triggers the remote end of the LSP to respond with a BFD message that carries the initiator's BFD identifier as well as its own identifier for the BFD session. Because the Echo Request can use the FEC information to uniquely identify an LSP, this provides all the function necessary to enable BFD. Additional minor protocol extensions are provided to allow LSP Ping to be used to verify the status of BFD between the end points and to disable BFD gracefully without generating any false negatives.

BFD is somewhat less intrusive than LSP Ping and is therefore more suitable for use as a connectivity monitor. The protocol can be run with a relatively fast timer enabling LSP failures to be reported rapidly and recovery procedures to be instigated.

10.4 VIRTUAL CIRCUIT CONNECTIVITY VERIFICATION

Virtual Circuit Connectivity Verification (VCCV) is a connection verification protocol developed specifically for application to virtual circuits such as pseudowires (discussed in Chapter 13). To operate successfully, such a protocol must first establish a control channel associated with the pseudowire, and it can then use this to manage the connectivity verification procedures.

As described in Chapter 13, a pseudowire is achieved by installing an MPLS LSP between two provider-edge LSRs and encapsulating the signal from a native service for transmission down that LSP. If BFD or LSP Ping packets were simply sent down the same LSP as the pseudowire traffic, the receiver would not distinguish them from normal data and would attempt to convert them into the native data format for forwarding through the client network. Fortunately, however, the pseudowire encapsulation technique includes a demultiplexer that allows control traffic to be separated from data traffic, and VCCV can make use of this feature to provide a control channel within the pseudowire LSP on which to operate continuity and connectivity checks. The advantage of this function is that the verification messages follow exactly the same MPLS path through the network as the data (at each hop of the pseudowire LSP they are treated in exactly the same way as the MPLS packets that carry the data because they use exactly the same MPLS labels), yet when they reach the destination, the control and test messages are demultiplexed from the data stream and are handed off to a control plane component for processing.

VCCV also needs a bootstrap mechanism, and this is provided by the MPLS signaling messages that are used to set up the pseudowire (see Chapter 13). These messages exchange information about the VCCV capabilities of the end points and negotiate the use of VCCV for the pseudowire. When the pseudowire has been set up, the controllers at each end of the MPLS LSP can start to send VCCV messages down the control channel within the pseudowire LSP.

VCCV can be used for fault detection or as a diagnostic tool for pseudowires. It combines the features of LSP Ping and BFD to transmit VCCV messages repeatedly on a timer or when requested by an operator. The MPLS TTL of the VCCV packets can also be manipulated to provide a traceroute function similar to that described in Section 10.2.

The content of the VCCV message depends on the function that is being tested. Two principal options are to include an ICMP message (exactly as would be used in IP forwarding) or to encapsulate an LSP Ping message, as described in Section 10.1, but using the correct pseudowire FEC to identify the LSP (see Chapter 13). When the VCCV message is received, it is passed to the control plane component, and the encapsulated message is processed exactly as it would normally be with the one exception that the response message that is built and sent is passed back to VCCV to be encapsulated and returned in a pseudowire control channel.

The control channel established for VCCV could additionally be used to carry native OAM communications for the emulated service. This allows the pseudowire to simulate the connectivity of the native client network more closely.

MPLS Security

11.1 INTRODUCTION

Security is arguably one of the most pressing issues in the entire field of networking. Users of networks are understandably concerned that they should not open themselves to attack when they connect their systems to a network. The introduction of a relatively new network technology, such as MPLS, raises additional concerns about whether the new technology is as secure as its predecessors.

The application that has contributed most to the deployment of MPLS is Virtual Private Networks (VPNs), and one of the major reasons to use a VPN is to obtain some measure of security. Thus, the security of MPLS networks has been an area of focus for both designers and users of MPLS network technologies for many years. In this chapter we will provide an overview of the specific security issues that affect MPLS and describe some of the techniques that have been developed to address those issues.

11.1.1 Scope

Many books have been written about network security, and many of the problems that affect IP networks in general are equally relevant to MPLS networks. In this chapter we will limit ourselves to problems that are unique to MPLS. Many of the specific issues affecting MPLS arise from the use of a label-swapping forwarding paradigm, which changes the playing field somewhat relative to the datagram model of IP. In addition, MPLS has its own set of control protocols, which also need to be protected against certain attacks. Finally, we note that there are specific issues related to the security of VPN services; these will be discussed in Chapter 12, where those services are fully explored.

Network security itself has a broad range of definitions. For example, a network operator might be concerned about the security of the network devices, such as routers, against denial of service attacks or other forms of compromise. A user of network services might be concerned that his systems should only be accessible by authorized users across the network. To understand what is meant by network security in the MPLS context, we need to consider a list of threats that we wish to address; this is the subject of Section 11.3.

343

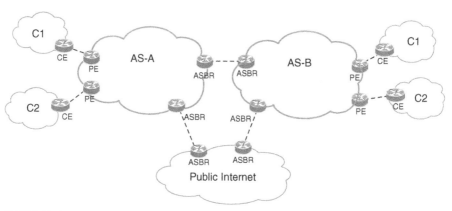

FIGURE 11.1

Network model for MPLS security.

11.2 NETWORK MODEL

Figure 11.1 shows a basic network model that can be used to illustrate various security issues related to MPLS networks. A few points to note about this model are the following:

- Customers connect to providers over CE-PE links. These links represent "trust boundaries" in the sense that a customer might not trust traffic that comes over that link as fully as he would trust traffic originating in his site, and the provider will certainly not trust traffic arriving over those links as much as traffic that is already inside his network.

- A customer, such as C1, can obtain service from multiple providers; in this picture, AS-A and AS-B could be operated by different providers.

- The links between providers (e.g., the link between ASBRs connecting AS-A to AS-B) also represent a trust boundary, and the issues arising at an interprovider boundary differ from those at a customer-provider boundary.

- Any provider might (or might not) have some sort of connection to the public Internet. This is yet another trust boundary and can raise additional security issues beyond those that arise at other inter-AS links.

11.3 THREATS

It is important to understand the potential threats to the security of an MPLS network. The set of potential threats includes:

- Observation of a customer's or provider's data while in transit
- Modification or deletion of data in transit
- Replay of previously transmitted data

- Insertion of data into the traffic stream
- Disruption of connectivity between customer and provider or between providers
- Degradation of quality of service experienced by traffic of one or more customers
- Unauthorized use or theft of provider network resources

Broadly speaking, we can divide the attacks that can be launched against the network into those that are launched against the control plane and those that attack the data plane. The following sections address these two categories of attack.

We also note that "attacks" might not always be active or malicious. For example, a misbehaving host at a customer site might be the source of an attack on the service provider's infrastructure. Misconfiguration of a service provider's routers might lead to some of the threats listed above—for example, by misrouting traffic from one customer to another. Thus, it is useful to have a fairly broad definition of threats and attacks.

It should be noted that many security measures come at a cost. This cost can be measured in terms of additional equipment, operational complexity, reduced performance, or lost functionality. It is important that the likelihood and severity of various attacks are understood so that sensible cost-benefit trade-offs can be made in deciding how and whether to secure the network against those attacks.

Finally, note that we are following the traditional approach in considering a list of threats before discussing how to protect against them. We urge you not to be alarmed by the list of threats, which can indeed be mitigated by the defensive measures described later in this chapter.

11.3.1 Control Plane

The MPLS control plane is composed of a fairly large number of protocols, each of which presents opportunities for some sort of attack. Any or all of the following protocols can be used in some capacity in an MPLS network:

- LDP
- RSVP-TE
- IS-IS
- OSPF
- BGP
- PCE signaling
- L2TPv3

Hence, attention should be paid to the security of all these protocols against attack.

Some particular types of attack are outlined in the following sections.

LSP Creation

If an unauthorized device is able to send MPLS signaling messages (e.g., using LDP, RSVP-TE, or BGP when it distributes labels), it might be able to create unauthorized

LSPs. At a minimum this represents a consumption of resources (label table space, cross-connect entries) that may be scarce; in the case of RSVP-TE it also represents a possible consumption of reserved link bandwidth. Creation of an unauthorized LSP might also provide a building block for other attacks, such as misrouting of traffic. Unauthorized LSPs might also be used as a way to effectively tunnel packets that might otherwise have been filtered out through routers at a trust boundary.

LSP Message Snooping

If an attacker is able to listen to the messages being exchanged by an MPLS signaling protocol, such as RSVP-TE or LDP (e.g., by tapping a cable or intercepting messages transmitted wirelessly), then he will be able to determine which labels are in use for various purposes. This can enable other sorts of attack, such as label spoofing, which is discussed in Section 11.3.2.

Control Plane Denial of Service

Various types of Denial of Service (DoS) attack can be launched using the MPLS control plane, much like many other control plane protocols. For example, CPU cycles and memory can be consumed just by opening LDP sessions or by sending RSVP-TE messages. In an extreme case, MPLS signaling messages could also be used to starve the network of link bandwidth. Note that this sort of attack is not all that specific to MPLS, but nevertheless it is important to bear in mind when designing (and possibly when configuring) the MPLS control plane protocols.

Cross-Connection of Users

Because the VPN applications of MPLS are specifically intended to provide isolation between the traffic of one user and another, attacks that (perhaps inadvertently) cross connect one user's network to another are particularly troublesome. This issue can occur in a number of different ways (many of them more likely to be the result of misconfiguration than deliberate attack), including:

- Incorrect interconnection of two sites by a point-to-point psuedowire
- Inclusion of a site in the wrong L2VPN or L3VPN
- Combining two (L2 or L3) VPNs into a single VPN (e.g., by incorrect route target assignment)
- Providing a data path from one (L2 or L3) VPN to another

MPLS VPNs are discussed in more depth in Chapter 12.

11.3.2 Data plane

Many attacks on the data plane are common across all types of packet network. MPLS networks can be subject to:

- Observation of data packets (resulting in loss of confidentiality)
- Modification of data packets

- Insertion or deletion of data packets
- Replay attacks
- Traffic pattern analysis
- Denial of service using the data plane

In all cases, these are reasonably similar to attacks against the IP data plane. However, the defensive measures differ for a variety of reasons, including different assessments of the cost-benefit trade-offs in an MPLS network as opposed to the public Internet.

A significant aspect of the MPLS data plane that distinguishes it from the IP data plane is, of course, the use of label swapping to forward packets. This presents some unique challenges because an attacker might be able to direct a packet to a particular destination by suitable choice of label. As previously noted, this might enable an attacker to tunnel a packet through a trust boundary, depending on how deeply packets are inspected as they cross that boundary. The use of label stacking further complicates the picture because a spoofed label might make its way to the top of the stack many hops away from where it was injected into the network.

11.4 DEFENSIVE TECHNIQUES

Now that we have seen the various threats faced by MPLS networks, we consider some of the ways to defend against those threats. As previously noted, the choice of exactly which defensive measures to deploy will depend in part on the trade-off made between the cost of deployment and the risk perceived from the threats that are to be mitigated.

11.4.1 Physical Security

While this might seem obvious, it is important to consider physical security as a first line of defense. For example, cables that run between routers within a service provider's PoP do not need to be secured against eavesdroppers if the PoP itself is physically secure (as it typically is). Similarly, some security measures for MPLS VPNs depend on the assumption that an attacker cannot change the physical interface on which his packets enter the network; this assumption holds true as long as the routers that form the outer edge of the service provider's network are physically secure.

11.4.2 Access Control

Standard access control methods (e.g., filtering based on IP address, port number, etc.) can be used to mitigate some classes of threat. For example, a provider can ensure that control connections to its core routers are not accepted from any routers outside the trust boundary. These techniques are not specific to MPLS, so we do not go into them further here.

11.4.3 **Control Plane Authentication**

Control plane authentication allows many of the threats previously mentioned to be prevented or mitigated. The basic idea behind control plane authentication is to only accept control plane messages or connections if the sender of those messages can be verified. By authenticating control plane messages, a router can prevent such attacks as the unauthorized creation of LSPs. Certain problems that arise from misconfiguration can also be prevented by authentication of the control plane.

Each of the MPLS control plane protocols (LDP, RSVP-TE, etc.) has a variety of authentication mechanisms. These are fairly similar to mechanisms that have been used for other IP control protocols. For example, LDP uses an MD5 signature scheme for TCP (as specified in RFC 2385) that is very similar to the one used for BGP. This scheme operates as follows:

- Use of the MD5 Signature Option for LDP TCP connections is a configurable LSR option. Two LSRs that are configured to use this option will agree to use MD5 signatures to ensure the authenticity of their LDP sessions.

- An LSR that uses the MD5 Signature Option is configured with a password (shared secret) for each potential LDP peer.

- Each LSR applies the MD5 hash algorithm to compute the MD5 digest for a TCP segment to be sent to a peer. This computation calculates the hash over the peer password concatenated with the TCP segment.

- When the LSR receives a TCP segment with an MD5 digest, it validates the segment by calculating the expected MD5 digest (using its own record of the password) and compares the computed digest with the received digest. If the comparison fails, the segment is dropped without any response to the sender.

- The LSR ignores LDP Hellos from any LSR for which a password has not been configured. This ensures that the LSR establishes LDP TCP connections only with LSRs for which a password has been configured.

This approach ensures that an LDP session can only be maintained with an LSR that knows the appropriate password. Because the MD5 hash is computed over the entire TCP segment, any attempt to modify messages in transit would be detected. Any device that attempts to spoof messages would have to know the "shared secret" or be able to produce the correct MD5 hash without knowing the shared secret. While MD5 is not believed to be as strong as it once was, this still represents a significant barrier to a would-be attacker.

RSVP-TE makes use of a somewhat similar approach, but authentication is performed on RSVP-TE messages rather than TCP segments because RSVP-TE does not run over TCP.

11.4.4 **Cryptographic Techniques and the MPLS Data Plane**

Whereas the authentication techniques used by IP control protocols can be fairly straightforwardly applied to the MPLS control protocols, the same cannot be said for the MPLS data plane. The MPLS data plane does not offer equivalent authentication or encryption options to the IP data plane (as provided by IPsec), and there is no obvious way that IPsec-like capabilities could be added to MPLS. However, we note that this does not appear to be a serious issue to date, for a number of reasons:

- It is possible to encapsulate MPLS packets in an IP header and then use IPsec to either authenticate or encrypt the packet, and this is quite a suitable approach in some cases. For example, one can use IPsec tunnels to carry MPLS packets across an insecure backbone from one PE to another.

- In many environments, the level of data plane security that MPLS provides is considered to be adequate, so the higher level of security provided by IPsec-like encryption or authentication (with the associated costs in terms of processing power and key management) is not required.

- Users of MPLS services are at liberty to use IPsec, end-to-end or site-to-site, to protect their data without relying on MPLS to do so, and this is likely to make sense if the user doesn't trust the provider.

11.4.5 **Security and Label-Based Forwarding**

Perhaps the important way in which MPLS networks differ from IP networks in terms of security is the effect of label-based forwarding. As previously noted, label-based forwarding enables certain attacks that are unique to label-switching networks. Label stacking further complicates the picture.

In some scenarios, label-based forwarding can be an asset from a security perspective. For example, in many MPLS VPN deployments, the CE-PE links should only carry unlabeled packets. Thus, the PE routers should be configured to drop any labeled packets that arrive from a CE. This ensures that customers cannot spoof labels, and it ensures that the P and PE routers will only receive labeled packets from other P and PE routers. Thus, the provider has a natural alignment of the network that lies within the trust boundary and the network that deals with labeled packets.

There are a few scenarios in which labeled packets must cross a trust boundary. These scenarios are discussed in more detail in Chapters 12 and 14. In certain interprovider VPN scenarios, labeled packets must pass between ASBRs. When a VPN provider offers a "Carrier's Carrier" service, labeled packets must pass over the CE-PE interface. In these cases, the PE routers or ASBRs should ensure that they only receive "legitimate" labeled packets. That is, a label on a packet is legitimate if, and only if, the PE or ASBR that receives the packet has advertised that label to the neighboring router that is sending the labeled packet. If the label is not legitimate, the packet should be dropped.

11.5 SUMMARY

Security is an important topic in any discussion of networking, and MPLS networks are no exception. Many aspects of security are common across traditional IP networks and MPLS, but MPLS also presents some unique challenges and requirements. The MPLS control plane needs to be secured, just like the IP control plane, and many similar techniques have been applied to achieve that goal. The MPLS data plane is quite different from the IP data plane, and thus it has both different threats and some different security techniques at its disposal. MPLS can also make effective use of IPsec to secure the data plane in various circumstances.

Finally, we note that there are a number of references that might be useful to dig deeper on this topic. At the time of this writing, the MPLS working group is developing an Internet Draft (for future publication as an informational RFC) entitled *Security Framework for MPLS and GMPLS Networks* by L. Fang et al. For general IP security references, we recommend Chapter 8 of *Computer Networks: A Systems Approach* by L. Peterson and B. Davie and *Cryptography and Network Security* by W. Stallings.

Providing Services with MPLS

This final section of the book discusses how MPLS is used to provide some key services in today's networks. Services are, of course, what it is all about. Networking is only of value for the function that it provides to the user, and only if the network has the capability to provide the necessary level of service as described in the earlier chapters.

The chapters in this section address the provision of Virtual Private Networks (VPNs), Pseudowires, Multi-Domain Networking, and Multicast and Point-to-Multipoint data distribution.

Virtual Private Networks

12

Virtual private networks (VPNs) are a major growth area within the Internet. Using standardized protocols, companies are able to connect their private networks using the economical and highly available resources of the Internet while, at the same time, protecting their data from prying eyes.

The growth in popularity of VPNs has been accompanied by an explosion in techniques for providing this function. Most of these techniques utilize standardized approaches, but each uses different protocols and each has its own benefits and disadvantages.

In this chapter, drawn from *MPLS Technology and Applications* by Davie and Rekhter, *Developing IP-Based Services* by Morrow and Vijayanada, and *The Internet and Its Protocols* by Farrel, we look at how MPLS can be used for supporting Virtual Private Networks (VPNs). There are several approaches for supporting VPNs that use MPLS. Even though these approaches all use MPLS, it is important to understand that MPLS is just one of the components within each approach; that is probably the only thing these approaches have in common. While in principle it may be desirable to cover all of these approaches, to do so at a useful level of detail would probably require an entire book. Therefore, we have chosen to describe one specific approach in detail rather than giving a superficial overview of all these approaches. Nevertheless, many of the general principles of MPLS VPNs will become clear in this chapter.

12.1 VPN OVERVIEW

12.1.1 What is a VPN?

Consider a company that has a set of geographically dispersed sites. To interconnect computers at these sites, the company needs a network. The network is private in the sense that it is expected to be used by only that company. It is also private in the sense that the routing and addressing plan within the network is completely independent of the routing and addressing plans of all other networks.

The network is virtual in the sense that the facilities used to build and operate such a network may not be dedicated just to that company, but could be shared with other companies that want to have their own VPNs. The facilities needed to build such a network are provided, at least partially, by a third party, known as a VPN service provider. The company that uses the network is known as a VPN customer.

Informally, we could say that a VPN is a set of sites that can communicate with each other. More formally, a VPN is defined by a set of administrative policies that control both connectivity and Quality of Service among sites.

It is quite natural that it is the VPN customer who sets up the policies that define that customer's VPN. With respect to who implements these policies, depending on the technology used, there could be a range of choices. For example, it should be possible to completely confine the implementation of these policies to the VPN service provider, so that the VPN customer could completely outsource the VPN service to the service provider. Likewise, it should be possible to distribute the implementation of these policies between the service provider and the customer.

With respect to the intersite connectivity, there is also a range of choices. At one end of the spectrum is complete mesh connectivity among all the sites, while at the other end of the spectrum is hub-and-spoke connectivity, where connectivity among the sites labeled as "spokes" occurs only through the site labeled as the "hub." Yet another example of intersite connectivity is when the sites are partitioned into two or more sets; in this case connectivity among sites within each set is a complete mesh, whereas connectivity between sites in different sets is indirect, only through a particular site.

While so far we've been talking about VPNs that span sites that belong to the same company, we see more and more cases where VPNs are also used to interconnect sites in different companies. The common name for the former is an *intranet* and for the latter is an *extranet*. The definition of a VPN given above applies to both cases. The distinction between the two cases is in who sets up the policies that define the VPN—in the case of an intranet it is a single company (or administrative entity), while in the case of an extranet it is a group of companies.

Our VPN definition allows a given site to be part of more than one VPN. For example, a particular site may be in a VPN associated with an intranet, and at the same time, it could also be in a different VPN associated with an extranet. In that sense VPNs could overlap.

Finally, we don't assume that a given VPN has to be confined to a single VPN service provider-facilities needed to build and operate a VPN could be provided by a group of VPN service providers.

The concept of a VPN is shown in Figure 12.1, in which two companies (imaginatively named Company A and Company B) each have two sites with private networks—the companies connect them across the Internet.

Such networks create the only illusion of being private. That is, the data that is sent between the private networks passes through the public network and is therefore vulnerable to interception, forgery, or accidental misdelivery. These networks

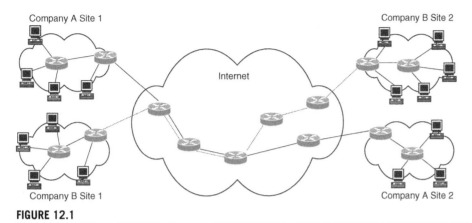

FIGURE 12.1

Virtual private networks consist of private networks connected together through a public network.

are consequently known as virtual private networks, and considerable effort is expended to ensure the integrity of the data sent between the private sites.

12.1.2 **Tunneling and Private Address Spaces**

One of the options provided by a VPN is that the addresses within the private networks may be kept private. This allows the companies in Figure 12.1 to use identical address spaces, and lets each have hosts that have the same addresses.

If the private networks were entirely distinct (that is, if their components were connected together using private dedicated resources) the use of identical address spaces would not be an issue and there would never be a problem distinguishing between two hosts with the same address. However, since IP packets from Company A Site 1 are sent across the Internet to Company A Site 2 there is obvious scope for confusion and misdelivery. How do the routers in the Internet know which is the real intended recipient of the packets?

One answer to this problem lies with tunneling using any form of IP encapsulation. This may be GRE, IP-in-IP, or a data-link layer mechanism such as the Layer 2 Tunneling Protocol (L2TP) or MPLS. So, in Figure 12.1, Sites 1 and 2 of Company B are connected by a tunnel represented by the dashed line. This tunnel could be seen as a virtual wire and some VPN management technologies allow the customers (that is the companies that own the private sites) to manage their connections across the Internet as emulated wires.

In fact, tunneling like this starts to address some of the security issues with VPNs since a properly configured router at the edge of the Internet will guarantee that the packets are kept within their correct tunnels and delivered to the proper remote edge router for decapsulation and delivery to the right private network. However, tunneling on its own does not provide a strong security model since packets within the Internet are still susceptible to interception, and the edge routers can still be misconfigured.

12.1.3 Solutions Using Routing Protocols

A serious concern with layer-two tunneling solutions to VPNs is that they don't scale well. Each tunnel models a wire or physical connection, so if there are *n* sites participating in the VPN there is the need to configure and manage *n(n − 1)/2* connections. An alternative is to provide a single hub node that acts as a clearing house for all data for the VPN—this cuts down the number of links to just *n* but leaves the hub node as a single point of failure that could break connectivity for the whole VPN. These topologies are illustrated in Figure 12.2. This is, of course, no more complex than managing the physical links that were needed in the truly private network, but since we are using the Internet, which is equipped with a host of automatic signaling and routing protocols, surely we can do better.

We most certainly can do better. Using IP tunneling techniques, it is only the end points of the tunnels that are nailed down; the actual paths of the tunnels are left up to the routing protocols within the Internet. Although this may reduce the configuration within the core network, it doesn't reduce the effort at each of the edge nodes. It is still necessary to configure mappings of private destination IP addresses into tunnels—that is, the IP address of the far end of the tunnel must be configured for the address of each node within the VPN. Although this process may be simplified by using suitable subnetworks, the configuration effort is still significant.

This issue can be handled quite elegantly by using the routing protocols that run over the Internet to exchange VPN connectivity information between edge nodes. In short, an edge node can advertise that to reach a certain set of IP addresses within a given VPN other routers should send packets to it.

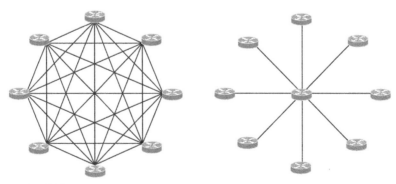

FIGURE 12.2

Full mesh connectivity with tunnels does not scale well, but the hub-and-spokes topology has a single point of failure.

There are two approaches to the use of routing protocols to support VPNs. Each recognizes that the edge nodes (the nodes that provide access from the private networks to the Internet) need to retain separate routing tables for each VPN that they support. This allows a packet from one VPN to be encapsulated and correctly routed across the Internet to the corresponding edge node that will forward it onward within the private network. The routing tables are often called *virtual routing tables* and are distinguished by unique identifiers assigned to each VPN.

The first solution uses a separate instance of a routing protocol to support each virtual routing table. Tunnels are set up between each of the edge points that provide access to the VPNs as before, but the configuration and management of these tunnels is greatly improved by running an Interior Gateway Protocol (IGP) such as OSPF through the tunnels. Each tunnel end point is presented as a virtual interface through which the IGP advertises its routing information. The tunnel appears as a single-hop link between the tunnel end points.

In this way, the full reachability information for the nodes within a VPN is distributed to every node that participates in the VPN, but is not visible within the core of the network and is not sent to nodes that do not participate in the VPN since the IGP only sends its messages on the virtual interfaces (tunnels) configured as part of the VPN.

Since a single edge node may provide access for multiple VPNs, it must keep the routing information for each VPN separate. Additionally, it must keep the VPN information distinct from the normal routing information for the core network. This can be achieved simply by using a distinct routing table for each use—the tables are usually indexed by a VPN identifier. A separate instance of the IGP is used to construct each routing table with each instance running on distinct interface be it a physical interface or a virtual (tunnel) interface. This is illustrated in Figure 12.3.

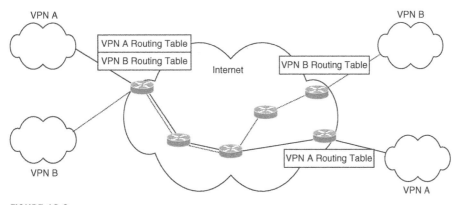

FIGURE 12.3

Separate routing tables are maintained for each VPN using information exchanged by IGPs along tunnels between VPN access nodes.

Distribution of reachability/routing information across a core network is one of the problems that the Border Gateway Protocol was designed to address. The second VPN routing protocol solution utilizes a single instance of BGP to distribute information for all VPNs. This approach is illustrated in Figure 12.4. It extends BGP to allow the inclusion of a VPN identifier in the information distributed. This immediately allows multiple virtual routing tables to be exchanged between all edge nodes, and with the minimum of fuss, VPN connectivity is established.

Note that in both cases, the routing protocol is being used to distribute the addresses of edge nodes that provide access to nodes within the VPN. IP tunneling is still used to deliver VPN packets across the Internet.

12.1.4 **VPN Security Solutions**

IPsec is essentially a tunneling protocol devised to securely transport IP across a public network. IPsec has considerable potential in VPN implementation because it offers a full suite of security features from encryption and authentication to protection against replay. A neat feature of IPsec tunnels is that they are connectionless and do not require that the tunnel end points store any protocol state information (although they do need to manage security information such as keys which may be distributed automatically or configured manually).

On the other hand, IPsec has the performance hit of encrypting all data—but since VPN data security is often a requirement, some form of encryption would likely be performed anyway. Another disadvantage to the use of IPsec is that it is hard to demultiplex data streams from a single IPsec tunnel, so a single tunnel may need to be set up between each pair of VPN nodes that exchange data.

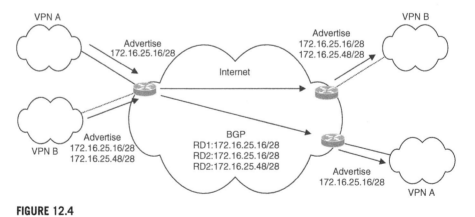

FIGURE 12.4

BGP may use Route Distinguishers to facilitate advertisement of addresses belonging to different VPNs.

Solutions to this second problem involve the use of some other tunneling mechanism in addition to IPsec. IPsec can be applied to the whole tunnel (that is, tunneling the tunnel itself through IPsec) or multiple IPsec tunnels can be multiplexed together into a single tunnel of some other technology.

12.2 **MPLS VPNs**

MPLS can be used to set up tunnels through an MPLS capable network as described earlier in this book.

These tunnels can be used to establish layer 2 VPNs in ATM, Frame Relay, or other MPLS-capable networks. Each tunnel provides a virtual wire between source and destination to connect different parts of the VPN. Alternatively, MPLS packets can be encapsulated in some other tunneling mechanism to allow them to be transported across the IP core network. This second choice may be particularly useful when MPLS is used within the VPN, or when many edge points each provide access to multiple VPNs, and it is desirable to reduce the number of tunnels across the network, as shown in Figure 12.5.

A hybrid VPN solution that utilizes both BGP and MPLS is described in RFC 2547 and is being further developed within the IETF. This solution is scalable and flexible. BGP is used to advertise which edge nodes provide access to which VPNs, the reachability information for addresses in each VPN at each edge node, and an MPLS label used to identify which VPN is targeted. Packets sent across the core are given an MPLS label that allows the receiver to immediately distinguish to which VPN it should deliver the data. As the packets traverse the core they may be encapsulated in IP, GRE, IPsec, or MPLS tunnels. An example of the information distributed for a BGP MPLS VPN is shown in Figure 12.6.

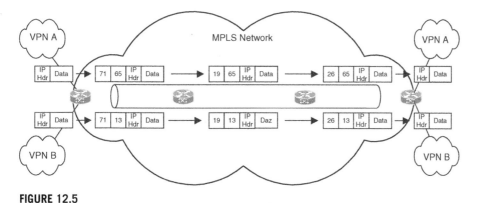

FIGURE 12.5

MPLS may be used to connect multiple VPNs through a single tunnel.

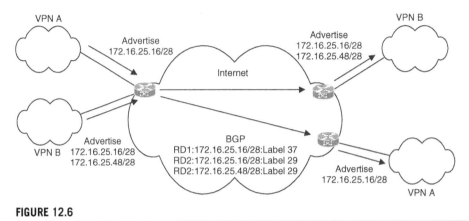

FIGURE 12.6

An example showing the information distributed for a BGP MPLS VPN.

12.2.1 **GMPLS VPNs**

GMPLS VPNs are a new concept originally concerned with the automatic pro-visioning of data services through an optical core. The networks that are being connected together in this case are likely to be fragments of a service provider's whole network. The core network providing the optical connectivity is sometimes referred to as a *service provider's service provider*. GMPLS may be used to estab-lish an Optical VPN and how the core network can be viewed as a single virtual switch switching data between access interfaces.

12.3 **MPLS VPN SECURITY**

Security is clearly an important component for any credible VPN solution. In the area of security, the goal of the BGP/MPLS VPN approach is to achieve security comparable to that provided today by Frame Relay or ATM-based VPNs. Specifically, the goal is to make sure that, in the absence of either deliberate interconnection or misconfiguration, packets from one VPN wouldn't be able to get into another VPN.

To see how we accomplish this goal, first observe that forwarding within a VPN service provider is based on label switching, not on traditional IP forwarding. Therefore, forwarding within the provider is not determined by the IP addresses carried in the packets. Moreover, observe that LSPs associated with VPN-IP routes originate and terminate only at the PE routers—they don't terminate in the mid-dle of a service provider network, and they don't start in the middle of a service provider network. At a PE router, these LSPs are associated with particular for-warding tables, and the forwarding tables are associated (at provisioning time) with interfaces on the PE router. Finally, observe that these interfaces are associ-ated at provisioning time with particular VPNs.

Therefore, when a PE router sends a packet to a CE router that belongs to a particular VPN, this packet has to arrive at the PE router either from another (directly connected) CE router or from some other PE router. In order for this to happen in the former case, both of the CE routers have to be within the same VPN and have to share the same forwarding table on the CE router. In the latter case, the packet has to be forwarded to the PE router via an LSP associated with a particular forwarding table, where the table is associated with the VPN at provisioning time via configuration. The LSP has to originate at some other PE; on that other PE, the LSP is associated with a particular forwarding table, and that table (via configuration) is associated with a particular VPN. On that other PE, in order for the packet to be forwarded via the forwarding table associated with the VPN, the packet has to arrive at that PE on an interface that is associated (via configuration) with that VPN. As a result, in the absence of misconfiguration, injecting the packet into a VPN could be done only through an interface on a PE router that is associated with that VPN. It therefore follows that packets cannot be maliciously or accidentally injected into some VPN to which the sender does not belong, just as in an ATM or Frame Relay network.

12.4 **QOS SUPPORT IN MPLS VPNs**

A VPN is defined by a set of administrative policies that control both connectivity and Quality of Service (QoS) among sites. In this section we look at the mechanisms that a service provider would use to implement the QoS aspects of the policies in an MPLS VPN. MPLS QoS is discussed in Chapter 6.

In the area of QoS, the challenge is to develop a set of mechanisms that supports QoS in a way that is flexible enough to support a wide range of VPN customers and scalable enough to support a large number of VPN customers. For example, a service provider should be able to offer its VPN customers multiple Classes of Service per VPN, where different applications within the same VPN would receive different Classes of Service. This way, for example, email would get one Class of Service while some real-time application could get a completely different Class of Service. Moreover, the Class of Service that a particular application would get within one VPN could be quite different from the Class of Service that precisely the same application would get within another VPN. That is, the set of mechanisms in support of QoS should allow the decision about what traffic gets a specific Class of Service to be made on a per-VPN basis. Moreover, not all VPNs have to use all the Classes of Service that a VPN service provider offers. Therefore, the set of mechanisms in support of QoS should allow the decision on which Class of Service to use to be made on a per-VPN basis.

Before describing specific mechanisms used by BGP/MPLS VPN to support QoS, we first look at two models that are used to describe QoS in the context of VPNs—the "pipe" model and the "hose" model.

In the pipe model a VPN service provider supplies a VPN customer with certain QoS guarantees for the traffic from one customer's CE router to another. In a sense you could represent this model by a "pipe" that connects the two routers, and the traffic that enters this pipe gets certain QoS guarantees. One example of the sort of QoS guarantees that could be provided with the pipe model is some guaranteed minimum bandwidth between two sites.

You could further refine the pipe model by making only a subset of all the traffic (e.g., only specific applications) from one CE to another CE able to use the pipe. The ultimate decision on what traffic could use the pipe is purely local to the PE router at the head end of the pipe.

Note that the pipe model is very similar (but not identical) to the QoS model that VPN customers have today with Frame Relay or ATM-based solutions. The essential difference is that with Frame Relay or ATM the connection is bidirectional, whereas the pipe model offers unidirectional guarantees. The fact that the pipe is unidirectional allows for asymmetry with respect to the traffic pattern, whereby the amount of traffic from one site to another may be different from the amount of traffic in the reverse direction.

As an illustration, consider the example shown in Figure 12.7, where a service provider supplies VPN A with one pipe that guarantees 7 Mb/sec of bandwidth for the traffic from Site 3 to Site 1 (to be more precise, from CE_{A3} to CE_{A1}) and another pipe that guarantees 10 Mb/sec of bandwidth for the traffic from Site 3 to Site 2 (from CE_{A3} to CE_{A2}). Observe that a given CE router may have more than one pipe originating from it (e.g., two pipes originate from Site 3). Likewise, more than one pipe may terminate at a given site.

One advantage of the pipe model is that it bears a great deal of similarity to the QoS model that VPN customers use today with Frame Relay or ATM. Therefore,

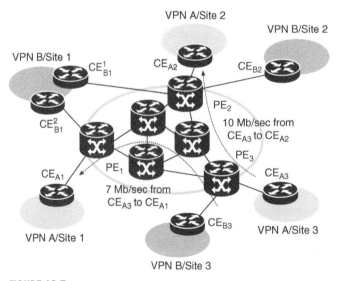

FIGURE 12.7

QoS pipe model-example.

it is easily understood by customers. However, the pipe model has several draw-backs as well. For one thing, it assumes that a VPN customer knows its complete traffic matrix. That is, for every site, the customer must know the amount of traf-fic that goes from that site to every other site. Quite often this information is not available and, even if available, could be outdated.

In the hose model, a VPN service provider supplies a VPN customer with cer-tain guarantees for the traffic that the customer's CE router sends to and receives from other CE routers of the same VPN. In neither case does the customer have to specify how this traffic is distributed among the other CE routers. As as result, in contrast to the pipe model, the hose model does not require a customer to know its traffic matrix, which, in turn, places less burden on a customer that wants to use the VPN service.

The hose model uses two parameters, Ingress Committed Rate (ICR) and Egress Committed Rate (ECR). The ICR is the amount of traffic that a particular CE could send to other CEs, while the ECR is the amount of traffic that a particular CE could receive from other CEs. In other words, the ICR represents the aggregate amount of traffic from a particular CE, while the ECR represents the aggregate amount of traffic to a particular CE. Note that, for a given CE, there is no require-ment that its ICR should be equal to its ECR.

To illustrate the hose model, consider the example shown in Figure 12.8, where a service provider supplies VPN B with certain guarantees of up to 15 Mb/sec for the traffic that Site 2 sends to other sites (ICR = 15 Mb/sec), regardless of whether this traffic goes to Site 1 or to Site 3 or is distributed (in an arbitrary way) between Site 1 and Site 3. Likewise, the service provider supplies VPN B with certain

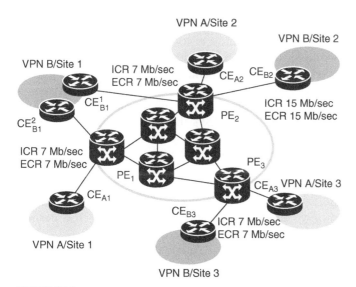

FIGURE 12.8

QoS hose model-an example.

guarantees of up to 7 Mb/sec for the traffic that Site 3 sends to other sites in that VPN (ICR = 7 Mb/sec), regardless of whether this traffic goes to Site 1, or to Site 2, or is distributed (in arbitrary way) among Site 1 and Site 2. Similarly, the provider provides VPN B with certain guarantees of up to 15 Mb/sec for the traffic that other sites send to Site 2 (ECR = 15 Mb/sec), regardless of whether this traffic originates from Site 1 or Site 3, or is distributed (in arbitrary way) among Site 1 and Site 3.

Note that the hose model closely resembles the IP Diff-Serv model. This model supports multiple Classes of Service, with the services differing from each other in their relative performance characteristics; for example, one service might have lower packet losses than another service. For the services that require "hard" guarantees (e.g., guaranteed bandwidth), the pipe model is a better fit. Note that the pipe model is closer to the IP int-serv model.

The pipe and hose models are not mutually exclusive. That is, a service provider should be able to offer to a VPN customer a combination of the hose and the pipe models, and it should be up to the customer to decide which service to buy and which traffic should be getting a particular Class of Service.

To support the pipe model, we use guaranteed bandwidth LSPs. These LSPs originate and terminate at the PE routers and are used to provide guaranteed bandwidth for all the pipes from one PE router to another. That is, for a given pair of PE routers, there may be multiple CE routers attached to those PE routers that have pipes between them, and rather than using a guaranteed bandwidth LSP for each such pipe, we use a single guaranteed bandwidth LSP for all of them.

For example, in Figure 12.7 there may be one pipe for VPN A from CE_{A3} to CE_{A1} and another pipe for VPN B from CE_{B3} to CE_{B1}. To support these two pipes, we establish a single guaranteed bandwidth LSP from PE_3 to PE_1 and reserve on that LSP the amount of bandwidth equal to the sum of the bandwidth of the two pipes. When PE_3 receives a packet from CE_{A3} and the packet is destined to some host in Site 1 of VPN A, PE_3 determines under control of its local configuration whether the packet should receive the guaranteed bandwidth Class of Service. If so, then PE_3 forwards the packet along the guaranteed bandwidth LSP from PE_3 to PE_1.

Using a single guaranteed bandwidth LSP to carry multiple pipes between a pair of PE routers improves the scaling properties of the solution. This is because the number of such guaranteed bandwidth LSPs that a service provider has to establish and maintain is bound (from above) by the number of PE router pairs of that service provider, rather than by the number of pipes the VPN customers of that provider could have.

To support Classes of Service that fall into the hose model, a service provider uses Diff-Serv support with MPLS. The service provider may also use MPLS traffic engineering to improve network utilization while meeting the desired performance objectives.

The procedures by which an ingress PE router determines which traffic receives a particular Class of Service, regardless of whether that Class of Service falls into the hose or the pipe model, are purely local to that PE router. These procedures can take into account such factors as incoming interface, IP source and destination addresses, IP precedence, TCP port numbers, or any combination of the above. This gives a service provider significant flexibility with respect to control over what traffic gets a particular Class of Service.

Although a customer signs a contract with a service provider for a certain amount of traffic in a particular Class of Service, the customer may send traffic in excess of this amount. To determine whether the traffic is within the contract, the service provider uses policing at the ingress PE routers. For traffic that is out of contract, the provider has two options: either to discard this traffic immediately, at the ingress PE router, or to send the traffic, but mark it differently from the traffic that is in contract. With the second option, in order to reduce out-of-order delivery, both in- and out-of-contract traffic should be forwarded along the same LSP. The out-of-contract traffic is marked differently, and this marking affects the drop probability in case of congestion.

Within the service provider network, the P routers may use Diff-Serv PHBs for service differentiation. Note that the P routers need only maintain queuing state on an aggregate (e.g., per-PHB) basis, rather than on a per-VPN basis.

12.5 CHOOSING A VPN TECHNOLOGY

VPNs are one of the biggest growth areas within the Internet. The solutions described in the preceding sections are only some of the popular approaches, and there are probably more methods available than there are vendors selling VPN-enabled equipment. As might be expected, the debate over which solutions provide the best connectivity, security, ease of maintenance, and speed of provisioning is highly colored by the implementations that the vendors have to offer, and is not necessarily influenced by reality.

Nevertheless, one of the most important factors in choosing a VPN technology must be its availability in proven and tested equipment. Table 12.1 lists some of the more important considerations when building a VPN and highlights which solutions are strongest for each feature.

Perhaps the most hotly debated topic is scalability. How much extra configuration is required? How much additional routing or signaling information must be exchanged? This issue affects the question of whose responsibility it is to maintain the VPN since the service provider's customers would like to buy VPN services without the need to configure their own equipment, yet they do not trust their service providers to protect their data from misdelivery or from hackers. Many tunneling solutions can be implemented by the Customer Edge (CE) equipment or by the Provider Edge (PE) equipment, further widening the choice.

12.5.1 The Benefits of MPLS VPNs

MPLS VPNs bring several benefits to the service provider and helps to create new services. VPNs provide data security and ensure that the network is isolated from

Table 12.1 A Comparison of Some VPN Technologies.

	Layer Two Tunneling	IP Tunneling	IPsec	MPLS	Virtual Router	BGP	BGP/MPLS
Customer Equipment Needs to Be Aware of VPN	Yes	Yes if CE manages tunnels, no if PE owns tunnels	Yes	No	No	No	No
Customer Equipment Needs to Be Configured for VPN	Yes	Yes if CE manages tunnels, no if PE owns tunnels	Yes	No	No	No	No
Network Equipment Needs to Be Aware of VPN	No	No if CE manages tunnels, yes if PE owns tunnels	No	Yes	Yes	Yes	Yes
Scalability at Provider Edge	Good	Moderate if CE manages tunnels, poor if PE owns tunnels	Moderate	Moderate	Poor	Moderate	Moderate
Data Security	Some based on integrity of hardware	None	Good	Some based on integrity of hardware	None	None	Some based on integrity of hardware
Traffic Engineering in the Network	No	Limited with DiffServ	No	Yes	Limited with DiffServ	Limited with DiffServ	Yes

other networks. Communication with other networks (e.g., the Internet) is done in a controlled manner. Traditionally, VPNs implement these features by using separate Layer 2 networks. This does not make it scalable for the service provider because the core network can no longer be shared among several services.

Scalable Core Network

MPLS VPNs help the service provider to implement multiple VPNs using the same core network by ensuring that the traffic from the different VPNs is isolated, even though all of these VPNs are implemented using the same core network. Moreover, the Routing Information Base (RIB) of the VPN is independent from the RIB of the core network. This also makes the core network scalable.

The intelligence is implemented in the PE routers. They maintain a separate RIB for each VPN. This helps to implement VPNs that have overlapping address space and still make use of the same core network. Figure 12.9 shows an example of how the MPLS VPN method helps to implement VPNs that can share the same core network and how these VPNs can have overlapping address space. The dotted VPN and the dashed VPN use the same address space. The PE routers PE1 and PE2 maintain separate FIBs for each VPN and ensure the isolation between the VPNs. The core routers Pl and P2 do not have any information about the VPNs in their FIBs. The core routers forward the VPN traffic based on the core label, and the VPN label is transparent to the core routers. The PE router inserts two labels to the IP packet before forwarding it to the core router. The inner label is the VPN label and is used by the PE routers; the outer label is the MPLS label that is used by the core routers to switch the packets to the PE router.

For example, for the traffic flowing from CE~ to CE2 (dotted VPN), P1 forwards this traffic based on the label for router PE2. For the traffic flowing from CE3 to CE4 (dashed VPN), P1 also forwards this traffic based on the label for router PE2. The inner label (VPN label) is transparent to the routers P~ and P2 and is used only by PE2. Irrespective of the number of routes connected to dotted VPN or dashed VPN or the number of VPNs connected to the PE routers, P1 and P2 forward traffic based on the labels for the PE routers. This makes the core routers stable and also scalable.

Security

Isolation of traffic between VPNs is implemented in the PE router. Only the PE routers have knowledge about the VPNs; they maintain a separate RIB for each VPN. The VPN labels are used to distinguish between packets from different VPNs. Unique labels are used to distinguish IP packets from different VPNs. This ensures that IP packets are delivered to the correct VPNs. For example, in Figure 12.9, the networks 11.0.0.0/24 belonging to the dotted VPN and the dashed VPN are connected to the router PE2. PE2 advertises the following labels to other PEs:

VPN label 1, for network 11.0.0.0/24 belonging to the dotted VPN
VPN label 2, for network 11.0.0.0/24 belonging to the dashed VPN

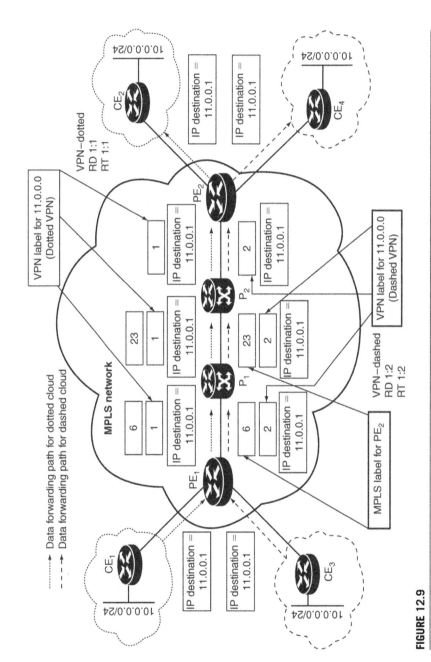

FIGURE 12.9

VPNs using the MPLS VPN method.

When PE1 receives a packet from CE3 that is destined for 11.0.0.1, it knows that traffic coming from CE3 belongs to the dashed VPN. It imposes the VPN label 2 and MPLS label 6 onto the IP packet and forwards it to P1. P1 and P2 forward the packets based on the MPLS label. When the packet arrives at PE2, it sees the VPN label 2 and knows that this label is for the dashed VPN and forwards the packet to CE4.

Extranets and Intranets

Other services that can be easily implemented using MPLS VPNs are extranets, intranets, and selective connectivity between intranets. Traditionally, extranets are implemented using policy routing, but it makes the life of the network administrator a nightmare to maintain all of the policies. Using MPLS-VPN, this can be done in a simple and easy manner. By selectively allowing certain routes to be leaked from a VPN to another VPN, it is possible to create extranets and connectivity between intranets. Firewalls can be implemented between intranets.

A typical application of extranets in the context of a large company would be in the data center where all of the servers are located. Some of the servers are dedicated to each department, and some of the common servers can be accessed by a group of departments. This can be easily implemented by creating a VPN for each department. The common servers are placed on a separate VPN (server VPN). The department VPNs cannot directly communicate with each other, but have access to the server VPN. Figure 12.10 shows the implementation of extranets.

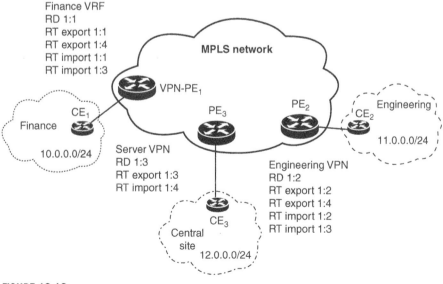

FIGURE 12.10

Extranets using an MPLS VPN.

Pseudowires

The concept of establishing a tunnel across a packet network to provide connectivity for a another network is familiar and produces virtual links in that other network. If the client network operates below the packet layer (that is, it is a sub-packet technology) and the server network is a packet network (IP or MPLS), the resulting virtual link is known as a *pseudowire*.

There is some slight confusion about the naming at this point. Sometimes a pseudowire is named by the service it provides—so that an SDH pseudowire is a virtual link in an SDH network provided by some packet network. Sometimes a pseudowire is named by the technology that provides the connectivity—so that an MPLS pseudowire utilizes an MPLS network to provide connectivity to some other network. Because this book is about MPLS, we shall adopt the former naming convention.

We should note that all pseudowires, by definition, constitute a form of layer inversion. That is, they tunnel a lower layer protocol over a higher layer (MPLS, in the cases of interest here). For example, an Ethernet pseudowire can be implemented over an MPLS LSP and connects two Ethernet switches; it is presented to those switches as a single hop Ethernet link that is accessed through Ethernet interfaces. Pseudowires can be constructed for any sub-MPLS technology that can be "packetized," that is, for any signal that can be reduced to packets for transport across the MPLS network and then reassembled to reconstruct the original signal with no nontrivial loss of information. At the moment, pseudowires are defined for Ethernet, Frame Relay, ATM, HDLC, bit-stream, and TDM (SONET/SDH). They have not been defined for all layer 1 technologies—no mechanism has yet been proposed to suitably packetize lambda signals, for example. Note that higher layer technologies that are already packetized (for example IP, or MPLS itself) can also be carried over MPLS networks by LSPs that are presented as single hops in the higher layer network, but these LSPs and the encapsulation of the payload signals that they require are just business as usual for the MPLS network—the LSPs are referred to as virtual links, hierarchical LSPs, or forwarding adjacencies (as described elsewhere in this book) and are not discussed further here.

Pseudowires are a booming market sector for MPLS equipment vendors and for network operators. They are typically used to connect disjoint network segments of legacy network technologies and form an essential part of migration strategies, allowing legacy services to be continued as underlying network technologies are changed.

This chapter provides an overview of the MPLS network architecture for pseudowire support and examines the two principal challenges: how to encapsulate payload data within a pseudowire; and how to set up and manage a pseudowire in an MPLS network. A final section examines the emerging topic of multisegment pseudowires.

13.1 PSEUDOWIRE ARCHITECTURE

The pseudowire architecture defined by the IETF is documented in RFC 3985 and illustrated in Figure 13.1. The customer networks operate some native service (maybe Ethernet, maybe TDM) and the customer edge (CE) equipment at each site needs to be connected by a native link. An emulated service is required between CE and CE.

The CEs are not MPLS-capable and do not play a part in the MPLS network. They have access connections to the PEs of the MPLS network, and those connections operate the native service. At some level, although the access connections connect the CEs to the provider edge (PE) equipment, the CEs and the wider customer network believe that the access connections provide direct connectivity between the two CEs. It is this illusion of a direct CE-CE connection that gives rise to the name "pseudowire."

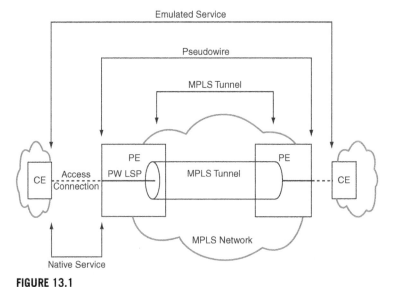

FIGURE 13.1

The pseudowire architecture.

Within the MPLS network, the PEs set up a pseudowire LSP (shown in the figure as "PW LSP") to carry the packetized traffic from one access connection and to deliver it on to the access connection at the far end of the pseudowire. The PEs are responsible for generating the MPLS packets and for converting them back into the native signal format. Other LSRs in the network do not need to understand or even know that the pseudowire LSP is carrying pseudowire traffic—they just handle it as any other LSP.

Finally, the pseudowire LSP is usually tunneled through the network over another LSP. This provides scaling advantages because more than one pseudowire LSP can be carried by a single tunnel. The tunnel might also be a traffic engineering LSP, enabling the advantages of TE (such as constraint-based routing, quality of service guarantees, fast reroute, etc.) to be provided to the pseudowires.

13.2 PSEUDOWIRE ENCAPSULATION

One of the key aspects of a pseudowire is how the native signal is taken from the access connection and placed into MPLS packets for transmission through the MPLS network. Figure 13.2 shows how the data protocols are arranged for normal encapsulation of a payload in an MPLS network—the payload data is encapsulated

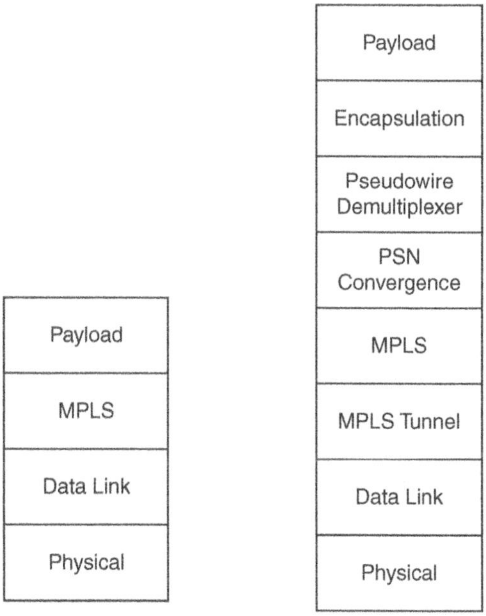

FIGURE 13.2

The protocol stack for a pseudowire in an MPLS network with the normal protocol stack for an MPLS LSP for comparison.

in an MPLS shim header, and this is carried in data link and physical layer encapsulations to deliver the traffic. The figure also shows the considerably more complicated protocol stack for a pseudowire with the following encapsulations of the payload:

- Encapsulation layer. The encapsulation layer is responsible for presenting the payload data for transmission. It can add extra information, not present in the payload itself, needed by the destination PS to send the payload on the physical access connection interface to the CE. If real-time synchronization support is needed, this is included in the encapsulation layer, but if no function is needed, this layer is empty.

- Pseudowire demultiplexer. Multiple pseudowires LSPs can be carried down a single MPLS tunnel and demultiplexed by their labels, but it is also possible to carry multiple pseudowires down a single pseudowire LSP if all of the pseudowires are for the same type of emulated service. In this case, a demultiplexer is required so that it is possible for the destination PE to assign the received packets to the right pseudowire and deliver the traffic on the correct access connection.

- PSN convergence. This layer provides any additional function that is necessary to enhance the MPLS network's ability to provide the right level of service for correct emulation of the native service. For some native services, the MPLS network already provides the right level of function, and this layer is empty.

- MPLS pseudowire LSP. The pseudowire LSP causes an MPLS shim header to be inserted in the label stack. The label identifies the pseudowire and is present at the bottom of the label stack (that is, the S-bit is set in the shim header).

- MPLS tunnel. If an MPLS tunnel is used, it introduces an additional MPLS shim header to carry the label for the LSP tunnel. This represents the top label on the label stack.

- Data link layer. The data link layer encapsulation performs just as for normal MPLS traffic.

- Physical layer. The physical layer performs just as for normal MPLS traffic.

13.2.1 Packetizing Data

Data is packetized (converted and encapsulated into packets) differently depending on the native format. Data that is already in packets (Ethernet, Frame Relay, HDLC, and AAL5 ATM PDUs) when it is received on the access connection can simply be presented as a packet for MPLS encapsulation. If the native format has padding or transmission overhead, this can be stripped at the head-end of the pseudowire and recreated at the tail end because it serves no purpose to transmit it across the MPLS network. Note that it is possible that the packets received on the access connection are too large for transmission within a single MPLS packet.

In this case the packet must be fragmented, but the technique used does not need to conform to the fragmentation rules of the native network so long as the data can be successfully reconstructed at the end of the pseudowire without changing its appearance in the native network.

Data that is presented on the access connection in cells (ATM data not in an AAL5 PDU) could be mapped to packets on a one-for-one basis, but this might make very inefficient use of the MPLS network. It is also possible, therefore, to buffer received cells and carry multiple cells in a single MPLS packet, but care has to be taken so as not to introduce cell delay to sensitive application streams. Some form of real-time support might be needed in the encapsulation layer to handle cell flows.

If the access connection is treated as a bit stream, then MPLS packets can be filled without regard to any framing in the payload. As with cell-based data, care might need to be taken not to introduce excessive delay to the data, and some form of real-time support might be needed in the encapsulation layer.

TDM access connections can be regarded as "structured bit streams." This means that the packetizing function can take advantage of knowledge of the framing within the bit stream to enhance the production of packets, make the job of the destination PE more simple (by preserving the framing), and discard any bits that do not need to be transmitted (for example, the section and line overhead). Some information, such as pointer justifications for SONET and real-time controls, can be included in the encapsulation layer.

13.2.2 The MPLS Control Word

One final note is needed about data encapsulation in MPLS LSPs. MPLS does not provide any protocol identifier to allow the receiver to distinguish what protocol payload is carried in an LSP. In theory this is fine if the LSP runs between two consenting LSRs that know to what use the LSP is put, and if the LSP carries only one sort of data (e.g., IPv4). But pseudowires might break this convention, and it is useful to be able to determine the payload type by inspecting the data itself.

In RFC 4385, the IETF has defined a control word for MPLS networks. This word is inserted in the data as the first four octets found immediately after the final MPLS shim header in the label stack. The structure and use of the control word rely on knowledge of the structure of the IP header for IPv4 and IPv6. In both of these protocols, the first nibble of the IP header identifies the IP version (0x4 and 0x6, respectively). Thus, the first nibble of the control word is used to identify the use to which the LSP is put; the values 4 and 6 are reserved, while the value 0 is defined to mean that the LSP is a pseudowire, and the value 1 defines an "associated channel" carrying data associated with the provision of a pseudowire but not forming part of the payload data. Other identifying first nibbles might be defined in the future.

The remainder of the control word is available to carry other information specific to the pseudowire encapsulation and might (to make efficient use of the bytes on the wire) mean that some of the protocol stack information is presented out of order.

13.3 PSEUDOWIRE CONTROL AND ESTABLISHMENT

Pseudowires, like any other MPLS LSP, can be created manually by provisioning the labels in the LSRs and defining the forwarding rules from an NMS. It is more convenient and less error prone to use a signaling protocol to set up the pseudowires. The IETF has selected LDP as the pseudowire control protocol, and in RFC 4447 it has made some small enhancements to the protocol elements to convey the additional information needed for this purpose.

The main objectives are to exchange the MPLS label that will be used to disambiguate the pseudowire from any other pseudowires carried in the MPLS tunnel, and to negotiate the parameters that define what the pseudowire LSP is used for and how the data is packetized and encapsulated.

Pseudowire labels are distributed by LDP using the standard downstream unsolicited mode of label distribution. This means that pseudowires are effectively established from their destination points toward their sources. Any further coordination of this process is outside the scope of LDP, but it can be assumed to be performed by the NMS.

The FEC encoding on the LDP Label Mapping message is enhanced to allow the FEC to describe the pseudowire as well as the source and destination addresses. With this simple modification, the Label Mapping message is restricted to a specific pseudowire rather than an address-based flow.

Only a few other minor modifications to LDP are required to define new error codes and a pseudowire status TLV for inclusion on the Notification message.

13.4 MULTISEGMENT PSEUDOWIRES

A new area of work is the multisegment pseudowire. The need for this type of service arises where there is a need to set up an end-to-end pseudowire across multiple network domains. Consider the architecture diagram in Figure 13.3. The same end-to-end construct of an emulated service is required, but the intervening MPLS network is broken into separate networks (in the example shown, these networks are separate routing areas, but they could equally be separate ASs). The MPLS tunnels are limited in this case to intradomain tunnels, so the pseudowire LSP emerges from the tunnel and is terminated only part way to its destination.

We define a terminating PE (T-PE) as one of the two PEs at the ends of the end-to-end multisegment pseudowire, and a switching PE (S-PE) is defined as any transit LSR that terminates an MPLS tunnel that carries pseudowires. We construct pseudowire segments as normal pseudowires between T-PEs and S-PEs across the network, and we concatenate these segments to form an end-to-end multisegment pseudowire.

It would not be unreasonable to consider the job of the S-PE to be to switch the payload data at the native level. That is, the pseudowire segment is terminated, and that means that the payload is available for switching. But this would mean

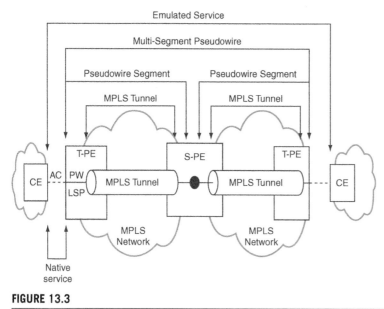

FIGURE 13.3

The multisegment pseudowire architecture.

that transit LSRs (in this case an ABR) would need to understand all potential encapsulation techniques and native payload switching paradigms. It makes far more sense, therefore, simply to stitch together the pseudowire LSPs by popping the label at the end of one LSP and immediately forwarding the payload packets into the next pseudowire LSP by imposing a new label.

In the case of a multi-AS environment, the architecture picture is only slightly modified. Instead of a single S-PE linking the two MPLS networks in the figure, there would be two S-PEs (these are the ASBRs) with an inter-S-PE link between them. The end-to-end multisegment pseudowire in this case is made up of three pseudowire segments rather than two, with the third segment running between the two ASBRs.

The multisegment pseudowire environment immediately opens up questions of routing and traffic engineering in a new network layer that could be called the "pseudowire segment layer." In establishing an end-to-end multisegment pseudowire, some decisions must be made about which tunnels to traverse and which transit S-PEs to use. In the future this might give rise to the invention of further LDP extensions to allow explicit paths to be encoded and quality of service parameters to be specified. Experts in ancient history might be reminded of CR-LDP!

Multidomain Networking

Establishing LSPs across domain boundaries provides a special challenge for the control plane and particularly for the signaling protocol. This chapter examines solutions to these challenges using some material from *GMPLS: Architecture and Applications* by Farrel and Bryskin.

A domain in the MPLS-TE and GMPLS context is considered to be any collection of network elements within a common sphere of address management or path computational responsibility. So, for example, a domain can be defined by the administrative boundaries within the network where those boundaries might lie between Service Providers or between subdivisions of a Service Provider's network. Examples of such domains include Autonomous Systems and IGP areas, but recall that there is a separation between the control plane and the data plane so that any division of either the control plane or the data plane can create a domain.

In practice, there are two important features that determine the relevance of a domain boundary:

1. Can the signaling message be routed to the next signaling controller?
2. Is it possible to compute the next data plane hop toward the destination?

Thus, it is most convenient to define a domain as a zone of routing and computational capability; a domain boundary is the point beyond which a signaling controller cannot see well enough to be able to reliably route a control message or compute the path of an LSP.

Signaling offers a core feature to help handle domains: the explicit path loose hop. Using loose hops, the ingress LSR can indicate a set of abstract nodes along the desired path (for example, the domains, or the domain border nodes, and the destination), but not specify the intervening hops. The details of the path are filled in when possible, usually at a domain border node.

Three additional tools enhance the ability to signal across multiple domains in MPLS-TE and GMPLS. The first allows an ingress to specify exclusions from a path. This is useful because, when only a loose hop is used in the explicit path, the ingress has no other way to restrict which links and nodes are included within the path. If, for example, the ingress knows that a particular link is unreliable, or if it is aware of the path of another LSP that supports the same service, it might wish to inform the downstream LSRs that will expand the loose hops of the links and nodes to avoid. This is done by the inclusion of a new message object which provides a global list of links and nodes to exclude (the Exclude Route object), or by the inclusion of special exclusion subobjects within the Explicit Route object.

The second utility adds support for crankback routing within GMPLS signaling. Crankback routing is not new—it has been used in PNNI and TDM networks. It facilitates "trial and error" progression of signaling messages across a multidomain network. When an LSP setup request is blocked because of the unavailability of suitable resources on a path toward the destination, an error report is returned with a description of the problem. A new path computation can be attempted excluding the blocking links, nodes, or domains. Note that the use of crankback routing within a single domain approximates to random-walk routing and is not recommended, and the same can be said of a path that crosses many domains.

Hierarchical (nested) and stitched LSPs provide the third building block for support of interdomain LSPs.

Another solution to the computation of the path of an interdomain LSP is provided by the Path Computation Element (PCE).

14.1 END-TO-END SIGNALING TECHNIQUES

RSVP-TE signaling (see Chapter 3) allows a user to specify the explicit path of an LSP and have the control plane establish the LSP through the network. However, when the LSP traverses multiple domains, it can be hard for the user to determine the path through anything apart from the initial domain.

Alternatively, the user can rely on the network devices to select a suitable path through the network. In this case, the usual mode of operation is for the ingress (that is, the head-end) LSR to compute a full end-to-end path across the network using some form of Constrained Shortest Path First (CSPF) algorithm, such as modified Dijkstra. In the multidomain environment this is impossible because, as we have defined a domain, the ingress LSR does not have path computation capabilities outside its own domain.

This section describes several techniques that can be used to address these issues.

14.1.1 Loose Hops and Per-Domain Path Computation

The desired route of an LSP is carried in an Explicit Route Object (ERO) in RSVP-TE. The ERO encodes the sequence of hops (network nodes or links) that must be traversed by the LSP. The ERO can state that the hops must be traversed in the specified order without intervening LSRs (*strict hops*), or it can be a series of links and nodes that must be traversed in the specified order but which can have intervening hops if the computation algorithm generates them (*loose hops*). This is achieved by flagging each hop in the explicit path as either strict or loose.

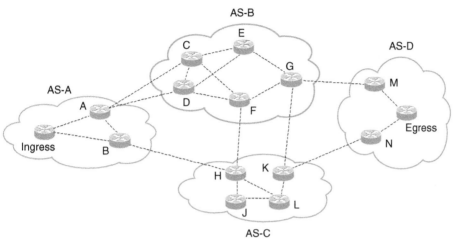

AS-B

E

C

AS-D

G

M

AS-A

A

D

F

Egress

N

Ingress

B

K

H

J

L

AS-C

FIGURE 14.1

Per-domain path computation.

The ERO can also contain nonspecific hops. These can be expressed as IP prefixes (allowing the choice of a range of addresses), or Autonomous System (AS) numbers (letting the route find its way through a distinct domain). Such nonspecific hops can be marked loose or strict according to whether they must be reached direct or can be arrived at indirectly from the previous hop, and multiple nodes within the nonspecific hop can be used before the next hop is used regardless of whether the next hop is strict or loose.

In practice, the network tends to be divided into *computation domains*. If the operator or application does not supply a full explicit path to the destination, then the first LSR in the computation domain will compute a full path to the end of the domain (which might be the egress of the LSP). This means that it is highly unusual to see LSPs signaled with no explicit route, and where loose hops are used, it is usually to identify a sequence of computation domains (perhaps by specifying the address of the entry point into each domain). This mode of operation is termed "per-domain path computation" within the IETF and is illustrated in Figure 14.1. In this example we want an LSP from the ingress LSR in autonomous system AS-A to the egress LSR in AS-D. The ingress LSR can only compute a path within AS-A, but it can know (through configured policy preferences) that a path through AS-B is preferred to one that uses AS-C. So the ingress can construct an explicit path that looks like:

- ingress
- node-A (strict)
- AS-B (strict)
- AS-D (loose)
- egress (loose)

Note that there are two possible connections from LSR A to AS-B. With the explicit route specified as above, the choice of link to the second AS is made by LSR A. If the ingress wants to control this choice, it must include an additional hop in the explicit path to either encode the link:

- link-AC (strict)

or to encode the first LSR in the next AS:

- node-C (strict)

Now, when the RSVP-TE Path message reaches LSR C and requests an LSP, the only information left in the explicit route is:

- node-C (strict)
- AS-B (strict)
- AS-D (loose)
- egress (loose)

LSR C must compute a path across AS-B toward AS-D. This process is repeated when the message reaches LSR M in AS-D. Thus, the LSP is signaled in one end-to-end signaling exchange, but the path of the LSP is computed in a per-domain fashion.

14.1.2 Path Exclusions

Suppose that the ingress node in the example in Figure 14.1 is strongly opposed to its LSP traversing AS-C. As already described, it can choose the next AS in the path (AS-B), but this does not prevent the selection of the path {Ingress,A,C,F,H,L, K,N,Egress}. That is, the ingress has not exerted control over the choice of downstream ASs.

The ingress can attempt some additional control of the path through the use of strict hops. For example, AS-D could be specified as a strict hop so that AS-B may not route the LSP to any other AS. However, in practice, the ingress might not want to exert such regimented control that would prevent AS-B from selecting other transit ASs.

To gain the appropriate level of control, the ingress is allowed to specify a list of path exclusions. This list looks much like an explicit route, but it is interpreted as a set of hops that must not be used anywhere along the path. The list can be nodes, links, or ASs. In our example, the ingress LSR could supply an exclusion list like any of the following (or any combination of these):

- AS-C
- node-H, node-K
- link-FH, link-GK

Path exclusions can be used to avoid domains or specific links or nodes. This means that they can provide a very fine granularity of control to an ingress LSR even when that LSR is not responsible for computing the path of the whole LSP.

14.1.3 **Crankback Routing**

During LSP establishment there is always the risk of a race condition. The path of the LSP is computed using the most recent TE information available from the routing protocol, but by the time the signaling message is propagated through the network, the resource (i.e., bandwidth) has been used to support another LSP or some link has failed.

When this problem arises in a single domain network, the error is returned to the ingress LSR, which computes a new path (excluding the failed link or node) and signaling is reattempted. But when the LSP is a multidomain LSP, it is not necessary to propagate the error back to the ingress—the problem can be resolved at some other computation point in the per-domain fashion.

Consider our example in Figure 14.1. Suppose the path for our end-to-end LSP is computed on entry to AS-B by LSR-C as {C,E,G,M,AS-D,egress} but that when the RSVP-TE Path message reaches LSR-E, the link EG is determined to have failed. Under normal RSVP-TE rules, this would cause a PathErr error message to be returned to the ingress LSR that would recompute and resignal. This is not only inefficient, but the key failure information might be lost by the time the new signaling attempt reaches LSR-C, resulting in a second attempt being made using the same impossible path (although route exclusions could be used to help with this as described in Section 14.1.2).

Crankback routing allows the computation point (LSR-C) to intercept the PathErr message and, instead of forwarding it toward the ingress LSR, it can have a further attempt at computing the path from that point toward the egress excluding the link EG, and if the computation is successful, to resume signaling from that midpoint. In our example, this would give rise to the LSP {ingress,A,C,F,G,M,egress}.

Now suppose further that when the RSVP-TE Path message reaches LSR-M it discovers that it cannot install the LSP on the link M-egress because there is insufficient bandwidth available. LSR-M could report a failure to its upstream neighbor (LSR-G) saying that the link M-egress is unavailable, but this would be of no use outside AS-D because no one outside the AS knows (or cares) about the connectivity within the AS. Instead, LSR-M reports that LSR-M itself is unsuitable for inclusion on the path. This information is propagated in a PathErr back up the route of the LSP and is intercepted by LSR-C.

If LSR-C has free choice of AS paths (that is, if the explicit path only lists AS-D as a loose hop and AS-C is not excluded) then it can compute a new path, perhaps using the link GK. On the other hand, if the original Path message constrained the choices available to LSR-C, either by requiring the inclusion of LSR-M on the path or by insisting that AS-C must be excluded, then LSR-C must forward the PathErr back to the ingress. The ingress then has the option to relax the constraints and try again.

14.2 **LSP HIERARCHIES**

Hierarchical LSPs are LSPs that are used to define data links that traverse the network between nodes that are not necessarily physically adjacent but, rather,

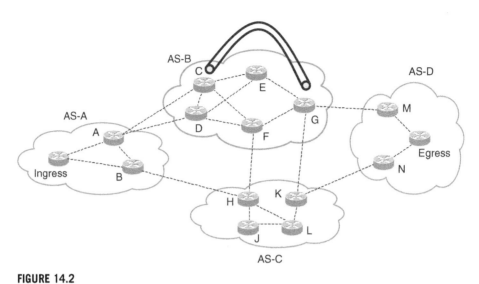

FIGURE 14.2

Hierarchical LSPs in multidomain MPLS-TE.

adjacent in a particular network layer. These data links are available to carry LSPs and form part of the network topology—that is, provide extra network flexibility—and are used during traffic engineering. In multidomain networks, Hierarchical LSPs form an important part of the TE mechanism and must be carefully planned (as is the case for the static topology) and advertised with their TE properties.

Hierarchical LSPs provide a significant scaling advantage in TE networks where they allow multiple end-to-end LSPs to be clustered and tunneled down a single Hierarchical LSP. This results in considerable simplification and reduction of the control and data plane state at transit nodes.

Chapter 2 explained how label stacks are used to nest LSPs. Hierarchical LSPs achieve this process through planning or controlled use of signaling protocols. Consider the network in Figure 14.2. As before, an end-to-end LSP is requested between the ingress LSR and the egress LSR. However, in this example there already exists a Hierarchical LSP in AS-B linking LSR-C to LSR-G; perhaps it has the nonobvious path {C,D,E,G}. When the Path message for the end-to-end LSP is received by LSR-C, it can decide to route the new LSP straight to LSR-G down the existing Hierarchical LSP.

Hierarchical LSPs are installed at their end points as virtual interfaces, and they can be considered to be virtual links between the end points. They can be installed as TE links (in which case they are termed *Forwarding Adjacencies*), but this is not necessary and is of no benefit for this multidomain use. To route the end-to-end LSP down the Hierarchical LSP and use it as a tunnel, LSR-C simply selects the virtual link CG and sends the Path message to LSR-G at the far end of

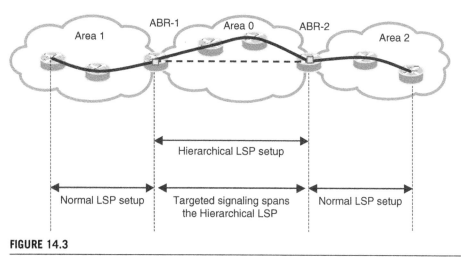

FIGURE 14.3

RSVP-TE signaling for Hierarchical LSP usage in a multi-area network.

the link. Note carefully that in unmodified MPLS-TE, this causes a problem because the RSVP-TE message would be forwarded through the IP control plane via router-E, which (being MPLS-capable) would intercept the message and either try to install the LSP or would reject the message as misrouted. However, the GMPLS protocol extensions necessary for the use of Hierarchical LSPs separate the control channel connectivity from the data plane connectivity and allow the use of virtual data links.

Thus, as shown for a multiarea network in Figure 14.3, the Hierarchical LSP is set up using normal RSVP-TE signaling (in this case between ABR-1 and ABR-2). When this LSP has been established, it can be used to support an end-to-end LSP. When the Path request reaches ABR-1, it is forwarded direct to ABR-2 (using the IP address of ABR-2 and without being intercepted by other MPLS-capable routers in Area 0). From ABR-2 the processing continues as normal.

The use of Hierarchical LSPs offers some significant benefits, especially for the operator of a transit domain:

- The amount of control plane state in the transit domain is significantly reduced. Only the state for the Hierarchical LSPs is needed. No state is required for the end-to-end LSPs within the transit domain.

- The transit domain can perform bulk repair of LSPs that transit it. That is, in the event of a failure, only the Hierarchical LSP needs to be repaired to restore all of the end-to-end LSPs.

- The operator of the transit domain can dedicate specific network resources to the Hierarchical LSP for use by transit LSPs, providing a simple thresholding and guarantee mechanisms in one go.

■ The transit domain can reoptimize its network without impacting the end-to-end traffic. Using make-before-break techniques, the Hierarchical LSP can be rerouted, taking all of the end-to-end LSPs with it. This gives the transit domain control back compared with a simple end-to-end LSP where only the ingress LSR can perform make-before-break operations.

Note that the transit domain can install multiple "parallel" Hierarchical LSPs between a pair of its edge LSRs, and it can decide for itself how to distribute the end-to-end LSPs between them. Further, the Hierarchical LSPs can be preestablished (as described above) or established on demand when a request for an end-to-end LSP is received.

14.3 LSP STITCHING

LSP stitching is an alternative to end-to-end LSPs and Hierarchical LSPs. A stitching segment LSP is set up across the transit domain just as for a Hierarchical LSP. And, indeed, the signaling of the end-to-end LSP also proceeds in the same way as shown in Figure 14.4. However, instead of using label stacking at the ingress of the stitching segment (as would be done for Hierarchical LSPs), the upstream segment of the LSP is "stitched" to the transit LSP. In this case, stitching simply means that the LFIB is set up to swap labels and forward packets. The same process is performed at the downstream end of the stitching segment.

In practice, this means that in the forwarding plane there is just a single end-to-end LSP with no label stacking, but in the control plane the operations are identical to those for Hierarchical LSPs. This results in one stitching segment being able to support just one end-to-end LSP.

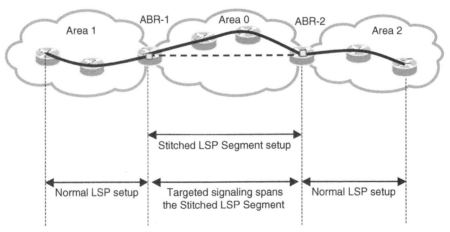

FIGURE 14.4

RSVP-TE signaling for LSP stitching usage in a multi-area network.

LSP stitching provides some of the same benefits as Hierarchical LSPs with regard to re-optimization and repair, and it helps the transit domain retain control of its resources. Although LSP stitching does not provide the scaling benefits of Hierarchical LSPs, by not requiring the use of an additional label the process might be more applicable to situations where a particularly large label stack needs to be avoided. It is, incidentally, the only option in homogenous nonpacket networks where LSP nesting is not possible.

14.4 THE PATH COMPUTATION ELEMENT

The IETF defines a Path Computation Element (PCE) as "An entity (component, application, or network node) that is capable of computing a network path or route based on a network graph and applying computational constraints." From that perspective there are several deployment possibilities for PCEs, and some include existing locations of path computation functionality. For example, in many systems the Network Management Station (NMS) has the capability to select network paths for LSPs based on its knowledge of the network topology and available resources. In this case, the NMS invokes its path computation function to determine a path that satisfies the service request and then commands the control plane to provision the LSP. Alternatively, the NMS can simply pass the service request to the control plane on the head-end LSR and leave it to the control plane to select a path by invoking a path computation function on the head-end LSR. In both these cases the PCE function already exists and has been deployed for many years—all the IETF specification does is formalize the functional decomposition within the existing implementations.

The IETF's work also recognizes that it would be possible to divorce the PCE function from the components that invoke it. That is, the PCE could be implemented as a separate and dedicated server within the network. Messages can be sent to the server (from, for example, the NMS or a head-end LSR) to request path computation for LSPs that are to be computed. This gives rise to the three deployment possibilities shown in Figure 14.5.

14.4.1 Per-Domain Path Computation With PCE

The per-domain path computation technique that has already been discussed fits well with the PCE architecture. Consider the example in Figure 14.1. When the Path message is originated, the ingress LSR needs to compute a path from itself to LSR-C. Similarly, LSR-C needs a path to LSR-M, and LSR-M needs a path to the egress LSR. Each of these paths could be computed within the LSR in question (meaning that the LSR has PCE capabilities), or a request could be sent to some remote PCE server within each domain.

In fact, it is normal to consider that a PCE has responsibility for just one domain. This is substantially derived from the definition of a domain at the top of

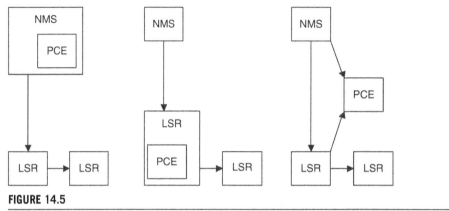

FIGURE 14.5

PCE deployment possibilities.

this chapter. At the same time, there may be multiple PCEs in any one domain to offer load balancing and redundancy. Because, as demonstrated, the interdomain case demands path computation at the domain border LSRs, a common deployment option is to place the PCE function at the domain border LSRs and allow it to be queried from other LSRs within the domain.

14.4.2 Cooperating PCEs

The per-domain path computation technique does not guarantee the selection of the optimal end-to-end interdomain path. Consider the simple two-domain scenario in Figure 14.6. Using the per-domain method, the ingress LSR sends a request to PCE-1 requesting a path from the ingress LSR to domain-B. The PCE will return the shortest path (ingress, LSR-A, domain-B), and the ingress LSR will signal the Path message to LSR-E, which will perform a further path computation to reach the egress, and we will end up with an LSP with path {ingress,A,E,F,G,H,J,K,egress}.

Clearly, looking at the whole network from the outside, we haven't derived the optimal (i.e., shortest) path, but by partitioning the information available to the PCEs, we have not been able to select a better route. An option, of course, is to make the full set of topology and traffic engineering information available to PCE-1 so that it can compute a better end-to-end path. In a simple network, such as that shown in Figure 14.6, this would not be a problem, but we must recall that the network has been split into separate domains for some very good reason. It might be that the domains are desired to preserve commercial confidentiality (for example, they might be ASs operated by different network providers), or it is possible that the domains exist to make the network scalable because there would otherwise be too much routing and TE information to be handled by the protocols (such as with routing areas). In any case, the definition of a domain that

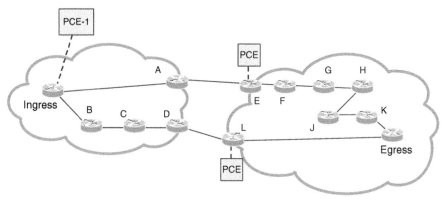

FIGURE 14.6

A simple two-domain scenario.

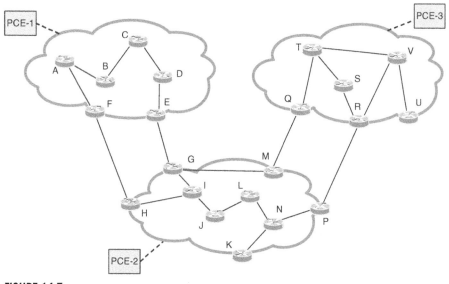

FIGURE 14.7

An example network for backward recursive path computation.

we used at the start of the chapter prohibits the case where PCE-1 can compute paths within domain-B—if it could, we would have just one domain, not two.

So how can we derive an optimal interdomain path? The answer lies in cooperative communication between PCEs and a chain of requests known as backward recursive path computation (BRPC).

Figure 14.7 provides a sample three-domain network for us to illustrate BRPC. An end-to-end LSP is required from LSR-A to LSR-V. The process begins with LSR-A sending a path computation request to PCE-1, which recognizes that the destination is not local and forwards the request to PCE-2, which is responsible for the downstream domain. PCE-2 forwards the request to PCE-3, which recognizes that the destination, LSR-V, is in its domain. Now the path computation begins.

PCE-3 determines an optimal path from each entry point of its domain to the destination. In this example it produces three such paths: {U,V}, {R,V}, and {Q,T,V}. PCE-3 returns the costs of these paths, along with their domain entry points, to PCE-2 as the computation response. Note that the internal details of the paths (such as the specific links of LSRs through which they pass) can be concealed from PCE-2 and replaced with tokens or cookies, as might be required for commercial confidentiality or to improve scalability. Now, let us assume that all link costs in our example are 1, so the path costs returned are 1, 1, and 2. At this stage, domain entry points LSR-U and LSR-R appear to be favorites, but LSR-Q is not ruled out of contention.

PCE-2 can now compute shortest paths from each of its domain's entry points not directly attached to the paths listed by PCE-3 to each of the entry points that are directly attached while pruning out the entry points that do not attach to the domain at all. That is:

- The path {U,V} is pruned because LSR-U is not directly attached to domain 2.
- The paths {R,V} and {Q,T,V} attach to domain 2 at LSR-P and LSR-M, respectively.
- The other domain entry points are LSR-G, LSR-H, and LSR-K.

So PCE-2 generates the following paths: {G,M}, {G,I,J,L,N,P}, {H,I,G,M}, {H,I,J,L,N,P}, {K,N,P}, and {K,N,L,J,I,G,M}. These paths can be spliced to the paths returned by PCE-3 to generate the optimum path from each entry point of domain 2 to the destination, LSR-V. Thus, PCE-2 returns three paths to PCE-1: {G,M,Q,T,V}, {H,I,G,M,Q,T,V}, and {K,N,P,R,V} with costs 4, 6, and 4. Again, the PCE does not need to return the whole path, only the entry point, a path token, and the cost to reach the destination. Now the entry points G and K to domain 2 look most favorable.

One observation at this stage is that this sort of multidomain calculation only makes sense if the domains use comparable metrics. That is, PCE-2 can only use the path costs that it received from PCE-3 to calculate sensible path costs all the way to the destination if both domains have a common agreement of what a link cost of 1 means or if there is some well-known mapping between the costs in the two domains.

Finally, PCE-1 gets to perform its computation from LSR-A to each of the entry points that connect to the paths supplied by PCE-2. It first prunes out the path from LSR-K because domain 1 does not connect to LSR K. Then it computes the two paths {A,F,H} and {A,B,C,D,E,G} and stitches these to the paths returned by PCE-2 to get the two candidate paths {A,F,H,I,G,M,Q,T,V} with cost 8 and {A,B,C,D,E,G,M,Q,T,V} with cost 9. So the optimum path can be selected using the domain entry points Q and H, neither of which appeared to be the best choice partway through the process.

Multicast and Point-to-Multipoint

15

Multicast and point-to-multipoint (P2MP) support was not included in the original MPLS specifications. Users wishing to send IP multicast traffic across an MPLS network were required to establish point-to-point (P2P) LSPs from the source MPLS PE (i.e., the entry point of the multicast traffic to the MPLS network) to each destination MPLS PE (i.e., to each exit point from the MPLS network). Effectively, this made the ingress PE the single replication point for all of the traffic in the multicast flow as shown in Figure 15.1.

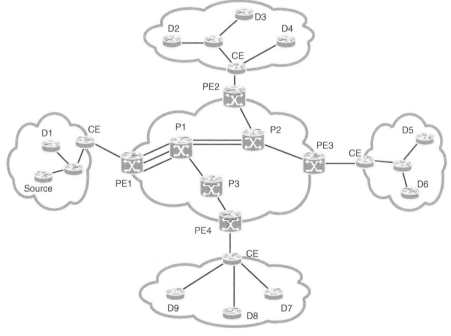

FIGURE 15.1

Legacy MPLS support for multicast traffic.

Although this function allows the effective delivery of multicast traffic, it is not efficient because the ingress PE is put under increasing strain by the addition of extra destination PEs and by the provisioning of new multicast flows. Just as important for the network operator is the fact that very poor use is made of the MPLS network resources, as can be seen from the example in Figure 15.1 where the link PE1-P1 carries three copies of the data (in the three LSPs: PE1-PE2, PE1-PE3, and PE1-PE4), and the link P1-P2 carries two copies of the data. As the size of the network increases with more and more PEs participating in the multicast distribution, this form of solution becomes unscalable, the burden on the replicating PE becomes too great, and the inefficient use of bandwidth is unacceptable.

However, multicast services are becoming increasingly popular with the MPLS network providers' customers. VPN services demand multicast support, and IP multicast must be carried across the MPLS backbone. Further, new services, such as video distribution, are entering the market, and the network operator needs efficient and effective mechanisms to deliver them across an MPLS network.

For these reasons, the IETF has recently been working to develop MPLS protocol extensions to facilitate the installation of P2MP LSPs within an MPLS network. MPLS-TE extensions have been completed, with RSVP-TE now able to set up P2MP LSP tunnels. At the time of writing, extensions to LDP are also well advanced, allowing P2MP LSPs to be constructed that follow the routing information within the network. There is also a set of extensions to the MPLS VPN architecture to facilitate the support of IP multicast services for VPN customers.

The remainder of this chapter introduces the extensions to LDP and RSVP-TE that enable P2MP LSP signaling.

15.1 P2MP LSPS IN THE FORWARDING PLANE

It is worth spending a few moments to examine the P2MP LSP as it appears in the forwarding plane. As shown in Figure 15.2, this is not particularly special. The LSP proceeds as normal from the *root* (LSR-A), through LSR-B, to LSR-C. The encapsulation rules at LSR-A are unchanged, and the forwarding rules at LSR-B are the same as for a P2P LSP.

However, LSR-C is a *branch node* on the P2MP LSP and is responsible for forwarding the packets to both LSR-D and LSR-F. It must replicate the packets and send them out of both interfaces. No mechanism for packet replication is specified within the standards, and this is likely to be a key element of market separation for equipment vendors because the replication process must not introduce excessive delay or jitter for any of the recipients, and it should be scalable to a large number of downstream branches for a single branch node. Note that the labels used on the downstream branches might be different because downstream label assignment is still used.

In this example, LSR-F is an egress (a *leaf node*), and it doesn't have to perform any special processing compared with an egress of a P2P LSP. However, LSR-F has

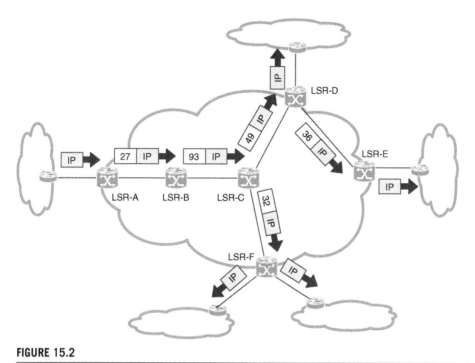

FIGURE 15.2

The forwarding plane and MPLS labels for a P2MP LSP.

two downstream IP networks that are both consumers of the multicast flow, and it must perform IP replication and fan-out after terminating the MPLS LSP.

LSR-D is a special case. It is both a leaf node of the P2MP LSP and also a transit point (because LSR-E is downstream). We call this type of LSR a *bud node*. LSR-D must forward the MPLS packets on the LSP, potentially to multiple downstream braches, and it must also make a copy of the packet for local termination.

15.2 **MULTICAST LDP**

LDP-enabled LSRs learn where to install labels based on the information distributed by the IP routing protocols and the labels advertised by LDP. Basic LDP LSPs actually have a multipoint-to-point structure in the forwarding plane because traffic that converges on a destination is allocated the same label. To install a P2MP LSP, some small modifications are needed to the protocol elements and procedures of LDP.

A new Forwarding Equivalence Class (FEC) protocol element is defined. This encodes a description of the multicast flow as identified by the source node or root of the P2MP tree and a set of opaque elements that can be used by an application to distinguish different flows and uses from the same root. The information in the opaque elements does not need to be decoded by transit nodes but is relevant at the leaves and the root. All nodes use a comparison of the whole of the FEC (including the opaque elements) to distinguish P2MP flows.

LDP label messages are enhanced to be able to carry the new P2MP FEC element so that LDP can talk about P2MP LSPs. A leaf that wants to join a particular P2MP LSP simply sends a label mapping message upstream toward the root of the LSP using the IP routing information to determine the next hop on the path to the root node. The label mapping message contains the P2MP FEC element and is forwarded by each LSR until either the root is reached or until an LSR recognizes that it is already handling the P2MP LSP identified by the FEC element and grafts a new branch on-to the LSP.

Note that a particular feature of multicast LDP is that the tree produced depends on the path from the leaves to the root, rather than from the root to the leaves. This is not normally an issue in a well-designed network with bidirectional links and is also consistent with the IP multicast architecture.

15.3 P2MP MPLS-TE

MPLS-TE LSPs are signaled by RSVP-TE using a Path/Resv message exchange initiated by the ingress of the LSP. To preserve the basic operation of the protocol, this basic rule is maintained for P2MP LSPs. As a result, the head-end (the root) must know which leaves are to be attached to the LSP. How this is achieved does not form part of the protocol specification and can vary depending on the application. For example, in video distribution, the attachment of a leaf to the P2MP tree could be achieved using a distinct application-level registration process that is subject to authorization, policy, and billing before the receiver can be added to the LSP. In other applications (such as the distribution of financial data), the definition of the leaves comes through an NMS, but in other environments (most notably, the support of multicast within MPLS VPNs) the routing protocol that distributes VPN site membership can also distribute multicast leaf information.

The basic mode of P2MP RSVP-TE operation handles each leaf separately. The ingress node computes a route for a P2P LSP for each source-to-leaf LSP and signals it. At each hop along the path, if the signaled LSP coincides with an existing LSP for the same P2MP tree, then resources and labels are shared. If there is no preexisting LSP with the same identifiers, the Path/Resv messages are treated as installing a new LSP, and a new label is allocated. This mode of operation makes the P2MP LSP almost identical to the P2P LSP. The only difference is how the LSP is identified (a few of the RSVP protocol fields are slightly modified) and how forwarding plane components are shared when two source-to-leaf LSPs for the same P2MP LSP share a hop. This technique also makes the addition and removal of leaves particularly simple.

However, there are some issues with the technique just described. First, the path of the P2MP LSP is not perfectly optimal—the tree computed shows "least-cost-to-destination" behavior, and this does not optimize core network usage as

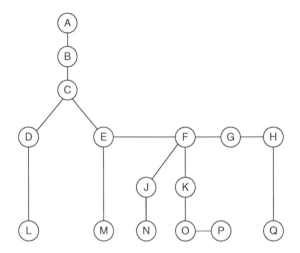

FIGURE 15.3

A point-to-multipoint LSP tree.

well as a computation that considers all destinations at one time to produce a Steiner tree.

Even if an optimal computation is performed, it is still possible to signal each source-to-leaf LSP using a separate Path message. This might be adequate for small LSPs (with a low number of leaves), but as the size of the LSP grows, the number of Path messages in the network can become unmanageable and, depending on implementation details, LSRs might be required to maintain excessive protocol state to support the different source-to-leaf LSPs.

As a solution to this problem, the new protocol extensions allow a Path or Resv message to carry information about multiple destinations (and the paths to those destinations) for a single P2MP LSP. Based on the Secondary ERO and Secondary RRO described in Chapter 8 for GMPLS segment protection, the P2MP tree can be encoded and carried on a single message. For example, consider the P2MP tree shown in Figure 15.3. Using the source-to-leaf signaling mechanism, we could signal six path messages with the following explicit routes:

- A, B, C, D, L
- A, B, C, E, M
- A, B, C, E, F, J, N
- A, B, C, E, F, K, O
- A, B, C, E, F, K, O, P
- A, B, C, E, F, G, H, Q

Using the SERO mechanism to compress the path information, we can signal a single Path message with the following path information:

- A, B, C, D, L
- C, E, M

- E, F, J, N
- F, K, O
- O, P
- F, G, H, Q

When this path information is processed by any LSR, it looks at each entry in the path list and determines as follows:

- If the LSR is the top hop in the entry in the path list, the LSR creates a Path message to carry the entry and processes the entry as a normal explicit path.

- Otherwise, the LSR searches for the Path message it has created that has a path list entry that contains the top hop of the entry in hand. It copies the entry in hand to the path list of the Path message it finds.

Thus, when LSR C receives the Path message, the path list looks as follows:

- C, D, L
- C, E, M
- E, F, J, N
- F, K, O
- O, P
- F, G, H, Q

LSR C processes the list as follows:

- C, D, L—Create Path message 1 to send to D
- C, E, M—Create Path message 2 to send to E
- E, F, J, N—Add path entry to Path message 2
- F, K, O—Add path entry to Path message 2
- O, P—Add path entry to Path message 2
- F, G, H, Q—Add path entry to Path message 2

Similarly, at LSR F, the following path entry list is received and processed as described:

- F, J, N—Create Path message 1 to send to J
- F, K, O—Create Path message 2 to send to K
- O, P—Add path entry to Path message 2
- F, G, H, Q—Create Path message 3 to send to G

Index

Printed and bound by CPI Group (UK) Ltd, Croydon, CR0 4YY

03/10/2024

01040317-0004